Sebastian

THREE

– The Accidental Steward

- The Return

A Liberal, Radical view of a reformed Euro, a Multispeed EU and realigned NATO. With the UK under a new constitution, at the heart of Europe.

The continuing Saga of Sebastian Edwards and his rise as a UK Liberal Democrat politician in 2020-22

By Julian Hamilton

January 2017

Disclaimer

This book is a work of fiction. Sebastian Edwards is a fictional character though he lives within a current known political environment. Almost all the information contained is already in the public domain. From the current date forward all names, characters, places and events are either products of the author's imagination or are used fictitiously. Any resemblance to actual events, locales, or persons, living or dead, is entirely co-incidental.

I am indebted to my wife Hilary Hamilton and my former secretary Mrs Marion Hawley for their tireless work in checking the proofs. As the writer is always the backstop any errors are mine and mine alone.

ISBN 9780993281792

DEDICATION - One

This book is dedicated to the UK NHS, Nottingham City Hospital, Haematology Department, brilliant Consulting Staff, excellent Day Case nurses, superb care in Toghill Ward and all those that have kept me alive for nearly ten years now beyond expectations, for which many thanks.

DEDICATION – Two

This is written from a modern European liberal perspective. At first in anger at the perceived destruction of the Lib Dems in 2015 but then in the realisation that the Coalition had failed to bring about the change members had sought for 40 years. The Lib Dems were not up to the task, only Vince Cable appeared to have a sense of purpose, the rest gambolled on the fringes of the 'quad' with changes any other Conservative government might have made anyhow. Tim Faron with a massive legacy which he tries desperately to keep alive, struggles hard to survive.

In writing this 'parallel' novel, which in fact involved a huge amount of research, I came to the conclusion that the 'Swabian promise' was at the root of the problem with the Euro which was so poorly protected that it was 'designed to fail' at the first shock. I saw that a derogation on UK Immigration was not only possible but very likely acceptable, furthermore that Mrs May had failed both to understand or firm up on controls and that this was crucial to the referendum debate. The Euro and EU are reformable and NATO is due a rehas. But the main problem is the UK's mental detatchment from the EU there's still a hankering for an (imperial) past long gone.

I remain convinced that negotiations with the EU can provide for a UK 'within' having all the freedoms we require whilst ourselves being able to change the EU itself, for the better.

Table of Contents

Chapter ONE – The call to the Palace

During the two days following the incident that lead to the Prime Minister's resignation on December 14th 2020 the whole of the political elite in the UK was on high alert.

The thirst of the national and international Press for even dregs of news of any kind was insatiable. Sebastian knew if the Press couldn't get news then they would invent it and the rumour mill would work overtime.

Superficially there was little change and the transition to a new Prime Minister was a strange anti-climax, under the political surface, there were frantic discussions urgent calls and angry exchanges, but the public saw none of this.

Sebastian Edwards had been appointed Deputy Prime Minister only 4 weeks or so before in Mid November 2020.

The Prime Minister Robin Turnbull had been quite clear about the reason for this, he had made a statement in the House of Commons at the time. He felt that the UK was failing to raise the country's international profile within Europe, the Commonwealth and the United Nations. It now needed a person of stature to raise the country's standing.

The position of Deputy Prime Minister was widely regarded within the country as a sinecure, entitling the holder to use the Country House Chevening or to entertain guests until the real Prime Minister became available or perhaps more mundanely just being allowed to play a game of croquet in one of the most sought after locations. One of the previous holders of the title had been photographed and splashed across the front pages of the tabloids, it had confirmed the general view that he and the office he held were a waste of space.

In short, within the UK, the position was everything and nothing or rather exactly and only what the PM decided it should be! Internationally however the position was taken at full face value so it was assumed that when the Deputy attended meetings abroad he carried almost the same weight as the Prime Minister himself. It immediately gave the Deputy precedence over mere Foreign Ministers in any international gathering. The Prime Minister had seen an opportunity for the UK to seize the lead in cases like Syria where there had been a clear failure of international diplomacy over several years. He had clearly thought that Sebastian was the man to do it!

As Sebastian Edwards was already the Foreign Secretary and the most senior Liberal Democrat Cabinet Minister by rank in the Coalition, he had welcomed the opportunity to launch a number of projects that had been agreed with the Prime Minister, Robin Turnbull. Sebastian and Robin had worked well together and there grew up between them an easy relationship but which, in the highly sensitive world of national politics, immediately drew either accusation of favouritism or of blurring the lines between the two parties in the Coalition.

To his Lib Dem colleagues in the meeting of Coalition Ministers, Sebastian had down-played the wider aspects of his new role, for example, as he told his party colleagues, since he was the Minister 'roaming the world' he had no expectation of standing in at Prime Minister's Question Time. This was the 90 minute 'trial by questioning' in Parliament when the Opposition Leader and other MPs are able to subject the Prime Minister to in-depth political interrogation. "It's unlikely I will be there very often!" In addition he had pointed out that the Prime Minister was both younger and fitter than he and that it was much more likely he would be off ill than the PM! "But I intend to use the extra weight the title gives me to push these projects further. We need, desperately, to improve our standing within Europe and to help reform it and we need to change UN perspectives with regard to the desperate plight of waves of migrants caused by ridiculous, devastating wars in Africa and the Middle East ."

However Sebastian was well aware of the jealously that this appointment had aroused amongst certain of his colleagues. Dan Stirling was in fact the Leader of the Lib Dems in the Country and indeed of the MPs in Parliament. He had therefore been the person nominated by Lib Dems for the position of Deputy Prime Minister, he had indeed occupied that position for over two years since the death of the former Lib Dem leader, the much lamented Tim Beaumond. However Dan Stirling and Robin Turnbull had found it very difficult to form a working relationship and their discussions and negotiations had often ended up in shouting matches so loud that disagreements were expected daily and, in Sebastian's view, this was damaging the efficiency of the Coalition. Earlier the Lib Dem appointee as Foreign Minister, David Billingham, had pointedly refused to project the UK on a global basis and had allowed his civil servants to run policy; he had scrupulously avoided taking the lead in any problems that emerged. In contrast when Sebastian was eventually promoted to Foreign Secretary he had taken on a very much more active role which immediately caught the headlines.

The Prime Minister had insisted on making changes. He told Dan Stirling he needed a new Deputy.

There was considerable relief around the Cabinet table when Sebastian was initially appointed to replace Dan Stirling.

Most other Lib Dem Ministers expressed the view that there were few other workable options available since the person had to be a Liberal Democrat and that Sebastian had indeed earned his spurs.

But Sebastian's preferment had caused a ripple of anxiety amongst senior Tory Cabinet Ministers. Although they could see that the easier working relationship between them was turning out well in foreign affairs, they knew that Sebastian had also been brought in by the Prime Minister for advice on other matters. Traditionally Conservative Cabinet Ministers had jealously guarded access to their Prime Minister. Although Sebastian made clear that he had never attempted to ingratiate himself with the Prime Minister, nevertheless it was obvious that they worked well together and frequently sparked off other actions as a result of casual discussions. Although Sebastian had never been accused of crossing the line and interfering with Conservative run Departments, they realised that he had in some cases supplanted their own advice to their Prime Minister. When they had made known their anxieties to Sebastian he had accepted their complaints with good grace. As a consequence most Tory Ministers had told Sebastian that they regarded his promotion to Deputy Prime Minister as a sinecure but done to gain more exposure to Britain's rightful place in the world. Some of them told Sebastian to his face that it was a good way to get Lib Dems 'out of their hair' and 'let them play around with foreign policy and leave running the country to us!' So his appointment as Deputy had gone largely unchallenged.

The sudden resignation of the Prime Minister Robin Turnbull had thrown everything into turmoil.

Dan Stirling, who clearly resented his own effective demotion, however had been the first to insist that Sebastian should enforce the legitimate succession. "A Deputy is there to Deputise for the Leader!" he insisted "Its obvious Sebastian should become the Prime Minister!"

Senior Tories immediately tried to press the view that Sebastian had never taken any interest in other Departments and, as a consequence, would be out of his depth Instead he should give up that role and return to the Foreign Office work. In any case he could not command a majority in Cabinet, so they could call for a vote and win any contest and dethrone him at any time. Also that, as a Lib Dem, Sebastian would be completely unrepresentative of the MPs and a backlash by the 1922 committee was more than likely."

The exchange of notes and emails between Cabinet Ministers on the day that Prime Ministers' resignation was notified to his Cabinet on December 15th, reached a fever pitch and this was exaggerated by the media who had somehow got wind of Robin Turnbull's intended visit to the Queen on the following day to resign.

Robin Turnbull had merely stated briefly publicly; "I understand and accept that I have to take responsibility for the project which I championed and of which I was the originator." He had told no-one of any recommendations he had made to the Queen.

The Cabinet Secretary, Sir James Knotwood, was consulted as were the Senior Law Officers. Sir James referred everyone to his booklet 'The Cabinet Manual' written by himself in 2011 during the earlier Coalition. He referred them to Chapter 2 'Change of Prime Minister.. during a Parliament' section 18, 'Where a Prime Minister chooses to resign... it is for the party or parties in government to identify who can be chosen as successor.' And then also to Chapter 3 'Deputy Prime Minister' section 11, 'The fact that a person has the title of Deputy Prime Minister does not constrain the Sovereign's power to appoint a successor to a Prime Minister'.

Nobody thought that any of that helped very much and that it was for the parties to get together and work something out.

Eventually all Lib Dems MPs except Sebastian signed a letter insisting that Lib Dems would hold the obvious succession as sacrosanct, a breach of which would mean the end of the Coalition.

The Tories realised that they could not gain the assent of other party leaders which would have been necessary to move for the early termination of the agreed 5 year Parliament scheduled to end in December 2022; and to move to a dissolution immediately. They had no wish, in the full glare of publicity of TV debates to go over and over the events leading up to the Prime Minister's resignation. In a General Election, this would surely overshadow the programme of success they would wish to present. The Tory hierarchy conceded that they needed time to repair the reputational damage caused.

Accordingly Senior Conservative Cabinet Ministers made known to the Liberal Democrats that they would go along with serving under Sebastian Edwards for a temporary period.

The Press assumed that one matter which weighed heavily in this decision was the Tories lack of any emergency procedure to elect their Parliamentary Party Leader despite being caught out in 2017 by a similar event. It would mean either putting in place a Temporary Leader yet again or riding roughshod over their own internal Tory constitution and electing a leader from the MPs without consulting paid-up party members. It was acknowledged that a contested election would probably take 12 weeks if the full consultation and hustings procedures were used.

At any rate, as Sebastian noted, all speculation came to an end when Her Majesty, on the advice, apparently, of the outgoing Prime Minister, asked Sebastian Edwards if he could form a Government on December 16th 2020. He replied that he hoped so, the indications were positive and he would confirm the position as soon as possible, probably within a couple of days, as many people had to be consulted in this complex situation.

They all realised that Parliament was due to go into recess on December 22nd and also that on that date, as Her Majesty's liaison officer at Buckingham Palace had advised the Cabinet Office, the Queen intended as usual to leave London to spend Christmas at the Country Estate at Sandringham in Norfolk. He had also casually remarked to Sir James that any major Government changes would be expected to be made and notified to her Majesty before then.

Neither Sebastian Edwards nor any of the Senior Conservative or Liberal Democrat Ministers imagined that they could interrupt the Queen's Christmas holiday and accordingly they knew that they had to formulate a new agreement between them quickly.

So if anyone was to prevent Sebastian taking over, they would have to act right away, denying Sebastian the position and allowing some other Minister with perhaps a better chance of forming a government to be presented to Her Majesty.

No other name was put forward.

For once in his lifetime Sebastian was remarkably laid back about the whole problem swirling around him. In just four years he had advanced a political career beyond his wildest imagination. When he had engaged his 'political motor' as he himself explained to his constituents, it had been to prevent what appeared to be the final collapse and elimination of the Liberal Democrats. It was only after some time that he realised that he was quite good at his job as a Minister. He had rattled through several positions; as Minister without Portfolio responsible for Devolution to the New Regional Assemblies, then Secretary of State at the Department for International Development and finally the Foreign Office. He attributed his success in these posts to his being very interested or absorbed in each of the topics, he had managed somehow to be acceptable to the Conservatives but he identified success primarily in terms of the achievement of a Lib Dem party goal, which he thought would also bring maximum benefit to the country, and that was to encourage a successful Coalition with which Lib Dems would be indelibly linked and from which they could gain identifiable political capital.

He knew that his wife, Sylvia, would support him if at any time he wished to resign and get out of politics, they had enough shared interests to survive and his financial position was strong; he owed nothing to anyone and due to their frugal lifestyle they were still saving month after month.

His big worry was how he would deal with certain projects in Cabinet to which he had personally been opposed. It was in those conditions where he felt he would be most ill-at-ease. As a Cabinet Minister of course he could and had just remained silent on issues that he did not support which had come up in other departments. He knew he would have been deemed to support agreed Cabinet measures in conformity with Cabinet collective responsibility but he had never actually to disown his previous view, he could and did simply remain silent... but this was different... could he actually table something as Chairman of the meeting, call for views of his Cabinet, summarise the arguments, reach a decision and yet suppress his own feelings and opinions?

At best he felt it would ruin his personal integrity at worst it would make him appear to be a hypocrite – it was when working as Chief Lib Dem Whip that he had come nearest to being, what he himself regarded as, a failure! He still found it difficult to be insincere, this showed in a certain hesitancy and lack of confidence which quickly became apparent.

Even if he was successful and guided the Cabinet as Prime Minister presenting of necessity some Tory policies, he knew that the pressure would be on him to shift his political spectrum to support or even promote Tory moves, the more he did so the more likely his own Liberal Democrats would eventually disown him and possibly turn on him.

His final worry was his own health, he had been ill several times in the last few years, and he knew that under situations of stress he did not perform well. Latterly he had been lucky, no-one had noticed and he had been able to recover without anyone drawing any long term conclusions as to his mental or physical robustness. But, as Prime Minister, Sebastian knew that he would face a relentless pressure from the press and come under the intense questioning of TV interviewers, he felt that any tiny crack in his armour would be seized upon and used against him.

Chapter TWO – Liberal Democrat discussions

Finally Sebastian still needed the assent and support of his party to these changes and accordingly asked the Liberal Democrat leader, Dan Stirling, to call a meeting of all Lib Dem MPs early on December 17th to discuss the political situation urgently and also for Sebastian to make known any other Cabinet changes before the Christmas recess also due on December 22nd.

Sebastian thought that his elevation would resonate better with the backbench Lib Dem MPs of which there were some 20, rather than with those 10 Minister MPs with whom he had been working on a daily or weekly basis. Seeing him designated as the 'First Ever Lib Dem Prime Minister' would, he knew, gladden the soul of every party worker and every constituency chairman and by extension every ordinary Lib Dem MP! Therefore with the full tally of 30 MPs he felt reasonably confident of a positive response to his assumption of the role of PM.

Dan Stirling, instead, set up a meeting with just those 10 MPs who were also in the Government as Ministers. Sebastian thought this would not favour him as he knew that at least two, Dan himself and Dave Billingham the former Foreign Secretary whom Sebastian had replaced would not support him on personal grounds if it came to any vote. Further he suspected that a third Minister, Saxon Bull, was less impressed by his, Sebastian's, past performance on the Devolution Bill than were the other MPs. Sebastian had successfully drilled through Parliament a Consolidated Devolution Bill but this had created a huge extra workload for Saxon who was extremely concerned about its implementation. He saw Sebastian as having escaped to other, higher roles leaving him, Saxon Bull as Minister for Communities and Regions to do the hard work of actually, physically, organising 12 Regional Assemblies and dealing daily with a large numbers of objections. Failure would irreparably damage his career. It was, they all knew, giving Saxon sleepless nights! There was another Minister whom Sebastian himself had proposed as his successor in DfID but who had inexplicably turned on him in his 'bumpy ride' that had nearly tipped Sebastian over the edge, Sebastian had no idea how that person might vote.

Sebastian thought he could count on the support of most of the rest of the Ministers. He estimated that in the end he could muster 5 or even 6 of the 10 including himself. However Sebastian spotted on the brief note which was sent around that the Lib Dem leader in the House of Lords, Baroness Sal Thrumpton would be there as would John Corn. He was Chief of Staff to successive Lib Dem leaders, and Sebastian rated him highly for his political nous.

They all met at 10 am in Lib Dem Headquarters away from the public gaze to ensure absolute privacy.

The room was hot and stuffy, Dan Stirling took the Leader's chair behind the desk and the rest, including Sebastian, sat in chairs around the walls.

Dan Stirling, Sebastian later remembered, told everyone to put old animosities behind them and asked everyone to move ahead to take advantage of the opportunity.

Dan himself raised the question of whether "We could do a deal", as he put it "giving up the Prime Minister post and the Deputy and, instead getting one other major Ministry like Defence or the Chancellor of the Exchequer, or perhaps instead trading off the posts for an agreed watering down Tory Policy like Trident, moving towards three not four replacements Subs with none on routine patrol".

Dave Billingham supported this move "We don't know how well Sebastian will perform in that role, he could get kicked out at any time or he could become marginalised by the Cabinet or indeed be so identified with their projects and that will not help us in electoral success. You are much older than the former Prime Ministers, Sebastian, and you could just get hounded out by the Press. Remember what happened to Menzies Campbell, after he was made Leader of the Lib Dems? He hesitated once or twice during a speech in Parliament and momentarily lost his spectacles; the Press immediately began a harassment which saw him terribly abused because of his age and they forced his resignation after just a few months!"

Sarah Driscoll the Housing Minister burst in. "I think you are forgetting yourselves, I give Sebastian the credit for demanding a Constitutional Commission in the first place, and actually guiding the Devolution Bills nearly through the House and there's no question but that he has raised the profile of the UK immensely as Foreign Minister, you started off, Dan, by suggesting that we should leave the past behind us, that does not make sense to me. Sebastian has been an outstanding success as a Minister. We should ride on that success."

Sal Thrumpton supported this line "I must admit that to begin with, Sebastian's efforts to tackle the devolution issues seemed to me to be amateurish in the extreme. Sebastian will not be aware of this but I was so disappointed that I tried to persuade Tim Beaumond to move him back to the Whips' Office. But he refused insisting that you, Sebastian, were the only man for the job. He was proved right. Occasionally in Politics there emerges a personality who appears to be exactly in tune with the times. Dan, Dave don't misunderstand me you have both contributed much to our party and indeed done service to the state. It's not that your performance has been poor, rather it's obvious that Sebastian's has been outstanding. Let's move on now! Can we vote please?

My proposal is simple let Sebastian negotiate the best deal that he can!"

There was a muttered approval from all those who had not, till then, spoken.

Dan Stirling sensed the will of the meeting, "No I do not think we need a vote. Sebastian we are in your hands, you have our approval to arrange the best deal you think you can!"

Sebastian thanked the meeting.

In the meantime Pamela Tressider was once again named by Conservative Central office as their Interim Leader.

Chapter THREE – Negotiations

Sebastian 'phoned Pamela and arranged a meeting for the following day Thursday 17th at 2 pm and, since this was to be a formal agreement, he suggested that the Head of the Civil Service Sir James Knotwood should also be there. They met in the Cabinet Offices behind Number 10 approached from Whitehall. Just the three of them.

Sebastian explained that the meeting had been delayed till the afternoon and moved away from Number 10 front rooms because the furniture and belongings of the former Prime Minister had just been removed that very morning but that Sebastian himself had no plans to move in until everything had been settled between them.

He continued. "I was sorry to hear of Robin Turnbull's resignation he and I had evolved a good working relationship. Of course he was a larger than life character and as such people are inclined to have clear-cut views of him both as a person and a politician; some good and others bad. From my own personal perspective he gave me responsibility for work that I found engrossing, interesting, enjoyable and mentally rewarding. I think, perhaps, this helped the Coalition to achieve certain successes?

The Liberal Democrats have, in my opinion correctly, suggested that as Deputy I should now take over the role of Prime Minister in accordance with that logic.

However it's plain that we Liberal Democrats don't have a majority of Cabinet and I have no intention of changing the mix to try to manufacture one nor of changing any already agreed programmes.

My proposal to you Pamela is that I remain Prime Minister for three months. At the end of that period the position of Deputy Prime Minister will, by agreement between us, not be used again to prevent the possibility of any future misunderstanding.

Accordingly at the end of March I will hand over to the person nominated by your Party, whoever that might be. In return I would like to make certain adjustments to the allocation of Ministries agreed between us. I wish to exchange the Department for International Development for the Home Office, which I would then transfer to in April.

My reasoning is this the limit of 200,000 net immigration was agreed as part of the deal with the EC have been breached and it's now well over 300,000 and unless we can show why it is so, it's likely to appear to the EC that we have simply exaggerated the case we made in order to reduce EC immigrants. This may, in turn, possibly end our agreed restriction on the Free Movement of Labour. If that ends, then the opt out clause cannot be defended, and the EU may ask for it to be finished. This would then kill any controls that the UK might have over immigration from the EU.

If that occurs then this will once again start the familiar accusation of lack of control of immigration and will probably lead to demands for yet another referendum.

In other words recent performance on halting immigration has failed to convince anybody that it was fair and effective but we cannot just drift into political chaos again, we must either resolve the issue and enforce our controls or renegotiate our position and justify a new set of limits."

Pamela Tressider seemed to Sebastian to be relieved at all this and stopped making notes. Sebastian knew that Pamela herself had been in charge of the Home Office, he suspected, indeed he had counted on the probability, that she was more than happy to rid herself and the Conservatives of the embarrassment of possible failure yet again on immigration.

So to the surprise of Sir James Knotwood who looked curiously at her she appeared to accept it.

"I suppose you mean by that the enlarged Ministry?" Sebastian knew this meant the Home Office as reconstructed by Robin which had incorporated several smaller units including the Ministry of Justice. This had been part of Robin's drive to reduce the numbers of Cabinet Ministers in order to improve decision taking.

"Yes that's right!" Sebastian replied.

"On the other hand" she quickly added "you are, as it were, giving us half a Department in return as the DfID was simply part of the FCO. Perhaps you would instead swap the whole of the FCO for the Home?"

Sebastian counter proposed, "No but we could consider swapping it for the Communities, Housing and the Regions?"

Pamela said quickly "No! No! We couldn't accept that!"

Sebastian knew that Pamela could not, would not, accept that. The final reading on the Devolution Bill was due imminently and there remained a core of Conservative MPs hostile to it, so to push back the Bills under a Tory Minister would mean that the Party would have to lean very heavily on its own MP's whereas, if this was shown as a Lib Dem inspired and directed Bill, a few Tories voting against would not create a visible Tory split. But the speed with which she rejected the idea gave Sebastian an inkling of what he thought was to come; without the support of the Labour Party and other MPs, the Devolution Bill would almost certainly be lost.

"Hmmpf" muttered Sebastian "but into the future you will not have an interfering Deputy PM will you? That must be worth something? So it looks like a trade-off between the enlarged Home Office including the Ministry of Justice and the DfID plus the position of Deputy Prime Minister?"

"Yes I would say so!"

"Then we would suggest a shift of Ministers of State from Education and Energy/Climate Change to Home and Ministry of Justice this would leave those other departments free of any Lib Dem interference and would allow us to bring forward comprehensive proposals for reform that would require interlinking between the Police and Prison services?"

"Yes such a move might help!" Pamela agreed. "But of course you would have to give us more details before we could agree to new initiatives that you suggest!" She asked in return "What about the London Airport, HS2 and Trident will you accept those continuing?"

"Well I have to tell you that I intend to honour an undertaking that I gave to the former Prime Minister that I would continue with the removal of London Airport to the Thames estuary and the establishment of a true green garden town at Heathrow. "

Pamela looked disappointed "I thought after the incident you might withdraw support for that?"

"No I have come round to the view that it's basically a good idea." Sebastian muttered "less of a security risk and so on, although I don't believe that all the necessary approach roads for the new Airport have been fully costed and this might ultimately take away funds from the HS2 extensions…. but we will have to see?"

Pamela nodded ".. and Trident?"

Sebastian coughed "Well nothing much really! Just a minor adjustment!" Pamela was silent but looked expectantly at him.

"Well I would like to see a break clause in the contract!" He finally admitted.

"Oh yes?" Pamela was all of a sudden taking renewed interest, she leant forward.

"Well I have an objection not to the agreement in principle because you have the largest slab of MPs in the House, it's up to you to work it as you think fit but where I do have a problem is in your desire to lock in future generations into the Trident deal."

"But" said Pamela "we do that all the time and in every Department, we are always doing things like large infrastructure projects which might both constrain and improve the life for future generations – we cannot simply just work in the lifetime of one parliament, if we did that no large projects would ever get done!"

"But" argued Sebastian "that's just the point that I am making. The British Government is a signatory to the Nuclear Non-Proliferation Treaty. Under Article 6 we agreed to move to disarming simply because the more nuclear arms there are the more likely it is that they will eventually be used, but the Contracts we signed for the Trident replacement gave not an inch to that idea. In deciding what our needs are for the future we should also have regard to the clear expectations from the past.

So" Sebastian continued "I want to introduce into any contracts for Trident a break clause in 10 years' time. This will allow the then Government in the UK to reassess the situation at that time without incurring huge costs for breaching these contracts which would otherwise make any reduction in those Nuclear Arms almost impossible! So if all Parties are aware of this then it's up to the then parties to build this into their manifestos and allow the public to decide between those political views. What have you got to lose? If your party is returned then they may just decide to continue- no problem!"

Pamela clearly did not like that approach "but you would have to put something into the break clause? If you allowed the risk to land on the contractors then the costs would rise astronomically!"

"No! No!" Sebastian hoped that he hadn't lost her attention "I understand that but the idea would be that those subs would be replaced by other work, other ships not carrying nuclear weapons, to the like value to the constructor."

"Oh well! I suppose so. Is that all?"

"Yes, except that I intend to take a lead on European matters, you will remember that it's the UK's turn to take over the rotating Presidency of the Council, it's a largely honorific post but allows one to take the initiative in posting the Agenda, we missed our last turn as we were in the middle of a referendum!

But Yes I'll keep faith with your projects if you keep faith with ours? The Royal Commission on Banking and the City is due out soon and I have no doubt we will not see eye to eye on all matters and then there will be day to day issues and I will, as you would expect, relate to those on an ongoing basis. We have still to pass the final part of the Devolution Consolidation Bill which also covers the House of Lords. Because of the situation I expect to be working with you on an almost daily basis."

Sir James Knotwood who had been silent throughout but making notes said "Well is that it?"

"Yes that's it! Why what did you expect?" Sebastian asked, Pamela nodded assent.

"So" Sir James was not finished yet! "Can you each carry your own parties with you on this?"

Sebastian replied simply "Yes"

Pamela said "I think so, I tell you definitely tomorrow morning!"

Sir James offered to prepare notes of the meeting, both parties shook hands across the table and the meeting ended.

It occurred to Sebastian afterwards that the Conservatives had feared that Dan Stirling would somehow get the upper hand in this renegotiation and demand the reintroduction of the bilateral discussions which had clearly not worked between him and Robin. Maybe that was the reason for their relief. Sebastian had not been at all clear of the benefits of pepper-potting Lib Dem Junior Ministers into all departments, instead he was concentrating them in fewer Lib Dem led Ministries. He hoped that it would lead to less friction within Departments and allow each party to concentrate on running their patch rather than in justifying what they were doing to someone from another party. Inevitably because the Lib Dems had always been outnumbered in each department they were either subjected to pressures to conform to the majority view or risk resisting it which inevitably led to potentially acrimonious confrontations.

Sebastian hoped that the Lib Dems would be seen as being responsible for whole departments thus giving them a higher profile but he knew he was taking a huge risk, he muttered to himself 'the enlarged Home Office had three problems, Immigrants, Criminals and…. Yes! Police' since they had always been difficult to control, he smiled 'without these it would be an easy ride!'

Pamela called Sebastian the following morning and said that there was just one sticking point.

"What if the Leader issue is decided quickly, can the time-frame of March be reduced?"

"No!" Sebastian replied "I don't think either Party should go through this problem again but I suggest that at the same time as the candidate consultation process takes place, your internal constitution is changed to allow an emergency procedure. I will put it to our Executive Committee to do the same!"

Pamela agreed.

Sebastian called Sir James Knotwood and informed him of their joint decision.

The Lib Dem MPs and Executive were informed.

Sebastian asked the Executive to change the Lib Dem Constitution so that the rules for the leadership election were changed so that in an emergency and subject to the agreement of 66% of the MPs and Federal Executive, instead of the formal procedures lasting between 8 and 12 weeks, using husting meetings and paper voting; the votes of members could be cast by email from a central database and hustings meeting would be available on line.

A formal note was sent to the Queen that Sebastian Edwards could and would form the next Government of the UK. This was acknowledged by a couriered letter from the Palace.

For the most part the news of the transition got lost in the build up to Christmas

A child's toy imported from the Far East had disintegrated and several children had nearly choked to death, the Press were harrying every stockist and shop to halt all remaining sales.

There were huge queues at all main line stations going east and south and there was a near riot as some trains to the south coast had, unexpectedly, been cancelled that day.

There was fog at Heathrow and several flights were delayed, causing thousands of passengers to sleep in the terminals.

In a few days the Press settled down The banner headlines had lasted just one day. The Stock Exchange after a sharp fall three days previously recovered to previous levels. The pound recovered to over $1.5 to the £, stronger than for several months. The Stock Exchange after a sharp fall three days previously almost recovered to previous levels dragged down of course by those many mining shares whose earning came mostly from abroad.

Chapter FOUR – Sebastian's own situation

By Friday morning December 18th 2020 Sebastian was at last able to consider his own situation.

He had asked his old flat-mate Bill Bennett if he would become his Parliamentary Secretary in effect his gatekeeper, someone to prevent everyone demanding to see the PM. If effective, he could find for Sebastian, amongst all the frenetic activity, 'space', time to think, but equally important was that the person should be able to maintain contact with Lib Dem back-benchers and so be the eyes and ears of the PM. Sebastian knew that falling out with one or two Ministers of his own party was forgivable but to fall out with all his back-benchers together was certain political suicide. Bill Bennett was, on paper at least, an ideal person for the post. He had been a party Whip and knew every back-bencher by name and also their strengths and weaknesses.

There was only one thing that worried Sebastian, he and Bill had become MPs on the same date and had shared the same flat since then, they got on well together and fed off each other's strengths. Bill was elected from a large urban part of Manchester. Sebastian thought he must have been brought up from his political birth on 'Focus'. This is the standard Lib Dem newsletter used in virtually every Lib Dem campaign for decades, its philosophy was simple. First find a practical problem no matter how trivial; do something about it; then shout about it in a Focus and finally bring it to the public by sticking it through as many letter-boxes as you can. If done correctly it has the power to win most local by-election at least those with any chance of winning. Sebastian joked that Bill was only really happy producing the next issue. Sebastian's Liberalism was more cerebral and he was always talking about ' strategic issues' and tactics.

Bill's head, Sebastian thought, was like a large boiled egg and he had never summoned up enough courage to find out if he was naturally bald or shaven; anyhow when embarrassed he noted that his friend's whole head reddened. Bill had never lost his Mancunian accent, he had a rather stern off-putting look, but when he smiled his whole face became one chubby grin.

Sebastian himself had seized every opportunity and his political advance had been dramatic, in contrast Bill's sole promotion had been from unpaid Junior Whip to Junior paid Whip. Sebastian was worried that his friend might be jealous of his own rapid rise and that if the relationship were in the future to become unbearable, he might turn against Sebastian and, because he would be in a position to know Sebastian's innermost thoughts and connections, any resulting press exposure would be devastating for Sebastian, indeed it might finish him completely. On the other hand Sebastian felt he had a moral obligation to help his friend, it was his friend's support that had rescued Sebastian when he was under a determined personalised attack just a few weeks before. Sebastian hoped that by bringing Bill to the centre of politics he could perhaps encourage his promotion to a junior Minister in his own right.

He was delighted when Bill immediately accepted the position offered.

He also offered Madge O'Connor, his long standing PA and assistant, the opportunity to become his SPAD – Special Advisor. She had recently obtained a position as SPAD but with the Liberal Democrat Housing Minister, he hoped to persuade her to re-join him instead. Not only would this mean that he would have around him a team he could trust but Madge also represented his link to his home constituency based on Middleton. Madge was a feisty character smallish with dark hair, a graduate who had moved from a psychology to media degree because, as she told Sebastian, she thought it more 'commercial'. She had once ripped out the final page of a speech prepared by Sebastian to prevent him delivering that piece. A former district Councillor she had also stood for Parliament recently for Lincoln, her home town but she was unsuccessful. One matter that did concern him was that Madge and Bill had become an 'item' and Sebastian had learned from bitter experience of the problems this could cause. Anger one of the couple maybe through a difference of opinion on some policy or other could have repercussions. At worst both of them might be switched off, and both might leave, this would be devastating in such a small team, on the other hand at best, one of them would cool the other down. It could either have a multiplier or dampener effect, but it would be a risk. He decided to go for it.

He knew that he was well within the numbers of staff permitted which previous Prime Ministers had used. Pamela Tressider when previously Interim Prime Minister had had 20 staff.

He offered the post to Madge who appeared to be delighted, she had already heard of Bill's appointment.

To these he quickly added to the team John Corn, the former Chief of Staff in the LibDem/Tory Coalitions whose views and good judgement Sebastian much admired, Jo Dyson John's former Deputy, Veena Peech the Lib Dem Press Secretary and finally Baroness Sal Thrumpton whom he knew would not be frightened to point out to Sebastian if, and when, he was making mistakes. He brought in Roger Collingham-Smith a former Lib Dem Euro MP and now Senior Lecturer in European Studies at a London University who was able to take a sabbatical.

He thus had a semblance of a team, he could, if necessary, tag on some more specialists later, but it was a mix, so he thought, of professionals and colleagues with which he felt comfortable. Madge called them and invited them over and they all met with Sebastian and accepted the positions offered. They agreed to meet on Monday afternoon at 2 pm at Lib Dem headquarters to preserve secrecy. For formalities' sake he also invited Dan Stirling who, he reminded everyone, was still the leader of the party. All Liberal Democrat Ministers were asked to meet at 3.30 pm and Sebastian said he intended to meet any Lib Dem MPs who were still in London and a couple more from the Lords at 4.30 pm. This was to outline his intended strategy.

Sebastian then had to work out where he would locate himself. He basically had four options, he could, if he wished, remain in his own flat but he thought that it would soon be made impossible if the Press were permanently encamped on his doorstep. He could make use of other Government owned flats perhaps in the Admiralty, that was where John Major had lived whilst Number 10 was being refurbished, that would be secure and trouble free but it would cut him off from all Press contact; that's not what Sebastian had in mind. Then there were the last two options, Number 10 and Number 11 Downing Street. Downing Street was where the world would expect him to live and it was gated so the press could only enter if he permitted it. Frankly Sebastian didn't like working over 'the shop', he had found that living some distance away from his work in the past had allowed him to wind down after a stressful day's work, just trotting up-stairs didn't seem to offer the same relaxation regime. Anyhow he would have to choose which!

Blair and Cameron had both settled for the larger Number 11 flat because they both had had children although it was technically reserved for the Chancellor of the Exchequer. As a consequence it had been much modified and enlarged into a modern 4 bed flat. So successive Prime Ministers had ensured that the kitchens were the most up to date possible. The flat over Number 10 was the much smaller 2 bed flat but it was nothing like as lavishly furnished.

Sebastian had always hoped that his wife would take to the London scene but despite his pleas for her even to visit Chevening, the Country House put at the disposal of Foreign Ministers when he held that position, she had never done so. Apart from odd weekends when he had persuaded her to stop over in London to see a show or reluctantly to attend official banquets, she had made clear that she much preferred to stay at home.

Accordingly Sebastian decided that the smaller two bed flat would do. He 'moved in' on Thursday evening 17th December. Although 'moving in' was perhaps an exaggeration, he left all his few bits of furniture, equipment and his files in his old flat and, much to the amusement of the watching Press, walked into Number 10 with just a couple of suitcases, whereas normally, a large furniture van had been needed for all previous Prime Ministers.

The following day the Tabloids had a laugh at Sebastian's expense calling him 'The Suitcase PM'

Over lunch on Friday 18th he discussed with Pamela, his Deputy Leader, the changes to fill Cabinet vacancies. Sebastian suggested transferring David Wires to Minister without portfolio as he intended that he would be central to Sebastian's desire to make changes to the structure and culture of the Banking sector which he hoped would come out of the Royal Commission due to be published in February, Saxon Bull was to move to the Foreign Office but Sebastian was to retain relations with the EC. Sarah Driscoll was to move to Secretary of State for Communities and Regions.

Dan Stirling was to remain as Chief Secretary to the Treasury and also to be the Lib Dem part of the Quad assisted by the Lib Dem Whip Jim Spiggot.

Pamela decided that she would retain her current position as Home Office Secretary until Match 31st and take on additional duties of Deputy Prime Minister, she asked for no other changes except that their Leader in the Lords had resigned following his part in the attempted impeachment of Sebastian and was yet to be replaced.

They agreed to hold a Cabinet meeting on the following Tuesday simply, as Sebastian put it, to reassure everyone that there would be no abrupt changes in priorities or policies. The Cabinet Secretary agreed to call the Cabinet as directed. After the meeting they would all go home as the House would be in recess as of Tuesday 22nd and the Cabinet was not expected to meet again till the first Wednesday in the New Year.

By 3.30 pm that day everything appeared to be in place and Sebastian was ready to wind down after a busy week. The Cabinet Secretary invited Sebastian to meet the Number 10 staff, some of whom he remembered from his time spent there in the early stages of the Devolution Bill.

By 4.30 pm he was beginning to wilt when Sir James Knotwood asked for a few minutes to go through some pressing matters. They met in the Cabinet Room so they could lay out any papers on the large table.

Sir James quickly updated Sebastian with some formalities. He took Sebastian through the standard emergency procedures, how COBRA the emergency Cabinet subcommittee dealing with emergencies worked and showed Sebastian the famous red button in its case which would launch a Nuclear Missile and what preliminaries would have to be completed before the nuclear deterrent could be released and how Nuclear Weapons would be armed. He was shown the confidential reports from foreign embassies and agents and the daily update on world trouble spots.

Sir James brought out from a pile of papers a black leather covered diary already emblazoned with the Prime Minister's name "So Mr Edwards here is your diary!"

"Thanks" but Sebastian was already pulling his own small diary out of his pocket "Snap!" he said and then explained, "I received some excellent advice after I became a Minister. That was to ensure that you always took control of your own diary, otherwise you will discover even your best Secretary will find interesting people for you to see and meet, with the result that you meet people who want to see you and thus have no time to meet those whom you want and need to meet to do your job! Then you are no longer master of your own time! Accordingly and as I have a Deputy, I shall go through every forward booking you have for me and I can assure you that a large number of meetings will be delegated in that direction!"

"I understand Prime Minister, shall we meet on Monday to do this?"

Sebastian noticed that Sir James seemed completely unfazed by any rebuff, probably he knew already from Sebastian's previous permanent secretaries exactly how he would work as secretaries were actually much brighter than the Ministers whom they served, they had to be, of course, to cope with the intricacies of the transition, of turning party manifestos into workable Laws and of being able to cope with often incoherent suggestions and abrupt changes in policy.

What all senior Prime Minister. His modus operandi would already have been common knowledge in Senior Civil Service ranks. Sebastian had no idea how they communicated amongst themselves but they did and very effectively too. Of course all MPs were well aware that almost all Senior Permanent Sec

 Civil Servants lacked, Sebastian knew, was political legitimacy and a link to the voter, they could only achieve anything through the Ministers, whom they had to influence and drive to what they perceived the country needed.

"Just one matter Sir James that I wanted to raise with you, I hope it still gives you time enough to do it for me?"

"Yes PM?"

"I have felt for years how dreadful it must be for those who have to work on Christmas day and even worse for those who are separated from their families. I always thought that if, in any far away dream, I would end up in a position of any power, I would try to thank them and empathise with them!"

"A very noble thought PM, I am sure we are all grateful for those that work in that way or are separated like for example in our armed forces, were you thinking of sending them a message perhaps?"

"No! not that, but Yes certainly!"

"PM?"

"Yes it's a good idea to send a message to all the armed forces –I don't want them to think that now there's a Lib Dem in charge they need to do their work in any way differently!"

"I'll organise something for Monday!"

"But that's not what I meant at all. I would like to drop in and visit a prison on Christmas morning and then a hospital in the afternoon."

"Are you sure that's wise PM, staff are unusually stretched at that time you know?"

"Yes! Well, that wasn't my first concern, it was for the prisoners and patients and how awful it must be for them, kids in children's' homes that sort of thing! Have you ever been obliged to stay away from your family at Christmas, Sir James?"

Sebastian stood up and walked towards the large window overlooking Whitehall, he watched the traffic passing and the sparkling decorations dancing from every lamppost.

"No, I don't think I ever have! PM!"

"It's terrible, terrible!"

There was a moment's silence as he plodded back to the chair – the only chair to have arms!

"Please do as I ask Sir James!"

"Are you sure PM?"

Sebastian did not reply "and can you tell me how I can make an outside call from this phone please?"

"You can do it through our operator here PM! We call it the 'Switch'"

Sebastian said nothing but continued to look expectantly at Sir James.

"Oh I think it's channel 1 then dial 4 and you are outside!"

"Thank you Sir James! See you Monday then at 10.30 am!"

He made the call at 4.55 pm and just hoped the person he was looking for would still be at work.

Chapter FIVE - The Family Problem.

"Hello I am looking for Ranjit Singh, is he in please?"

"I am afraid he is busy, who is that? Can I ask him to call you back? He is still in the building."

"Yes this is Sebastian Edwards!" There was a pause as if the receptionist was consulting someone.

"Oh Yes? What is it about please?"

"I had several meetings with him about 6 weeks ago – we called it 'bumpy ride'".

In fact Ranjit's shrewd and cool handling of the case had helped Sebastian enormously and not for nothing was Ranjit Singh noted as the sharpest brain in the sharpest legal practice in London.

"Just a minute please!"

"Hello Ranjit Singh here! Is that Sebastian Edwards?"

"Yes and can I thank you again for helping me when I was at my wits' end before."

"No problem! Glad to see you have the promotion which we all thought you would get – but how can I help you now?"

"Have you a few minutes? It might take me some time to explain!"

"Yes carry on! I was just about to go home anyway. You have probably saved me from standing in a crowd for 20 minutes at the station!"

As quickly as he could Sebastian began to explain the problem with his wife's brother in law Ahmed.

"Let me stop you for a sec' all this sounds confidential are you sure you should use the phone? Look we could meet at a pub somewhere, but No! I can see now you are such a high profile person that's simply going to attract attention. Isn't there a back entrance to Downing Street? I think there is!"

Sebastian replied that he was quite relaxed about it, "If the line is bugged then so will the premises at No 10 be!"

"OK" Ranjit gave in "let's continue and if at any time I think you are relating some compromising details then I'll stop and we will have to meet here at my offices OK?"

Sebastian explained how his wife ran a charity for Asian women who were subjected to abuse usually for perceived transgression termed 'honour' matters, refusing to marry designated husbands or having relations with men of other casts or religious affiliations. She had bought what was in effect a 'safe house' where girls could feel safe. They stayed there for as long as necessary, often months. Some went out to work and they paid the charity as much as they could afford. In order to hide their presence as much as possible, they preferred not to go shopping or to visit banks and pay in their savings over and above their 'rent' to the charity. Sebastian had resigned as a Director several years previously when he had become a Minister but his place as Non-Executive Director had been taken by Ahmed, his wife's young sister's husband. He, Ahmed, had suggested that he would pay those savings into each of the girls bank accounts for them. But the Charity later learned that Ahmed had, in effect, stolen that money!"

"OK let me stop you there! So you are not directly involved at all?" Ranjit was obviously relieved.

"Yes! That's right, but I was concerned from three points of view; first that Ahmed knew there was no pay for his services but he had apparently right from the start pestered to be paid and Sebastian was not sure that his wife, Sylvia, had actually told him outright No! or if she had just deferred the discussion; second that any criminal case would almost certainly lead to a court case which would badly damage the charity, exposing the 'safe house' meaning the whole thing might have to be reset somewhere else at huge cost and third; it appeared that Ahmed had traded on his links to Sebastian so that Ahmed had received greatly extended credit and they had found out that he was in no position to repay the total amount owed."

Sebastian added other details of the case.

Ranjit sucked through his teeth "I see – nasty!"

"So, I agreed to step in, pay the money back to the girls, pay off Ahmed's creditors and even gave him some living expenses to tide him over till he got a job!"

"Oh, Oh dear, Hmm. So have you told the local Police?"

"No not yet, this all happened after the 'bumpy ride' at that time if you remember I thought I would be rather lucky to remain an MP, this thing wasn't even on my worry list! I thought, look if it's just money then let's just pay him off and walk away!"

"And now?" Ranjit asked.

"Well it all looks a bit more dangerous! I am afraid I don't trust Ahmed as far as I can throw him! If he is minded to he could invent all sorts or stories about what he did for the money I agreed to give him and could then sell stories on to tabloids. He could blackmail me, if he thought that my 'payoff' was to keep him quiet rather than me just trying to help him. He could just borrow even more trading on my connection and, ultimately, his creditors could come back at me as if I were his guarantor or something? Yet the whole thing seemed containable at the time and I did not want the consequences of a court case for either him or the charity"

"Have you paid him anything?"

"No nothing much yet just £1,000 but I paid the girls the money he took from them – and I promised that I would pay him the rest £19,000!"

"Oh well at least it's not the lot!! Now what precautions have you taken?"

"Nothing much. Oh but he's no longer a trustee of the charity!" Sebastian muttered.

"Have you had another Audit of the Charity carried out? You need to make sure that he's taken nothing else and you need them to carry out a systems check to make sure there are no other loopholes in your system! Understood?"

"Yes" Sebastian meekly replied.

"And you have to get that done very quickly, find a replacement Director, and then file a report with the Charity Commission. You need to assure them that you have fixed the problem as far as they are concerned, OK?"

"OK I'll get that started immediately".

"As far as the remainder of the money is concerned, don't pay him a penny more until I have had a chance to consider this and work out a plan that will get you out of harm's way. I think maybe we should get the chap 'Ahmed' you say, to sign a letter? We need to meet soon. Monday? No? then right now, can you manage that? It's important to get it sorted out, delay will not improve matters and will leave you exposed."

"I'll send a car over to collect you, see you in 15 minutes! I don't want to run any risks over this getting out!"

Sebastian informed the Secretariat of his plans so that the MPS security people could track his movements.

The car arrived and within 15 minutes he was looking at a draft letter which had been prepared in the meantime. Ranjit Singh asked if he had the whole story, Sebastian agreed but he suggested a couple of small changes. Sebastian told Ranjit that he had not been at any of the meetings of the Charity Trustees since he resigned 3 years ago and that he was not at all clear what had been said between Ahmed and Sylvia his wife. Ranjit assured him that it did not matter. "Can you get him to sign it? Some people are as slippery as fish when faced with something like this!"

"I'll try and if that does not work, Ranjit what then?" asked Sebastian.

"Well we will see, one step at a time but if necessary we will have to go to the police or risk doing nothing and finding the whole thing exploding in your face."

Within minutes he was transported back to Whitehall.

Much to his surprise he was easily able to pick up his car from the Car Park beneath the Commons forecourt as there was little traffic. He drove back to his home in Nottinghamshire on Friday arriving home at 9.00 pm.

As there was another MPS located on his road in the house opposite, the London MPS decided not to tail him but sent messages to successive Police forces up the M1 and he was tailed by one Police Car until another took over on entering another County right up to entering Nottinghamshire past the M 69 when the Notts Police took over.

Chapter SIX - At home in the constituency

Sebastian was turning the Car into his drive when he was stopped by the police who had taken up residence in the small house across the street a couple of years before.

His Ministerial Protection Squad was headed by Superintendent John Denny, a local bobby with whom he had worked for several years.

Before Sebastian became a Minister, Inspector John Denny, several years ago helped when Sebastian's house had been attacked in a drive-by incident, a Molotov cocktail had been exploded in his garden. The local police had asked them to move to premises which they considered they could more easily protect. Initially, the purpose had been to protect Sebastian's wife who had been targeted by those with a more strict Asian cultural code for whom Sylvia's work was a complete anathema.

Sylvia had refused to move.

John Denny had been transferred from the local police to the MPS and as a result he was promoted to Superintendent when Sebastian had become Foreign Secretary. Again they had asked him to move as the place was difficult to protect completely

This time Sebastian had refused.

He had lived in the house for nearly 20 years. It was a small place with a lounge, an attached dining area and a small kitchen on the ground floor and two bedrooms and bathroom on the first floor. There was a small patch of grass at the front alongside the drive that lead to the single garage built into the house and a larger lawned area at the back just over that fence the main road ran alongside a few feet away.

"It's not much but it is my home, and I refuse to be bullied out of it by anyone!"

When out of work 20 years ago, Sebastian been forced to sell the larger family house and downsize to this.

So the Nottinghamshire police had first rented, then bought out, the small house which stood at the entrance to the cul-se-sac on the opposite side of the road from where Sebastian lived with his wife.

They had always enjoyed cordial relations with the police, often they knew there was just one local patrolman there as evidenced by his low powered vehicle in the drive. Sometimes there was no-one and neither Sylvia nor Sebastian had been troubled at any time since the police had taken up residence. In fact they were both given bleepers to use if there was any trouble. These had been directly connected to the Police Station less than a mile away.

Since becoming Foreign Secretary just a year or so ago Sebastian now fell under the full security of the MPS the Ministerial Protection Squad and as Prime Minister he knew this would be upgraded even further.

On this occasion there was a fair old traffic jam in the cul-de-sac and Sebastian counted three police vehicles plus two outside on the main road.

He was warmly welcomed by John Denny who formally waved him to a halt. "First of all congratulations Sir on your promotion. Of course now that you are PM we have to complete yet another form! Please let us know, if you can, before you intend to leave the house so that there is always someone within reach? Just a few minutes notice means we don't have to have a mad scramble and can contact London. They have told us that we always have to know exactly where you are now and where you are going. If we lose you we know they'll go nuts in London! Otherwise just do your normal thing. We'll try to stay out of your hair as much as possible!"

Sebastian thanked John Denny and got out of his car and shook hands with each of the officers individually.

They had a peaceful evening and Sylvia did one of his favourite hot curries. They watched TV and went to bed.

All hopes of a work-free weekend was ended by the arrival on Saturday morning of 5 red boxes which had been specially driven up from London. He threw these into a corner of his lounge and at 10 am went to the constituency offices which were literally heaving with people due to Sebastian's expected arrival.

He met his key supporters Tim Holland and Mohammed Rahmam as well as his assistant Madge O'Connor now newly appointed as Sebastian's SPAD.

Sebastian started an impromptu speech in the rather untidy ground floor which was used as the production area to print off the Focus leaflets but there were still many more members and well-wishers outside. So Sebastian was obliged to move onto the pavement so they could all hear, and the crowd spilled over onto the road. Madge had a better idea, and running upstairs, she opened the window directly over the shop and shouted to Sebastian to join her. This he did and addressed his supporters from the first floor window.

Sebastian mused this was all rather nineteenth century as politicians like Gladstone, his hero, frequently addressed the public from a first floor balcony of suitable buildings.

The road was effectively closed for several minutes whilst Sebastian gave a speech thanking everyone!

The local Press and TV were across the road and caught scenes of clapping and waving. The Press were eventually asked in after the crowds had dispersed and Sebastian gave a fairly downbeat interview simply describing the process, where he would be living and what he would be doing over Christmas.

He said that he hoped to arrange visits to places where people had to work over that period and could not be with their families. He declined to elaborate as to what that might mean and where he would be visiting.

Some fish and chips were brought in and Sebastian sat munching his chips which he had ordered vinegared and with just a tiny bit of salt!

He had a quick word privately with both Tim and Rahmam and told them to email him if they thought he could help. Tim told him that the Unitary Councils measure was going through, but still that he and other Lib Dems were expecting some backlash. The closure of District Councils had been unpopular with local politicians of every hue. Rahmam gave him better news, he related that at last the Middleton Neighbourhood plan had been approved and voted on in a referendum, that this had indeed increased the CIL, developers tax, and that they hoped to set up the Car Park soon. This was seen by everyone as absolutely necessary for the town.

He drove back home by 2.00 pm and immediately felt he had to start ploughing through the red boxes, he thought if he could clear the majority now they might give him some peace over the Bank Holiday for he knew he would be busy on Christmas Day.

The Red Boxes contained all manner of things; what Sebastian described as 'his homework', a mixture of papers from Cabinet Ministers, other documents he had requested earlier (in this case on the Rail chaos on station south of the River), and statistics; piles and piles of statistics, the numbers of Prisoners, Prison Staff, Police, Armed Services, rehashed budgets of this and that. Letters from senior members of the diplomatic corps, notice of changes of Ambassadors and bits and pieces that appeared to need his signature, update of his security clearance. Invitations to Lunch and carefully selected letters from other MPs and letters from important bodies like the Stock Exchange and Lloyds, several letters from Chairmen of larger corporations offering their advice as to how he should run the Country. Several Senior lecturers of various Universities at home and abroad asking for his political view of this or that policy or strategy.

Chapter SEVEN - The Cabinet Secretary, meeting Sebastian's Team

On Monday morning December 21st 2020 at 6.00 am he was collected by the official car and driven to London; Sebastian was still not quite sure of the system used to allocate cars or how they were organised.

As Foreign Secretary he realised that, as a department, they appeared to have a different system, the reason for which had never been explained but it had been relatively easy to understand and organise; if he had to be somewhere abroad or in London then he would simply leave it to his staff to organise, but when he went home or back to London he would use his own car, by agreement with the MPS. He was met at every county border on the M1 by a new police force being passed on from county to county much as passenger aircraft are passed from one flight control centre to another. He thus had the use of his own car whether in London or at home.

He realised that as PM he was much more likely to be taken anywhere in the country at any time. If he was always based in London then that did not pose much of a problem. Having his home split between London and near Nottingham, Sebastian realised, was going to make his logistics much more complicated. If he didn't have his own car in London then he would be entirely dependent on the Government Car Service for every little trip or use a taxi which he would have to share with his MPS. On the other hand being near Nottingham for the weekends didn't stop the seemingly endless supply of red boxes arriving daily by chauffeured limousine to his doorstep. 'That's as barmy' thought Sebastian 'as the Royal Regalia, that is the Imperial State Crown, being carried to Westminster in its own state coach'. He could of course take the train but he would still be accompanied by the MPS. He decided he couldn't work out how to manage things, but he was quite well aware that there was a published list of car costs allocated to Ministries which, from time to time caught, the eye of the Press and gave their editors acres of column inch space for text and pictures highlighting excessive costs incurred by certain Ministers. He expected sniping attacks like these towards the end of his 13 weeks as PM but he wanted to avoid unnecessary own goals and told all LD ministers to watch their official car usage, for now he'd just go with the flow!

He was driven direct to Number 10.

He met up with the Cabinet Secretary and they worked slowly through the diary. In attendance was a 'proper' secretary taking notes.

Sir James first pointed out what he considered the 'must go to' events – they went through these, weekly audiences with Her Majesty, regular Cabinet Meetings, COBRA Meetings, expected visits by Foreign Heads of Government these were marked as 'MUSTgt' so that staff could be advised how to organise his movements. Where he was speaking for the Government in an official capacity, then speeches would be prepared for him, all others, like political speeches he would have to be responsible himself through his team.

"The key item that you have to decide PM on this list is what you want to do about the EC, you will know that the UK was to have been the EC's President of the Council back in 2016 but due to the first referendum the UK waived that right but then, after the second referendum which re-engaged the UK in the EC, we re-joined the list of revolving Heads of States. This next year 2021 is our turn again. Now the position of President has become more complicated as it's actually a sort of triumvirate or 'trio' as they call it, there are three states, ourselves and two others, who work out the long term goals and prepare the topics and major issues for the following 18 months agendas between them, that's to provide some continuity. The other two are Portugal and Slovenia. Unfortunately, as you are aware, the previous Prime Minister Robin Turnbull was a Brexiteer not very EC focussed and had actually missed one or two meetings."

"Yes" Sebastian put in "I remember that I had to deputise for him in November – we didn't actually discuss much."

"That's right PM. Anyhow the others are by now aware of your promotion and it might be as well if I sent them a message of your willingness to fully contribute which is, I gather, your intention following your desire to retain control over EU matters?"

"Yes! Please, Sir James, ask both of their secretaries to dig out the latest agendas and add a note to them that I will need an additional 15 minutes in my speech to raise a number of issues on the future direction and development of the EC and the UK's part in that?"

"The first meet isn't until the end of February, PM, it's held in Brussels at the Justus Lipsius building, I think?"

"Oh and please ask the FCO to dig out the latest EU 'barometer', it's a sort of public interest poll and gives the 6 most important issues as seen by EU Citizens, it's updated every 3 months or so?"

The secretary nodded.

Sebastian turned to Sir James and passed him a card, "Could you please get this person now?

"Yes PM" Sir James nodded to the secretary, she returned minutes later whilst they were still discussing the remainder of the diary bookings.

"Now let's go through some of these other meetings shall we Sir James? Shall we designate these "MAYgt"

About half the meetings he suggested should be delegated and Sir James agreed to discuss these with the Deputy PM.

The phone rang and it was passed to Sebastian "Ah! Bonjour Jacques". There followed several sentences in franglais which confused the position even more than had they each stuck to their own language; eventually Sebastian put the phone down. Sir James leant forward quietly "I understand from this, PM, that you have asked for a private meeting with the French President using the good offices of the French Health Minister you met some time ago!"

"Exactly Sir James!" said Sebastian, quite unabashed.

Sir James raised the matter of the other countries within the UK, Scotland, Wales and Northern Ireland, "It's tradition to meet with each of them, probably at a time when their representatives also meet."

"Yes I am aware of that, but with all the travel and an overnight stay… that's a minimum of two days each about a full week if I visit each independently! But I have only got 13 weeks; that's nearly a tenth of my time unless I can manage the whole lot in two days? So maybe I could fly up Sunday night, Monday morning Scotland, afternoon Stormont, Tuesday Cardiff back here Tuesday lunch. Can you work on timing for that and come back to me?"

"I shall be here for most PMQs and, when I am, I will require the morning beforehand for a full briefing with my team from 10 00 am and a meeting with the Chief Whip at 9.00 am on his own."

Sir James raised an eyebrow which Sebastian had already learned meant 'Surely not!' This obliged Sebastian to repeat the instruction for clarity.

"And I will need from Friday 12 noon to Saturday 12 noon blanked out"

"Would you be going home then PM? To arrange cars? Will Mrs Edwards be joining you in London?"

"No! Probably not." Again the eyebrow!

"Any more?" Sebastian enquired. "These would be the NOTgt?"

"Well there are the usual stock of important Employers Groups and various 'chancers' from well-known charities just gambling that they might be lucky, your presence could earn for the charity £50 per seat more! See here is one from a children's charity, there is another from a young offenders rehab scheme?"

Sebastian said "Let's have a look! Hmmh!"

Sebastian winked at Sir James "I have always wanted to do this! Please get me Lord Jacob of whatever, you know S & G the largest clothes retailer?"

"You mean Lord Israel Jacob of Golders Green?"

"Yes that's him!"

"Now Prime Minister?" again the raised eyebrow.

"Yes right now – if he doubts it is for me, please get him to call back, the code is 'Remarkable stallholder' Sir James nodded to the secretary who reappeared a few minutes later.

"He is calling back Sir!" she said.

The call came in Sebastian asked "How do I use speaker phone?" Sir James pressed the buttons.

"Can you two please give me a few minutes – it's a private matter!

"Hello is that the PM, Sebastian Hughes, or something?"

"Edwards, Sebastian Edwards" Sebastian broke in.

"Yes, yes. What's the matter? Haven't I paid enough taxes? Are you looking for an extra cheque for staff wages to carry you over to the new year, or something!"

"No! It's not that, I have an idea" said Sebastian.

"Ha! That's a good one, is an idea the same as a promise then?" asked the Peer

"No you can't break an idea!"

"Well normal people can't but I am sure a politician can if he really tries," joked the Peer "OK let's have it!"

"Well I have always bought your kit, suits, shirts, trousers, jackets shoes even dinner jackets!" Sebastian started to explain.

"Bully for you, you won't be surprised when I tell you that's what everyone says to me when I meet them!" retorted the Peer. "OK OK, go on!"

"Well I want to suggest that you start a new brand called PM Premier or First Minister or something aimed particularly at my ageing generation; pre and post retirement, the grey hairs market".

There was silence "and" the peer asked "where's the catch? Are you looking for free clothes or something? Look I know they don't pay you much but we have our own sales staff you know!"

"No no! It's not that, I'll pay for all the kit I buy, after all that's what I have been doing for 40 years!"

"So what's the game?"

"You add 10% to the selling price and give the difference to a designated charity, showing this on all of the dedicated range that you sell!"

"What charities?"

At least the Peer had not said No! and that was encouraging! "I don't know!"

"How long did you say you were going to be PM for?"

"Till March 31st!"

"Thirteen to fifteen weeks only! Hummph – just a minute!" it sounded as if he was muttering to someone nearby. "OK I'll send the Senior Men's buyer and Design Director around – tomorrow! "

"I am a bit busy then – what about 6.00 pm tonight?"

"OK where should they go – Oh I get it Downing Street! Look, Mr Edwins, I'll get my guys to look at it and see the stuff you like and what we think suits you, what might be in the range and then I'll get my marketing guys on it. OK? Tell you after Christmas OK? Just give me your measurements will you?"

Sebastian did so and there was a mild "Huh! Oh dear!" Then the phone went dead.

Sebastian was taken to Chelsea Barracks at 1.00 pm and there gave a brief message that would be relayed to all military units, air and naval bases and barracks at home and abroad on Christmas Day. It was simply stating that he had been Foreign Secretary, then Deputy Prime Minister and was now Prime Minister and that basic policies were not going to change and that he in turn would hand over to a new PM at the end of March. He thanked them for their service on behalf of the State.

He then rushed back to Lib Dem Headquarters.

His entire team was assembled at 2 pm on Monday December 21st.

The venue, whilst away from prying eyes, was the same stuffy cramped room they had used before. At Dan's suggestion three of the Cabinet Ministers were also present. In view of his position, as Party Leader, Dan Stirling took the seat behind the only desk and, as a consequence, when Sebastian stood to make the introductions his papers cascaded onto the floor, so immediately Dan suggested to Sebastian that they change seats. Sebastian was then able to lay out the papers in front of him.

Sebastian immediately launched into his theme.

"At our recent meeting it was Dave Billingham who questioned my ability to take over the position of PM. I have thought about it long and hard and he is right, in part. However I think I know myself but I cannot be sure how well I will succeed under extreme pressure. The purpose of this session is for you frankly to discuss my strengths and weaknesses, I hope constructively and then after this I want to put a proposal to you which I think is the only one with which I feel happy, to gauge your reactions. The comments can be either your own or what others have told you about me, but be as honest as you can."

"So start me off, Madge would you list the items on a flip chart please? And by the way make sure they are destroyed immediately afterwards – we definitely don't want to gift this to the Tories or let it be found on some tip!"

Madge collected the comments Positive on one Flip Chart and Negative on the other. Quite a number were painful and made Sebastian wince, but he didn't argue with any of them.

After about 20 minutes of this Sebastian spoke again "Well it's a bit like gymnastics I suppose let's cut off the very worst and very best comments about which frankly I can do very little. What I pick up from this is that I am likely to be poor at Prime Minister's Questions and formal speeches unless, as one of you said, I am really passionate about something. I am at my best in raising off the cuff matters and sparking discussion and lateral thinking. My very worst aspect is in trying to push something through with which I am not in favour, it's likely I would get caught out by a persistent TV interviewer if repeatedly asked 'But do you yourself agree with this?' So I have to avoid general TV interviews which involve answering unscripted questions from aggressive reporters."

Now here is how I see it, at PMQ I am going to need considerable coaching and rehearsing and I am going to have to rely on my team for that.

First I will of course ensure that we proceed with LD policies like; Devolution to the Regions, Reform of the House of Lords, massive Affordably or Council House build. If ever these are threatened, I will inform the Party Leader and ask him to reform this committee. Then we will all decide how to proceed and if we wish to break the Coalition.

I expect major problems with the next Spring Review which is due in my term. This is where any new, overtly Tory, bias is likely to show itself.

As far as passing overtly Tory policy in Cabinet is concerned, I shall simply advise the Deputy in advance that I want her to take the lead, I hope this will diffuse much Tory energy trying to entrap me which I feel sure they will. In HS2 of course they still have a massive 'elephant trap' of their own making. There are Vehicle blockages around Manchester and huge problems on the train service to the South Coast but instead they intend to throw money at a vanity project which has other Tory MPs openly grumbling.

There are times, of course, when I will be unavailable anyhow due to my being President of the EC Council and I will need considerable time as you will see to do my bit on the EC.

However the Prime Minister is in a unique position in that, although Cabinet Ministers are obliged to refer to him on any speech they might want to make, and the PM can in the Press trump any Tory minister trying to do his own thing, the Prime Minister is not obliged to do the same. He is able to raise any number of points without contradiction, or at least he can do so at the moment. My idea therefore is to have a whole list of pre-prepared issues which can be made into Press releases or form the basis of an agreed single issue interview. Also I shall endeavour to meet such Press as are in general favourable to us and particularly develop Regional Press and TV. Here is the list."

He handed the list around. There was a mixture of nods of approval, gasps and grimaces. "This isn't a list set in concrete far from it, I'll have to be guided partly by what my team thinks and partly by views from members."

Dan Stirling had obviously been holding back "But some of these are not Lib Dem policy at all why not just take all our policies and just use those, why try to invent stuff ?"

"Well I am not trying to impress Lib Dem members and voters with Lib Dem policies, I am relying on you all to do that. It will destroy my value to you if I just spout propaganda. I am trying to show that I am interested in the people's problems, that is what concerns them! Trying to connect with a wider audience. Look at one item for example, the shocking performance on what used to be Southern Rail. Trains run late or are arbitrarily cancelled and, if you can get on one, at peak periods, you'll be squashed like a sardine in a can. I mean if anyone had a big blow out on dozens of curries the night before the whole carriage would faint? – there's no Lib Dem policy for that is there?"

There was a subdued laugh and muttering around the room.

"But" a Cabinet Minister interjected "what would you do about it? Would you be able to solve the problem? Wouldn't we just look silly saying we would do something and then do nothing?" .

"Well maybe and maybe not, so what I intend to do as of now is to take a journey from Brighton to London at peak hour, myself. Maybe that way I can embarrass the train directors to do something; maybe I can change the definition of what late means; maybe I can offer the travellers a discount – but I am bloody well going to try to do something!"

"Hmmh" there was a general assent around the table.

"At least in this way I hope to be able to stay ahead of the game, constantly raising new issues; several will fail but I hope many will succeed. I can raise one or just possibly two issues a week. I think Friday lunch is possibly the best time as the Sunday papers are looking for stories to fill their pages. I reckon that I will have a chance to push out 5 or 6, possibly 8 at the most, before the Tory Cabinet Ministers twig and try to constrain my activities. I am pretty well resigned to the fact that the last 4 or 5 of the 13 weeks are going to be rather savage – hell you might say! As they try to unseat me after the Tories have agreed their new leader."

"Why's that?" someone asked.

"If by then they have already elected a leader they are going to hit me every day with 'your job's done move over!' Or, frankly, some much ruder comments. I will be under attack from the 1922 committee, some Cabinet members and very many Tory back benchers. Press and TV will want to crown the next PM not waste time on an old one passed his sell by date! The loyalty of senior civil servants is going to move into sharp decline, they may deliberately simply miss me off meetings and refuse to follow up initiatives which they were happy to do the week before. They'll start talking to the next PM behind my back to check if so and so which I requested, should in fact be done and is really needed! In short my power will fade. I expect major problems with the next Spring Statement which is due near the end of my term.

There are several things that I can do to counteract that. They still need our support in the Commons and I am sure that the Lords, where following the strict party line is seen as frankly a bit tacky, would resist any attempt to undermine a published agreement, which is what we have, were it not for the fact that I am trying to abolish them! So if any of you have any other bright ideas now's the time to come forward. I am hoping Dan Stirling will protect my back everything ultimately will go through the Quad and it will take great judgement from him to know when to settle with the Tories and when to raise a formal objection."

Dan Stirling nodded his approval

"Anyhow that's my plan, I won't issue much advance notice on any of these issues or interventions as I will call them, but I will have them researched and hope to be able to launch them within a 24 hours' notice!

Now I am well aware as they say 'the road to hell is paved with good intentions'. I am told that Gordon Brown had a similar sort of wish list for his first 100 days – apparently he just got thrown off course by the 'banking problem' and was never able to get back on track!"

Sebastian did not go into all these tactics with the other Lib Dem Ministers but moved to explain the changes in ministerial positions.

At the later meeting of the MPs he thanked them for their patience, asked them to support him at 'this crucial time' and suggested that a time would be set aside where any MP could request a 10 minute meeting with him, booked through Madge, to discuss any pressing matter, though it might have to be at a weekend. This seemed to cheer them. Sebastian knew that communication within the Party had not been good recently, he hoped to show each one of them that they were important to him.

Sebastian pulled Madge aside "Look I want to arrange a small family party here in No 10 for next Saturday, could you arrange it? He gave her the list. Minimum publicity! OK?"

Madge agreed.

Then he was back at Downing Street for fitting jackets and trousers by the retailer's staff. An estate car arrived with the retailer's name emblazoned on the side and the bemused photographers clicked a small team of people taking rails of men's clothes into No 10 and then an hour later taking them out again.

The Design Director was heard to say to Sebastian on the doorstep "That'll be £2000 for that lot, thanks! – No I am only jesting!"

Sebastian was heard to say "Well I hope so!"

Speculation soon grew that something was afoot but no-one quite worked out what that might be!

Chapter EIGHT – 1st Cabinet, Chilcot discussions with Cabinet Secretary

The Cabinet meeting was held on Tuesday December 22nd at 10 am. It was, as Sebastian, had advised, merely to settle people in new Cabinet positions. He paid tribute to Robin Turnbull and said that he intended to work with all ministers towards the goals that had been agreed by the Coalition.

He declared "I am the accidental steward and I shall do my best to hand back my stewardship in as good or better state than when I took this office!"

He pointed out that he was going to continue with the smaller Cabinet and was intending to introduce a couple of minor alterations which he wanted first to run past Sir James Knotwood, the Cabinet Secretary, and that Cabinet Members would receive a paper for discussion quite soon.

He finally assured the Conservative members of the Cabinet particularly that he hoped for a smooth transition at the end of March, "I hope, by then, to have made some headway in a few directions, of which I hope you will approve."

With that he wished them all a Merry Christmas and Happy New Year and hoped to meet them again on Wednesday 6th January 2021.

The meeting closed at 11.30 am so that newly appointed Ministers could spend more time within their departments and pick up various ongoing projects.

He asked the Chief Whip, Sir John Hopkins MP, to hang back and asked Bill Bennett who, as his PPS was also there, to arrange a meeting for his team for lunch at 1.00 pm. He asked to see the Cabinet Secretary at 2.00 pm for a brief meeting.

Sebastian had met Sir John Hopkins many times in 2018 when he has served under him briefly as the Lib Dem Chief Whip. That had proved a difficult period for both of them but Sebastian had had to admit that Sir John's recommendation to the then PM had been to promote him away from the Whip's office, as he was not considered to be suitable material. But then the Whips' office was renowned as either a cul-de-sac or part of the promotional ladder, good Whips were rarely successful later on as ministers because they had evolved different skills. It had actually been the start of Sebastian's rapid ministerial promotion. Nearly two years later when Sebastian was going through his 'bumpy ride' as he later described it, Sir John was one of those who had unexpectedly come to his aid!

Sir John was an old military man, of average height and was prone, to dress, when the House was in session, in a smart three piece dark subdued tartan suit. His tie, Sebastian knew was of some Guards regiment. He had a military moustache. He was ruddy faced and his sloping forehead and brow were clear of hair. Apart from his brow, a shock of white hair, almost crew cut, covered his head. He always spoke with a clear parade ground voice, his instruction to Sebastian had always been precise.

"Hello Sir John" started Sebastian when the room had cleared. "I just want, belatedly, to thank you for your support a few weeks ago. It was much appreciated!"

Sebastian was aware that any Tory found helping a Lib Dem couldn't be openly thanked. Anyhow, Sebastian wasn't sure, but he thought he saw a blush of embarrassment flash momentarily across the man's face, but of course it couldn't be, could it? but in an instant Sir John regained his composure.

"Hello er er.." Sebastian knew Sir John had always called him and everyone else of lower rank, 'dear boy!' and he could see that he now had had to modify his previously automatic introduction "er Sir, Prime Minister?"

"Well", Sir John "You were quite right! I wasn't cut out to be a Whip was I?"

Sir John relaxed somewhat "Well it's not a role for everyone is it, but congratulations Sir!"

"Sir John, you and I have a particularly difficult three months ahead of us! For my part I am committed to continuing with the Coalition's objectives. You know I got on well with Robin Turnbull and I am sorry that he had to go, but there really was no way out for him. So now I'll hope to run a Cabinet most of whom are Tories; if I lean too far that way my Lib Dem friends will cut me to pieces, too far the other way and by a simple majority in the Cabinet I could be unseated. All this I am afraid makes your job more complicated I fear…"

Sir John interrupted. "No No! not at all, Sir. I am the Government Chief Whip and you represent the Government, until I am instructed otherwise, and if I am so instructed I'll let you know immediately, my role was, and is, to serve the Prime Minister!"

"Thank you Sir John, you will appreciate that near the end of the three months it's likely to get a bit hectic, tricky, there will likely be some plots…"

"Now don't you go worrying about that Sir, they'll have to get past me first!"

"Thank you Sir John!" As he turned away Sebastian thought he saw a tear slowly dribble down the older man's cheek, silly he thought, it must be the fading light.

Sebastian's team met at 1.00 pm, Sebastian thanked them all for their work so far and promised, "more of the same in 2021". They then transferred to Lib Dem headquarters at 1.30 pm where all the Liberal MPs and staff were gathered and he made a speech of thanks, asking them to "Go back to your constituencies and double your membership and your work!" He promised them a different kind of government and some early changes.

At 2.00 pm he was back to one of the smaller rooms in the Cabinet office for the discussion with Sir James Knotwood, Sebastian asked the 'proper' secretary taking notes to leave.

"Sir James, its many years ago that I was called out by the Conservative Leader in Middleton District Council for criticising the officers there. I was told that it is bad form to attack those who are unable to defend themselves. I think the Leader was possibly right, although I had no forum for adequately questioning him and when I did I was merely brushed off, like a person might brush off say a ladybird! In practice of course the Civil Service has many ways of getting back at a politician but I don't want to go into that now!"

"So how can I help Prime Minister; what are you thinking of? I hope during the last few days I haven't given any caused for complaint?" His eyebrows positively jumped in alarm.

"No No! this is not personal in any way, any way at all because it concerns your predecessor, actually predecessor but one!" Sebastian coughed he knew he had to introduce the topic slowly. "I was reading through the Chilcot papers…"

"Ah! Them!" said Sir James as if in dread of the whole Iraq problem being raised again.

"Yes! exactly, them, particularly the testimony of the then Cabinet Secretary, actually held on 13th January 2010 almost a decade ago; you see the Cabinet structure and process has changed very little since then hasn't it?"

"Yes I suppose so, though we have strengthened the committee structures and sorted out the hierarchy problems within the Secret Services!"

"But that's not the direction of my enquiry with you! Of course Tony Blair did a lot of silly things, agreeing to support Bush 'whatever' and seemingly going for regime change which appears to be outlawed, not to mention whether or not he caused the dodgy dossier to be sexed up or wilfully convinced himself that there was, or would be, WMD found!"

"So the opprobrium is heaped on Tony Blair and by extension his Cabinet for failing to check, criticise, question what was going on around them, some of which they didn't know anyhow!"

"So I ask myself, Sir James, how this could have happened? You know it's the sort of scenario that could have been much more serious, for example, if somehow the game had been uprated to launching heavier, more lethal missiles, and then what?"

Sir James looked annoyed and was about to reply but Sebastian held up his hand to stop him. "Wait a minute please, the purpose of my question will become clear very soon. As you know I agreed with Robin Turnbull that the Cabinet was too large and unless it was reduced in numbers there never would be an opportunity to interrogate, criticise or even improve proposals put to it. So firstly I will propose that for any future Military intervention, by that I mean use of force, where the government of the country concerned has not invited us in, that involvement by representatives of certain ministries will be included in a special Cabinet Subcommittee whose meeting would be formally minuted. This should improve the very poor and selective planning that did take place. However, here in the UK, Prime Ministers who have won a second election believe they are invincible, that their judgement is infallible and they take short cuts as Tony Blair did. In effect he avoided those who questioned what was happening. The PM worked only with those, on an Ad Hoc basis, whom the he could trust and who fed him what he wanted to hear.."

"That's not altogether true, Prime Minister, I have been over that same transcript too and some matters were questioned indeed, to quote Lord Turnbull 'there were 24 key moments of endorsement'…"

Sebastian pulled out his copy of the transcript of the interview.

"Well how about this 'I think they were quite familiar with that style of working by five years yes!' This was about 'sofa government, when key decisions were taken by individuals, working in little Ad Hoc groups'? As Lord Turnbull said 'I think once the ministers had coalesced people said 'there is a settled policy' and you are not encouraged once this thing has settled to go on arguing that we shouldn't have done this.' So it became a series of updates not decision points?"

"So, Mr Edwards where does this all lead?" Sir James questioned, clearly tiring of an unaccustomed interrogation.

Sebastian replied quickly "It leads directly to exactly what the Head of the Civil Service was doing? Let me quote one more of Lord Turnbull's comments, towards the end of the interview he suggests that even had there been more 'sharing (of information) between the insider group and the outsider group, I don't think it would have made much difference'.. because they were operating on false information but he continues 'The only way it (carrying out a reality check) would have happened is if there had been somewhere close to the Prime Minister, saying, you know 'You need to think about'…

"So my question is why did not the Head of the Civil Service provide that role?"

Sir James was silent waiting for what, he knew, would be Sebastian's main thrust.

"Let me take you back right to the start of the interview Lord Turnbull defines the role of the Cabinet office he stated it is 'on its website it says…' Look here I have listed them down for you!" Sebastian read out the list of roles;

1) *It is supporting the Prime Minister in leading the Government*
2) *Supporting Ministers collectively*
3) *Providing the fora to take their decisions*
4) *Resolution of disputes*
5) *Co-ordination*
6) *Using the five secretariats (I am not clear what that is?)*
7) *It is (sic) development of capacity in the Civil Service*
8) *And it is the guardian of the rules of propriety.*

Sebastian handed the list to Sir James and continued "Then, he immediately states 'It is the first two that are relevant' In my opinion that's nonsense, Sir James, he failed to carry out 'resolution of disputes', one Cabinet Member resigned, he failed to ensure that 'co-ordination' was carried out between departments for planning e.g. troops not adequately equipped', there was no adequate discussion on the legal issues, so no help to provide the fora to make decisions, but there was, of course, an awful lot of railroading! And no application of the rules of propriety!"

Sir James was clearly annoyed and stood back arms across his chest in a petulant attitude, "Prime Minister, I object, you are certainly wrong if you are implying the Civil Service acted inappropriately."

"My vision of the Civil Service is that it operates for the good of the UK, OK through the Government of the day, duly elected, but in my opinion the then Cabinet Secretary seriously lurched way off-line following a Prime Minister whom the Civil Service knew was not adequately consulting some Ministers, such as Claire Short or even whole Departments!"

Sebastian knew he was winding himself up and any further direct accusations could likely lead to Sir James' withdrawal. The moment that that happened Sebastian realised, he would lose his own moral authority, so he withdrew from the frontal assault and planted the blame firmly at the door of the instigator of the problem.

"I have to repeat yet again for the sake of clarity that, of course, the majority of the blame rests with Tony Blair, but the Civil Service Head would have seen all this confusion, stretching of the truth, hopeless lack of planning and yet, he simply stood by?"

Sir James' eyebrows shot up again, but Sebastian realised that he had gone too far now to pull back.

"The Cabinet office did not in fact have complete ownership of the project did it? and to that extent it's wrong to blame them wholly. But nor was this project apparently Lord Turnbull's primary role! He was asked by Sir Lawrence Freedman, see here it is I have underlined the passage, 'Can you give us some idea generally how much of your time was being spent on Iraq issues, say from the point of time you came in, in early September, through to the start of the war itself?' Lord Turnbull replied 'I don't know, I'm not sure. It wasn't the biggest part of my job – two things, one is, in effect, I was the Line Manager for 30 Permanent Secretaries and I spent many hours working on the SAS Committee, and on the Delivery and Reform agenda.'

So you see he wasn't even there for some of the time and wasn't fully switched on, he didn't and couldn't question everything, he allowed the decisions to be made outside of any formal structure!"

"So that's you conclusion Mr Edwards?" Sebastian sensed that the old Civil Service knack of hiding behind questions was going to make it difficult to engage in discussion so he quickly came to the crux of the matter.

"Yes it is! Sir James, and, in order to prevent its reoccurrence; first there must be one Lead Minister (who must not be the Prime Minister) taking responsibility before Parliament for the whole mission pre and post intervention and; second there must be one Lead Civil Servant (who must not be the Head of the Civil

Service) co-ordinating and if necessary organising the process. Indeed the Head of the Civil Service should designate one of the Permanent Secretaries for that role and he himself should have oversight from reports as to what is going on. It's then for the Head of the Civil Service to question if the plans are wide or deep enough and to ensure himself that the majority of the Cabinet are aware of options and costs so as to enable them to come to a political conclusion, and indeed to ensure that the operations are, in fact, legal!"

"Hmmh So the purpose of this meeting?" Sir James seemed relieved but he began to drum with his fingers on the desk, which he immediately ceased when Sebastian noticed. Sebastian thought that Sir James was rattled, but how would he now behave, would he walk away or engage, if he did the latter it could only be as an admission of past civil service failings.

Sebastian tried to help "Well next is for you to declare, having discussed this with your Permanent Secretaries by your usual process of osmosis, what changes the Civil Service will make if the situation recurs. I will match this by stating at the next Cabinet that a formal Cabinet Committee must be established that has the full information satisfactory to make a Cabinet decision. The whole new procedure will then be wrapped up in a formalised package which will also be sent to all opposition parties whom I have every reason to suspect will endorse it. This will then become the standard default procedure for any future military foreign intervention. It becomes a format to follow? Let's be clear it cannot constrain the actions of a future PM but it will clearly lay down an expected pattern of behaviour which any Cabinet member can refer to! As I said at the start I have no wish to openly argue with the Civil Service.

I'll send you my proposal over Christmas and I hope we can promulgate that at the first Cabinet meeting?"

"So what is your opinion Sir James?" Sebastian felt things were coming together but he was not sure, he twiddled the signet ring on his little finger, which he knew he always did when nervous or agitated.

Sir James spoke at last. "It may surprise you to learn that I agree with most of it, it was never really under full Civil Service control and by flitting about Tony Blair was almost impossible to control, nor could anyone, certainly not any cabinet ministers, manage to sit him down and make him look at the whole thing himself. Sorry to sound obstructive, I thought your line of questioning was leading somewhere else!"

"Where?" Sebastian enquired quietly.

"I wasn't sure; possibly you insisting that a special meeting he held of Privy Councillors before any such venture is launched, or additional staged votes in parliament, maybe a neutral committee chair or publication of secondary justifying information – none of which I could have supported since they would have been brushed aside by any Prime Minister who had 'the wind in his sails". Sir James sounded profoundly relieved.

"But we agree?" asked Sebastian "After all this reinforces Civil Service control in that very sensitive area?"

"Yes I agree! But it also puts us Civil Servants in the 'eye of the storm' and for what? A second general-election-winner rampant PM can believe he has the trust of the people, which justifies him acting out his vision of how the world ought to work. But, at least, it sets a standard!"

As Sebastian left the table he offered his hand to Sir James which was taken immediately.

"No offence meant" Sebastian stated.

"None taken," came the reply.

Sebastian was however concerned, the Civil Service disliked Politicians reworking what they did, he shrugged his shoulders.   As he climbed the stairs to the flat above, he muttered to himself, 'he has every opportunity to get even, silly of me to have raised it right at the start of my term, or, am I already getting slightly paranoid?'

Later there were several private email exchanges with Tories until an agreed, joint statement was prepared.

Chapter NINE – Christmas Day – Prison Visit

Sebastian was up and had finished breakfast by 8.30 am. He opened the front door of his house. It was cold and wet and he could see his breath like a mist in front of him.

He went across the road and knocked on the door of the Police House. A sergeant popped his head round the door and they briefly discussed where they were going and the expected route.

The head, this time with its cap, on popped out again "OK be with you in 5 mins, Sir!"

Sebastian went back to his car and waited. A couple of burly policemen emerged and went for the souped up Land Rover. They were fully equipped with body armour and what looked to Sebastian like canisters of pepper spray, or maybe they were Tasers, over the body armour. Across their chests they both carried snub nosed sub machine guns. They drew up alongside and the Sergeant lowered the window.

"OK Sir just follow us nice and easy, don't stop or vary your pace. If we choose to do so we may change the route, if we do it'll be deliberate and for a reason, just follow us as before. There is a police helicopter on call a few minutes away so don't worry even if anything happens to us, just keep moving! Don't stop unless we instruct you to do so! OK?"

There was hardly any other traffic on the roads. There were a few pedestrians walking purposefully about, Sebastian thought maybe to Church, and a couple of children had clearly insisted going outside to try out their new bicycles as soon as it was light. They tottered unsteadily along the pavements, guided by reluctant and sleepy adults.

They arrived at the Prison in the East Midlands early

The police car remained in the car park and Sebastian moved to the massive grey painted door set into a Victorian entrance gate built of sandstone blocks, which Sebastian noted were blackened on the right hand side of the door, presumably he thought, having caught the sooty air from the town, in the prevailing wind. He could see that there was a smaller wicket gate inserted into the larger door.

He pressed the buzzer and explained he had come to see the Governor. The door opened inwards and he found himself in an enclosed inner courtyard with another large metal gate ahead.. A door opened from the side and a large dark blue uniformed prison guard asked him through, explaining as he did so: "Hello my name is Mister Macwigan I am an OSG that is an Operational Support Grade officer. The Governor knows you are coming. You appreciate, Sir, that normally no visits are permitted on Christmas Day. So this is the staff entrance but I am afraid we still have to search you as indeed we do all visitors. I hope that is alright, Sir?"

He was lined up against a white wall subjected to a 'rub down' and a metal detector was passed over him. "Just like at an airport, Sir" Macwigan added cheerily.

Sebastian tried to engage him in conversation but he saw that the OSG needed to process him quickly so all he was able to say to him was "Nice day, thank you for your work today."

The OSG shot him a confused look and Sebastian deduced that maybe he had not been told the purpose of his visit.

Sebastian forgot to place his keys, money, notepad and propelling pencil on the tray, so the process had to be repeated. "Sorry" he said.

He was given the all clear and passed into another room where another OSG asked for some identification. "It's standard procedure, Sir". After all the publicity of the last few days, it had not occurred to Sebastian that he might have to justify who he was, he was momentarily baffled. The OSG handed him a long plastic coated typed list of 'papers required for identification'…. 'Passport, Driving Licence, Utility Bill' and so on'.

Sebastian searched his pockets and luckily found his driving licence card and a phone bill from the shared flat in London. "Sorry about this, Sir, but the Governor said I should treat you as any visitor".

"No, that's fine" replied Sebastian "it gives me a feel of the process that others go through!"

"Now, Sir, would you stand against that wall, all visitors have to be photographed." A fixed camera flashed and the OSG immediately lifted the phone on the raised dais and spoke "OK he is ready!"

"There's just the book to sign, Sir – and with the number of the car?" He was passed a list to print his name and sign, then a portion was torn off and inserted into a plastic badge headed 'VISITOR'.

Another uniformed guard entered. "Good morning Mr Edwards, I am a Miles Hopkins, prison officer, actually I am a custodial officer." Sebastian could now see that this man had several stripes on his epaulettes. "I am sorry we had to put you through all that but its standard practice; apparently you did ask to be treated as any visitor? Just follow me, Sir, please. The Governor is J.C. Bromwell."

He was shown through another door along a corridor up some stairs and into an impressive room. The person whom Sebastian took to be the Governor stood up from behind his desk and moved forward shaking Sebastian firmly by the hand. He was dressed in ordinary clothes, tweed jacket and dark trousers, he was open faced and dark haired, Sebastian thought he was in his late forties but he could see that he was not at ease. The Governor dismissed the guard "Thank you Miles! Is the tour nearly ready? Perhaps you could return in 15 minutes?"

"Well, welcome to our prison Mr Edwards. It was built in the 1890s, reconstructed in 1912 and until 1997 was a training prison for adult males but it was later rebuilt completely and reopened in 2010, the entrance gatehouse is the only part of the original building that still remains. There are 7 wings here which hold up to 1100 prisoners, there is a lifer wing holding 104 and a vulnerable prisoner unit holding up to 140. It's what is classified as a 'male local' prison."

Sebastian felt he had to but in. "Well thanks for that! I should perhaps explain the reason for my visit. In past Christmases I have always wondered about those who work or are held in prisons. Freedom is something I hold to be very important. So I came here to thank you and your staff for the very necessary work you do and also to empathise as far as I can with the inmates here. I think the idea was that I could perhaps make a quick trip around the facility, then speak to some prisoners?"

"Yes, Sir, that's the idea. We have arranged a tour for you and we have invited 3 prisoners of varying categories to meet with you for about 10 minutes each. It's a Sunday regime so they are on lockdown and there's no opportunity for you to address them all together. The whole visit will take about 50 minutes, I hope that is OK? We are, as you appreciate, short staffed over Christmas and frankly don't get many important visitors though I believe Justine Greening did visit a prison some time ago! To be honest with you we try over Christmas to release as many prisoners as we can so they can spend time with their families. Fewer inmates means fewer guards so that gives us all, as it were, more time to be with our families."

"Yes I understand" replied Sebastian and trying to put the Governor at ease, "Well it looks fine and the staff seem friendly enough!" On this J. C Bromwell appeared to relax. "What do the people here call you?"

"Ah well formally speaking I am 'Gov' actually the 'Number One Governor'. We have several Governors here each with a different role but I suspect that they call me 'JCB' or 'Digger'! Though here we encourage every member of staff and all inmates to behave with respect so we don't use nicknames or first names, people are referred to as 'Mister.'

"Yes I can understand that! How many of the cells are single and how many have to share?"

"We have three types of beds single cells and two types of doubles, bunk beds and flat doubles! They each have toilettes with a privacy screen".

"Is it normal to have to share?" asked Sebastian.

The Governor was evasive. The 'Certified Normal Accommodation' for this prison is for 718 males but the number actually held is 1048 so you can see we are pretty full!"

"Would you say that's overcrowding?" asked Sebastian

"We are similar to other prisons and using our prison service definitions there is an overcrowding rate here of around 50%"

"That sounds high?"

"Well" replied the Governor "there would be no one happier that I to see a rate of one person per cell, but, Mr Edwards, I guess the Government of the day has a list of other things that they would rather spend their money on!"

Sebastian nodded "Yes that's true enough, there are many more ways to spend money than earn it! How long are they 'banged up' for?"

"That depends on several factors. This is a Category 'B' prison which means it's one down from the worst category. In this case, 'B' means 'Escape must be made very difficult.' Here we have 95 Category 'B', 460 Category 'C' and 12 Category 'D' prisoners and several not yet assessed and some have indeterminate sentences. 'D' is the 'Trusted' category, suitable for 'open conditions'. As to routines; generally the prison day will start at 8.00 am with work or education. Those not in either role return to their cells at 8.30 am when they will be locked up. Lunch is at noon, afternoon activities start at 1.15 pm.

Evening meal is at 5.00 pm. There is a period of association from 6.00 pm to 7.15 pm. Most prisoners will be out of their cells between 8 and 10 hours on at least two days a week, those not working will have much less – 5 hours out of cell. Those prisoners on basic level of incentives might have as little as one hour out of cells and this applied to 12.5% of prisoners".

"Humph" said Sebastian" that doesn't sound very good!"

"Well it's quite complicated working out these various regimes. The problem is one of staffing and supervision! We currently have between 166 and 200 prison officers – clearly our first priority is safety and that means public safety, making sure that they do not escape, as well as safety of the staff, safety of prisoner on prisoner and prisoner self-harming. Educational and vocational training comes after that and remember we have to patrol the visitor centres for meetings between prisoners and visitors whom we have to check out, as well as supervising the sending and receiving of prisoners, who have to be assessed and processed relatively quickly."

"And the training you give to prisoners?" asked Sebastian.

"Well, it may not sound exciting but staff provide training for a BICS qualification, that's on Industrial Cleaning, and we also do training on Bicycle Maintenance; though we have recently put in for more vocational training courses at higher levels."

"Humph well I hope you get those!" Sebastian sensed that he was still nervous, probably fearful of what Sebastian might report to the Justice Minister, his ultimate boss.

"I am sorry, I hope I have explained everything. In fact I have only been here a few months and there has been quite a turnover of Governors here recently!"

"Yes you have been very kind and I am sorry that I have, if anything, made your Christmas Day more complicated than it might have been. I am sorry for intruding!"

There was a knock at the door and Miles Hopkins returned.

Miles was noticeably much more relaxed than the Governor and answered Sebastian's detailed questions on the incentive scheme and how that worked. Sebastian learned that to an inmate things like clothes were important. Miles explained that most prisoners could wear their own clothes rather than the standard issue of grey or blue T shirts and blue or maroon jogging bottoms.

They discussed the importance of visits in holding the families together and how that in turn appeared to result in nearly 40% less reoffending, as families were something to work for. They toured one particular wing and saw the canteen, kitchens, education rooms, workshops, chapel/faith centre, sports area, showering areas, library and the medical centre.

Miles explained. "The prisoners are on lockdown, working on a Sunday regime when the day starts one hour later, but there is no work or education today, however the amount of time on association when they can leave cells will be increased by one hour today. Of course the priority for most prisoners now is the call home and there will be long queues for this. On some wings the prison officers may encourage games like quizzes to pass the time." They turned the corner and he continued "So now I am passing you over to a wing officer Mr John Salmon." And with that he unlocked another set of gates and was introduced to a Mr Salmon. "When you are finished with him John call me and I'll relieve you and you can take him back to the Governor"

Sebastian introduced himself.

"You want to meet some prisoners I think?" The Prison Officer said.

"Yes that's right I think that even prisoners ought to know that we are interested in them and their welfare and they should know that we are always looking for ways to improve the service."

The Prison Officer did not directly reply but eyed Sebastian closely.

Sebastian asked some details about the numbers of prisoners held on this wing, the staff, helpers of various kinds and the sorts of crimes for which prisoners were held.

The Prison Officer replied in a matter of fact voice and gave Sebastian updated lists of the cells and prisoner details.

"I asked around and there are three prisoners willing to meet you, the first two you will be meeting in their cells and the third in a small meeting room. Come with me please!"

Sebastian tried to engage him in conservation as they walked along the corridors.

"Where do you come from?" - "Nottingham!"

"How long have you been in this services ?" - "Eight years",

"Do you like the work here?" - "Must do or I wouldn't stay would I?"

"Have you ever been threatened by a prisoner?" - "Often"

"Have you ever been terrified?" - "Yes but you get over it!"

"Are there going to be any special activities today?" "What for them? – no not here but they can do something between them if they wish! We are short staffed you see, they have to be locked up so that the staff can have their Christmas. We don't usually have visitors today you know!"

They entered the wing which had three levels with outside landings, in effect balconies, with the centre opened up, each level was reached by a metal stairway from the floor below, netting was stretched as each level to prevent falls. A pool table was situated at the far end and there was a trolley with library books which a prisoner was distributing. There was an orderly queue of prisoners waiting to use the phone.

A cell door was unlocked and opened. Sebastian could not help noticing that there was a certain smell, he knew what it was, a mixture of sweat, damp drying clothes and urine with some disinfectant as well.

The prisoner, a thin man with crew cut hair was dressed in his own clothes; he invited Sebastian in. It was small, a single bed cell. The metal framed bed was along one wall, the heating pipes were covered by perforated metal along the shorter side under the window which was set high up with three panes of glass, the centre one of which appeared to the hinged. The lighting was adequate as it was now around mid-morning and there was some sunlight. There was some form of mesh on the outside of the window. Across from the bed there was a plastic chair and against the other long wall was a desk with a TV on it, which the prisoner switched off as Sebastian entered. Behind the door was a toilet. There was a T shirt hanging from the end of the bed. There were a few pictures on the walls that looked like family members. The walls seemed to Sebastian to be freshly painted in an off-white colour, 'probably magnolia' thought Sebastian.

Sebastian immediately held out his hand and they began a discussion, Sebastian learned that he was called David aged 30, his job in prison was on the catering staff. He was spending his tenth Christmas in prison under a life sentence, he had been allowed out earlier that month under a special escorted leave programme. David said that his family had not seen him since. Later on that day he would be cooking the staff lunch whilst most prisoners would eat in their cells with the food delivered on hotplates. Sebastian asked if there was any special reason why he wanted to talk with him. "Well we have had a number of different Governors recently, maybe that's part of the problem, but there's a lot of violence here, I mean prisoner on prisoner. Frankly I don't feel safe. I was attacked, that's why I have a single cell, so I feel more protected but, of course, banged up on your own for 20 hours or so today isn't a heap of fun, so I thought any opportunity for some intelligent discussion would do. What are you an MP or something?" Sebastian nodded, "I thought so I could have sworn I saw you on the TV recently!"

The conversation was soon finished and Sebastian walked to the door which was ajar. The Prison Officer was outside. He said nothing as he led Sebastian to the next cell which had been selected. This was Tom aged 31 he currently worked as a cleaner in the prison; he had been convicted for conspiracy to supply drugs several years previously. His was a cell with bunk beds, a new

cell mate was expected after Christmas, but the layout was identical to the previous one. "Of course I am awaiting my turn to phone home, we take Christmas seriously in my family and there will be a 20 people dinner, it's a reason for a big get-together, so I am missing that. Here my big complaint is that often they start the lunch far too early, so we may eat at 11.30, evening meal can be brought forward too so I get hungry at night. Also it's very difficult to get into the library, as the opening hours are restricted for some reason!" Then he blurted out "You are older than you look on TV!" Sebastian said he would notify the prison of the problems.

Sebastian knocked on the door which was opened and the Prison Officer took him to the third appointment, there was no-one there. It looked like an interview room. The Prison Officer told Sebastian to sit on the chair nearest the door "Underneath the table, just by your right knee where you are sitting, there is a button which, if you press, sounds a bell in the adjoining room to alert staff if any help is needed! OK, understood?"

Sebastian nodded he thought he was getting used to discussions with prisoners, it was easier than he had expected so he was not worried by the thought of another.

The Prison Officer then announced "The next person is Mister Wallace – John Wallace" and before Sebastian could say anything the officer was muttering into a phone attached to his uniform, Sebastian heard him say "OK I'll be right there!" then to Sebastian "I am wanted elsewhere I'll be back in a couple of minutes, just remember what I said!"

He left and ushered in a prisoner. "John Wallace this is the Prime Minister Sebastian Edwards!" and then left clanking shut the door behind him.

The man who came in was dishevelled, the much stained T shirt was partly hanging out over the jogging bottoms which Sebastian noticed were prison uniform, there were stains over his trainers which were untied. His long hair was ungroomed and hung about his unshaven face which was scarcely visible.

He marched over to the chair on the other side of the table to Sebastian sat down and began waving his hands around in an exaggerated and disjointed manner.

"So yo' are the Prime Minister 'that right? So yo' are the one that sticks people in 'ere, what have yo' come fer'? To crow over my misfortoon? Bollocks you are all a bunch of wankers! Yo' couldna' give a shite about us could yo'? Yo' prat aboot in yor wam offices stuffing all t' secriteries so I's told and riding around in posh cars on expenses! There's thousands uv bankers making millions yet it's us werkers what gets thrown out o' jobs! I couldn't get a job – see I got no qualfication, that's all they wanted esperiunce and qualifcations. So I get by nicking stuff, last time I were out they woun't even pay me the dole, thay said I hadn't tried to get a job so I was sanctioned! Yes that's what it was sanctioned! No money. No bloody money!"

He got up and started circling the table, pacing backwards and forwards, Sebastian noticed, he was coming between him and the door. John Wallace then began shouting "Yose' all a load of fucking wankers! That's what yo' are! Yo' know that?"

He seemed to be unsteady on his feet but he was getting nearer and nearer to Sebastian who was by this time thoroughly alarmed. He pressed the button by his knee expecting at any moment that the Prison guard would return.

Nothing happened, the prisoner sat down again throwing his large frame into the chair and placing his elbows on the table in front of him and stared directly at Sebastian "So yo' cum 'ere to see wha'? Well this is what it is, see! It's a crap place, foodz lousy and the company's lousy too!" Sebastian could see that he appeared to be quite fit and he was of athletic build.

Sebastian had so far said nothing, he pushed the button again – long bursts. "Yes, the company's not the best!"

"Ah! So the person speaks Eh? Not t' best! Ha! They'll nick anything from yo', so they will," with that he put his head in his hands and began to sob deeply.

Then just as quickly yelled in Sebastian's face "It's not my fucking fault! Yo' bastard!"

He waved his hands about within inches of Sebastian's face. He got up and prowled around behind him again. Sebastian was well aware that if the prisoner made a sudden lunge, he could easily grab him round his neck, get him in an arm-lock and break his neck within seconds.

Sebastian pressed the button again, he nervously twiddled the signet ring on the little finger of his right hand, he knew it was a sign of his nervousness, it was an automatic reaction.

He had to think. Think for God's sake. Think! 'I have to engage him somehow!'.

"Do you have any family John? I know it's terrible at Christmas being separated. That happened to me many years ago!"

"Oh yea I can't see someone like yo' getting in trouble with the nick"

"Well I very nearly was"

"Nearly, nearly what's that mean? Nearly! Did you nearly commit a crime, nearly bash someone did yo'?"

Sebastian knew the sneering was intended to provoke him.

"Well sort of!" Sebastian then related the story of how he was out of a job, feeling depressed and went to the doctor for some pills, he went out that evening and entered a pub Quiz, he shouldn't have drunk but he did, they were doing so well winning nearly every round. But he realised he should be home, he started back, he was sick several times and couldn't find his keys; even so he tried to get into the house. He didn't remember much after that. Next day, his father-in-law told him there had been some sort of a fight and he had broken his son's arm. He himself was covered in blood falling against the window in the door. His father-in-law then threatened to call the police. His wife walked out the following day! Both his sons followed her and he didn't see them for over 20 years. "The five Christmases following were the most dreadful in my life. Do you know what I did?"

There was a pause and Sebastian noticed that the prisoner was calmer now.

"I just went walking, walking, I'd walk for miles and miles until I was exhausted then I would walk back, if I could remember where I was. That was terrible, especially at Christmas day lunch, it hit me year after year!"

Sebastian was silent, he just looked at the prisoner intently.

The prisoner stopped pacing the room sat down again and eyed Sebastian closely.

"Yeah, well, whatever! Foods crap and laundry's slow and who wants to be a bicycle mechanic? I ask yo' a bike mick?"

"Sorry I cannot make up for time with your family!"

"Yeah well, stuff happens" but his attitude now changed just as quickly as it had exploded in the first place, "Hey Mister er er Edwins – er Oh! would yo' sign mi T shirt?"

"Sure!" Sebastian replied and was getting out a felt tip pen when they heard the bolt shot back and the Prison Officer John Salmon returned and took him back to the Governor's office.

"So how did things go, Mr Edwards? The last person you saw was John Wilson wasn't it? A lovely old chap, spent more time in prison that out I think, sees this as his real home!"

"No I saw John Wallace for about 20 minutes, he's suffering some problems I think?"

"Surely it was John Wilson?" the Governor sounded worried and visibly blanched. He turned to the Prison Officer. "John! What happened here?"

"I am sure you said John Wallace, Governor and it could only have been 10 minutes – I was called away to another wing"

"You mean that Mr Edwards was shut in with John Wallace for 20 minutes!"

"Ten minutes I am sure no longer, I thought it was strange you suggesting John Wallace he's in drug rehab! Just been re-categorised from 'B' to 'C' because we wanted to move him to another prison remember?"

"Oh I am sorry Mr Edwards, are you OK? We are several staff short today!"

Sebastian had to think fast, was it just a mistake, carelessness or was it a deliberate breech of the rules? The guard getting back at him for making his Christmas day more complicated! If it was the latter he should surely complain or report it? But then the Prison Governor would get it in the ear from above and it had not been Sebastian's intention to carry out an inspection; he had been trying to thank the staff not report on them. In any case what could be proved? He had no doubt that the prison guard would have a ready defence. So he just said rather lamely;

"Yes I am OK thanks Governor, a bit shaken I suppose, but OK and I want to thank you and all your staff for the work you do!"

Was there a smirk on the guard's face? Or was it just that the man had moved from the window and a shadow fell across his face? Sebastian couldn't be sure.

Anyhow he made a decision there and then that his naivety had showed through again, he had not, in fact, achieved much at all, it had not been a good idea. These people were not at all thankful for his visit, for them it was just an unnecessary extra task and he had seen so few prisoners that it would hardly make a difference!

Sebastian left the Prison and was briefly interviewed by a TV reporter who had been previously tipped off by his staff in London.

Sebastian appeared ashen faced and mumbled just a few words about "If others have to work on Christmas Day then I felt I should show willing, to at least spend my Christmas in the same way!

Inside here are the guilty ones put away according to our laws. Each of them has a family, wife, mother, father, brothers, sisters, children. But those are also punished, there is an empty chair at home for lunch today, the pain is spread through the whole family but particularly the children who will grow up much more predisposed to criminality than the average person. So the cycle continues its dreadful turn."

Sebastian thought 'Well at least if I wasn't able to get through to people in the prison perhaps those at home watching TV would understand what I had intended to do!'

The TV reporter disappeared and Sebastian drove off following the police Land Rover to their second appointment of the day at the General Nottingham Hospital.

On the way there Sebastian suddenly felt queasy, he veered across the road and made for a layby which he knew was there, he had passed it daily going to work years before. During a road straightening programme in the 1990s there was a bend in the road which the new, straightened road had left isolated but which was used by cars and over-night trucks.

He drove in there, stopped the car at the side of the road next to the hedge, opened the door and began trembling, he couldn't stop, then he was violently sick. He knew it was an attack of nerves; a reaction to prisoner number three.

By the time the escort caught up with him seconds later with sirens on and flashing blue lights previously hidden behind obscured darkened glass, he was sitting on the car seat with the door open, a handkerchief to his mouth.

The two officers of the Protection Squad pulled up alongside him one of them started ticking him off "No! Look Mr Edwards I thought the understanding was that under NO condition would you veer off like this! You cannot just change…."

The other officer stopped him and pointed to the puke on the ground in front of him, still steaming on the frozen ground. It had unfortunately also caught Sebastian's left trouser leg. "Are you alright Mr Edwards? You look very white! Do you want to cancel the Hospital visit, Sir, if you are not OK?"

They switched off the sirens and lights. Sebastian took a few minutes to recover.

"No! Let's complete the day's work, though I need a wash basin to wipe this stuff off! I feel much better now – it must be something that I ate for breakfast." The policemen exchanged worried glances.

In a few minutes they resumed the journey but more slowly. On arrival at the Hospital, one of the policemen cleared a way and Sebastian went through into the A & E side into a toilet where he managed to clean his trousers and swill out his mouth.

They then went out of the building and in again through the main reception. There he met the CEO of the Hospital Trust who was waiting. Sebastian explained how he was needed elsewhere and could only unfortunately spend half the allotted time with them.

He walked around several wards, chatted to a few patients, thanked the staff for their service, posed for a photo for the Hospital's magazine, spoke briefly over the Hospital's radio system and selected the next carol, then, as quickly as he could, he extracted himself and returned home.

Sylvia his wife, knew immediately that something was wrong but he said he would be fine with a few hours' sleep, he drank some milk and munched some cheese and biscuits.

Through habit he turned on the TV and caught the news, it appeared that, due to the lack of other stories, his brief prison visit interview was shown in full on the main channels; he looked ill. He grunted and then went upstairs and fell asleep immediately.

Chapter TEN – Boxing Day - Sat. 26th December 2020 – Relatives

At breakfast the following day he told his wife what had happened. They were both sitting at the small dining table finishing tea and toast.

"Sebby you cannot punish yourself like this, ease up for heaven's sake, it is barely a month since your last episode, stop playing the hero, as Prime Minister you should be the one setting the pace!"

She told him she did not think it would make any difference what she said and that she supposed he would continue as before! Sebastian could see that she was very frustrated by him.

He then broached the problem of Ahmed. "I spoke with the solicitor in London, you know Ranjit Singh; this problem when it broke was, well, embarrassing for us perhaps but not serious, but as Prime Minister it could get me into all sorts of problems, I mean, me paying Ahmed directly could easily be misinterpreted you know. Look! If someone steals something it would be unusual to 'pay him off' unless you have something to hide?"

Sebastian was struggling to explain why he had had to change tactics.

"Neither of us has anything to hide I know but that's not how the press might read it, nor the public and I couldn't do with another 'bumpy ride', at least not yet!"

"Not ever Sebby!" Sylvia agreed, "Not ever – I don't want to see you like that again!"

".. and we don't know", continued Sebastian, "who else has got his claws into Ahmed? Suppose they are part of a ruthless gang, and Ahmed is in fact up to his neck in their mess or he's even been inveigled into other tricks! Are these other people not going to realise that I am an easy touch and, if they too think that I am covering something up, then they might come back for more! In other words I could be blackmailed for being kind. Also we have no idea that he hasn't done something like this before, have we? I mean neither of us have questioned how on earth he earned enough to buy his posh house, did we?"

"So what are you suggesting Seb? You know, if you appeared to renege on the deal now, both Ahmed and his wife would be very upset, they are counting on your help to dig them out of the hole!"

"But just imagine, dear, come April, when it's likely I will become Home Secretary, in charge of Police, Prisons and the Justice System and this thing blows up in my face? Unless everything is clear and clean the Press will take me to the cleaners and I will not survive. There are lots of ways to end a political career, Sylvia, but being caught out by Ahmed's mess is not something I like the sound of!"

"So what do you propose Seb?"

"I don't know but as I was saying I saw the Solicitor a week ago Friday, you know Ranjit Singh, the chap who helped me over the impeachment thing, you remember? His advice to me was just to cut the whole thing and report it to the police and let justice take its course. Incidentally he wants you to make sure your charity accounts are OK and to get a special report from your accountants as to how the theft occurred and to cast an eye over any other possible weaknesses in your internal controls! Could you do that? The Trustees of the Charity should acknowledge the incident, how it was dealt with and then properly minute it so that it's all declared?"

"I suppose the accountants will ask for another fee?" suggested Sylvia.

"I am afraid so but with that we can then report the matter to the Charity Commissioners. If you tell them, look, this has happened and these are the checks we have run to ensure that we are alright into the future, then I think it will be OK. We tell them you see! It's much better than someone else tipping them off – and the Charity Commissioners then demanding a report from you, that would suggest you are covering up something! That would make a juicy press story, if anything leaked out?"

"OK I will do that Seb as soon after Christmas as the firm is back at work!"

"Good, so going back to what I was saying, I told Ranjit I didn't want to go back on the deal, so he then insisted that I must get Ahmed to sign an agreement. Then at least we would have a clear story. But do you think Ahmed would sign that?"

"What would it say?"

"Well, he prepared for me this letter, here it is, it's a draft, on the basis of what I told him about the case. It's really the whole story as we know it, it includes his theft of money and how much he owes right now and that he will disclose to me to whom he owes the money and what the terms are, so that if there is any come-back at least we know exactly where we are! Here take a look!"

Sylvia glanced at the letter briefly which she saw at the bottom had places for signatures of herself, Sebastian and Ahmed. "You have thought about this a lot Seb, is there any alternative?"

"No I cannot see one, except for halting any further payments and reporting it to the police; but will he sign it?"

"I don't know". Sylvia hesitated "He was so wild and out of control when we caught him out, but in signing it he would, in effect, be admitting his guilt to you in writing! Something that anyone could hold against him in the future! He might just explode in fury as he did before! If he did sign would that mean we would not have to report the matter to the police?"

"I still don't know about that, according to Ranjit, hundreds of cases of fraud every year don't get reported. He says it's a 'judgement call' as he puts it, so there seems to be no necessity to do so under law! Ahmed has actually stolen money from the girls not the Charity, although the Charity was responsible because Ahmed was acting in his capacity as a director. The girls could have sued it directly if we hadn't repaid the cash. So it's primarily up to the girls and, if they don't complain, then probably the police would not get involved.." Sebastian continued.

"..But if they did, then Ranjit told me what he thought would happen next. The case would go to 'Action Fraud' a unit which decides which force will pick up the investigation, that unit actually comes under the City of London Fraud Squad. They would go into the case in more detail, check Ahmed's birth or immigration status and his relationship with fraudsters who might be loaning him the money and also any previous police record that he might have. They would go into where he got his money from for his house and his ability to pay back for this and any other crimes he might have committed. A Senior Investigating Officer (SIO) would question the girls and you and all trustees as well as myself, because I will have implicated myself in paying him off, which they may well take as a sign of my guilt in anything else Ahmed might have done!

The SIO will then prepare a case and pass this to the Crown Prosecution Service (CPS). If it did come to court Ahmed might be imprisoned if he has 'previous form' that is previous convictions but, if not, he might be let off with a warning but by then the reputational damage will have been done. I cannot tell if exposure to police and a legal case might blast open the 'safe house' you have established with so much care. Of course any solicitor employed by or for Ahmed might deliberately use that as a bargaining chip, knowing that the threat of exposure might well end the charity for good and in any case damage any possibility of future fund raising!

"One final matter" Sebastian added looking at the letter again "The police themselves are leaky; if you remember, the Leveson inquiry found that several police were paid off by the Press for inside information. There can be no absolute guarantee that, with such a magnificent prize as the PM's scalp up for grabs, someone might not spill the beans and sell the story to the Press, they would get a lot of money!"

He looked up and saw that Sylvia was crying, tears were rolling down her cheeks, Sebastian had never seen her in such a state before. He rushed around the table and immediately hugged and kissed her.

"Oh Seb is all this worth it?" Pointing at a few red boxes in the corner of the room.

"Look, I cannot back out now, there are too many people counting on me. But this I promise! When the next General Election comes in 2022, I shall stand but only as an MP I will not seek a Ministerial position again. I have to live out the next 13 weeks but after that things should be easier!"

"Oh Seb!" She rushed past him upstairs to their bedroom. He found her there still sobbing, he hugged her again until her choking sobs subsided. "Hey look, I have an idea, you remember my half-brother from Nigeria,"

"You mean Massa Edwards Gombe, Seb? Yes he really was nice, I felt he had been as badly hurt by the event as you, you know – I could tell that, he was somehow so very sad!"

Sebastian said cheerily "Let's get him over and have a family reunion in No 10! We could ask Rupert to come as well! Let's look on the positives. Let's give the Press something really to talk about!"

Sylvia was suddenly positive again. "Yes no point in moping is there, just look at the time? I have to make a dozen curries for lunch, we have ten people coming!"

"Including Ahmed I suppose?"

"Yes him too!"

"Well I'll have to raise it with him, there's no point in delaying, I'll wait till everyone has gone and ask him to wait a bit, then go through it with him and hope I can make him see sense!"

By 1.00 pm the cars started to arrive and Sebastian met each of the groups at the door. There had been four sisters, after Sylvia was abused by her father she had left home and hadn't seen them for 20 years, she had been fearful that her father would keep to his word and kill her if he found her. The sisters were all younger but in turn they got married and had children, so by the time the family was reunited, the father was long dead and Sylvia found that she had a ready-made complete family.

Every year they would meet up on Boxing Day and every year Sylvia would cook, every year everyone agreed it was good, very, very good!

They all sat on cushions around the room with Sebastian in the dining alcove pouring and passing out the drinks whilst Sylvia sat by the open door jumping up every few minutes to bring in more dishes which were laid on a tablecloth on the floor.

Sebastian had remembered to clean his hands well, the first time after the reunion of Sylvia's extended family he hadn't done so. He had been messing about with his bicycle and hadn't realised that hands were used as much as forks in these events, unfortunately he hadn't scrubbed as well as he should and there had been the lingering taste of machine oil on the rice. He had felt too embarrassed to excuse himself so soon after starting; the others noticed he hadn't eaten much but he had waited for a full half hour before getting up and washing off every trace of oil!

With the buzz of chatter and with the attention to his drinks duties, Sebastian was able to avoid getting into detailed discussions with Ahmed, who appeared to be unduly deferential to Sebastian, calling him 'Sir' all the time but as they were all constantly interrupted by the grandchildren who were aged from 6 to 26, there was in any case no pause in the conversation, which was all about relatives.

As the first of Sylvia's sisters was about to leave with her family, Sebastian went outside to see them off and bumped into Ahmed and asked him to stay back to finalise some of the details. Ahmed looked alarmed and it appeared to affect him, he was noticeably quieter after that.

When the families had been reduced to just Ahmed and his wife, Sebastian nodded to Sylvia who immediately got her youngest sister and her children to help clear away the plates, wash up and put away everything else.

Sebastian drew Ahmed to one side and suggested that they go upstairs into the other small bedroom where they could chat. In fact it was a small room, chocker-block with piles of papers, magazines, books, files, odd chairs, lamps so there was only just room for two chairs which Sebastian had placed there before the families had arrived.

Sebastian started off but was almost immediately interrupted by Ahmed who started to congratulate Sebastian saying he was a fine gentleman in the purest tradition of everything that was good about England.

Sebastian stopped him and tried to explain that his new position as Prime Minister left him vulnerable to political attack. He would have to be very careful. Ahmed offered to help him in whatever way he could, that it was marvellous to have such an exalted man in their family and that his friends had all marvelled at his good fortune in having such connections. Even the village in Pakistan from which they all came were considering having a celebration.

This obliged Sebastian to explain that what Ahmed had done might be a considerable embarrassment to him if it was used by his opponents. It seemed now to dawn on Ahmed that the situation had changed, he blurted out "But I always had intended to give back the money I would never have stolen it from them, just until my affairs are settled."

"However events have now overtaken us" and Sebastian began to hint that he later might be in charge of the Ministry of Justice and could not afford to be misunderstood.

"Oh No! you are not going back on your word No! Oh No!" Ahmed wailed and appeared to become defensive.

"No that's not what I intend to do, I do intend to keep to the deal, however I have been talking to solicitors and they have advised me…."

"Oh No! No! are you going to call in the police surely not, Sir? This was to be a private deal between our…!"

"But it still can be Ahmed, what I need from you is for you to sign this letter so that we know exactly where we are."

"Letter, what letter?"

Sebastian drew it from his pocket "This is the draft we ca,...." But Ahmed was no longer listening he was reading.

Ahmed's brow became wrinkled and his eyes narrowed and turned into boiling pits of anger.

"No! No! No! you want me to confess – I cannot sign that. I am not a thief, that is what this suggests, I just borrowed it – I know you are trying to find some reason to get out of the deal! You LIAR!" he shouted.

With that he got up from his chair grabbed the door handle and rushed downstairs shouting instruction for the family to follow him immediately.

Sebastian scrambled down the stairs after him and made the front door as Ahmed's alarmed family were getting into the car. Sebastian walked to the driver's side.

Ahmed leapt out of the car with such vigour that he nearly bowled Sebastian over. Ahmed rushed up to Sebastian and shouted "LIAR, LIAR" He then, with exaggerated swipes of his arm, tore the letter that Sebastian had handed to him in half and then half again, shouting at him "You are breaking the deal – don't you dare do that to me, my whole family depends on this NOW, I need it NOW!" and he was shaking his fists at Sebastian.

All the while Sebastian could see out of the corner of his eye that the police had been alerted by the noise and had emerged from the house across the way.

Sebastian tried to calm Ahmed down, but it seemed to have the reverse effect and the shouting and aggressive behaviour continued. Ahmed raised his hand with the remaining bits of paper in one hand and appeared to reach into his pocket for something with the other. A young policeman who had quietly walked around behind Ahmed literally pounced on him and tried to wrestle him to the ground. Sebastian shouted "No! No!" but Ahmed was too strong and managed to get free and made a dash for the open car door whilst his terrified family looked on from inside the car. The policeman jumped up and held him against the car struggling to get the cuffs on Ahmed who stretched his arms as wide as he could to prevent it.

There was a brief pause.

Sebastian pleaded, "Officer please release him, we were merely having an argument which got out of hand, he is my wife's brother-in-law, it was a simple misunderstanding!"

"Well sir a misunderstanding it might be but this isn't". The officer turned around and Sebastian could see that there was blood pouring from his nose and it seemed as though Ahmed must have landed a punch during the tussle, as the officer's right eye did not look good.

The officer completed putting the handcuffs on Ahmed and pushed him into the rear seat of his own police car.

He then immediately called for back-up which arrived a few minutes later. The young policemen and the senior officer exchanged words some way off and Sebastian was relieved to see it was Superintendent John Denny.

The young policeman explained that he saw Ahmed behave aggressively and seems to reach into his pocket and draw something out. "I had to act!"

Superintendent Denny took Sebastian aside "Look we don't really want to interfere with a 'domestic' but as the young officer believed you were in danger. He had to act; indeed had he not done so and you were assaulted then he would be severely reprimanded. I shall have to refer the matter upwards and the case will rest with him and the Notts Police who are his employers as to whether to take this further. Now can you tell me what this was all about?"

Sebastian took Superintendent Denny over to the police car where the young officer was standing by the open rear door.

"Look" said Sebastian "We were having a nice Boxing Day family lunch, but then we had a disagreement over some property. I want to thank you young man for acting so promptly and I am sure that Ahmed here will apologise, I think you caught him from behind with no warning and he reacted automatically which of course he should not have done. You have the names and addresses of everyone so you can always get back to us to answer any questions. Is it possible to release Ahmed and let him take his family home? They have been a bit traumatised by the whole affair."

Ahmed at last seemed to have regained his composure and briefly apologised to the young officer and pointed out that he was trying to produce his diary at the time which he now brought out. "I intended to discuss with Mr Edwards a possible date for a future meeting!"

This seemed to satisfy the policemen, Ahmed was duly released and was allowed to return home with his family.

Sebastian moved towards his house where Sylvia was waiting in the doorway.

One of the two remaining neighbours on the cul-de-sac had been altered by the noise but turned and went into their house after a friendly wave from Sebastian.

Superintendent Denny stood for a while watching the various parties leave the scene. He paused for a moment deep in thought before returning to the police house on the other side of the road.

Sebastian told Sylvia what had happened and Sebastian said that he was now more determined than ever to get Ahmed to sign, his volatility suggested to Sebastian that he was completely unreliable and he had no alternative but to cover himself in that way.

On the following day, Sunday, they went for their traditional walk to Wollaton Park off the Ring Road in Nottingham.

Early the next day, Monday, at 10.00 am he called Ranjit Singh as had been agreed between them, Sebastian suggested one small change inserting the words "Ahmed declares that it was always his intention to return the borrowed money" and an amended email attachment was sent to him the following afternoon.

Sylvia then spent over an hour on the phone to her youngest sister. Ahmed's character had now changed again and he was in grovelling mode, probably, thought Sebastian, now desperate for the money Sebastian had promised. Eventually the letter was signed by all the three parties and it was with some relief that Sebastian believed he had now closed the whole affair.

He stressed to his wife however that there was nothing that he could or would do to determine if the local police wanted to take further the matter of Ahmed's assault on the police officer. "I have no power or influence over the local police. They already incur costs of hundreds of thousands of pounds monitoring and maintaining local surveillance for us." He said "It would be incredibly stupid of me to start attempting to give them instructions as to how they should do their job".

Sylvia told Sebastian that she would not discuss that possibility with Ahmed yet but hoped everything would now blow over.

Sebastian and Sylvia spent Monday and Tuesday night, December 28th and 29th at an expensive hotel in Derbyshire, they went for a couple of long walks and managed to escape any publicity, spending the evening in their bedroom. He returned to the family home in Middleton and began sorting through the red boxes which just appeared almost every day.

He returned to London on Wednesday 30th December and went straight to the Downing Street flat. He had a meeting arranged with Roger Collingham-Smith for 3.00 pm

....

It was in fact several weeks before they heard anything more about the incident by which time Ahmed had been interviewed twice more by the police.

Ranjit Singh acting on behalf of Sylvia, as a relative, attempted to find out what was going on. The word came back 'There's previous' indicating that Ahmed had a police record of some kind.

Sebastian and Sylvia did not discuss the matter again, they agreed that it was now out of their hands.

Chapter ELEVEN – Internal Lib Dem email – warning of under-cover stings

Sebastian was concerned about the possibility of a 'sting' or other scam being worked against them. The problem with Ahmed showed how easy it was to become tangled up in a dubious situation. He discussed the matter with Dan Stirling, the Party Leader, who agreed that they should at least warn all senior Lib Dem staff and Ministers.

Accordingly they had sent out under their joint names the following email

To Inner Circle of contacts – from Sebastian Edwards PM and Dan Stirling Party Leader.

URGENT - POSSIBLE POLITICAL STING AND FUTURE L/D CONTACT WITH MPs

We are most concerned about the possibility of us being caught out by a political sting. All senior LD Cabinet Ministers, including myself as PM and senior staff are all 'sitting ducks'. We are more open than other parties and tend to welcome new ideas and particularly new donations. As we move towards the end of the 12 weeks we think it's highly likely that the Tory Press will try very hard to catch us out. An 'exclusive' piece on the PM or any of us doing something wrong or saying the wrong thing, like maligning the Coalition, is bound to be worth 'a packet' to a leading Newspaper!

We have seized the opportunity for me to take over as PM but in the warped mind of some Tories that is wrong and that alone gives them the chance to justify their actions under the pretence of 'Public Interest'. We can expect what the Leveson enquiry said was part of the 'journalistic dark arts' although those that do it tend to use the rather grander title of 'Investigative Journalism'. But it sells Newspapers!

So please be on your guard, if someone offers money or favours for something, or access to me of Cabinet colleagues... BE SUSPICIOUS!

After discussions with our security, the essential features of a sting seem to be:

1)   They (most often it is two people – probably reporters) have to inveigle their way into the trust of a person whom they consider to be influential and who is known to senior Lib Dems

2) They will offer a bait, which is probably money (or if it involves several stages then it could be, regular smaller inducements like tickets to a show or sports event which might be repeated)
3) They may take weeks in planning this, it will likely mean they will need several meetings to build up credibility with you - not just one day.
4) They will work out what they want, some revelation they can sell, disagreement within our party or within the coalition or disclosures of secret meetings like Cabinet meetings, or 'buy' a place on the prospective MP candidate list.
5) They will need evidence, hearsay isn't enough, that means getting something in writing or on a tape recorder or camcorder, but even simple phones could be used to take a snap.

There are certain things we can do to protect ourselves,

a) If you are not sure of your audience wait till you are, before sounding off
b) Don't 'bad mouth' other Lib Dems or the Coalition unless you are in secure surroundings
c) If someone not known to you asks to meet a specific person or do a specific thing ask for identification. Be suspicious, always take a phone number and call it back.
d) We should all start using a visitor's sheet which asks the person 'to give personal details and then confirm that they are asking for this meeting for themselves and, they are not employed by any news agency or newspaper and have no intention of using this information for personal gain.'
e) Make sure you separate the visitors from their hats or coats, bags or briefcase which might have recording devices and put them furthest from any meeting e.g. near a clothes stand.
f) If you are at all concerned about the possibility of a scam then change the date, or venue or people at the meeting, it'll give you more time to check things out.
g) If you are concerned bring in any other member of staff, use a prearranged code word for 'Sting'.

AND NOW VERY MUCH MORE IMPORTANTLY – communication with YOU,

We intend to report back to you regularly and to hear your comments about how things are going. We'll use any ideas you have that might be useful to amend government proposals.

Dan Stirling will organise and chair a regular weekly event for all our MPs and 6 top staff in a private room somewhere for a Lunchtime meeting?

There will be regular weekly Webinars every Friday 2.00 pm, either Dan or myself or another Cabinet Minister will preside, the country will be divided into 4, so every region and constituency will have the ability to have direct access to our top people at least every 4 weeks. Make sure that every member linked in is properly accredited, please, and you know ask real questions and tell us how you think we are doing, give us feedback!

Either Dan or I will be available for one on one meetings with all our MPs and will allocate a time, probably Friday pm. Please book through my PPS Bill Bennett or Madge O'Connor.

Sebastian Edwards, Dan Stirling.

Chapter TWELVE – EU Discussions ONE - Temporary derogation explained

They met in a small room off the Cabinet Room on Wednesday 30th December 2020 at 3.00 pm.

Roger Collingham-Smith was tall, Sebastian thought six foot three inches perhaps, and thin with a wiry figure. He had a receding hairline and the hair, once black, was now interspersed with white particularly around the temples, giving him a rather patrician look. His brow was furrowed. He had a rather long nose and thin ears which were almost flat against his temples. Although clean shaven he was clearly one of those to whom two shaves a day would have been normal as there was already the shadow of growth. He wore a smart dark green suit and highly polished shoes, a white shirt and a nondescript tie.

They had met several times previously but only briefly. Roger had been a Tory MEP until he realised that the Conservatives appeared to have absolutely no interest in the EC at all. He had, almost in desperation, switched to the Liberal Democrats but was knocked out in the 2014 elections to the European Parliament. The Lib Dem vote had collapsed to just 6% and the number of Lib Dem MEPs fell from eleven to just one.

At the time Sebastian had in part blamed the Lib Dem leadership for their failure to project a positive future within the EU. He had queried how the only fervently pro EU party had failed to capture the Pro EC vote, which at its lowest was 40%. Sebastian remembered that Roger had simply disagreed, "It's much more complex than that!" he had said.

They had both been on the hustings for the first referendum in October 2016 when the Brexit vote had won but by the narrowest of margins, a difference of 130,000 votes or 50.2% to 49.8%. The Prime Minister had decided that was not a decisive enough vote to untangle such a huge and complex relationship. The vote in Parliament agreed with him, only 75 MPs could be found to try to force an exit and use Clause 50 and begin the extraction process. As one paper quipped at the time 'Look the government would probably have had to hire at least 40,000 more staff to try to unravel all the EU laws and mandatory rulings and replace them with new ones. The costs would have been astronomic'.

Whilst the Government did indeed set up an 'Out' department to cope with such an eventuality, their main thrust and effort had been to bolster up the Conservative Leader's demand for a better deal. The EU leaders knew that unless they did give way, then the UK Parliament would have had no option but to apply for Clause 50, the pressure now came on the EC to bend or be blamed for splitting the EC.

The UK Prime Minister's task had been made easier because the referendum had revealed the precise weak points that the OUTers had used to devastating effect.

Although Sebastian had not been involved with the successful 2017 re-negotiations, he knew that Roger Collingham-Smith had been. Sebastian was now, by virtue of his being the UK Prime Minister, one of the EC Presidents, there were five in total for different institutions of the EC. He was the rotating President of the Council of Ministers, the small group made up of one representative of each country – a sort of Cabinet. It was a largely honorary and ceremonial role – a rotating office which had nothing to do with experience or skill or aptitude but was simply a 'buggins turn'. Though, as Sebastian pointed out, amongst the motley crew of EC Prime Ministers there were some very intelligent people – the problem was nobody could identify who they were! Sebastian intended to use his position to directly address the EC problems and propose changes. So he hoped to draw on Roger's extensive experience and use it to the advantage of the UK.

Since his failure to get re-elected Roger, as an MEP, was making a successful career as Senior Lecturer in European Politics at London North University. They had given him three months leave of absence basically to support Sebastian as PM. He told Sebastian that it would in any case provide him with a final chapter on a book on the EC which he had already started.

Roger started off the discussion.

"Let's just recap shall we? Well we knew we had a year from the date of the first referendum to the second, That focussed our minds and also those of our negotiators in the EC at Brussels. We knew that it was not possible to formalise any changes we might wrest from them within an enduring contract. If it was substantive then it might have to run the gamut of gaining assent from each of the Member State's Parliaments or even referenda. So it was decided, right from the start, that it would be unwise simply to use a permanent opt out as a reason, but rather that temporary exclusions, or 'derogation' as it is called within the EC, would be sought which could be carried by the Qualified Majority voting within the Council of Ministers, so it would not require unanimous approval of all member states which was notoriously difficult to obtain.

If it were later made permanent this could then sit alongside all other major constitutional changes and be welded into them and therefore not stand out as a specific British request.

The UK was notorious for its 'Opt outs' and many, even, the few allies that the UK did have, quipped that 'Perhaps the best way would be for everyone else to consider 'Opt Outs' whilst the UK tells us what are their 'Opt Ins'!

At that time the UK case was put by the Chancellor of the Exchequer, a Europhile only in the sense that he thought extracting the UK from the EC after 40 years as 'conjoined twins' was an horrendous task and he thought life after 'exit' would be economically ruinous and disastrous, disrupting existing trading patterns.

The Chancellor had discussed the tactics with his small cross-party team. He knew that, although there were some dreadful and senseless EC anomalies which drove the UK Press frantic, like packs of salmon having to state 'this packet contains fish', most of those were a trifling inconvenience nothing more, but without bringing home some restriction or cap on migration his case would be lost. Tinkering about with immigrants' benefits to make UK seem tougher on casual immigrants arriving without jobs simply hadn't worked. To be blunt, what Cameron had negotiated had not, in most people's view, been worth a row of beans. Some other ploy had to be carried out to bring back a meaningful gain for the REMAINers.

Someone came up with the idea of using article 100 A(4) of the Single European Act to get a temporary derogation which might then later be made permanent" Roger read this out.

'If, after the adoption of a harmonisation measure by the Council, acting by a qualified majority, a Member State deems it necessary to apply national provisions on grounds of major needs referred to in Article 36 or relating to the protection of the environment, or the working environment it shall notify the Commission of these provision.

The Commission shall confirm the provisions involved after having verified that they are not a means of arbitrary discrimination or a disguised restriction on trade between Member States.

By way of derogation from the procedure laid down in articles 169 and 170 the Commission or any Member State may bring the matter directly before the Court of Justice if it considers that another Member State is making improper use of the powers provided for in this article. '

Roger continued, "This article had been actually introduced by Denmark and was used later by the UK to avoid being pushed into the final stages of monetary union.

The element on which the UK based its case was one of population density leading to poor working conditions both for migrants and the existing residents, exacerbated by other contributing factors".

He went on, "We managed to convince the EC that Wales and Scotland contained much rugged hilly countryside which was unsuitable for any substantial increase in population which was likely from an EU open door immigration policy. In any case migrants would inevitably make for England where the work was. We constantly stressed that whilst the principle of freedom of movement of people was fine, it was clearly posing a perceived threat to people in the UK and we in the UK were bluntly running out of space to build."

He continued "I was there supporting as part of the UK Team. The Chancellor pointed out that there were various reasons why the UK, and in particular England, was so attractive, this was a paper that he had prepared and which formed the basis for his appeal. Let's look through it."

Roger handed a copy of the case to Sebastian, who read through it all very carefully.

THE UK CASE FOR LIMIT OF FREEDOM OF MOVEMENT OF PEOPLE FROM THE EU MEMBER STATES TO THE UK. (October 2017)

1. *Attractiveness of the English Language. A proficiency in the English language could be a unique advantage to a migrant in several ways. Several international bodies use it exclusively throughout the world, like Air Traffic Control, and it is used extensively by the United Nations as a lingua franca. It is needed to gain working entry to USA and several other countries but more importantly any USA or other Foreign Direct Investor setting up operations in any country within the EC would likely ask first for those speaking English. Indeed that international demand for English language tuition was so great that a very large number of colleges had been set up in the UK to cater for it; many had been found to be bogus and had to be closed. The advantages of gaining a knowledge of English for a migrant far outweigh the benefit of learning Dutch, or Swedish or indeed Portuguese where future opportunities for use are far more limited. So many people coming here believe that they can, whilst earning, learn English, it's a double advantage This is one of the UK's unique 'magnets'.*

2.   *Attractiveness of UK growth in jobs compared to EC growth. The UK growth and particularly growth in England, and within that London, has been substantially higher than in other countries recently. 1.8% compared to 0.6% So there is a perception from the migrants' view that they have a much greater chance of finding a job in the UK than in areas which were struggling economically like France or Italy. The UK became a magnet for those looking to better themselves.*

3.   *The UK is seen as a tolerant and accepting society. The UK has, in the past, accepted the open door policy and hundreds of thousands of people from Poland, a country which held the UK in high regard due the circumstances of the war had been largely well received and welcomed into the UK with relatively little friction. They have, without doubt, assisted in the UK's increased GDP. But the volume of people coming here with no restraint in numbers has often swamped the services of the local population in areas such as Boston, Lincs, and later flows of people from the latest Euro Member States have not been so well received, as there was less of a historical link and their customs were slightly different. The strict adherence of Poland to the Catholic Church found a ready acceptance in UK communities. Historic and religious connections helped integration and led to further migration..*

4.   *The lack of cheaper housing in the UK. One of the major problems in the UK has been the failure of successive Governments to build enough houses for the existing population. There are various estimates of shortage but probably most would not disagree with a figure of 250,000. We are still not today building enough houses. The cumulative effect of this has been a sustained and rapid increase in house prices where even the most miserable shed in London would sell for over £200,000 or maybe 250,000 Euro. The problem is particularly acute at the cheaper end of the market where, due to the earlier sell off of the Council owned properties, the stock of social housing has, in effect, been progressively reduced. There are thousands of people on the shortlists of most councils waiting their turn to get occupancy of a house. A rapid external interference is bound to have consequences. In actual fact it appears that many casual immigrants live in appalling squalor in private landlord premises. Another problem is that local people fear they might lose their place in the queue and be condemned to share their parents' house for yet another year, as foreigners who had amassed more points jump the queue. This is an unresolved problem area – a shortage of resources.*

5. *The lack of suitable land. The shortage of houses is directly linked to the lack of available land, even though a landowner, when selling land for building purposes, may receive a multiple of ten times the value of the the plots compared with agricultural land value. There is still a shortage in supply of land. There is no doubt that part of this may be due to developers' hoarding of land in the hope and expectation that house prices will rise even further leading to even greater profits, nevertheless several councils are having to give consent to build on 'Green Belt' areas which have previously been designated to be free from development between cities. Very often too these protect small hills and valleys of some beauty as well as lakes, rivers and woodland. Green Belt was brought in over 50 years ago to prevent the growth of creeping development which would otherwise see endless suburbs linked together making one major city indistinguishable from another. Germany has endless miles of a sandy plateau where a whole town could be built without even anyone hardly being aware, it would be simply lost in its setting, the same is true of Poland. Another unresolved UK problem affecting scarce resources.*

6. *The recent austerity measures in the UK have reduced certain services. The latest open door to new immigrants happened at a time of austerity in the UK. These cut backs were particularly severe for Social Services and many poorer people were affected directly and some services were withdrawn. Benefits payable to poorer people and to some disabled were under threat. It's normal and usual that this causes suspicion and jealousy that others might be obtaining preferential treatment and there is always a case reported somewhere of individuals receiving something out of the ordinary. The unplanned and unplannable nature of the arrivals has meant that the local councils are often not able to cope and prepare for an influx. The numbers arriving from Poland was miscalculated by a factor of 10. The lack of planning has not enabled the UK to cope with an unregulated influx, the timing of a surge did not allow for restrictions of services within the UK which might have enabled migration to take place more easily.*

7. *Fear that immigrants are taking UK jobs. It is probably fair to say that the UK has/ never had an adequately integrated work training programme. However what plans there have been, for example, by local colleges offering basic skills training or training in particular trades, like plumbing or electricians, have been made almost impossible by the rapid influx of trained tradesmen from Eastern European countries. Whilst there is no direct evidence that immigrants have directly undercut UK wage earners, this is not entirely clear because once some foreign workers are accepted*

in one sector or company it is possible that their friends are taken on under private deals through what might be called a 'syphon effect'; so that immigrants attract other immigrants to the same places exacerbating existing problem. These later arrivals might suffer at the hands of less scrupulous employers, agencies and landlords, earning below the minimum wage and being housed in poor conditions often keeping the agency's introduction fee for themselves. Whether immigrants will accept this depends on the increase they would earn over their home wage. But there is another more serious problem, for any recently trained young British worker entering the labour market. Because the wage differential is so high between some countries and the UK, the people attracted to work in the UK might have a much higher qualification than their British competitors for the same job. For example the immigrant might have a degree and several years of work experience. If within the UK the employer wants to take the best person for the job, he might in those circumstances hire the immigrant. This might leave the local person unemployed, on benefits and a burden on the state. The cost benefit analysis evaluating the contributions of immigrants to the UK economy in terms of taxes and increased GDP does not appear to take into account this substitution effect in financial terms nor in the emotional terms of the person in the UK who fails to find employment. <u>Experts are not clear on the benefit from immigrants to the host nation.</u>

8. *<u>It's the surge in immigration that cannot easily be coped with</u>. It is simply not possible to assume, as the freedom of movement of people does, that the receiving areas will not be affected. Immigrants arrive and use facilities before they can be fully accommodated in terms of schools, medical and training facilities. The EU offers nothing with which to back up its guarantee of free movement of people. It gives substantial grants for regional developments in poorer countries but offers nothing to wealthier countries on the basis that the costs of immigration can either easily be found by them or are self-financing from increasing tax and higher GDP. The EU fails to understand such inconveniences. It is apparent that the greater the difference between the average pay in the UK and the average pay in the country of origin, then the greater the likelihood that those who seek to better their circumstance would be attracted to move. The initial members of the EEC, as it was prior to the recent enlargements, had wealth that was very similar so there was little benefit from a country move. Where the GDP is different by a factor of 2, the flow is likely to be more intent and protracted. <u>So the UK finds it difficult to plan for and absorb these surges.</u>*

The UK has been unable to predict and plan immigration and the perception is that it is out of control. But these issues are what directly led to the recent negative referendum result. The feeling within the UK is that the UK is powerless to manage its own affairs, which might run out of control, and that the EC has failed to recognise the problem or assist countries which are destinations that have problems in shortage of significant infrastructure facilities. The main difficulty is that immigration has become such an emotive word that those opposed to immigration are too easily named racist or chauvinists when even making the simplest and most innocuous comments about it. This in turn has hampered our ability to recognise the problems arising and cope with them.

London is by far the most international Capital City in the EC. Members will however have to set this against the undoubted fact that, for example, London is the most metropolitan city in the whole of Europe; it already has the highest proportion of foreign born residents of any of your own capital cities. By and large we have opened our frontiers to the world, there is scarcely a country in the world that is not represented in London.

We already have a huge unseen City of illegal Immigrants. Apart from all other considerations most people believe that there are at least a further 250,000 and possibly very many more illegal immigrants living here who are never recorded in any statistics.

The UK has no intention of halting immigration. You will recognise that we are not halting immigration, that would be impossible both from the point of view of allowing UK citizens to bring in relatives, our own need to recruit for an expanding economy and to encourage entrepreneurs to set up businesses here. Allowing immigrants to fulfil our proven needs will surely still require people from the EC. There will be no halt on immigration unless further austerity reduces our GDP and this then affects employment and the lure of jobs available.

The UK will tighten up controls and put in place a fair review system for Immigrants.
The UK will have to put in place a much more rigorous immigration control system.
You have no reason to suppose that any rules which we do apply will be discriminatory. Indeed our record is that we have had the most unregulated labour market of any country in the EC.

The alternative of Brexit might cut off some immigration completely
*If you do not accept some limitations then, as you have all predicted that dire
consequences would follow for the UK, you have to set a limitation of the
number we can admit whilst a member of the EC against the high probability
that in the event of a Brexit and economic collapse there will likely be no
immigration at all from any of your countries to the UK if unemployment in the
UK rises substantially.*

*To reinforce the comments I am making to you. Forecasts suggested that
England by 2030 will have the highest number of inhabitants per square
kilometre of any country in Europe. Twice the density of Germany and France.
You might have imagined that Holland had the greatest density, but that will not
be so.*

*The UK seeks a temporary derogation from the free movement of people. It is
under these conditions and for these reasons that we now seek to limit the net
immigration to the UK to 200,000. Basically we have nowhere to put them and
can no longer guarantee the reasonable working or living environment for an
unregulated supply of immigrants. Accordingly the Government of the United
Kingdom seeks an emergency derogation in this respect for a period of 5 years
or later until new constitutional changes are introduced when this item will be
part of the changes on which each Member State's Parliament may be entitled
to vote.*

Review by the EC Court of Justice
*Any system of controls by way of visas, evaluative points system or system to
match skills with specific job requirements will be presented for approval to the
Council of Ministers in due course. We are aware that any Member State may
challenge the controls used by the UK and should they decide that our systems
are discriminatory, if this challenge is successful this derogation might be
suspended or withdrawn.*

*The position of the City of London. The only other matter on which we seek your
assurances is for the preservation of the financial skills of the City of London.
The volume of financial operations there are much greater than in any other EC
country. We need the assurances, even should further steps be taken by
Eurozone member states to continue their march towards a federal structure
having, for example, a single Eurozone Finance Minister, that whilst the UK
remains within the EC but not in the Eurozone, 'The City of London' would be*

included as an honorary member of the Eurozone committees, able to vote in its own right on matters directly affecting it..

If these matters are consented to then the UK Government will formally propose these changes for acceptance by the people of the United Kingdom in a second referendum to be held in November 2017.

They both put the paper aside. Sebastian asked him to explain several points which he did, he continued. "Well, Sebastian, as they say the rest is history. We did receive the derogation and enhanced full consultation for the City of London if the EC were to move to a Federal Status, but the decision was close and several Member States voiced their opposition.

Meanwhile our net immigration has failed to reduce below even 250,000, despite our theoretical powers to contain it, a main problem being that there was a surge in GDP increase in the UK following the second referendum. This has been exclusively attributed to the UK being seen by all Foreign Direct Investors (FDIs) as the country of choice for their 'Launchpad into the EC'. All of these FDIs have insisted that they must be allowed to man their operation adequately and, if trained UK operatives are not available, to be able to select accordingly and if necessary bring in their own staff, at least for the initial period after commissioning. This in effect has placed the FDI companies in prime position to determine the level and source of immigration for many new businesses.

Also there is no view that foreign students should be prevented from coming to the UK, they are generally welcomed, so the thought is that they will simply be re-categorised out of the immigration figures, but cynics say that would be done just to show something has been done when it hasn't .

The main problem is now that the 5 years derogation will expire in October 2022 and, as far as I understand it, we are currently unable to state what mechanisms we have in place to police the opt out and to prove that there has been no overt discrimination. Certain Eurozone Member States have already advised us that they intend to bring the matter to the Courts of Justice, particularly if we should pretend that we can continue without explanation or permission into the future.

So there is a lot of work to do, otherwise we face a resurgence of anti-EU scepticism here in the UK!

The rump of UKIP are obsessed by it claiming that the actual level of immigration proves that it was a 'stitch up' the Derogation they claim was all for show proving the UK was back in control in order to win the second vote, but the UK government was just play-acting, going through the motions. You can be sure that UKIP will continue to fly the 'too much immigration' flag again and again, but our case looks weak.

But events have changed within the EC too, you might have thought that migration from Eastern Europe has been a great benefit to those countries, well superficially it has been largely through remittances back to their families and those countries are defiant in their desire to uphold their right to their populations' free movement, but that's just re-iterating their public's desire. The reality is quite different, some have calculated that the effects on some of these countries whose population move abroad, will, by 2029 mean a fall in their GDP of 4%. Yes a fall! There seems little doubt that the IMF findings are correct when it suggested that post-communist emigration from eastern Europe countries had stunted their growth, strained public finances and accentuated demographic problems. So when Germany hails the benefits of migration from other EU countries improving their demographic profile they don't seem to care that it in effect destroys the demographic profile of the donor/ emigrant states. The French Government is itself stirring the pot when it backed new EC rules that would force companies sending employees abroad to match local wages. Syrian and other immigrants will be given short shrift in many Eastern Europe countries."

"Hummph!" snorted Sebastian "Well I have been concentrating on other matters for the last two years, I didn't realise it was that bad! So you mean that although we had powers to control immigration that we failed to do so? So the only real benefit is that this time it's our own failure and cannot be placed at the door of the EC! It's hardly surprising that, when I suggested that I could later take on the Home Office, which is of course responsible for immigration, there was little or no objection or obstruction! But do we have any other armour to help us Roger?

"Well, Sebastian, it just depends on how rough you want to get? We will come to the 'Four Freedoms' in more detail in our next sessions, these are Movement of People, Finance, Goods, and Services. The EC has been laggard in opening up 'Services' because of its sensitive nature, it would mean for example opening up government departments to foreign bidding for supplies, such open-ness as there is might mean application being made in specific languages and in a certain legal format: but no-one takes issue with them for that. Yet they try to enforce the 'movement of people' even when in some cases it is counter-productive to do so. It's an unbalanced growth, but probably UK is bearing the brunt of criticism because it is by some measure the 'opt out' leader in the EC and we haven't 'opted in' even where we have a clear leadership role to play! The UK are far ahead in 'openness' the rest play 'stumm' when it suits them.

Of course immigration has to be seen also in the long term, the large waves of immigrants from Poland, Romania and Bulgaria of course were caused by suddenly opening frontiers and due to the major enlargement eastwards, it's conceivable that provided there are no more countries with high populations and low GDP joining the EU, immigration surges to the UK will likely not be repeated and that immigration itself will level off.

Eastern European countries might well increase wages to prevent us taking their skilled people. Furthermore the treatment of Syrian refugees has shown some of those countries to be hostile to taking those from a different culture, that's something that can perhaps be turned on them?"

"Anyhow thanks Roger it's been very helpful – next session we'll look at the Military and how that's all tangled up with NATO and er, oh! yes Turkey!".

Chapter THIRTEEN – EU Discussions TWO - Turkey

They met again on the following day Thursday morning December 31st 2020.

Roger explained "This is going to take time as it's a complex matter and not at all as obvious as it should be, Sebastian. One of the problems with the EU is that there's an element in the mix which is pure emotion and doesn't appear to be derived from business or finance or growth or anything like that which you would have thought stemming, as the EU did, from the European Economic Community, i.e. fundamentally an economic grouping".

Roger continued..

"Let's look at how the controversy started?

Of course Turkey was raised as an issue several times here in the first of the two recent EU referenda in 2016.

It became a matter of some contention and was never satisfactorily resolved by either side.

A junior Brexit minister claimed that Turkey was going to join the EU and that the UK could not stop that, the assumed intention being to conjure up a vision of hordes more immigrants arriving in the UK that we could not stop. Turkey has a population of over 70 million and would be the second largest country by population in the EU so it was a statement and a challenge that deserved some response. Within the institutions of the EC, it would overturn the balance of QMV and would change the balance in the EP and render smaller member states virtually insignificant.

David Cameron's response was two-fold a) that the UK had a veto over new countries joining and that it was impossible for Turkey to join without our consent. (Indeed he was right on this part, the decision on new Member States has to be unanimous it is not one of those matters subject to QMV, Qualified Majority Voting) and b) that it was not a problem as it would be decades before Turkey was ready to join – if ever.

That was seen by most people as, at best, an ambivalent response. It simply begged the question, if the UK had the veto and were against Turkey joining then why had they not used it already? That would have clarified the position to Turkey, and indeed to everyone in the UK and removed the spectre of further surges in immigration.

But the UK didn't. In fact quite the contrary, Brexiteers found that David Cameron, on a visit to Turkey, had stated in 2014 that Turkey was 'Vital for our economy, vital for our security and vital for our diplomacy'. This didn't seem to mesh with the throwaway line 'if ever'.

That allowed the Brexiteers to claim that there was a possibility of immigration from that direction.

Reasons for the ambiguity.

Now to understand the reasoning behind the apparent ambiguity of the UK's position we have to go right back to the 1980's when Turkey first put out feelers about joining, these were not totally rebuffed.

Later there came into being the 'Copenhagen Political Criteria' and this laid out minimum standards that any country had to reach to be acceptable as an applicant but this didn't exclude Turkey which is of course 95% in Asia and it laid down clearly understandable criteria for a candidate country to achieve - the various accession chapters, the famous 'acquis'. These cover a huge variety of topics and some of them are, in fact, negotiable.

During the next few years Turkey's interest waxed and waned and it was apparent to both sides that Turkey was not ready for a number of basic reasons relating to its state of development.

However Turkey's application was taken seriously enough by 2004 for the EU to have then prepared a very detailed report and good analysis of Turkey as a possible EC candidate. The paper was entitled 'Issues arising from Turkey's membership perspective'.

One matter of importance was that about half of Turkey's imports and exports in 2004 were to the EU-25 – so there were established trade links.

You might think that this EU report dealt overwhelmingly with the economic advantages to both parties but that is NOT the case. Hidden within the summary of the main issues is this statement:

'The economic impact of Turkey's accession on the EU would be positive but relatively small, both due to the modest size of the Turkish economy and the degree of economic integration before accession.'

It is therefore in economic terms an asymmetric economic gain, *'i.e. small for the EU-25 as a whole and much larger for Turkey' (para 2.2).*

Of course the same might have been said for other countries' applications, but there was for all of them a geographic contiguity which is, simply for the outside reader, not at all apparent in Turkey's case. For example ultimately it seems to most people that all the former pieces of Yugoslavia are likely to be accepted when they reach the criteria because they are nearly surrounded by existing EC countries. A swift study of a map shows that Turkey shares only a tiny border with EU member states and that it is mostly in Asia surrounded on all sides by other Asian or Middle East countries.

Indeed it would be difficult to find a country more different in outlook, religion, structure, geography size, state of development, current GDP, than Turkey and the EC, certainly compared with the original Rome Treaty member states.

Nor is it as if there were a number of EU states demanding Turkey's admission; on the contrary a number of EU states have at one time or another voiced serious concerns. These include Cyprus, Germany and France and, more recently, the clear obstructionism of the Visegrad States to having even a few Asian migrants, previously sent to Germany, dumped on them, suggests that immigration to those countries from Turkey would probably not be welcomed even resisted. Hungary voted massively against any immigrant allocation of those that supposedly came from Syria neighbouring Turkey where the same tribes lived on either side of the border, even though as it failed to reach the 50% turnout and, therefore was not legally enforceable.

Other reasons for allowing accession.

So we can assume that there are some other more deep reasons for encouraging or allowing Turkey's application to proceed.

Of course instead of Germany's 'Merkle moment' in 2015, what logically they might have done would be to have re-enforced Greece's dreadfully weak border guards, activated their own military to assist and taken the refugees back to the country from which they set off for Greece and Italy, mostly Turkey and Libya, at the same time as providing for camps in those countries. They didn't do this. Another course of action might have been to engage with the UN to resettle the refugees elsewhere. Saudi Arabia has, for example, taken in none at all. Yet again the UN, might have directly attempted, by diplomatic or military means, to have resolved the root of the problem – the war in Syria. They did none of those things.

As you know, as the German embarrassment grew they eventually realised that they could not accept a further one million migrants in 2016, so they then bribed Turkey to prohibit refugees from setting out from there on the basis of allowing in a much smaller allocation of refugees from existing refugee camps that were proved to come from Syria. Another aim was to encourage Turkey to actively pursue ISIS, which it had been dilatory in doing, permitting them to operate through or near Turkey's borders. Part of the bribe was in cash but part was also that the EU speed up the process of granting Work Visas to the EC for Turkish citizens hinting too they would probably move towards completing the 'acquis' for EU accession for Turkey. Erdogan has openly stated that he has earmarked 2023, the 100th anniversary of the founding of the Turkish republic, as his target date for accession, this has never been challenged.

So now the EU appears to be embroiled in Turkey's accession from which it will find it extremely difficult to extract itself as the 'acquis' chapters move ahead.

So the question needs to be asked as to why Turkey was ever considered to be a 'runner'? Indeed the whole 'old EU elite' appears to be wedded to the idea including all leading political parties in the UK.

EU's Geopolitical reasons

To see why, we have to return to the 2004 report which clearly identifies the reasons, which I'll attempt to summarise below. These are all basically, what you would call, 'geo-political'.

Turkey as you know sits at the cross roads between Europe and the Middle East. All the EC elite in almost all countries EC repeatedly say '…and there's Turkey'. That elite has convinced itself that were Turkey to join the EC it would form a bridge into the Middle East and bring the EC to the centre of much of the world's oil, protecting possible pipelines.

It would also control of the Bosporus and could throttle Russia's incursions into the Mediterranean, commercially or militarily.

It would be a fitting reward for Turkey, having been a loyal outpost under NATO, which is important to the USA. It had for decades formed the shield to NATO's Eastern flank which earlier had physically restrained the USSR's desire to dominate the area and destabilise the West's oil routes.

Another reason, sometimes quoted, is that allegiance to the EC would prevent any possible Axis forming between Turkey and Iran or any other grouping of Muslim states which might lead to a new and more dominant and uncontrollable political or military alliance, so it would, from the EC spectrum, deny any other country dominance in the area.

Turkey is an observer to the Arab League and despite it's past as an oppressor empire is regarded as being partly, at least, in sympathy with Arab political thought but it is the only Muslim country to have established working relations with Israel which the EC is keen for other countries to emulate.

Although it is never stated that it would allow the EC to dominate trade there, Tukey does however control important water resources which drain into several countries.

As a Muslim secular country with a functional, if somewhat paranoid, democracy Turkey is a factor for stability in the region, it might encourage other Muslim states to follow when the populations see wealth being more equally distributed.

Development of that position might even encourage the restarting of the Arab/Israeli peace process which has been at the root of the problems there as it shows Arabs at their weakest and most unstable. For most Middle East countries the treatment of Palestinians is an enduring humiliation.

So generally EC Member States seem to overlook the enormous problems that Turkey's access would cause.

The nature of the challenge.

The EU 2004 Report suggested that accession would be 'challenging'.

Turkey is huge, at over 70 Million people, much larger than any other state in any enlargement so far, and is as large as the last 10 new Member States admitted combined. In comparison Germany has 80 Million, France and the UK 65 Million.

But, within Turkey, there is a constant question mark over its adherence to 'Liberty, Democracy, Respect for Human rights, Freedom and the Rule of Law' – something that was made worse by Erdogan's crack down on a major newspaper, his reforms away from a completely secular state and his willingness to attack Turkish Kurds with tanks and deny them any sort of regional democracy. The 2016 coup against Erdogan and his vicious response, including imprisoning judges, indicate to most Europeans that Turkey is simply not suited to the co-operative style of the EC and is unlikely ever to be so. So there are question marks over Censorship there, Women's rights and even the 1920s Armenian genocide which has never been formally acknowledged.

There is a huge mismatch between the GDP of the EU and Turkey, 32% in 2004. This was still about the same 10 years later. The 'Employment rate for Women' was half the rate of the then 2004 EU-25. In 2004 33% of Turkey's employment was in the agricultural sector compared with just 2.1% of the EU-25 in 2004. As a result there was a huge disparity of GDP between the industrialised and the more eastern agricultural regions in Turkey.

This suggests that it would cost the EU millions of Euros for 'Regional Development'; massive grants would be needed for years but the EC doesn't seem to cost this out and consider its effect on Member State contributions. As a guide some Eastern European Countries currently, in effect, receive a subsidy of E400 per annum per head. 70 Million times that does not even bear thinking about!

There would be a massive additional border to secure for if Turkey's GDP were to rise significantly it would itself suck in the poor from the surrounding countries. But Turkey's borders are porous and, whilst the sea, at least, holds back some migrants from entering Greece, there would be no natural boundary to hold back streams of economic migrants.

But key is, if they did join, would Turks integrate easily?

At present Turks are the largest single group of third world people in the EU due to their longstanding 'Gast Arbeiter status' in Germany which encouraged their admission to supply manpower due to Germany's increasingly aging population. There is some doubt that the Turks in Germany have been successfully integrated.

They appear for the most part to be Turks in Germany rather than German Turks.

There must be at root within the EC, a fundamental concept that; say Poles working here in the UK and remaining for 5 years will transfer some of their loyalty to the state in which they live, contributing to life here, their offspring educated here and feeling in every way equal to other citizens for promotion and voting. Individuals have to relate to the state where they live in order that its laws are observed and understood. But what happens if some groups specifically refuse to integrate in that way?

There have been many studies of the Turks in Germany and although the position might slowly be changing, one of the reports suggested that 'whereas 59% said two years ago that they wanted to belong to German society, 75% say so now (2012) that is encouraging. But some of the information that we do have is more disturbing. For example those that regard themselves as strictly religious increased from 33% in 2009 to 37% in 2012. Whereas 21% said they saw Germany as more of a homeland than Turkey in 2012, that number has now dropped to 15%. Another earlier report said 'but immigrants from Turkey are very poorly integrated—they are worse educated, worse paid and have a higher rate of unemployment. And it doesn't make much difference how long they have been living in Germany. But many Turks who came to Germany as guest workers decades ago didn't want to become part of German society, they wanted to earn money there and return home. That didn't happen. The Turks stayed on but their original attitude hasn't changed. They formed ghettos and didn't establish much contact with Germans. Two thirds of immigrant children can't read adequately at the end of their fourth year in school. 'A new statistical survey shows that 36% of ethnic Turks live below the poverty line compared to 25% of migrants from the Balkans and southwestern Europe'.

As recently as 17 October 2010 AFP in a Press release headlined 'Merkel says German multi-cultural society has failed'. Merkle admitted that Germany's attempt to create a multi-cultural society has failed, Chancellor Angela Merkel called on the country's immigrants to learn German and adopt Christian values. Merkel spoke after talks with the Turkish Prime Minister in which they pledged to do more to improve the often poor integration of Germany's 2.5 million-strong Turkish community.

Originally the Turks in Germany were not allowed to cross into other EU states but they are now permitted to do so. Whereas they were the exclusive problem of Germany, now they are an EU problem!

An additional problem for Germany is how would it's 3 Million Turks react to seeing Turkey permanently excluded from the EU? That is a greater number of Turks, apparently with no political voice, than several existing small EU states which have a skewed disproportionate political weighting! Anyhow the Turks in Germany are almost totally politically voiceless.

Potential immigration from Turkey

The EU 2004 report suggested that 'Since the 1980s the flow of net migration leaving Turkey amounts to 40,000 to 60,000 persons per year; almost all of this migration takes the form of family reunification. In 2002 about 3 million Turkish Nationals were officially registered in the EU-15. The main recipient countries were 77.8% in Germany, 7.9% in France, 4.7% in Austria and 4.4% in Netherlands'.

The 2004 report suggests that 'The estimates for the long term impact, i.e. by 2025/2030, based primarily on income differences tend to give varying figures (ranging from broadly 500,000 to 4,000,000 potential Turkish immigrants to EU Member States and… Based on the experience that Turkish workers tend to migrate alongside networks of already established relatives, the biggest share of additional migrants to the EU would most likely go to Germany, France, Netherlands and Austria'.

It suggests that 'There are perceptions that a possible substantial and uncontrolled increase in migration to the EU could lead to serious disturbances in the labour markets of some of the Member States'.

To my mind, Sebastian, 'serious disturbances' suggests some localities would be swamped.

Turkey's current progress in 'acquis'

When I last checked, and this information is from 2016, Turkey had yet to complete by negotiation 33 of the 35 chapters of the 'acquis', the accession process. Four were at early stage and Four were well advanced and the rest were somewhere in the middle, some chapters have however been blocked by Cyprus. You will remember before Cyprus' accession both Greek and Turkish speaking parts of Cyprus held referenda on a new agreement for a reunified Cyprus. Turks voted for; but Greeks against, primarily on the grounds, so it's said, that they were not prepared to permit Anatolian, that is mainland Turks, who had arrived after the invasion, to remain.

My understanding – a Summary"

Roger continued "my own view is that not many countries want Turkey in the EU for the huge cost and disruption it would cause, but they recognise the pivotal position of Turkey in the Middle East. Surprisingly perhaps Greece is in favour largely, it seems, for the EC's oversight to prevent continued tensions and conflict between Greek and Turk which are legendary. Various other states such as Spain appear to support the application.

Merkle herself has steadfastly opposed Turkey's accession, as in 2013 did Wolfgang Schaube who famously said 'Turkey is not part of Europe!' He is the hard man of Germany with a tough attitude to Greece, he's the German Finance Minister aged now 76, even so he is seen as a possible contender to succeed Merkle. As the largest number of Turks are now in Germany and are likely to increase as a result of a successful application and because Germany is so heavily involved with the 2016 Syria migrant deal, nobody else seems to want to take issue over Turkey's future membership.

It seems that most Member States are hoping that another Member State will use its veto, but no-one does, so that for every year that goes by the embarrassment becomes greater and no-one else appears to be able to have the courage to say 'Look! Turkey just does not fit!'

Then in the autumn of 2016, the European Parliament voted for delaying any future deal with Turkey as an EC Member but based on the wave of arrests and poor human rights record. The immediate response from Turkey was to threaten the deal over Syrian immigrants. A British Foreign Secretary at the time was much derided by the EC for praising Turkey the day before the EP vote.. but there is still no decision on the matter.

Turkey has been strung out so long that their Prime Minister is entitled to feel grossly annoyed if they were now to be fobbed off, nobody knows how he would react.

It's a train crash waiting to happen, the EU elite, and the USA, can see the geopolitical advantages but seem unaware that the people below may simply recognise what their political masters cannot – that it's a bridge too far.

A rational person would conclude that the EC has problems enough without deliberately taking on what would be the largest Member State, a country with undoubtedly the greatest cultural difference and the greatest difference in wealth, at a huge cost to the EC if the EC should attempt to introduce measures in time to equalise GDP across all countries.

Is there an alternative?

Turkey would be the overwhelming gainer from joining, but a rejection of Turkey as an applicant raises uncomfortable questions for the EU. Any exclusive club clearly designed to significantly improve the lot of its citizens has to decide sooner or later how it faces up to the rest of the world and particularly its impoverished neighbours.

Perhaps instead the EU should be aiming at encouraging further trade and investing in these poorer countries? Merkle probably came nearest to this when she proposed instead a 'privileged partnership'. If such were applied to all neighbour countries this could lead to an outer ring of influence and engagement which might in fact help to limit and constrain foreign relationships and help focus the EC's mind on the enormity of the problem it faces. But we will come to that in a couple more sessions' time.

<u>So in short – answering the original questions:</u>

Yes! The UK can stop Turkey's admission but

No! It has shown no inclination to do so at all, the UK actually appears to have encouraged it and

Yes! there's likely to be huge surge of Turks to the EC on accession - but

No! It's unlikely they'll come here, they'll probably go to countries where Turks have already settled.

But of course there's no guarantee, and under 'free movement of people' we could not stop them coming here, if they wanted to do so.

However this matter is of great importance because for many in the UK our ambivalence on this matter allowed many people to infer that we could be swamped by Turks. It has apparently little significance in Whitehall but enormous importance in places like Boston, Lincs.

The issue has to be burned and buried!"

"Hummh, that doesn't sound good!" said Sebastian " but is there no way of offering the Turks some form of associated status?"

"Well" Roger responded " the EU does in fact have a European Neighbourhood Policy but it doesn't operate very well, it was this that was offered to the Ukraine and which appears to have provoked Putin into taking a more active role there to prevent the Ukraine falling into the EU orbit."

"Hmmmh! Well I hope the military issues are going to be easier? See you later Roger!"

Chapter FOURTEEN – EU Discussions THREE - Military

Later on Thursday afternoon Roger continued:-

"At first glance, Sebastian, it might appear that a proposed EU Military and NATO might be rivals.

But in my opinion that's substantially overstated.

NATO has been around almost since the end of the Second World War. It was a buttress against the USSR's attempted domination of Western Europe.

At the heart of NATO is the USA which is the dominant contributor in money, in military and in political power.

There seems to be no intention to supplant NATO, other countries might occasionally 'sound off' but the USA's contribution, at over 4.4% of its GDP to its total Military budget, far exceeds any other contributors. The UK's is 2.4% and whilst there are a few countries near that % like Greece, Poland and Estonia; most of the rest are half or less than half the UK's contribution. So if any Euro Army were to supplant NATO it would almost certainly mean a massive hoist of their military spend. There is no sign of that happening.

NATO remains the only effective military force with a command structure and commitment to fight in the EU states' areas.

There has been for some time a recognition that something should be done to 'enhance the EU's military capability', what was previously called a European Defence and Security Identity.

From this arose in 2002 what was called a Berlin Plus agreement which was, in effect, an EU-NATO security agreement, there were seven major parts to it, most of it was related to exchange of information, planning capabilities, joint use of assets and consultation process. This meant that if NATO refused to engage then the EU force could use those assets, but all NATO members would have to agree. The EU did in fact carry out limited operations in some states of the former Yugoslavia under EUFOR.

This was followed by the EU Lisbon Treaty which includes a clause to the effect that 'If an EU country is the victim of armed aggression on its territory, the other EU Countries have an obligation to aid and assist it by all the means in their power, in accordance with Article 51 of the UN Charter'.

If, as the EU elite had hoped, the EU were to evolve into a Federal Structure rather than the Confederacy that it more closely resembles now, then it would be a natural thing for it to want to defend itself. In the same way the EU has taken faltering steps to start a foreign policy with a designated 'High Representative'.

Indeed in 2016 one of the political groupings in the EU, the EPP Group, launched a paper 'Towards a European Defence Union'. It says 'It wants to end the uncoordinated and isolated islands of military co-operation, high priority has to be given to the launch of Permanent Structured Co-operation (PESCO).' But it is also clear that it is intended to compliment NATO. 'Europe must match its share of responsibilities and act as a strong defence pillar within the the trans-Atlantic security community' but it then adds 'with the ability to conduct CSDP (Common Security and Defence Policy) missions and operations with its own resources'.

This is where the UK seems to draw the line, building up the 'defence pillar' is OK, but carrying out 'operations with its own resources' seems to be supplanting NATO and is not OK!

Part of the problem stems from the fear of Poland and the Baltic States that Russia might try to use the indecisive nature of co-operative agreements within NATO and EU to launch a surprise attack.

NATO responded to Russian sabre-rattling by temporary assignment of forces to the Baltic States, indeed the UK sent a squadron of RAF Typhoons to the Amari Air Base in Estonia to help monitor Russian probes and mock attacks around the Baltic States. This was part of the move by the alliance to allocate four battalions or 4,000 troops, 650 of them British, into the Baltic States. This move was met from Russia by a statement accusing NATO of 'focusing its efforts on the containment of a non-existent threat from the east'. Moscow has been railing against NATO for more than a decade claiming that the alliance's eastern enlargement, NATO's acceptance of the Baltic States into the alliance, puts Russia's security at risk!

But the USA has been ambivalent about buttressing their forces in Poland. The US and Germany have unequivocally said that NATO will not build new bases in Poland, citing tactical and political reasons, but Poland's Foreign Minister said he wanted 'presence, presence, presence and once again presence' of NATO troops to act as a symbol of readiness to defend the eastern flank.

The USA has 38,000 troops in Germany, most people seem to believe that the cost of these troops is partly paid for by the host country but this is not so, the actual cost to the USA of keeping them in Europe is between $10,000 and $40,000 per head more than it would cost if they were at home!

Article 42 of the Treaty on the EU provides for substantial military integration within the institutional framework of the EU, but it requires unanimity and this move remains gridlocked because of the known opposition of the UK.

There are already a number of bi-lateral agreements like the German/Dutch Corps, European Gendarmerie Corps, European Air Transport Command and a Maritime Force (for humanitarian missions) and a Movement Co-ordination Centre and there is a Franco-British Joint Expeditionary force involving all three military arms but it is not a standing force but rather available on notice. This latter was agreed only in 2010.

Of course after the first UK Referendum in 2016 the other EU Member states became fearful that the UK, perceived as having one of the major high quality military forces and one of the few with almost constant combat experience, might duck out of its European obligations as part of its rejection of the EU. They sought to take the opportunity of the UK's absence to rethink what they wanted to do, being then free of the UK's persistent opposition to a EU Force.

The second referendum in 2017 reconfirming UK's presence in the EU, nevertheless did not make up for the earlier shock of the UK's possible departure when it might well have taken on a more global role turning away from Europe. The UK is still perceived as lacking commitment to developing, or even blocking, a European Army. The need for which appears to arise from a desire from several states for some deeper protection which has gained momentum after the Ukraine crisis.

With your knowledge of Russia and Ukraine, Sebastian, you are possibly the most experienced person at ministerial level in the EC to deal with this problem since you have a better understanding of Putin's motivation. However to return to the case; the UK carries out a Strategic Defence Review every few years, the last in 2015, and this is intended to match the UK's perceived defence needs with its existing military strength. But this document does not even acknowledge the existence of any other European Military organisation than NATO. True, it mentions 'our allies in Europe', and in response to Russia's exercises, it mentions NATO many many times. There is a collaborative treaty with France to develop technologies for maintenance of Nuclear stockpiles and also a joint venture with them developing military drones. There is an obvious strengthening of the Northern Group within NATO covering the Baltic States responding to the recent Russian sabre-rattling.

But as the review states clearly 'NATO is at the heart of the UK's defence policy'. It states the UK will continue to foster co-ordination and co-operation between the EU and other institutions, principally NATO, but it's clear there's no intention to join any separate EU force.

Indeed the Press in the UK were openly hostile to any deeper EU military structure 'EU parks its tanks on NATO's lawn with European army plan' and 'EU army plan sets alarm bells ringing on NATO's front line'. Of course it didn't help that it was the UK's bête noir in the form of Jean-Claude Junker who is an out and out Federalist, appeared to be the instigator of renewed moves towards a functioning European Army. He urged 'Europe can no longer afford to piggy-back on the military might of others, we have to take responsibility for protecting our interests and the European way of life!' The plan suggested a military structure to be able to 'act autonomously' from NATO. But this move does not have support of all member states, some Eastern European countries fear that the plan could become a 'phantom' allowing Germany and France to neglect their duties to NATO.

"This is just another example of the UK's past lack of leadership", Roger exclaimed rather passionately, "apart from pottering about here and there we have really done nothing to engage positively in the discussions, it should have been quite possible to evolve structures which did increase the military defence at ground level in Northern Europe AND to ensure that it was integrated into NATO. Sadly we lost that initiative, most EU countries believe that even now our commitment to the EU is less than whole-hearted. You can see yourself that the USA is being challenged in the Far East with a podgy adolescent trying to make nuclear war-heads and delivery system to hit the USA, and China, whose march to realising its position in the world will surely lead to confronting the USA sooner or later. It's likely then that the USA may well reassign troops from Europe to the Far East, much as, long ago, the Roman did from Britain when they had other enemies to fight. If that happened there would be a military void here in the EC!"

"You can test this yourself, Sebastian, in principle what is wrong with the EU trying to take over greater responsibility for its own defence? We are all aware that some countries spend much less than say the UK on Military spending? Perhaps with an initiative like this their defence spending might improve especially if it were 'sold' as THE EU defence plan?

As part of the EC's desire to keep itself informed it carries out regular citizens' reviews or opinion polls through sample groups in each country. One of these was on a common defence policy; this revealed that 73%, of the EU-28, favour a common defence policy, for the UK it's 61% despite the UK's consistent rebuttal of a Euro Army on the grounds that it might undermine NATO. That's simply a further indicator that the UK's position is seen as illogical.

I see this as a vacuum waiting to be filled. If NATO doesn't want to expand into North East Europe then it seems that the EU will. Of course from the USA's perspective they don't want a military alert being triggered off by some half-cock reaction by any blundering EU army to counter, say a Russian feint, such as what you yourself witnessed over Belarus in 2020, which gets out of hand and they then come screaming to the USA for help. That would leave the USA to ride to the rescue and deliver diplomatic and military defence! NATO was designed to act as a threat to war but the EU 'army' would have to be strictly controlled if it is to work and be knitted into NATO! There is a sneaking suspicion too that some of the European soldiery are chocolate box, week day, soldiers without consistent combat experience which would in any case collapse in front of any Russian incursion. Leaving the USA plugging gaps in emergency.

But are the UK political and UK Military using the USA reluctance merely as an excuse to prevent an EU force becoming established? and why would they do that?

I think, because the UK knows that recognition of an EU army will mean a commitment of UK troops it would constrain it's supposed global reach. After the last manpower reductions any permanent allocation there would leave the UK with no ability to serve its other tasks set out in the Strategic Defence Review, which are now clearly still within its mental, if not physical, compass. Generals want to believe they can 'go anywhere, do anything'. After all the UK Government has coughed up for two aircraft carriers to prove it! Everyone else sees it as hopelessly out of date – fading dreams of an Imperial past. But the USA does not object they support UK's military spend. For them it appears to mean the UK getting stuck into just about any fight that's going for which the USA request us as allies! 'Allies' of course prevents the USA being seen as a dominant threat and exposed as a solitary policeman. A substantial permanent commitment to any EU army would probably prohibit future UK engagements such as Iraq and Afghanistan.

A heavy commitment to defend Europe wouldn't need those aircraft carriers and expensive dedicated aircraft, their sole role is to carry out 'global tasks'. For which frankly we have no longer the military nor financial capability."

"Hmmh" coughed Sebastian, "So more troops locked into Europe may not be a bad thing? OK that's even more for me to think about, thanks anyhow! Are you going to continue tomorrow, Saturday morning? I feel I have to get to grips with this quickly."

Roger replied "Look I'll be here in London just as long as these sessions take! In any case in the period around Christmas and New Year is just about the only time, I guess, when its peaceful here with no interruptions?"

"OK then I'll call home, Roger, see you tomorrow unless you want to stay the night – foods limited as all staff are away but I should be able to rustle up something. There's a spare bed!"

"No that's kind, let's take a break and see you Saturday morning then – say 9.30 to 12.30 will that do? I suggest we go over together 'What's wrong with the EU' then on Monday if you are game, I have a case study I want to show you on the German Motor Industry and how it has adapted to the single market and Eurozone; then, in the afternoon we had better try to work out, let's say, 'an improvement plan'. Obviously as a former Foreign Minister you'll know a lot of this but it's perhaps just as well to see it from a distance, let's hope it's more objective that way!"

Chapter FIFTEEN – Personally planning ahead

Roger went home and Sebastian spent the evening trying to arrange things for the following day. Saturday afternoon and the whole of Sunday he had set aside for the family reunion. Madge was in charge of the logistics and she had agreed to drive down with Sylvia whilst Bill Bennett collected Massa Gombe from Heathrow Airport and deliver him to Downing Street. Then Madge and Bill would disappear to Sebastian's old flat.

Sebastian hoped that Madge and Sylvia would mend some bridges, Sylvia had convinced herself several years before that, Madge was out to capture her husband, and she positively winced at even the mention of Madge's name. Sylvia was right of course although she never knew it for certain and Sebastian had no intention of ever mentioning it – it was a one-night stand, it meant nothing.,

Sebastian had had to use all his powers of persuasion to get her to come. Sylvia had initially decided not to, then decided to come by train or even bus, until Sebastian had offered to himself drive back up to Middleton on Friday and then back down the same day. Sylvia of course said that was impossible! Sebastian knew there were no pool drivers, he had been consulted by the Cabinet Office and suggested that the drivers be let go over the long weekend. But he knew he had to go through the next Euro session on Saturday, so there was a logistics problem.

Sebastian emailed Dan Stirling asking him to set up the train trip from Brighton on Thursday week and to a Moslem neighbourhood the following week and to organise Constituency Dinners for the two following Saturdays, he added.

Email to Dan Stirling and Staff:

Dan I may as well start off on the plan as discussed with you, well see how far we get?

On meetings, can you try to get 2 LD constituencies, one winnable and one where they've just got 'hopes', within 75 miles of home?

Remember, best if I meet separately with Councillors and Committee before the meal and for photos.

Then I prefer written questions which I can consider and answer after the meal, frankly local press would make a meal of any off the cuff asides I might make replying to verbal questions.

For the meal just stick to basics, chicken or beef or vegetarian – definitely no offal please, that means no liver, kidneys, brains, pigs trotters, black sausage or tripe. OK?

I'll speak for 20 mins no more.

Check with Bill and Madge transport arrangements – got to be back home at 10 pm OK?

Please reply by Monday so I can book the diary which is already getting filled up

PS Don't be surprised if you see photos of me popping up in odd places!

Sebastian Edwards.

Chapter SIXTEEN – EU discussion FOUR – What's wrong with the EU?

Sebastian took New Year's day off to go through the Red Boxes and prepare for the week ahead.

They resumed discussions on Saturday, January 2nd 2021. Roger brought with him two briefcases stuffed with files which he laid out on the Cabinet table.

"Well, Sebastian I was writing a book on it, as you know and here's all the research!"

"By Gum! Do we have to go through all that?" asked Sebastian concerned it might go on into the afternoon.

"No! No!" Roger assured him "that's in case you ask detailed questions, I have a paper prepared anyhow. Let's run through it, stop me whenever you feel you need to OK?

But, Sebastian, this is where it gets difficult, the Euro Referenda in 2016 and 2017 were all about whether we wanted to be 'In' or 'Out' not what sort of EU it was going to be!

A lot of the very poor discussion, for which frankly the TV is largely to blame, came down to 'Immigration' and the rather irritating but never defined 'Interference from Brussels'. There was no time given to look at the EU, see how it operated and to highlight its strengths and weaknesses. There was absolutely no vision or plan by the 'Remainers' to show where the UK might be within the EU and more importantly how they would expect to change it! At best it was for them a 'dead cat bounce' a half-hearted reluctance to even endorse the EU 'Look we are in it now, there'll be a dreadful mess if we leave!' doesn't sound a dynamic reason for staying! Does it? … and to have added truthfully 'but there'll be a dreadful mess if we remain!' probably would not have helped much, would it?

There are lots of people who want to 'have a go' at the EU as The Economist declared recently 'Cheerleading for Europe has become an almost impossible job: No one will stand up for Europe these days', but there are dozens of Euro-Bashers. In order to bring the discussion to a reasonable format, Sebastian, I have chosen to group the main accusations of what they say is going wrong with the EU under three headings which cover, I think, most items.

1. **The EU's structure is all wrong, leading to Policy gridlock, lacks legitimacy, democratic deficit**.

2. **The EU is unpopular, people don't want further integration and loss of sovereignty.**
3. **The EU (a) Economically doesn't increase GDP enough, and (b) the Euro is a failure.**

Well let's not pre-judge it yet but conundrum is that changing the current situation of poor performance to something that would deliver increased wealth, might demand changes so great that the people may not be willing to accept them. This is why many observers suggest that the EURO's collapse is, in the end, inevitable, others suggest that it can and will survive!

But to look at the EU we have to go right back to the beginning.

You, as any educated UK citizen, will be aware of the origins. German Industry destroyed by war, French Industry pillaged of its equipment, millions of dead, The UK bust, all populations at a low ebb, bitterly aware that the many conflicts had led almost to the ultimate destruction of a way of life and if they continued in that vein there was only misery ahead. Europe was in fact saved by the USA Marshall aid in 1947 an act of unparalleled generosity.

THE EU timeline

In 1950 came the ECSC. The Governments of both France and Germany provided first a vision, through its founding fathers Jean Monnet and Robert Schuman, a practical way of preventing such recurrence by pooling all coal and steel production under one joint authority.

In 1952 the Treaty of Paris also brought in Belgium, Holland and Luxembourg who already achieved some integration though bilateral agreements in 'Benelux'. Then Italy came in.

In 1957 the Treaty of Rome was signed, it incorporated the famous phrase the 'ever closer union.' It began as a Political act of faith although it was termed the European Economic Community. Slowly institutions were evolved which seemed to mesh with unfolding needs,

In 1965 the Council of Ministers seemed an appropriate way to formally bring together countries into a standard format away from the personal contact between the leaders which had been there from the start, a nascent European Parliament was intended to capture the public interest and grow into a key part of the structure.

In 1973 Denmark and Ireland, plus the UK, who had initially been rejected by de Gaul, finally joined. This was followed by Greece, then Portugal and Spain, which had all been at one time under fascist governments, they became locked into the EEC's democratic format.

In 1986 the initial chumminess whereby decisions could be made by leaders around a dining table was ended by the Single European Act which aimed to establish a single market, also introduced Qualified Majority Voting (QMV)so that the majority could work around any single country's objection on certain matters.

In 1990 the reunification of Germany saw East Germany added within the German Federal Republic which bore all the costs rather than the EEC, this in fact ended a 'Europe of the Regions' that had been a possible route of development based on Regions being represented.

In 1992 the single market was introduced, mostly prodded by the UK, this was designed to set a level playing field across Goods and Services to encourage competition and efficiency.

In 1993 the Maastricht Treaty was signed which previewed monetary union and introduced some further political themes such as common citizenship and policies on internal and foreign affairs. The 'Copenhagen criteria' laid down the basic rules for applications from any European State, these were contained in the chapters of the 'acquis', rule of law, human rights, protection of minorities, market economy etc.

In 1995 Austria, Finland and Sweden joined and the Schengen agreement came into effect allowing for passport free travel between the original 5 plus Spain & Portugal.

In 1999 the Euro was formally launched, it came into common currency in 2002.

In 2001 The treaty of Nice changed the QMV.

In 2004 came the huge increase of 10 new member states basically the CEE, states formerly under communist rule, again latching into a clear democratic future with the EC, plus Cyprus and Malta. This added 20% more population and made it the largest grouping in the world.

In 2007 came the accession of Romania and Bulgaria and the Treaty of Lisbon which created a new post of President of the council.

In 2013 Croatia was admitted

In 2015 the President of the Council suggested that there would be no further admissions of states for a period of 5 years but there's a waiting list of Balkan States and of course Turkey.

You can clearly see a pattern, a clear path, a trajectory which ultimately leads to a sort of United States of Europe.

This might be a 'federal' structure built on common standards and laws throughout driven from the centre, near a single state, or whether it might fall short of that in a looser 'confederacy' permitting some individuality, allowing decisions to be made by each member state, is unclear, but there is no other conclusion that one could draw.

As a representative of the European Trade Union Confederation (ETUC) put it in March 2016 'The EU is much more than a trading block. It is the most successful example of long-lasting, voluntary and democratic international co-operation in the world, and that's why it continues to exert a strong attraction for neighbouring countries and populations. That's something worth saving!'

The ruling elite has some very clear guiding beliefs which can be described as 1) the desire to avoid another European war, 2) the idea that it is natural for Europe to be united, 3) the concept that, in economics and politics, size really matters, 4) the notion that Europe needs to be united to compete effectively on a global basis with Asia rapidly challenging, 5) the idea that integration in Europe is inevitable.

Alongside these are the 4 principles, the 4 Freedoms. 1) Freedom of movement of people, which is clearly almost an EC obsession, 2) Freedom of movement of Capital, not really developed much, 3) Freedom of movement of goods, which has been mostly delivered and 4) Freedom of movement of Services.- this latter has hardly been touched.

What has gripped the imagination of the elite of the EC is that this is NEW, it's a NEW Relationship, using NEW Rules and there is this momentum amongst the core believers that they work desperately to be inclusive and to co-operate, but they will not be blown off course, they will feel their way around problems, pause, rethink and reconsider, then move ahead again.

If you are inside this bubble there is still a measure of excitement and of innovation.

If you are outside the bubble it can feel like a remorseless snowball threatening to crush you under its path into the snow and squeeze any individuality out of you.

Some in the UK suggest that either the EC will disintegrate or that the Eurozone will collapse. They are, in my opinion, hopelessly wrong, so out of the loop that it shows a total lack of understanding of the generations of Europeans who are striving to an ideal. Most see the UK as an outsider just hanging on by its boot straps but always rather detached, lacking that element of commitment all the time.

You can get the level of commitment by one of the top countries in Angela Merkle's statement 'If the Euro fails Europe fails!'

The question is can the EC move forward or does it by doing so endanger the ideals of voluntary co-operation which was its basic tenet. That's the paradox.

Here are some of the main criticisms of the EU, its institutions, aims and processes.

1. The EU's structure is all wrong, leading to Policy gridlock, lacks legitimacy, democratic deficit.

Most observers agree that the EC has rather stumbled into its current structure, adding and improving as the various new themes and modules were brought into play.

As several have said it is now almost a state but it's not quite complete yet, so it has emasculated member states of some of their powers without finishing the job.

What is also clear is that EC has struggled to transform itself from a group of 6 states sharing certain common ideals, similar or at least well understood cultures and potentially similar wealth into a group of 28 member states which a much broader range of cultures, histories and GDP. It is at base an economic grouping but it has clear political objectives too. It has attempted to be co-operative and democratic. It has endeavoured to ensure that every state and every political party has representation. Over time political views and objectives have changed. The running repairs to its structure have not all been successful. In attempting to ensure that no state is overridden the processes have. Qualified Majority Voting has been used so that progress can continue around blockages.

A process of derogation or exemptions have been permitted in order to ensure that states are not compelled to enter processes which they find objectionable.

The institutions have themselves evolved in time. But the EU is now at a cross roads. It appears stuck. It seems either unable or unwilling to go forward to its logical conclusion.

Let's be clear what the structure is and what the main problems might be. I'll just run through the main points using the institutions as a guide. I have taken most criticisms from authors who have studied the EU and you can see the references that I used, (the details of the names in brackets in the notes at the end of the book).

The **European Council (EC)**, made up of the heads of state or government of the EU Member States, the president of the European Commission, and the president of the European Council, sets overall EU policy and is the highest political authority in the EU.

Thomas Piketty suggests that the heart of the problem is the Council of Heads of State, 'we pretend that it can take the place of a sovereign parliamentary chamber as if it were a chamber representing states, alongside the European Parliament representing citizens.. This fiction doesn't work and never will… it leads to clashes of national self-interest and to collective impotence'.

In practice many key decisions are made on a bilateral basis (R.B) and don't use the Council.

EP tries to influence the EC by presenting 'two-files' and bargains acceptance of one file against another (J-C Piris) in this way it puts pressure on the EC.

Beneath the European Council, the EU's law-making process involves 3 main bodies.

European Commission: The executive branch of the EU, the European Commission proposes legislation, manages the Union's day-to-day business and budget, enforces the rules, and negotiates international trade agreements on behalf of the EU.

There's a view that the Commission has been weakened since the move was made to change the number of Commissioners from two to one (J-C Piris) then to a rotating system of less than one to 2/3rds, then back up to one, this leads to an overlarge group with inadequate time to discuss important matters and work through key issues, moreover each commissioner becomes a 'representative of their state despite theoretically being independent from governments. As it's one man one vote a small number of commissioners representing a few % of the population could act as a block, The counter argument is that a country without a representative is 'unprotected' and countries cannot mandate others to protect them if they are not there.

The Commission can be and has indeed been removed by the EP, so the commissioners are not protected and are not the 'college' suggested in the Treaty. Larger states put pressure on their appointee. To counteract that influence the president of the EC speaks directly to the heads of the largest states (J-C Piris)

The Electorate cannot dismiss the EC as they can their own national Government (R.B)

Council of the European Union: Made up of ministers from the 28 Member State governments, the Council adopts laws in conjunction with the European Parliament, coordinates the Member States' broad economic policies, concludes international agreements between the EU and other countries or international organizations, and approves the EU budget (jointly with the European Parliament).

A potential hazard for the UK was thrown up from a Review of the Balance of Competencies UK/EMU carried out by HMG in December 2014. A formidable part of this Council is called ECOFIN, it is the meeting every month of the EC's Member States Finance Ministers. They carry out briefings on the existing situation. Soon after the Euro was launched and it hit some financial turbulence, the members of this group which had adopted the Euro, formed themselves into a EUROGROUP a sort of subcommittee but the meetings are held in camera. This group meets before every ECOFIN meeting, which is therefore joined later by the non-euro Finance Ministers. Of course there's a possibility that the Euro and non-Euro parts would tend to drift apart although HMG was given repeated assurances that this would not happen.

However the Council adopted Qualified Majority Voting, this was deliberately to avoid one or two members holding out rigidly for a particular course of action which might happen if every country had its own veto. Now the effect of later changes to this QMV meant that 65% of the total EU population could carry the decision. Member states that adopted the Euro can now achieve that figure on their own so as a group they could, if acting together, win every vote. This is disturbing for the UK which has signaled its intent NOT to join the Euro for the foreseeable future. But it might be stuck with decisions made by ECONFIN driven by the EuroGroup steamrollering the UK which would be in no position to halt it in any way. Several people have suggested that being sidelined is very unlikely since it would require all EuroGroup members to have achieved the same level of development and unity which there is no sign of then doing and then operating directly against the express wishes of the UK.

Whilst on the whole the UK has accepted assurances that they would not be treated as second class members, there is still a nagging doubt that the institutions were set up assuming ever closer movement and that therefore the EuroGoup might well instinctively adopt new policies designed primarily to resolve issues around the Euro and thus taking their eye and effort away from the continuing development of the Single Market which has still many defects. It is only through the further development of the Single Market and its opportunities for further increased trading in Services that would maintain the commercial interest of the UK.

Hence pathways of the Euro and Non-Euro Groups might well be diverging although not by any deliberate act. The Non-Euro Group is hampered in that some of its members are 'sometime but not just now' whilst others are 'not now maybe never', so it seems unlikely that all the Non-Euro member states would want to form a unit in contradiction to the EuroGroup.

There is an acknowledgement from the UK that the EuroGroup is likely to be further enhanced by a move to a full time Finance Director, taking further powers away from the Euro States Governments in order to improve the controls needed on every Euro State. The UK also concedes that a healthy Euro is required for the EC to function adequately. So the UK has no wish to prevent the centralisation of further powers within the EC for Euro area countries.

The European Parliament, 751 directly elected members from all member states. It shares with the Council the power to legislate; it exercises democratic supervision over all EU institutions, it has the power to approve or reject the President of the Commission and Commissioners; it shares authority with the council over the EU budget.

MEPs are not elected with the same constituency quota of voters. The smallest country has 6 MEPs, the larger countries have disproportionately fewer, this reduces the legitimacy of the parliament and weights it to the smaller states. (J-G Piris). Although the US Electoral College is similarly biased, so the USA President is not elected by direct voter mandate, that only occurs every 4 years! In the EC it distorts the voting for Chairmen of committees in Parliament. Also decisions are not necessarily equally representative of all the people. This warping does not increase democratic legitimacy. In the EP there is no parliamentary majority to support a government.

Although there are 7 cross-country political groupings, given the large linguistic and cultural differences, these make little impact in the member countries themselves (R.B).

Nor is there in any sense an 'opposition' whose task would be to test all proposals to prevent steps in the dark which might risk the EC. and if necessary to subject proposals to aggressive criticism. The Brussels Elite consider that the main opposition is 'inertia'.

The EP has the power to increase spend but has no responsibility to find ways of funding that (J-C Piris).

A majority in the EP now has the potential to choose its own Commission President and Commission and also enact policy proposals that are opposed by a minority of governments in the Council (S.Hix) due to QMV, so the gridlock has nothing to do with the institution. The main cause of policy gridlock... the problem of how to reform existing policies when one group of governments and parties want policy change in one direction while another group wants policy change in the opposite direction (S.Hix). When the opportunity for reforms opened up in 2005 the EU lacked the legitimate mandate to make major changes that would be against the interests of any of the big players (S.Hix) .. in this case France.

In addition to the UK being possibly sidelined in ECONFIN there is also a move afoot by the Governor of the Bank of France to support the move to the appointment of a Finance Minister and to support this democratically through 'institutionalising the euro area format of the European Parliament' this would in effect leave the UK in a very secondary position, probably with reduced influence in practice whatever guarantees to the contrary may be offered..

The EP does not deal with those issues that are the most important for voters, employment, taxes, labour market, health, education of foreign policy, as these are not within their remit.

Other major EU institutions include the Court of Justice of the EU, the highest EU judicial authority; Each country regardless of size, supplies a judge, but the quality is variable, some had no experience. This scarcely enhances the Court's performance or its reputation (R.B). It has been accused of going beyond its remit and to advance European integration (R.B).

the European Central Bank, which is responsible for monetary policy in the 19-nation euro area; It has worked well (R.B). but it now belatedly has independence and more powers.

the European Court of Auditors.

It's often argued that the EU's budget both has and hasn't been signed off by auditors for years.

Both sides have a point. The EU's Court of Auditors regularly "signs off"—in its own words—the reliability of the accounts themselves, and has given them a clean bill of health for the last eight years. But it has consistently found significant errors in how the money is paid out since it began giving opinions in 1995. Ultimately, it depends on what you think the term "signed off" implies about the accounts.

This seems to be a huge point for the Brexiteers made as constantly as the second 'home' in Strasburg, but they are essentially peripheral matters, there is scope for improvement but is it critical for the health of the EU? I don't think so!

Overall (1) the urge to harmonise, naturally implies integration… this leads the EU into obsessing about various sorts of trivia (R.B)….. however they have never been able to bring the same energy and drive to implementing effective economic measures, as they have to the various political projects egg The Lisbon Agenda (R.B). This agenda was thought by many to have been moving the EU in the right direction as it laid down economic growth target of 3%, employment targets, increased spending on research, support to SMEs, saving energy promoting environmentally friendly technologies (R.B). This Agenda was not implemented.

Overall (2) with the reforms of the EU treaties in the last 20 years, the institutions are far less consensus oriented than they used to be. The main reason for the gridlock (failure to address integration of energy and service sectors, internal market in financial services, reform of agricultural services, reform of effect of social regulations on small businesses) is that the policy agenda has shifted from creating the internal market to economic reform (S.Hix).

Overall (3) The democratic Deficit is that there is no open competition for control of Political Authority at European level. (S.Hix). As pointed out, it's not just a democratic deficit, it's about subjecting proposals to rigorous testing.

2. The EU is unpopular, people don't want further integration and loss of sovereignty.

There is a lot of information available to test this. The information shows a depressing pattern, a growing gap between the direction of EU travel and people's expectations. It's not all downhill however and support varies considerably from country to country.

Voting patterns

First we can trace what has happened in the voting patterns for the European Parliament Elections, we can see that, for example, the turnout has declined from 1979 with a turnout of 62% to 2014 with 42.5% - a 30% decline,

The UK's vote varied between 24% and 36%.

Strangely perhaps almost all the later enlargement countries, excepting Malta, had, in 1974 a similarly bad turnout as the UK in 2014, dropping to as low as 13% for Slovakia to the mid-30s% for Bulgaria and Romania, bearing in mind that these countries stand to gain substantially from the regional development grants and an eventual lifting of their GDP, it seems, if anything, scant return for the EC's huge investment in time, energy and funding of these peripheral countries. There seems to be something wrong with the reward/cost ratio somewhere, either the EU vision is not getting across or the vision doesn't relate to peoples' perceived needs.

The results of the Euro Election in 2014 simply re-endorsed this decline, 'roughly a quarter of all seats in the European Parliament in 2014 went to parties sceptical of the EU or protest parties.'

Simon Hix carried out some research marrying support for the EU with the EU's economic growth, this suggested that initially until 1992, they correlated fairly well as growth increased so did support but later despite an upturn in growth towards 2000 support continued to decline and did so across most countries.

Simon Hix then analysed what he termed the 'elites' using a Euro survey in 1996, this covered, politicians, senior civil servants, media owners, business and trade union leaders etc., this showed that whilst only 48% of the public supported the EU a massive 94% of the elites did. Further analysis followed which indicated that people were beginning to evaluate whether or not they stood to gain personally from the EC, higher income earners, being more able to take advantage of opportunities, were in favour whilst manual workers and public sector workers in the 'older member states' were more likely to feel threatened due to their lack of flexibility and by the new states whose cheaper wage rates threatened their jobs, so they were broadly speaking against.

Referenda Results

Of course this failure to form a positive pro-EU base in the national electorates has had a very damaging impact when referenda are held to ratify the structural changes intended by the EU in cases where such ratification is required by a country's legislation.

Apart from Norway, where there were special consideration with its offshore oil and gas reserves and fishing, most countries when tested initially returned substantial referendum majorities.

But then Maastricht was carried in France in 1992 by just 51.1%, Denmark rejected it initially and only voted for it by 56.8% with the benefit of opt outs. In 1994 over the Enlargement, Finland and Sweden gave approval of 56.9% and 52.8% respectively not the ringing endorsement expected. Then in 2001 Irish voters rejected the treaty of Nice by 53.9% and only gave it approval on a second referendum when they obtained an opt out on defence matters. On the moves to the Euro both Denmark and Sweden voted against its use.

By 2004, however, it seemed that perhaps a corner had been turned when all referenda were carried for the major Enlargement, in the accession countries.

But then the EU development hit a basic problem and shock to the system as both France and Netherlands voted against the adoption of the European Constitution which caused the whole module to be dropped.

Ireland voted against the Treaty of Lisbon, but then given certain assurances on the number of commissioners, voted in favour in 2009.

Various other referenda have been held recently on Enlargement, Croatia; on the European Fiscal Compact, Ireland; on the Uniform Patent Court, Denmark; all of these passed with around 60% to 66%.

Famously Greece rejected its bailout conditions in a referendum but then the Greek Parliament over-ruled that result and accepted it.

In 2016 the Dutch voted against the Ukraine-EU agreement, primarily it seems due to the Dutch view that the Ukraine Government might have been complicit in the downing of the aircraft. Later the Dutch voted against and in support of the same agreement.

In October 2016 Hungary voted against in a referendum accepting migrant quotas, thought it didn't achieve the minimum to give it legal approval.

Finally of course we have our own referenda, the first UK vote in October 2016 rejecting the EU and the second after opt-outs, in November 2017 in favour (as the reader may have picked up from reading the first Sebastian novel which was published in December 2015).

So you can see the pattern, the nearer the EU moves to transferring further sovereignty the narrower become the margins of acceptance and even often now referenda results in failures.

The EU is no longer able to create new or changed institutional structures at will and depend on a cohesive response such that public referenda necessarily follow a country's leaders represented at the EU at the European Council. The Elites views have not been transmitted to the average citizen

Opinion Polls and Research

This is the final part of the information system. There are two specialist sources here but the main one is the EC's own polling research. It has a large and sophisticated, regular, in depth unit which publishes many reports on diverse topics in its 'Eurobarometer' series, perhaps 12 studies every year. A primary report for our purposes is 'Europeans' and its detailed interpretation 'Europeans and the European Union'. (Other reports, for example, were on 'Enlargement' in 2006, and 'Europeans, Agriculture and the CAP' 2015).

This study, for example, in its 2015 edition asked what were the two most important issues facing the EU, the polling groups identified the leading items for the EU in total as 'the economic situation – 28%'; 'the state of Member state's finances – 26%'; 'immigration- 25%'; 'terrorism – 24%'; 'unemployment – 22%'. The same questions were asked in every EU state – 'immigration' was the highest ranked item in the UK with 31% ! Signs were there of impending trouble for the first UK referendum, people either ignored it or suggested it was 'racism' and beneath contempt to take seriously, it was a fatal mistake!

A more damaging simple question was asked 'In general are things going in the right or wrong direction in the EU?' The overall response was '25% were RIGHT direction, 39% were WRONG direction'. For the UK the answers were 17% RIGHT and 44% WRONG. So there was plenty of warning about the UK disaffection! The questions go deeper; 'Does the EU conjure up, very positive, fairly positive, neutral, fairly negative or very negative image?' The overall results were '4% very positive, 33% fairly positive, neutral 39%, fairly negative 28%, very negative 4%'. So approximating; 1/3 for, 1/3 neutral, 1/3 against, you can see that the huge neutral figure slopping about in the middle, makes any Yes/No adjudication very precarious.

For the UK alone the answers were '5% very positive, 23% fairly positive, neutral 37%, fairly negative 23%, very negative 9%'. And that was the rather wobbly base from which Cameron insisted a Referendum must be held!

Within this report there's a whole host of detailed comments and quotations.

So anyone studying this detail, would not have been surprised, by the initial UK referendum results in 2016, it's all there, as also is that the people's perceptions of what the EU was expected to do fell short in actual achievement!

Of course these Reports are not designed particularly to hit at the heart of some EU institutions or policies so the detailed report on the CAP, fails to ask a key question 'would you prefer that part of the 40% of the budget sent on CAP is instead spent on employment generating investments?'

Sebastian interjected "but perhaps this gap is, in reality, caused by a failure to deliver expected economic gains? People think that the weak returns don't justify further pooling of sovereignty. So the solution here is to release the growth potential, it is only that which will persuade people to continue to deepen and widen the single market and increase wealth and ultimately increase GDP!"

"Well" Roger replied quickly "that's what we are going to cover next!"

3. The EU Economically a) doesn't increase GDP enough, and b) the Euro is a failure

(a) Economic Gain

What we can say with some certainty is that initially the EEC (as it then was) showed plenty of signs of success; from 1957 to 1973 the GDP of the six original countries grew by an average of 4.9% in the same period the UK trailed behind, growing at only 2.8%. Of course it's impossible to state that the playing fields were level, as the six had suffered considerable damage during the war and had started to re-equip with new more efficient plant, so there was some catch-up; but never-the-less the momentum was with them rather than the UK, much of whose equipment had not been replaced and was jaded after years of severe austerity, rationing and exchange controls.

However between 1980 and 2007 the EU growth rate lagged slightly behind the UK's 2.4%.

It's difficult to disentangle from this the different styles of economic management, Mrs Thatcher shifted the UK economy away from subsidising industry, this put a hammer through several major companies but allowed others to flourish; whilst in the EC, the countries continued supporting declining industries for much longer. A report by Professor Crofts of Warwick University suggested that the UK's early adoption of ICT was partly responsible for UK's strong showing and that the increased competition brought about by the UK's accession removed the industrial relations problems which had blighted UK industry for decades. Later UK financial services made another significant impact after deregulation.

It's almost impossible to get anyone to state categorically how much of the UK's GDP growth can be ascribed directly and only to the EC because no-one can say what would have happened if we had not joined. The CBI estimates a 4 - 5% GDP gain, a Government report in 2005, in a paper 'The economic effects of EU membership for the UK' suggested that trade with EU was estimated to have been boosted 7% and that a further 7% increase was due to the Single Market. The Centre for European Reform in 2014 after extensive modelling suggested that UK 'trade is 55% higher than one would expect given the size of these countries' economies'.

Opponents quote other data giving a loss of GDP of between 1 and 3%. The largest element of this being CAP, the Common Agricultural Policy. It is acknowledged this increased the costs of foodstuffs by 0.5% of GDP. There are also EC administrative costs.

Even the Government's own report in 2013 'Review of the Balance of Competences – The Single Market' which was intended to be used as the basis for Cameron's renegotiating prior to the referendum, failed to make the picture any clearer but it states that 'the most commonly cited study by Ilzkovitz, Dierx, Kavocs and Sousa in 2007 suggests that in 2006 EU GDP was 2.2% higher than it would have been in the absence of the Single Market, with an additional 2.75 million jobs created and a 0.5% boost to total factor productivity'. Unfortunately the only evaluation for UK's specific gain returned a negative!

Certain commentators suggest that the EU social policy costs including Working Time Directive, gender equality, guidelines on working conditions, agency employment, transfer of staff on a change of business have together cost a further 0.5 % holding back our GDP. Although it's by no means clear that the

UK would have escaped these changes even were UK outside the EU because of the changing social mores at the time in the UK.

Opponents claim that the EC's performance is faltering and that the EC's share of world trade is in fact declining, though this seems largely due to the rise of the BRICS (Brazil, Russia, India and China) in that period. In fact the explosion of the BRICS GDP, increased from $ 2,268 Bn to an estimated $ 21,736, much of this was increased supplies at lower cost, to the developed world, so it's difficult to read this as implying that the EU lost momentum because the BRICS operated from a much lower cost base. Then too the financial banking collapse, hit several EU countries like a shock for which the Euro area was totally unprepared, one estimate suggested it cost the EU 10% of its GDP.

However for the UK there are some other very significant gains, it's only after 1973 and the shock of entry that the UK started to feel competition from Europe and started to raise its quality and efficiency, without it, it's likely that the UK would have become totally uncompetitive. The Commonwealth could never have provided an adequate competitive spur.

Most importantly the UK attracted a significant portion of FDI Foreign Direct Investment, people often buying bases in the UK from which to manufacture and sell into the EC, 60% of this is in services.

One also has to 'Services' contributes 60% of GDP, this is where the UK, through its language and IT skills might be expected to out-perform.

So overall there has been a significant advantage to the UK of having EC membership, it provides a huge potential market of 500 million people. Currently of our exports to the EU over half is to Germany and Holland, we have not yet really scratched the surface of what we can do, but it needs working at. Just because we are in the EC doesn't mean that it's a free meal ticket!

However one also has to bear in mind the views of a 'proper economist 'Thomas Piketty, probably the leading Economist in France, in his seminal tome 'Capital in the twenty-first century' suggests that the likely growth rates are much lower than suggested above. He says 'if we looked only at a continental Europe we would find an average per capita output growth rate of 5 % between 1950 and 1970 a level well beyond that achieved in other advanced years over the past two centuries.'..' In continental Europe and especially France, people quite naturally continue to look on the first three post-war decades… as a period blessed with rapid growth.'

In the USA and the UK post-war history is interpreted quite differently, between 1950 and 1980 the gap between the English-speaking countries and the countries that had lost the war closed rapidly. In the UK GDP per capita fell below the level of Germany, France, Japan and even Italy. It may be even that this being rivalled played an important part in the 'conservative revolution, (Margaret Thatcher and Ronald Regan promised to roll back the welfare state.

In fact neither the economic liberalization that began about 1980 not the state intervention that began in 1945 deserves much praise or blame, France Germany and Japan would likely have caught up with the UK and the USA following their collapse of 1914 – 1945 regardless of what policies they had adopted.

He concludes that 'it is highly unlikely that per capita output in the advanced countries will grow at a rate above 1.5% per year, but I am unable to predict whether the actual rate will be 0.5 %, 1.0 % or 1.5 %. The median scenario, I will present here is based on a long term per capita output growth rate of 1.2 % in wealthy countries which is relatively optimistic.

(b) The Euro

One of the key factors leading expectations of the benefit of the introduction of the Eurozone was the work of Professor Andrew Rose. This is the so-called 'Rose Effect'. In a work in 2000 'One money, one Market' – the effect of common currencies on trade, described by Professor Frankel as 'the most empirical paper in the field in the last decade', Rose estimated that 'monetary unions triple trade among members.' His study was based on a panel of 186 countries analysing their behaviour over the period 1970-1990 every 5 years. The drivers for such increases were considered to be the reduction of trade costs and higher competition. This, as it turned out, hopelessly distorted expectations of what might be achieved.

For several years that was believed and it formed the basis for 'success' in many peoples' view. It was a figure enthusiastically taken up by many economists. As soon as data was available the actual effect of the Euro's introduction and its influence upon trade became the object of intense empirical research.

Alongside Rose's outcome which was latterly regarded as seriously flawed, the actual results were much lower than expected. Prof Jeffrey Frankel of Harvard University in 2008 suggested that Rose had used data from many previous monetary unions but these were small-country results (also very poor areas) which it was thought may not be useable for larger countries, there were several other criticisms, the data may have been faulty and there was considerable difficulty in disentangling the effects of Monetary Union from a customs union effect, break up of states, switching away from USSR orbit, etc. However studies concluded that trade rose by 15% beyond what would have been expected by normal growth, with what he termed consensus in the first 4 years 'significant, but small, of 10 to 20%'. But using later data he concluded that the gain appeared to have levelled off and, including all developed countries, the effect was 10%. But he, as most other economists, still believed that it was an unsolved mystery – why was the actual increase so low?

One commentator, Mark Havel of Trinity College Dublin (Euro at 10 years), suggested that the lack of common language might be a restraint on trade, (other explanations included local differences in legal systems, financial structures and local buying preferences) another reason might be that even at 10 plus years old the Euro is still a 'new' currency and there could be a time lag effect. Another is that the gain has largely been to the original 'core' members for example Germany's trade imbalance has grown substantially since the Euro. He also argues that the Euro brought in cheaper interest rates and that financial markets trading in bonds, equity and banking assets, were substantially reduced. He suggests that the 10 - 15% gain, at least some of which must have come from the Euro, should not be regarded as a failure.

In 2008, Professor Rose recalculated his figures based on 26 of the most recent studies and reached the conclusion that that the Euro has influenced trade by between 8% and 23%

Allister Heath writing on 27th August 2014 in The Telegraph was more devastating suggesting that 'Intra-Eurozone exports peaked at around 52% of the total in the late 1990s and have been in decline ever since. They are now down at least 5% from their peak'.

Tsl Sadeh of Tel Aviv University suggests that 'the Euro increased trade among the periphery countries of the Eurozone (Greece, Italy, Ireland, Portugal and Spain) more than among its core member states' between 2004 and 2006.

Saving on currency conversion costs with a monetary union is estimated to be 1% of GDP (economics – Help) of course the basic case in favour of monetary union rests on the desirability of eliminating exchange rate uncertainty which is alleged to hamper trade and investment. The EC in 1990 estimated this transaction cost as one quarter to one half of 1% of GDP. As an additional benefit in 2001 the ten year bond rates from many joiners fell from between 4%

and 11% to just 1% allowing saved interest to be used elsewhere. (Although some country rates rose rapidly later). Or, like Ireland and Greece stupidly spent on their own little foibles, housing and huge pensions.

Two economists Juliana Cindea and Moise Cindea probably came nearest to the truth, they suggested that the effect of increasing trade was anticipated by measures such as the Single Market and that trade integration began in the period 1992-1998 but that this was difficult to separate from the effects of the Single Currency as the implementation of EU directives varied from state to state. The intra area trade had increased significantly before 1990 and the marginal increase in recent years was more limited.

When, Sebastian, we look the German Motor Industry in a separate case study, we shall see that this is what appears to have happened in practice, German manufacturers sought to reduce costs by shifting production to cheaper labour areas and were probably reacting to their own internal needs like increases in volumes and costs and seeking out suitable factories in the CEE areas where suitable quality could be achieved, in many cases this occurred before the Euro was introduced. They did not need to wait for the formality of the Euro.

What was clear however was that the increase in GDP over that period in the UK was higher than in the Eurozone area. This gave an immediate boost to those in the UK who in any case wanted to leave the EC. It was their 'proof' that the advances being made by the EC towards harmonisation and integration were neither necessary nor desirable. However it appears that perhaps a substantial element in the UKs figures was caused by the increase in Service Transactions outside the EU 28 and that the UK's figures may therefore have been partly caused by one off factors not related to the EU particularly in the Financial Services Sector.

So there is a basic problem, contrary to expectations the introduction of the Euro has not led to the huge increase in trade that some had expected.
There is, after all, not much point in losing the sovereignty and control that one had before, then move into the Eurozone and find that the economic benefits do not match such a loss. Many observers have suggested reasons why the gain is so poor.

Jean Claude Piris cites a 2010 report to the then head Jose Manuel Barroso 'A new Strategy for the Single Market' this identified 'gaps' and 'missing links' that hamper the functioning of the Single Market.

In some areas the Single Market 'exists in the books, but in practice, multiple barriers and regulatory obstacles fragment intra-EU trade and hamper economic initiative and innovation. In others, the potential for greater economic gains is frustrated by lack of physical and legal infrastructure or by absence of dialogue between administrative systems.'

Another sector missed out from the Single Market is ITC which did not exist when the single market was initially conceived.

A further report, 'Monti', identified 50 possible proposals for improvement, this covered a wide range of items, patents, copyrights, internal market of the services sector (which the Economist 16th July 2016, says is 70% of the EU economy), e-commerce, internal market on transport, public procurement legislation, professional qualifications, basic banking services, internal mortgage market, dispute resolution. To this might be added educational and technical qualifications. To these The Economist (16th July 2016) added energy, digital services and Europe's fragmented capital markets. The Economist quotes the commission as saying that simply by implementing current law on services and digital market could boost EU output together by 4.8%. Other commentators have added potentially the ceasing of protection of agricultural products and services.

So basically it has been much easier to liberalise trade in goods than in the 'jealously guarded protected services markets'. The easiest, low-hanging fruit has been plucked.

Problem – Currency no State and Country Interest Differentials. However whether or not the Euro has increased trade, it has, as Thomas Piketty amongst many others have pointed out, some serious flaws. 'The basic error was to imagine that we could have a currency without a state, a central bank without a government and a common monetary policy without a common fiscal policy. A common currency without a common debt doesn't work. What was not foreseen was that speculators on exchange rates would be replaced by speculation on seventeen different interest rates for public debt…that makes it impossible to arrange an orderly balancing of our public finances.'

Problem – Management of the Euro. Martin Sandbu in his books which tracked the Euro from the start, makes clear his accusation; it's the management of the Euro rather than the structure which was to blame. He suggests, as does Vince Cable, that the 'one size fits all' for fiscal tightening failed completely. The Greek 'salvation' was a botch because the Germans refused to take a haircut on Debt. Greece was left in a similar position to Germany after Versailles unable to survive because of the Debt mountain. Germans treatment of Greeks was appalling 'infantilisation'. The ECB run on German rules threatened to end operations of the banks there and elsewhere 'conform or else'.

German fiscal tightening was wrong. Academic research estimated that the Eurozone's GDP in 2013 was 7.7% lower than it would have been without the fiscal consolidation. The second Euro recession was entirely self-inflicted. As one buff said 'You may have saved the Euro but you forgot the people'. So far Germany has refused to mutualise debts across the Euro area, which is seen as one sensible way out of the conundrum, but that would require trust between countries, Germany regards it as a 'moral hazard' that if it is there, invites its use. The Euro is driven, reluctantly perhaps, by Germany who the rest look to as the only member big enough to underwrite the Euro. Germany therefore insisted on the Euro blindly following its basic tenets in all the rescue deals it does. (The reluctance of the Hegemon). France meanwhile remains almost invisible going along with Germany but unable or unwilling to challenge Germany's leadership, some say because France fear the same treatment given to peripheral states as it adjusts its fiscal data (The Duumvir that abdicated). For some Euro members it is 'Voluntary Servitude'. Threats and abuse of democracy, like getting rid of the odd Prime Minister and bullying another, have ruined any sense of co-operation. The mythical behaviour of 'Swabian' women to which the Germans refer to as a prudent spendthrift has proven a disaster as a model for Europe. It seems that all German politicians swore that nobody was going to weaken its rules applied to the EU, they were not going to weaken the currency by subsidising weaker state. Merkle meanwhile seems happy to proceed in this incremental way with no major constitutional changes that might run the risk of being overthrown.

Problem - Germany's Trade Surplus. But there is another fundamental problem Germany, and to a lesser extent Holland, has now built up a massive trade surplus on its current account balance of 7% of GDP. This is mostly explained by the efficiency of German's industrial model (see German motor industry). Vince Cable explained in his book 'With monetary policy set centrally and exchange rates fixed, the clear conclusion is that the periphery (Greece) should have tightened its budgets, while Germany should have done the opposite' allowing them to import more. But that didn't happen mostly for German cultural reasons. This huge balance threatens the Eurozone structure which means that 'Germany must either increase its savings reserves or be a net exporter of capital', lending money to other countries, to allow other countries to buy German goods, or otherwise the German people will need to shift their economies towards increasing domestic services, buying more and increasing their wages to support domestic consumption and draw in more inputs.'

So there we are, at our next session we will go through some possible solutions to these problems. I understand, Sebastian, that you intend to add your weight as Rotating Head or President of the European Council to try to shift attitudes, as you know very little has happened since 2016, virtually a year was lost by the EC renegotiating the UKs derogation clauses which had to be endlessly discussed within all the institutions of the EC and since then the EC's momentum has stalled, partly due to the lack of confidence which was caused by the UK's shock possible Brexit and partly the EC Elite has been hoping that brighter news on increasing GDP would provide a base from which a new momentum could grow."

Sebastian rubbed his chin ruefully, he had been so tied up in his work that he had never bothered to take a rain check on the EU. He had however one advantage during his year at the Foreign Office he had assiduously cultivated most EU Foreign Ministers inviting them for weekends at Chevening, the Foreign Secretary's mansion, which his staff called as a result 'Hotel Europa' and taking them to London Shows. He hope that these personal contacts would be of help!

Chapter SEVENTEEN – The family reunion

It was after 1 pm when Roger disappeared.

Within minutes the small party began arriving. Madge delivered Sylvia and had difficulty getting through the Downing Street gates even though Sebastian had notified the police there of all the arrivals.

Sebastian immediately showed Sylvia upstairs to the kitchen of No 10 and she immediately began to prepare the evening meal, most of whose ingredients she had, in fact, brought down with her in the car. She had appeared to be happy and Sebastian noted with relief that having unloaded the car she returned specially to thank Madge for driving her down, or up as Sebastian corrected himself!

Then Bill arrived with Massa Edwards Gombe and finally Rupert Edwards drove in with his souped up 'F' Type Jaguar. Sebastian took Rupert on one side and reminded him that Massa Gombe was his half-brother, a son of Leonard Geoffrey Edwards and that everything would be explained shortly.

Whilst Sylvia prepared the meal, Sebastian showed the other two around the various rooms, sat them both at the Cabinet Table, reminded them of some of the decisions that would have been taken in this room, showed them the old doorkeepers' chair still kept in the lobby, showed them out into the lawned area and pointed out where the IRA mortar had landed. Sebastian mentioned the various pictures on the walls for which he had to refer to his notes, then they proceeded up the stairs past the photographs of previous Prime Ministers and so to the small but well-appointed flat. Sebastian showed Massa Gombe to his room as he would be staying for a couple of days.

Sebastian was dressed in informal loose yellow sweater and blue cotton trousers with brown casual shoes. He pointed out that this kit was supplied by S & G the UK's biggest clothes store. This outfit was, he suggested, their best casual kit and Sebastian described the deal he hoped to put together to raise money for charity.

They went into the small lounge and Sebastian offered them both drinks.

Within a few minutes Sylvia declared the lunch ready and they all trooped in.

Sylvia was wearing a tunic and trousers, she did a swirl at her husband's request, "It's a Punjabi Salwar Kameeze" she declared. The top was a half sleeved orange tunic embroidered at the neck and with loose fitting green silk trousers collected at the ankles.

"Very smart!" declared Massa Gombe who was dressed in his Saville Row best suit.

The food was, as Sebastian had suggested, a mix of many different varieties of curry the smell was nose-tingling and all pervading.

Sebastian joked of his first embarrassing encounter with curries how he had previously been trying to fix a gear on his cycle and so his hands were ingrained with oil. That incident reminded him to wash thoroughly before any curry even though this was a plated meal.

Sebastian recounted the recent events and everyone listened intently. Rupert and Massa Gombe congratulated Sebastian on his new position. Massa Gombe then related the story of Sebastian's father Leonard Geoffrey Edwards and the affair with Massa Gombe's mother.

Rupert was clearly startled by these revelations and asked several deep questions. Massa Gombe replied with an air of exasperation 'but I was only four or five years old, everything I have told you has come from my mother! But I know this, I can be sure that Sebastian's father would have been so proud of him now!"

Sebastian filled in a few blanks, that, following Massa Gombe's grandfather's assassination in the first Military putsch in Nigeria, his mother and Massa Gombe had had to lie low for almost twenty years before the country came to its senses and began to take democracy seriously. The area was often in the hands of Muslim or Christian leaders and as the result of a mixed heritage Massa Gombe would have counted as neither.

Rupert then explained the family breakdown and how his grandfather had brokered a deal that meant the family would split. Rupert and another elder son, Alexander, would move with their mother to his mother's family and that William Jefferies her father, who was in fact very wealthy, would give the two boys the best education and in time would pass on his wealth to them. Then Rupert had tried to find his father decades later and had tracked him down and indeed worked for him two years ago as a Special Adviser.

Sylvia related her own story of a dominating father who had determined that his eldest daughter would marry a much older friend of the family. Sylvia had rebelled and tried to run away but her father had caught her and badly damaged her arm. He had threatened to kill her because of the shame she had brought to the family. She told of finding at last a safe house and how she went to work and some years later met Sebastian, how she passed messages to him because she thought he was being tricked by the directors of his company.

Sebastian in turn related how he had in peculiar circumstances managed to save the life of a Russian policeman and had later been delegated by his UK employers to grow a company in Russia. It was involved in mineral extraction, how they had employed a person called Jeffrey Pardoe who turned out to be a British spy and how Sebastian had gone near the Ukraine border to get him out, but as Sebastian said, "I then was introduced in Kiev to a man that I cannot name who told me the person that I had helped did not exist, was never in Russia and that the information that he had recovered could not be acknowledged.

However," Sebastian added walking over to the table drawer and bringing something out, "Here is the Russian Police Medal which I received from the hands of Medvedev himself, and here the English OBE – when I was leaving Kiev the man I cannot mention called after me, 'We'll make it up to you!' I replied as I remember, 'Oh Yea!', and here they both are!".

By about 4.00 pm Sebastian noticed the time, "Come on now family!" They followed him downstairs and out into the roadway in front of No 10. There were just two members of the Press and several photographers. Sebastian told everyone "This is my family!" and briefly introduced each of them. The flashes went off and Sebastian was asked to make a statement as it was indeed January 1st 2021.

"I have about 90 days in office as PM by agreement, I am not going to drown you in quotes or platitudes which I might not be able to keep, I am determined to try my best to help the country, parliament and the people and that I hope you will lend me your support to do so!

I wish you all the best for 2021. Thank you!"

They returned upstairs and later just snoozed in front of the TV.

Sebastian had of course timed the Downing Street presentation just perfectly. The Sunday papers showed what they all described as the 'Odd family' together with Sebastian's brief speech which, of course, was published complete! He knew right enough how the Press worked. A small snap of four people didn't take up much space nor did the press statement, he knew the editors would just reduce a larger photo and pop it in just as Veena Peech the Lib Dem Press Secretary had suggested 'maybe the third page' she had indicated.

Sebastian had no need, right at the start, to make Conservatives feel that they had made a big mistake. He had not intended to dominate the Press, at least not yet!

On the following day Sebastian took the family on a rather cold walking tour of the main London tourist areas, limited of course to important buildings or rather important Ministries which they could only see from the outside, but it was a pleasant walk and they had muffled up well to avoid public attention. They scarcely noticed the MPS, the Ministerial Protection Squad following discretely behind.

On the Sunday afternoon Sebastian took Massa Gombe aside for a few moments and told him that he had further plans to re-engage in Africa and asked him to take a letter to the President of Nigeria. This indeed he agreed to do but he sat for a few minutes and just roared with laughter something that made his otherwise sad face light up. "Hah! I should have known, Sebastian, that you would have a task for me, same as your father, my mother always said he'll ask you to do something but usually there's an ulterior motive as well, as she said 'he never missed an opportunity'.

Sebastian began to excuse himself "I just thought that as you know the President that you could as it were…" but then stopped abruptly and also laughed out loud. "You're right! Of course!"

Chapter EIGHTEEN - Press Comments etc. on Sebastian's promotion

In the first two weeks of January Sebastian studied the responses to his rise to being PM. They came from home and abroad, a file had been kept by Madge O'Connor of press cuttings and comments received, to these she had added some notes. Some came through Government channels and were passed on.

For most of the International Press it was all a bit of an anti-climax. The Foreign correspondents agreed it was really 'business as usual'. As far as the key politicians were concerned it seemed to be just a matter of musical chairs, a few people changing seats and there would, it appeared, be hardly any policy changes.

The National Press decided for the most part there was no point in lashing out about 'The Lib Dem takeover' because the swapping of the Ministries between the parties was not due to take place anyhow until March 31st, nor about a Liberal Democrat Leader potentially 'running amok' because he would be out of office before any newspaper campaign to sink him could really take effect.

The Press had been more interested in heart-warming Christmas or New Year stories, they were switching off politics altogether for the short season.

The Conservative broadsheets 'almost to an editor' decided to downplay the whole episode. In the coming days they would, as Sebastian noticed, show a photograph of Sebastian and then run a caption 'The Prime Minister' or the 'Coalition Prime Minister'; they refused to add the label 'Liberal Democrat' as if by ignoring it they could imagine it had never happened.

The tabloids called him by fits and starts 'Mr Boring' or 'The Comet' depending on the context; if it was a complicated matter it was 'Mr Boring'. They had begun this as soon as he had been made Foreign Secretary. Sebastian realised that he had partly brought that on himself, he never ever joked about anything or even smiled, his delivery, he knew was often flat and matter of fact, his speeches often lacked energy. If it was Sebastian introducing a matter with which that paper did not agree then it was 'The Comet did, this or that' ridiculing his position.

Liberal Democrat magazines, newsletters and Focuses were instructed not to glory in the first Liberal Prime Minister in 100 years, so as not to deliberately antagonise Conservatives, not to, as it were, stick their face in their own mess! The Deputy had merely taken over as Leader since that Leader was no longer available. Every Lib Dem constituency had had its own stories of how local Tories had in the past had deliberately belittled their efforts. Tories liked to project an air of natural right to rule, and they told Liberal Democrat supporters that they merely got in the way of their real battle which was to attack their natural enemies, the Socialist or Labour party supporters. So this 'Lay off the Tories' request from Party HQ came, to most Lib Dem activists, as a bit of a surprise.

The Labour Party themselves refused to distinguish Lib Dem from Tories, it was 'The Conservative led Government'. Whatever Bills were passed they would all be opposed even if they were patently of genuine benefit to everyone. As the weakest link in the Coalition all Lib Dems were to be attacked indiscriminately whenever they spoke or, better still, Labour MPs were to use it as an opportunity for them to noisily walk out of the Chamber or rustle their papers and mutter as loudly as possible so that the Lib Dems could hardly be heard. All Labour MPs agreed with Conservative MPs on just one thing, Lib Dem MPs were a superfluous nuisance and must never be accorded any praise for anything, at any time, that would merely give them credibility which must be denied them at all costs! Though at the mention of Sebastian Edwards the sleepy Labour Party Executive Committee opened its eye and wondered if the Devolution Bills setting up Regional Assemblies might not be worth voting for? Not to make a big fuss in support of course! They knew the more Labour suggested they would vote for it, the more likely the Tories would try to ditch it, therefore if they wanted to pass it they would use a 'free vote', not nailing the Labour Party to any result. That way they didn't have to openly support Lib Dems or by extension the Conservatives!

For the SNP, the coalition was still 'The Westminster Government', the ultimate bogeyman who was to be blamed for every and any failing in Scotland itself. It was obvious that all problems were caused either by a failure of the UK Government to provide sufficient funds or Westminster's obstructionism in blocking some logical plan or imposing a restraint which Scotland regarded as important. They didn't care about who was who in the Coalition. They were all "Sassenachs".

The Greens and rump of UKIP did not even mention the event they just continued to quarrel amongst themselves respectively; as to what sort of Green Policy was best; and who should be the leader!

International leaders however had different views.

The view from the EU was that for the first time there was a UK leader fully committed to Europe. Some countries like France coolly wondered if this meant that the UK would become more involved, something they did not particularly want. The French still believed that France was one of the original

Treaty founders and only it and a few others could interpret it's soul. Sebastian knew that raised the old spectre of the British spoiling the special German-French accord which had driven the EC politically right from the start. For other countries like Poland there was genuine delight for Sebastian 'Welcome back!' was the brief message received from Warsaw. Sebastian was aware that he was the only large country EC politician to have registered their plight and understood the Polish fear of the looming presence of Russian military might. Several East European countries sent messages of encouragement 'hoping that an empowered UK would help resolving their EU problems' by which Sebastian knew this meant helping them fend off interference from Brussels, for example in the 'redistribution of Merle's immigrants' which had been forced on them, and which, even now, years later, still rankled!

The Kremlin noted with surprise that a minority party politician in the UK had managed to force himself into such a position. Of course they knew of Mr Edwards from years back when he ran a business in Russia from the UK. The first Deputy Minister of Foreign Affairs responsible for Europe, Dimitri Tatov, in a message through the embassy welcomed the change and suggested it was an opportunity to reconsider and refocus UK/Russian relations.

The White House was too careful to say anything but they had privately noted Sebastian's previous tendency to plough a separate UK furrow and wondered if he was likely to be as malleable as all the other UK Prime Ministers before him. Most USA Presidents had simply to use the phrase 'Of course there is a special relationship with the UK' in every discussion or Press release for all UK politicians to come to heel. The USA naturally expected to have the UK Prime Ministers giving them their support in the UN. The UK was regarded as the one dependable ally so they trotted out the same words as usual, hoping for the same result.

Most African Commonwealth leaders did not greet Sebastian's elevation with absolute enthusiasm. He, it was, who told African leaders rather bluntly not to use grievances of their time within the Empire, under British Rule, as excuses for their poor current economic performance. They should, instead, work out how they could improve their own situation. Development Grants were still there but they had to be earned not assumed. Of course the UK still had the huge development budget to dispense so any criticisms were muted. Most simply acknowledged the 'temporary' change.

The UN did not even acknowledge that any change had taken place. Sebastian Edwards did not even show on their 'Dashboard' of important people. True he had spoken at the UN but so had literally hundreds of leaders over the years.

Each of the UN's massive departments regarded themselves as immune to change, at least on anything forced on them from outside. Even though the UK registered as one of their major financial supporters, the UN was not about to be nudged in any particular direction. The UN had become used to attempts to oblige them to change direction and were equally adroit at carrying out minor modifications to give the impression of change but in fact doing nothing at all. The UN constantly invented new initiatives or launched increasing demanding 'achievable targets' which they played up and asked loyal countries to support, most did so unquestioningly. Everyone recognised that the only thing that constantly saved the UN was the fact that they were always there somewhere in the background at any catastrophe and nearly every war, and it was difficult to argue with their full time staff, who were highly regarded worldwide as honest and dedicated. Although the UK registered as a major supporter of the UN their influence appeared to be waning. It was widely recognised that, on any changes in the Security Council to reflect the changes in world population and wealth, Britain and France would both be relegated to the second division and would lose their right to veto. The UN of course never itself raised the issue head on. UK and its prime ministers of whatever colour were generously listened to but they had not for 40 years done anything spectacular, nor did it look as though they now would!

Chapter NINETEEN – A Quick Trip to France

At the end of the week Sebastian advised his MPS of his intended visit to France; he asked Madge to co-ordinate with the Cabinet office.

On the Saturday morning the allocated driver picked Sebastian up at 8.00 am and they drove to Folkestone; they used a pool car so as not to attract attention. The PM's much larger and heavier official armoured Jaguar would stand out a mile; much too obvious for an informal little trip.

At the insistence of the Permanent Secretary of the Foreign and Commonwealth Office (FCO) Keith Williams, Sebastian was accompanied by an interpreter who was introduced simply as Michelle who sat in front. The Deputy Head of Mission in Paris, called David Morton who had happened to be in London, sat in the rear with Sebastian who was told that David had joined the FCO in 2002. Previous to that he had been in the Army and he was the former military attaché in the Hague. He was dark haired, thin and wiry of average build, he was always looking around nervously. He had asked Sebastian what the mission was about but in an oblique way "Is there anything I should look out for Prime Minister?" Sebastian just put his finger to his lips.

Sebastian just busied himself with his papers which he took from time to time from a rather battered briefcase with large leather straps over the top.

They took the car onto the Channel Tunnel train at 12.50 pm.

Sebastian began to unwind as soon as they were on the AutoRoute system in France.

"Well Mr Morton, I have three things to discuss and perhaps Michelle you might listen into this as you'll know what words to use? All this is pretty tentative stuff, I am really testing out the French to find out if they are willing for us to really enter into the spirit of the EU or whether they continue to see us as interlopers to the German/French Alliance."

"You mean" said David, "Can you join their game and what the price of entry might be?"

"Well that's something like it but I have got some lures which I hope the French President will attempt to reach out for. If he doesn't take the bait then we just quickly pack up and go home, without damaging anything except perhaps my reputation! One of the people who might be there is Jacques Dupuis and, watch out Michelle, he tries to speak terrible English, almost as bad as my French. I met him some 4 years ago when we were both Junior Ministers of Health and I was doing a comparison between the NHS and its French equivalent. I had several chats with him about sharing Nuclear Weapons systems, but that came to nothing".

"So what are the three topics?" asked David

"Boko Haram is one" offered Sebastian.

"That's the terrorist group in Africa!" David piped up perhaps for the benefit of Michelle.

"Yes, you will remember they caused great destruction and took 218 girls hostage, some of whom the Nigerians later exchanged for four captured Boko Haram commanders? At the end of 2016 it appeared that they had been militarily defeated, but they soon popped up again, they were based in Northern Nigeria but operated also around Lake Chad which is surrounded by Niger, Chad and Cameroon. For various reasons the Nigerian Military took a long time to get to grips with it, part of the reason appears to have been that the Police and Local forces who were often the subject of the attacks, often took revenge on the local population – that didn't help! Also apparently weapons designated for the Nigerian troops never arrived seemingly either stolen along the way or maybe they never existed!"

"Drones is the next" said Sebastian listening for the explanation

"That's the joint development and manufacture of pilotless attack aircraft". Said David proudly- "that'll be the update to the previous agreement".

"Yes that's correct David…er?"

"Morton Sir, David Morton"

"Yes there was a contract review date in 2020 which we missed and I am anxious to show that it's important to us and that we can do business with the French!"

"And UN development", said Sebastian wondering if his assigned assistant knew about it.

"Is that on the Security Council or about repatriation of refugees? Sir?"

"Both" Sebastian responded. "there's a lot of chatter about reform of the UN Security Council and I want to find out if we are still on the same wave length as the French and I am trying to propose initiatives to push responsibility for migrants back where it belongs and I hope to get French support for this."

"So your role, Michelle, is to translate for me, I'll go slowly over technical matters". She blushed and murmured "Thank you Sir!"

"Yours David is just to witness what's going on, listen and make notes. We are not making any new initiatives. It's really to let the French President know that I am who he takes me for, an EU supporter. So it's more of a personal visit than anything. I was obliged to bring you otherwise it's clear that the FCO would have tried to prevent this meeting or raise its status to a formal intergovernmental session which I wanted to avoid. So if I should wave you away, particularly if he asks about internal UK politics, just take it in good faith OK?"

French security police were obviously appraised of Sebastian's arrival, and joined at the front of the little convoy whilst the UK cars were briefly stopped at the side of the A 26 AutoRoute, so they led Sebastian's pool car with the MPS bring up the rear.

The weather was good and it was still daylight, there was little traffic on the roads and they had a clear run. They turned off at the N 17 for the short run to the centre of Arras.

It was mid-afternoon before they met up with the French President in the centre of the town where the mayor had kindly offered the use of his grand committee room on the first floor.

Sure enough Jacques Depuis was there as were two others, one of whom was in military uniform. David tapped Sebastian on the shoulder and told him these were the 'big cheeses' senior ranking officials in the Diplomatic and Military services, the military one was, he thought a General, the other a senior official in the French Foreign Office, whom David had met. They were soon introduced.

They sat down around the mayor's large, oak, mid nineteenth century table. The French President himself described the building. It was completed first in 1571 then reconstructed by Napoleon III, finally it was burnt down in 1914, due to a bombardment, and restored afterwards.

It was, Sebastian suggested a magnificent building, the size of a large church but sideways on to the large square. The ground floor externally consisted of stone arches, above that there were several large windowed rooms, in one of which they were now sitting. It had a huge stone fireplace at one end and greenish wallpaper on the wall facing the windows. The main building had a circular tower at either end. The roof was steeply sloping and was punctuated by two rows of garret windows.

"Magnificent!" Sebastian declared, the French President courteously congratulated Sebastian on his appointment. Sebastian walked over to Jacques and warmly shook him by the hand and muttered something which the interpreter failed to pick up properly "'ens teet" he said laughing aloud.

After a few minutes generalities Sebastian launched off at a cracking pace, he pulled a rather scruffy map of Northern Nigeria from his bag. He described how the Nigerians had insisted in 2016 that Boko Haram were defeated but they were back again this time with some returnees from the Syrian War. He was attempting to describe how he thought the Boko Haram were attacking and retreating, often into Chad and the Cameroons, playing hide and seek with the frontiers and that no country had wanted to chase them out, so Boko Haram were deadly and elusive. He jabbed his finger at one spot. "It's here! It's got to be here… lightly armed forces….desert attack groups…..leased from Nigeria…..training ground for the UN for African troops, whose deployment has not been successful, covering all this area,…. joint military group with France also shutting off the base of the human trafficking arm that went north to the Mediterranean".

The French group leant over and peered at the spot indicated. "A long lease military base at the edge of Lake Chad that would give quick access to all surrounding countries including Niger".

"But" asked the French General "You could do this yourself, why do you need us?"

"Two reasons, General, Firstly frankly we have no idea what's happening North of Nigeria where it runs straight into what I would call the Mediterranean Arab Muslims, we have always regarded this as your area of operations! You had a successful military intervention there 'operation serval' I think, in Mali? and you are well aware of the different local military groupings, your military intelligence there is far superior to ours.

Secondly Nigeria was slow to react but in the end activated ECOWAS which attempted to cover that area, but was not very successful. The cause of that was the rivalry between Francophone and Anglophone blocs. A joint task force might settle the whole area down and allow countries to deal with a likely famine there. At present only half of the NGOs operate in that area. Regular supplies of food and grain to grow might convince the local population to turn away from Boko Haram for good! It would benefit Nigeria, Niger, Chad and Cameroon and greatly add to our prestige in that area! What's more all these states are fragile; stability will allow them time to develop economically and politically!"

The French Group stood aside for a moment and returned "We'll consider this!"

Next he moved on to joint manufacturing of drones, "In the agreement with David Cameron signed on the anniversary of the battle of the Somme in 1916 there was a clause indicating a technical review in 2020. We missed that due to our internal problems but wish to confirm to you our desire to continue with the project. We want to bring forward the date of introduction from 2030 to 2028, we also want to consider the introduction of smaller specialist drones. We want to start planning for identical factories on both sides of channel, the output could be used by either side in case of need, we would have to introduce a restriction of sales to other countries in case they as could soon be used against us".

Again the French Group stood in a little huddle, the General shrugged his shoulders "Sounds OK!"

"Finally", said Sebastian "I wanted to raise the issue of the effectiveness of the Security Council and how it might be changed, my understand whilst I was at the Foreign Office was that we had very similar views, this was to increase the numbers of the Permanent members from 5 to 10 by the inclusion of Germany, Brazil, India and Japan, plus a permanent representation for Africa on the Council?"

"Yes that's correct" the French Diplomat spoke.

"You'll be aware that there is anger amongst those countries being left out and they will block that reform so I cannot see that happening. However there's another proposal which apparently has the approval of 129 out of a total of 152 voting; that is to leave the veto countries as they are but to increase the term of other Council members from 2 to 3 years and the number of non-permanent council members, from 5 to 13. This would give these extra countries a voice but no vote, it would increase the embarrassment of any of the permanent members who attempted to force a veto without justifying their position! It would include more member states and involve them in key decisions, this would break the UN out of its cocoon which the rest of the world thinks is driven exclusively by and for the West with Russia and China acting as some sort of deadweight."

"Yes we will consider it".

"And as you know I am keen to make changes to the UN to compel those countries who carelessly make life so bad for their own people that they join the endless stream of migrants trooping towards the safe haven of the EU. I am looking for your support for that?"

The French President nodded then tried his bit of English.

"And Hinkley Point it is proceeding OK?"

"Not really, but it's too early yet to say – I fear it's going to be years behind before it delivers electricity to the grid – but that maybe too late, you know we will not subsidise it further? If you think it's going to fail it had better be acknowledged soon to save us both embarrassment. As you know the drastic and sustained collapse in the oil prices has apparently made it uneconomic, we should instead have copied your development of tidal race systems!"

The French President smiled and nodded wearily.

Jacques then jumped in "And the Force de Frappe? You are nuckle ar subs." He said slowly in English..

"Yes well maybe why not, perhaps a bridge too far right now but it'll come!"

"But how long will you be there, Mr Edwards?"

"Just less than 90 days, but all changes have to start somewhere? With a permanent base in Africa right in the trouble spot we should gain commercial contracts and head off Chinese development there. With UN changes we might get more action on migrants, with a leadership in Drone manufacture we shall save the lives of some of our soldiers!"

"Have you got any sign of interest from Nigeria yet, Mr Edwards?"

"No not yet, I am expecting to see them in the next two weeks!"

"That's 75 days left!"

"Yes but I am starting to move elsewhere too!"

"Where Mr Edwards?"

"I cannot say, it's too sensitive, but I'll let you know!"

The French President looked at Sebastian rather sadly, "Well we will look all of this and let you know in a week!"

"Thanks that's all I was expecting, Mr President!"

The meeting ended, as the French President turned to go down the stone staircase Sebastian saw him, ruefully rub his chin.

Sebastian's group had a brief discussion amongst themselves and decided to return home that same night.

On the return journey David Morton tentatively asked Sebastian why the meeting had been over so quickly.

Sebastian offered the view that "The French President expected me to indulge in some discussions about how the workings of the Euro could be repaired and what role there could be for the UK within the EC, but I decided not to go that far."

Sebastian knew that it would take more than this casual chat to convince the French that the UK was, this time, playing the EC game in earnest. If he could not do that the chances of the French President wasting time on a country, that they regarded at best as a competitor and at worst as a time wasting interloper, was unlikely.

They arrived back in London at midnight. Sebastian asked the driver to take his staff to their homes. .

Chapter TWENTY - EU Discussion FIVE - How German Motors coped with change

Roger Collingham-Smith continued, "Whilst it's possible to see the EU as a comparative failure, where as you have seen, there's plenty going wrong, it's important also to understand that several industries within the EC have not only weathered the storm but are taking maximum benefit from the enlargement. One such industry is the German Auto Industry.

Germany has become, pretty well, the EC's and possibly the Worlds' leading Auto Hub. In 2014/5 it had a production of 5.4 million units against a German own registration increase of 2.9 million units, giving a net export of 2.5 million units. No other EC country comes near to that level of dominance. In the UK we think we do very well if we make 1.5 million units and register 2.2 million new number thus importing a net 0.7 million units.

Quite why the UK is in that position is the subject for another day. Basically after the war we were the only European Auto Industry that remained intact, we were the second largest car manufacturers in the World. Then several things went wrong and the industry was plagued by a switchbacking £ which constantly undermined exports, rampant unions which had a deliberate policy of aggressive disruption to increase pay without increasing productivity, poor technological design and degraded production facilities due to lower Research and Development. The UK government interfered first forcing Rootes to expand near Glasgow hundreds of miles away from its Coventry base, arguably Rootes never did control that plant. Also Government tried to help by forcing Consolidations into one big Car group, unfortunateatly it had no designs for new models!. This lead to a fatal Corporate collapse and the UK car Industry was only resurrected by German, Japanese, French, Indian, Malaysian and USA companies who came in initially to scoop up any unprotected market. We still have a few fringe UK owned businesses which are almost living antique period, hand-built pieces. Basically we produce cars here mostly, in what I call, 'slave factories.' We make to the order of foreign owners who provide, the brains, technology, design, marketing and management skills, often using foreign designated machine tools and production equipment imported for the purpose and using many imported car components. The exception may be Jaguar Landrover which we will look at later.

I am sorry to be so depressing, Sebastian!"

"Yes well anyone who has lived through the last 40 years has watched the whole sorry saga. But let's move on, you are going I suppose to show me how well the Germans have done? It's going to make me even more depressed, I suppose!"

"The German Auto Industry employs about 815,000 people. We here come fifth equal in the list by volume, with Czech Republic with around 141,000! But bear with me please, Sebastian, there are several very important lessons we can learn from this! Note that in discussing this foreign owned car producers like Ford and GM, are treated as if they were German because they inhabited exactly the same German industry environment and are driven by the same factors.

Earlier when Spain and Portugal joined the EU several Car cos opened units there or like Volkswagen took over Seat the Spanish Manufacturer. Labour costs in Spain were around 50% of those in Germany in the 1980s, but since then the wage level in Spain rose substantially.

However the CEE Countries of Eastern Europe had an even more advantageous rate at just 10% of the German Rate.

The German Auto Industry had two basic options. 1. Complementary Product Specialisation – putting the production of sub-compact and low priced cars in CEE Countries, partly to encourage those countries to buy those products and so increase the market and to the take-over by VW of Skoda the Czech company with a long and proud history of engineering quality. Or 2. Parallel Production, placing production of well-known brands split over two or more countries to encourage competition both in grants and labour costs. This was an approach used by Opel with its Astra model.

Generally direct relocation of complete plants took place in only a few cases. Opel shifted production of Zafira from Germany to Poland, part of Astra went to Poland and the UK. VW moved part of Golf and Passat to Slovakia.

In general the production of low-priced, small and compact cars was shifted gradually to Eastern Europe.

So what in fact happened was that the production of premium brands increased over a period of 20 years from 1990 to 2010 whilst the production of volume brands reduced.

However in order to keep the premium brands price competitive, major components for example like engines were shifted by Audi from Germany to Hungary.

The Auto industry uses a large quantity of production line robotics and other specialty machine tool equipment. Almost all of this equipment required for new foreign plants continued to be built in Germany. In 2010 almost a third of export of the German metalworking machinery went to Eastern Europe or Asia.

Meanwhile suppliers of parts to the Car Industry began to shift production to the low wage countries away from Germany. Between 1997 and 2001 between 25% and 38% of this production was moved out of Germany, this included first the labour intensive and lower skilled jobs like the wire harness systems which was despatch to Portugal and North Africa. Car Seats for the high volume products were sent to East Europe. In this way the share of component imports grew from 9% to 40% from 1995 to 2012. Nearly 50% of German component imports came from CEE Countries., three times higher for example than French Car Companies.

Initially in the middle of the 1990s this transfer was limited by the number of suitable quality component plants. But in the second half of the 1990s the location of Auto factories there meant that they could also buy locally produced components. As a further extension of this move certain items like IT services and some R & D work was also relocated there although these had a subordinate function, for example adjusting an existing product rather than developing new models.

This relocation began to decline around 2005 after the 2004 enlargement and this coincided with the economic crisis in 2008 which hit volumes. It appears that this surge in relocation is now finished.

So what remains in Germany are 1) Premium Brand Car production, 2) Customised production of high quality components 3) Most R & D work including innovation an new models 4) Machine Tools and flow-line production equipment.

It seems unlikely that there will be further significant shifts until volumes rise again and the next cheaper suitable labour market, like China, has been evaluated.

I must now take you back to Germany in the early 1990s. Agreement had been reached with the Unions there, called 'employment protection agreement' by local agreements at plant level which meant they accepted wage and working time concessions. These in turn lead to the increasing use of less secure employment forms such as agency workers. In effect there was a 'dualist' system split between core and non-core employees.

So what has happened to the employment of different types and categories of worker within German Automobile and supplier sector is that the number of unskilled workers has increased only modestly by 15% and the number of skilled workers by 16%, but the white collar workers with simple tasks has declined by 55% as most of these went eastwards but, there was a substantial increase of white collar workers with 'complex tasks' this included more R & D aimed at innovating new components and developing new models, and management to control the supply to foreign based operations; this category rose by 50%

The German auto industry was in danger of pricing itself out of the market raising prices caused by union agreements. Internally within the Motor Industry these constant moves or threats to move production away from Germany towards lower rate countries, appears to have influenced the bargaining process with the dominant union, IG Metall, and it agreed an 'opening clause' permitting employers to increase the 35 working hours a week to 40 hours for up to 18% of the employees. At the same time local agreements gave concessions in return for deviations from the strict industry wide agreements. In exchange for the employers relinquishing the right to collective dismissals the works council offered concessions on wages and working hours.

As far as the rates of pay were concerned, in the 1970s and 1980s, the workers employed in the German Auto Industry earned more than shown in the industry level collective agreements. Subsequently this premium of 30% to 40% was reduced in stages but as general industry wide increases occurred at the same time the effect was to award no reductions in pay for some time. But new employees suffered the reduction. VW negotiated a separate deal increasing its average hours per employee from 28.8 hours to 33 hours for no increase in pay. Overall what happened was the real wage increase halted whilst productivity grew. The result was that over ten years to 2010 the effective labour cost rose only slightly whilst in France they almost doubled.

The German Industry agreed more flexibility agreements for example by increasing hours at times of peak demand without paying overtime but allowing these hours to be banked and reduced by time off when production was lower. Such 'stored hours' in the case of some plants can amount to 400 hours; at VW for example.

The main squeeze factor in the move of production eastwards was the flexibility of the Agency workers. As part of the agreements, agency workers were exempt from the standard Union rates and different collective agreements were signed for agency workers which effectively avoided them being paid the going union rate, in effect paying them much lower wages. So there was a double benefit for employers using Agency staff; a cheaper cost and greater flexibility. At one stage, something like 40% of employees were Agency Workers., several plants however limited their number to around 5%. Agency workers' pay gradually increased over the years. In effect the works councils had to agree the use of agency workers but it's clear that the agency workers are not allowed to 'put at risk' wages and working conditions of regular employees. There was a clear pecking order. In principle agency workers had to be offered a job if they had been with the company for 24 months, but most agency staff, it appears, stayed for less than 12 months.

So this is important to show how Germany has successfully worked its way through to find a strategic development plan. Retain Premium Brands in Germany, offload components and high volume production to cheaper wage rate areas. The German Motor Industry now employs more highly skilled and better paid workers.

The German training and education system churns out thousands of staff trained through the-on-the-job schemes plus a huge number of degree-qualified engineers to support this.

However it should be noted that many of these changes appeared to have occurred before the Central European States joined the EC in 2004 and most before they joined the Eurozone Slovakia 2009, Slovenia 2007, Estonia 2011, Latvia 2014, Lithuania 2015, Poland and Czech Republic are still not Eurozone members.

The argument, you remember that I raised earlier, Sebastian, suggesting that the impact of joining the Eurozone had turned out to be much less beneficial than previously expected? You can see here why that was. The German Auto industry was way in advance of these EU moves and worked on the basis of obtaining access to cheaper wage areas whenever that proved advantageous, that was the major driver rather than the formal country/agreements on EU membership or the Eurozone."

"OK" Sebastian agreed "points taken! Has the UK motor Industry been able to do anything similar?"

"No I'm afraid few of the UK car volume manufacturers have been able to set up foreign plants, that's largely because none of them are UK owned, so major strategy changes are not determined here and fall into line with the requirements of the foreign owners, some of whom have plants in other EU countries, others use the UK as a base to supply into the rest of the EC – so the UK motor industry was, by and large, unable to emulated the German Industry and move its production into the higher added value work!

The sole exception is possibly Jaguar Land Rover which is actually owned by Tata Sons an Indian based mega millionaire which has done extraordinarily well. Some Land Rovers may be switched to a plant in Slovakia. It has recently attempted to introduce an electric car, but its development will be hampered by the lack of UK skills in consumer electronics. It is understood that their first electric car 'I-Pace' will be built under contract in Austria. However JLR has nothing like the volume or depth of management or range of products of the largest German Car Manufacturers. "

"That's disappointing I suppose? – So next we are working out how to turn the EU around!"

Chapter TWENTY-ONE – EU Discussion SIX - Possible Solutions

Well, Sebastian, we have fairly well taken the EU apart but now we have to try to put it back as best we can so that you can target what to say at your presentation as the rotating President of 'The Council' which is attended by ministers from each member state who have the authority to commit their government to the actions agreed. So you will have to gain cabinet assent to what you are going to say and do. By then you must have persuaded your 'trio', that is the former, current and next Presidents of 'The Council', who together prepare and issue the agenda, that your item should be included.

You will act as chairman. You meet in mid-February I think?

There you will have 30 minutes at most to make your case.

So it's important if you aim to try to change the direction of the EC that it clearly identifies what has to be done and what changes you are requesting.

So we have to assume that these suggestions for improvement we have today represent as it were a 'clearing house for ideas' from which you will have to select the best for your purpose which will then have to be honed, nuanced and balanced to give the dynamic presentation you require?

I suggest that we first identify what we think the EC has to do. From that, I think, a lot of things will logically fall into place, then after that we can see how the UK is likely to fare and what your proposals might be. Do you agree with that line, Sebastian?"

"Yes, I think so, we clearly have to prioritise something or we will be going around in circles!"

"OK let's start with what might be considered as the core of the problem – the difficulties within the Eurozone itself?"

"OK So from what I understand" said Sebastian "the Euro was launched too quickly, Germany "the economists" in principle wanted internal price stability and the co-ordination of economic policy by the elimination of differences in wage and price behaviour before launch. France "the monetarists" emphasised instead the importance of exchange rate stability stating that prior convergence was unnecessary."

As Santos makes clear in his book that's much too simplistic, France and Germany spent ten years try to find some common ground. But it seemed to be hopeless as each country had different objectives. France wanted a low interest rate to encourage growth, Germany didn't mind having a high interest rate because it wanted to stamp out its bugbear inflation, so Germany's Bundesbank without saying anything would raise its rate which if France followed would ruin its growth. They were like two cats in a sack.

But they were aware that what they were all doing was quite unique and had never been attempted before, but they didn't recognise the fatal structural flaws that it was simply unreasonable to expect, as the French economist Thomas Piketty has said, "to have a currency without s state, a central bank without a government, a common monetary policy without a common fiscal policy"… and a common currency without a common debt. They might have got away with it had the GDPs expanded as fast as some had expected. But that didn't happen, instead there came this plague from the USA attacking the banking structure which came as a shock, which cruelly exposed these flaws? I think I have that right Roger?"

"Dead right", said Roger "but then they had to try and correct for those problems, and move ahead. But Germany whom they induced to in effect underwrite the currency, exacted a terrible price, demanding fiscal consolidation. When trouble came as Greece, which had seriously over borrowed, faced collapse in 2010. Germany demanded through the ECB that Greece's Debts be honoured but the deal was so tight that it spelled doom for Greece. Germany were deaf to all protestations. The deal eventually costs much more than it otherwise might but Germany made clear it did not want to support profligate countries. It is estimated that German & ECB management might have cost the Euro area 7.00% of GDP. France, thereafter, appeared to have gone into its shell and in effect took no major role in the events but was, in effect, a bystander

They could of course try to unscramble the Euro, but not only would that be very difficult but it would also be an admission of failure, something that would stand out so raw that it would never ever be repeated and it would be the end of the "United States of Europe" dream for good". Germany will not allow that to happen and Germany rules.

"So now what is left is to carry out running repairs, there's nothing original here but what needs to be done is now much clearer and has been for the most part well signposted. There are if you like two options, first 'Fiddle about a bit'. Being effectively in charge of the Euro and overseeing the application of the fiscal rules, Germany seems willing and able to carry on as they are. They, in effect, lay down the rules, police it and bully the other countries into submission. This way the Euro would probably survive, the bulk of the procedures have been improved and QMV probably with one or two acolytes will ensure they continue in control. There need be no changes to the existing structure which is cumbersome but bearable to the Germans, this means there is no risk of the structure being rejected by any individual country or parliament. Change will come by modest steps.

Second, but to regularise the situation the Eurozone will have to acquire that attributes of a state, there's already an urge to draw together the Euro Finance Ministers in EUROFIN and agree a structure probably appointing a full time Finance Director whose role will be to ensure that each Euro Member State adheres to the agreed financial disciplines and is able to impose direct financial penalties for failures. The European Bank would then change into being the lender of last resort to that EuroGroup. EuroBonds would be issued equalising the interest rates for all Eurozone states. This poses a risk for Germany, apparently their voters have been promised that German money will not be used to bail out, lazy or idle nations that cannot look after themselves. Constitutional changes anyhow run the risk of being overturned by national parliaments etc.

A mechanism would have to be found to address the large balance of payments imbalances within the Eurozone, this will mean three things a) Germany and Holland – citizens spending more b) Commercial Loans to encourage businesses in the deficit countries c) Probably relocating military or other bases from the surplus North to the deficit South to act as a permanent spending bias but that's for the EuroGroup to do. But none of these options seem to worry the Germans, although they have offered a modified 60% supported EuroBond.

"OK so far, Sebastian?"

"Yes I think so, Roger, but the second option looks less likely because of the higher risk of being kicked out by the Electorate, so anything that needed a treaty change or reference back to the various nations will not be their preferred option?"

"Well, Sebastian, we will come onto treaty changes a bit later, but you are right to question if it can be achieved. Will the prudent Germans spend? Will they allow high spenders like Greece to be funded in an way that means Germans would in effect guarantee their spend? Something that the Greek Loan crisis threw into high profile? Then the German fury at Greek profligacy was visible for all to see! The answer is that they probably would if the structures were in place to hold it all together, France's diminished role is more of a psychological problem as they have to accept the German dominance, as a once equal partner, that's near humiliation. Smaller states would perhaps begin to feel very insecure as increasingly decisions would be made in Brussels or rather Frankfurt which they could not individually control. As usual with such things luck and perseverance play a part; several years of good GDP growth ahead could well put a new light on things – presumably that's why they have done very little for the last three years from 2017 to 2020."

"But does this affect the other institutions of the EC?" asked Sebastian.

"Yes, there are already calls for the Eurozone members of the EP to have a separate group, this means their own review committees, so Yes! To ensure that the legitimacy flows through they are going to develop Eurozone Groups in every one of the Institutions, that's the logic of the move, in fact a move towards a partly Federal Structure. As David Osborn appears to have said 'the remorseless logic points that way'. It's not possible to judge how far that march would go but it would probably be by fits and starts, it unlikely those states would want to have their discussions interrupted and affected by those not in the Eurozone."

"So where does that leave the UK, Roger?"

"Frankly not well placed at all, the EC have promised that the 'ever closer' bit would not apply in reality, David Cameron sought reassurances before the first UK EC Referendum on being able to continue the Euro opt out and that the EC would not realise the UK's worst fear of being treated as a second class state, being dragged along and outvoted by QMV because the Eurozone members have enough weight between themselves to carry the day. Imagine what that might happen to the City of London, if its status could be changed or new taxes applied without the UK being able to protect it? The problem is that after a while, even if they do not do so now, it's likely that Eurozone states will act in concert to protect their position, unless there is a structural filter in some way, there can be no general guarantee that we will not get left behind and our key aims by-passed.

This is a real problem, the Commission wants the 28 member banking union to be supervised by the European Banking Authority, this would shift the power to supervise Europe's biggest banks from national regulators to the centre, this would mean passing power to Brussels. The UK, with the EU's largest Financial Sector, favours a banking union for the Eurozone only, this would mean that the UK would be excluded from the perhaps more rigorous deeper convergence, claiming that the UK's own strong Banking Regulation is both more advanced and more broadly based! In its way the UK proposal though merely puts Banking Regulation of the Euro zone beyond reach of the UK who would be unable to control developments. It is noticeable that the least developed of all the 'Four Freedoms is the opening up of Services. Jealousies of the UK's huge and highly profitable Financial Services will surely eventually lead to the deliberate or accidental marginalisation of the UK's most valuable commercial sector.

You can forget words like honour, co-operation, consultation, after the treatment handed out to Greece, frankly I would not bet a penny on the City surviving, apart from anything else the EC blames the deregulation period in the UK for paying massive bonuses and salaries to Bankers and they don't want to import that!

It's likely then that either the Commissions view will prevail leading to institutional control from Brussels or that the UK's view will prevail and that Brussels will only control the Eurozone Banking, this would leave the UK's sector unprotected, uninvolved in any changes and prey for sniping from France or Germany. It's really a heads they win or tails we lose."

"So Roger that does not sound too good and the only other option is for the UK to join the Eurozone or have the £ pegged to it in some way. Our last attempt at pegging nearly broke our economy through high rates, a speculators' dream, I do not think we would do that again. There are no takers to adopt the Euro in the UK in any political party, but of course times and circumstances do change and, as all politicians repeat endlessly, never say never!"

"Well what we are left with, Sebastian, is a two speed Europe!"

"It sounds messy and fragile from the start, would that not do exactly what the UK elite feared, Roger? Make us into a second Division Euro team?"

"No I don't think so, if it was negotiated correctly, it could leave us with the best of both worlds!"

"Carry on, Roger, I am still listening."

"Which is access to the single market in goods and services – and the latter is most important because 60 to 70% of UK GDP comes through services which are far behind in being opened up in the same way as goods. Whilst the EU could out of spite deliberately try to crush our Financial Services they have many other problems to deal with. We still have a huge lead in Finance and Digital and English the dominant second language in the EU which we can exploit to our advantage. Membership of the customs union is important. It's possible we could ease the continued temporary derogation from total freedom of movement of people over time to existing EU members only or use some other filter. We might perhaps continue to pay towards the EU budget on an 'as used basis' – that is a proportion of the trade carried out over and above the existing trade. Let's say for example it were 1%, although it would sound like a tariff, it would be much cheaper that being outside the EU and facing a tariff wall, there is an EC common external tariff (CIT) of 6.7% calculated on a weighted average. Of course we could recover some of the latter by imposing our own tariffs on imports. The 1%, I would imagine, could be overcome by increasing out productivity or adjusting the exchange rate!"

"Well that sounds a bit more attractive but would that be acceptable to the EC?" asked Sebastian.

"Surprisingly perhaps a 'two speed' or as some would have it a 'multispeed' Europe has a good pedigree.

In 1974 Willy Brandt developed the idea of splitting Europe into two groups, Eurozone and the rest. The idea was really to allow the Eurozone members to move forward creating a stronger union; to follow a path of deeper economic and political integration without constantly looking over their shoulders at the other states. It's clear that the economies of the EU member states do not move at the same speeds. Weaker Euro members could fall out of the Eurozone into the second grouping so ensuring that the Eurozone is not held back by those who cannot take the pace. At present there is no fall-back position; no Euro member state can escape the Euro except by exiting the EC one of the reasons why Grexit was so messy.

Nicolas Sarkozy in 2011 called for a 'federal core' of the then 17 members of the Eurozone with a looser "confederal" outer core. 'You cannot make a single currency without economic convergence and integration. But on the contrary, one cannot plead for federalism and at the same time for enlargement. It's a contradiction we are 27, we will obviously have to open up the Balkans, we will be 32, 33 or 34, I imagine that nobody thinks that federalism – total integration – is possible with all those countries…. There will be two European gears, one gear towards more integration in the Eurozone and a gear that is more confederal'. Observers felt that he was against the enlargement in Eurozone membership believing that a much smaller group of more similar positioned states would be able to be much more flexible

In 2015 Mr Junker declared that "..eventually, it will no longer be possible that 33, 34 or 35 states will proceed with the same speed and the same momentum in the same direction."

In August 2016, that is between the UK's first and second EU referenda, a paper was published by well-respected individuals within the Breughel Group suggesting a somewhat weaker linkage between the UK and EU, it was to be called a 'continental partnership', a collaboration giving UK access to the EU goods and services but with some say on EU policies. "this results in a Europe with an inner circle, the EU, with deep and political integration and an outer circle with less integration." This might also cover relations with Turkey and the Ukraine.

In practice there is already within the EU a motley of opt outs and various countries have extracted some form of derogation, some would argue that it's really multispeed already, but its membership of the Eurozone that in fact is a clear dividing line between federalists and the confederacy.

However there are powerful forces against the two speed Europe, the well-respected Manuel Barroso was quite certain "A split union will not work. … an integrated core but a disengaged periphery – a union dominated by an unhealthy balance of power. All these are unsustainable and will not work in the long term because they will put in question a fundamental principle – the principle of justice, - of the respect of equality, - of the respect of the rule of law!, though several Eurozone members would argue that the Euro Zone rules and how they have been applied contradict all three"

Merkel herself seems far from convinced that there is a need to make a great leap forward towards deeper integration, preferring small steps and intergovernmental agreements to new treaties

But the problem is that once the Director of ECOFIN is established, that is the signal of the intent to create a 'single fiscal authority' then there is already an inner core and it will be logical to carry that though all institutions for legitimacy sake.

Of course the UK could itself propose a two speed Europe and this could be enhanced for example by discussions with other EC non Eurozone members to agree some format for any new structures, clearly Norway and Switzerland might also be interested if they could be members with lesser EC controls but with a presence within the EU to make their views felt.

Let's examine the possible format it might take. First there is a case whereby no treaty changes are required. A Euro group could function mostly within the current structure. If the closer group was an informal arrangement then there is apparently nothing to prevent this, so that within each institution say Heads of State could meet and discuss matters of concern. This has already taken place by the EuroGroup setting up the European Stability mechanism affording a 500 Billion lending capacity. In any case there is nothing to prevent member states putting in place higher standards on social policy, pensions, environmental policy, public health, education, culture, and civil protection.

It might be possible then for the Euro Group to put together an informal arrangement, this might take the form of a 'Political Declaration' of what areas they intend to cover. The problem with this arrangement is that the work carried out would not be legally binding, as it is outside the due EU decision-making process and would be outside the control of the Commission or the Court of Justice. So all measures would require mutual agreement and compliance could not be guaranteed. However as far as the Council is concerned in cases of 'enhanced co-operation' such as these, the treaty provides that only participating member states have the right to vote on the Council. No such option is available for the European Parliament and no segregation there is currently possible.

None of this however would ensure that the UK in the 'confederacy' would not in time be side-lined by the 'federalists'.

But we should not ignore the UK's standing in the EU, despite our tendency to opt out frequently yet we are seen as by and large honourable and whose advise for example on the bail-outs might have yielded a better and more nuanced approach. In Europe the UK have never done things which others have hated that's why even some German's cried when the first EU Referendum results were announced. When we are motivated to get interested, they listen to our advice. We are big enough not to be bullied.

So the Confederacy Group might also use the same mechanism that is an 'Enhanced Co-operation' and similarly form a 'Political Declaration' and attempt to have them enshrined in a right which could be enforceable through the EU Courts of Justice. In other words it would state that the existing rights afforded to the Group within the existing treaties are legally enforceable. This would cover matters like the objectives of the single market and its eventual development so as to cover all financial services and also Bank supervision and control mechanism.

So if this arrangement were acceptable then for example to formalise economic and fiscal convergence in the Euro area would require a treaty change and each institution would have to be redefined in terms of what was and was not subject to the new rules. The Institutions could meet in a different group and then together as the whole EU. It would be necessary to grant the 'confederacy' group some form of guarantee that their rights would not be ignored and these rights could then protected by the EU Court of Justice. It might be possible to enshrine these rights as a temporary derogation through the Council in some way.

There is one problem in this route the 'enhanced cooperation group' was intended for the faster group. To create such a group out of the rest will require nine member states. Only two states have opted out of the move to the Euro and another one is in permanent suspension all the rest are in the process of moving towards it, partly it's true because that was the expectation when signing up to enlargement. Perhaps given the option of a looser arrangement they could well be encouraged to join, provided the option to join the Euro was always, later available.

Initially changing to a Two Speed EC might be possible without treaty changes.

But that's the point formal structural changes to institutions and changes in their powers and formal guarantees will require Treaty changes. In view of the low standing of the EU in many countries such changes cannot be assumed".

"Hummph" mumbled Sebastian. "So I can possibly lead the call for a review towards a proper two speed EU, I can see if I can make common ground with Denmark and Sweden, who must be as equally concerned as we about the direction of the EU. Poland is not yet committed. I can discuss the situation with Norway and Switzerland to see if they are interested in this. Well" Sebastian suggested hopefully "at least it gives me a sporting chance?"

"You? What do you mean you? Frankly, Sebastian, you don't stand a chance of doing this on your own, with a possibly divided cabinet?

I can play a leading role, perhaps, in the EU Military, that might get me more leverage? I can relate better to existing Euro Leaders as I have met several of them - a year ago I held 'open house' and invited many of their foreign ministers to London for weekends, and I can perhaps do or at least try to do what no previous UK Government has done to obtain the assistance of a former leading light in the EU and see if he can give some inside advice and assistance. Do you know of anyone?" asked Sebastian.

"I agree" Roger said "If you are convinced that you are going to try, then you are certainly going to need some inside help otherwise you have no chance set against the probable hostility of the EC elite!" Roger thought deeply for a full minute. "Hmh there is Payunk Wask," he said at last "at least that's how to pronounce it, it's spelled Pajuk Lask, an Anglophile and Europhile, former Prime Minister of Poland until the country turned to the right, more nationalist, he then became a President of the European Council from which he retired several months ago. Some years ago I had several sessions with him, so I know him reasonably well. Shall I sound him out for you?"

"Yes that would be helpful, I may have to go to Poland anyhow on the military matter, so I could meet him there?"

"OK, I'll try that, Sebastian. Is there anything else we have to go through?"

"We still have to resolve the Turkey issue! Until that's dead and buried there certainly is no hope that the rump of the Brixiteers will accept that the temporary stay on freedom of movement of people, even though it seems that even with our control we could still not prevent a net increase of immigrants! But Turkey is the test piece, solve that and what we say will be believable, fail and it leaves a huge open unanswered question. What can we do with that?"

"So I have been giving some thought to that, Sebastian. Outside the EU there is already something called the 'Neighbourhood Grouping' which was an earlier attempt to have some sort of outreach to neighbours. It covers mostly states around the Mediterranean shores. It would certainly make sense to enhance that and provide for Loans and Grants to countries beyond the boundary of the EU to spread the accumulated EU wealth more widely and encourage the establishment of more businesses there leading to more employment which would assist in the economic growth and political stability. By increasing work opportunities there it might also ease the endless flow of migrants attracted by our increasing wealth."

"Yes that's what was at the back of my mind – also I would like to see this extended to Ukraine and Yes Russia!"

"Hold on now Sebastian are we not going a bit far? The EU is mostly convinced that Russia under Putin is the Russian bear!"

"It's not my view, he will not last for ever and we have to end these games he is playing and show him that there is a bonus for good behaviour, friendship brings wealth, even if his entourage don't see that the ordinary voters will!"

"Ok that's up to you Sebastian, I think we have done? Well frankly I am just about done in! You can see, Sebastian, how these changes will affect many other items on the list which we started off with?

In a sense many smaller structural changes like making the EP more political and driving alternative programmes will probably occur with the next major treaty change which has to come. For the moment I think everyone is hoping for an improvement in the GDP across the board to encourage people to believe that future Treaty changes are desirable."

"I agree Roger, it's been a good session. For the moment I am in really no position to do the twidley bits, like eliminate the use of Strasbourg which consistently infuriates the UK Press nor eliminate the two additional bodies particularly the commission of the regions, although oddly with our own Regions just starting it might actually be helpful to give them a new aspect on their work and a new connection to the EC. What I can still do within our constitutional reform Bill is to introduce a formal review of ongoing EU legislation requiring the presence of the UK Commissioner and the MEPs to come before the UK Parliament to explain the current and ongoing changes likely to affect the UK. This might give TV time to better explaining the changes."

"But there's a warning Sebastian, the EU regular panel feedbacks give you the information that I am told you have long been concerned about, although Lib Dems have been consistently pro-European that does not appear to have yielded Lib Dems the votes they might have expected, that's because only 5% in the UK are 'very positive' about the EU. Within your poll ratings of 8% to say 12%, you probably already have as many EU strong supporters compatible with the the negatives from the rest of your policies which would prevent them voting for you. Presumably the 'fairly positive' are not positive enough to make them change their voting habits given that, Tory and Labour also officially support the EU membership! – So there is here a warning however hard you try to set the EC to rights, you will be very unlikely to shift those who are hostile to the EU. So is your effort really worthwhile, it's unlikely to double your vote! You understand that?"

"Hmmh!" Sebastian muttered "That's sad but you don't know for certain – all we can each do is to do our best – I cannot do more than that!"

Then there are a number of other points we have not cleared our way, though key is that the EU lacks a democratic base, frankly I think that's right the European Parliament seems somehow disjointed from the rest. There are strange proposals for, somehow, basing the EC Commission on a competitive bidding say a three way corner fight between Socialists, Conservatives and Liberals but I cannot for the life of me see why the existing EU Institutions would put up with that. But there is without a doubt a gaping hole – there is no 'Opposition' to test out and challenge the sometimes very bad ideas put forward by the Elite. That's extremely dangerous. During the Greek mess no-one was looking out for the total cost everyone was shamelessly concerned with their own patch. There was no independent observer. Greece should have been allowed to relate repayments to increasing GDP for example. One European Bank Chief was heard to comment that his participation in loan swaps discussions 'were as voluntary as a confession during the Spanish inquisition.'

Also the people are fed up with promises and assumptions of growth which always seem to be made inferior to economic targets they all understand the EC needs completely refocussing, I can and will remind them of that!"

"Bravo, Sebastian that's the spirit show them what the UK can still do even though missing all those years!"

"And Roger, Germany has to break out of its culture mode which has damaged the Euro and terrified his so-called allies. Greece's FDI inflows of capital dropped to one third of prior performance. Investment in the periphery must, must, must, be done!, I'll have to show them how!"

"Sebastian, I think you have passed out, grade 1, now can I help you draft your speech?"

"Yes please Roger, I'll have to choose my words carefully if I am both to have an effect yet not immediately get peoples backs up!"

Chapter TWENTY-TWO – Cabinet Meetings format, CHILCOT and MIPG

Sebastian welcomed the Cabinet back from the recess and handed out the one page paper on Military Intervention Planning Group.

"Before I go any further I would like to tell you about a change in your roles. As you know I have sat through Cabinet meetings for some years now and discussed with Robin Turnbull several times how these meetings worked and whether they were effective.

Many commentators have suggested that the meetings which now last 90 minutes are really a Prime Minister's updates compared with those under Thatcher which used to last two or even three hours but which often contained substantive discussions and where decisions were sometimes made. These days with a Quad system in place, policy disagreements between Lib Dem and Tory are ironed out before matters even become public. The tendency then has been for updates and for each Minister to operate within his own silo. Cabinet meetings are not used generally to criticise or improve any proposals.

The worst case of this was probably the whole Iraq war affair and the paper is designed to make sure that, in any future Military intervention in another country, we raise the expectation of how we operate in Cabinet, so that there is proper consultation across ministries, proper planning and proper checking of the operation. So this formalises that a Cabinet Committee will be used as the driving force under one Minister, appointed for the project, who will be answerable to Parliament, just as each of you are. Similarly there will be changes in the Civil Service structure so that one Permanent Secretary will be appointed to ensure co-ordination for the project and also to review the steps in the process. The Head of the Civil Service will then be able to review it with a hands-off and more objective role.

At least it's a framework, and with your consent I will invite comment from opposition parties so that it can become a standard procedure.

Perhaps we could take a vote on this at the end, leaving you more time to consider matters?

This leads me directly onto the next matter. How do you wish us to proceed with these Cabinet meetings?

Unlike the previous Prime Ministers I have no power to oblige you to do things, even should I want to, not only do I not have power to replace Conservative ministers, I don't have the power to replace Lib Dem ministers either, as I am not the Lib Dem party leader. In any case I regard the update as a waste of all of your good intelligence. I am sure that many Bills could have been improved had more lateral discussion been encouraged. The classic case was David Cameron's decision to hold the 2016 Euro referendum, it wasn't discussed in Cabinet. Even had you all acquiesced to it, you might have changed the wording, established some threshold % or turnout % or considered lowering the voting age for those affected for a generation; or empowered those living in the EC who might have been directly affected by the result. You might have done this as part of the trade off in allowing the referendum to proceed. But you did none of those things because by the time the decision came here in Cabinet, it was already a done deal!

It's obvious why these meetings have become dumbed down. It's much easier for the PM, it requires a good agenda and perhaps 20 minutes preparation of the chat which he will give. There are, or rather were, so many ministers around the table that, all the PM had to do was say 'Sorry we don't have time for that now, see me after please!' and any opportunity for discussion was lost.

Open discussion might mean protection of pre-held positions, critiques and maybe heated discussions leading to decisions and changes of direction, on the hoof. Considering that possibility last night, I realised that it would have taken me hours to prepare for questions and to pre-think my responses. Each of you would have had to be prepared to defend and promote your own Department's plans and views.

Previously of course such open discussion has been taboo, Conservatives not wanting to acknowledge differences of opinion in their ranks, which Lib Dems might use to embarrass them publicly and Lib Dems hiding behind the Quad where, because of equal numbers, there's estimated to be a 50/50 chance of success whereas, subjected to an inbuilt Conservative majority here, they might get nothing through at all! So open discussion is even more muted.

Earlier Roger had decided to reduce Cabinet numbers since he was well aware that with nearly 30 in the room, it would be impossible for all members to have their say. This is why there were several departmental amalgamations to attempt to reduce the number nearer to 15.

But if, of course, we are moving towards governments run by coalitions, then we shall have to find a way around this problem.

It is a problem only made worse by countries of the UK being run by parties not here present. So their case is never adequately put. Of course we know what we think is good for them, that's why we have Secretaries of State for Scotland, Wales and Northern Ireland but you, as a Cabinet have no opportunity to hear it from 'the horses' mouth' have you? and there's a clear danger of a gap emerging between 'us' and 'them' which is unhealthy and unwise.

Finally there are similar problems that will arise when the regional assemblies start operations. It's likely we will be faced with regions wanting to do different things, how to raise money for example or changing national standards because the existing size does not fit all, maybe shifting segments of staff between Councils and NHS. We will be called upon to adjudicate between regions and between different departments in regions.

For all these reasons these Cabinet meetings will have to change and I hope for the better. For the moment I do not intend to change anything or oblige you to alter your ways. It is perhaps a process of evolution? I will have further discussion with my deputy, if any of you wish to make any observations please do so through the Cabinet Secretariat."

They then went through the likely business in the next two weeks and the status of the major projects, New London Airport, Heathrow Garden Suburb, HS2, Trident and an update from the Chancellor of the Exchequer on the financial and monetary position.

Sebastian advised that he was considering setting up a small permanent base in Northern Nigeria near lake Chad. This was to prevent Boko Haram rising again. It was scheduled to be a joint venture with France who had successfully intervened in Mali. Most charities would not work in the area because of the lawlessness and violence there. It was thought that some 250,000 people were at risk of starvation there. This is just a possibility at this stage, with apologies to the Defence Secretary, who I will undertake to keep informed. At present this is in outline discussion with the French and Nigerian governments..

There were no interventions or discussions.

At the end Sebastian called for a vote on the MIPG paper.

It was approved and was later sent to all other UK based political parties, who almost unanimously supported it.

Inevitably someone leaked it to the press where it was agreed to be 'At long last a sensible move to put into place some of the Chilcot proposals and improve Cabinet collective responsibility'.

Chapter TWENTY-THREE – The crowded Train Trip

On Wednesday evening it had been pre-arranged by his staff that Sebastian was invited to a Liberal Democrat constituency event in Thrussleton near Brighton. He was warmly welcomed there and he explained the reason for his trip. He commented on the apparently dire performance of the rail franchisee, Govia, particularly with regards to the overcrowding of trains from Brighton to London during the morning peak travel times. He said he hoped to do something about it but first, as was his habit, he wanted to see the problem for himself.

The whole visit had caused some consternation for the MPS (his Ministerial Protection Squad) and Sebastian had had to stay a night in a budget hotel rather than with the constituency chairman, with the MPS dossing down in the next room. When the MPS had further learned that on the following day Sebastian intended to catch the 7.00 am Brighton to Bedford service, Sebastian could tell that the whole system of carefully controlled surveillance was about to have a fit. There were several attempts to dissuade him, which became even more heated when the MPS realised that the service was going to be jam packed. They protested that they could not adequately protect the PM. They had suggested that instead he take the train two hours later, he could always of course be at the station at 7.00 am and be snapped appearing to get on the train and then taking a later one, appearing in London to get off an identical train. That way his personage could be securely protected and he would get the publicity he needed.

Sebastian and Madge had spent some time explaining that the whole point was to subject himself to the same frustrations as normal passengers. Did they not know that this train was the most over-crowded train in the UK. It would carry around 300 extra passengers on this trip? They proposed instead that Sebastian could take a First Class seat which the officers could better protect, as there would probably be no passengers standing. But Sebastian was having none of it. He was going to travel Second Class the same as most passengers. Eventually it was agreed that Sebastian would stand at one end of the carriage with two plain clothes men alongside him and two more uniformed men would stand just inside the doors.

Sebastian was taken to the Brighton Station for the 7.00 am train the next morning and from a huddle on the platform, they joined the crush on the train. Everyone was packed so tight that it was impossible to move, indeed Sebastian felt something jabbing in his ribs and realised it was probably one of the policemen's pistols. Several people were startled to see the Prime Minister on the train. One lady standing a few feet away, in her forties perhaps, wearing a black suit and white blouse, alarmed the policemen as she kept looking at Sebastian and then looking at something in her hand. Sebastian was relieved to see it was just a newspaper, it seemed she was comparing him 'in the flesh' with a picture in the paper. At the first opportunity, when several passengers got off, she managed to grab a seat but kept on looking at him as if he were a mirage and would surely fade away. There was a constant jostling for position as people moved near to the door to make their escape or tried to hold onto the coach fittings. Nobody said anything except for 5 schoolchildren, girls Sebastian noted, all wearing the same red school blazer who happily chatted away to each other even though there were people between them, no-one seemed to object. To pass the time Sebastian tried to listen in to their conversation, he could hear the words but couldn't make sense of anything they said, they spoke so quickly that in the end he gave up. Sebastian tried putting his weight on one foot then the other but that didn't help much and he had realised that it had been silly to have bought even a small bag with him for his over-night kit. There were no overhead racks within reach so he had to hold it all the way, on one occasion the bag seemed to be walking off on its own until Sebastian realised that it was wedged between two people who were trying to move to the door. He said "Excuse me I think my bag is caught" at which at least thirty pairs of eyes swung round to see what was happening, noticed the problem then reverted to the glazed look which he saw everyone had adopted. It was 'I'm awake and my eyes are open, but I am focussing on a piece of carriage since it's taboo to directly look at anyone, that's staring, and certainly not directly in their eyes'. Clearly something dreadful would happen to them if they did, as if a magnetic force would be exerted and capture them. Sebastian noticed that many of them were reading paperback books usually held about 6 inches from the end of their noses; one person managed to flip over a page by using his chin which Sebastian thought seemed to be a well-practiced move. One, a taller well-dressed man, had managed to drape his news*paper over the baggage rail, but every so often he had quite a trouble turning the pages. Others had ear pieces and would occasionally mouth some words so Sebastian deduced it was probably a song; some possibly had radios but the reception seemed to be, on occasion, rather poor and they would cup a hand over the ear. Sebastian could not tell why they did that. Whenever of course the train went around a curve there was a deafening squealing of the metal wheels against the rail, and there was a clatter as the train rode over points, everyone would sway and return to the upright position. Of course one or two people had mobile phones, the various ring tones would go off and then there was a struggle to actually get hold of it, which often meant the person turning around to put their hand in their pocket; most conversations were restrained. One person, a young coloured girl, seemed to be giving a running commentary of nearby buildings. Apparently she needed warning of which station was next to get off, she wanted East Croydon; a tall young white lad with blonde hair had obviously left home forgetting to bring a package with him so he spent a few minutes imploring the 'other end' to call ahead and say he wouldn't have it.

At several stations when the train stopped passengers would try to get on and one or two appeared to succeed but there was a sort of "Hnnn" from the people inside and many made no attempt to squash any further up the carriage. There was clearly a limit and the passengers knew what that was, they were not going to give way, so passengers on the platform could be seen dashing up and down the train trying to spot a weak link in this passenger defence system.

The rows of seats were laterally placed except near the entrances where they were against the side of the train. There was a peculiar piece of looped metal protecting the ends of the seats which some people rested against. Those who sat in the seats engrossed themselves in a book, or just held tight to a bag across their knee. Sebastian noticed an inverted blue triangle which he knew meant the seat was reserved for disabled people, but the person sitting there clearly had no intention of looking around to see if there was anyone more needy than himself – of course there couldn't be, they would be mad to travel at this time!

The carriage became rather hot and stuffy and Sebastian cursed that he had put on his outer coat over his suit, he soon felt a driblet of sweat forming on his chest, he had amassed some fat in his mostly sedentary job as a minister and it felt damp and uncomfortable. He had been persuaded to wear a hat as a disguise but it did not quite fit and drooped over one eye which he had to rearrange every so often. One arm was getting numb through holding onto an upright pole; he counted at least 4 more hands there, if he lost grip he feared he might lose his position, so he had to put up with it. The bag in the other hand was getting heavier, he had tried to put it down but it merely landed on someone's foot and there was a sort of jabbing movement before he picked it up again. The two policemen didn't like it either, in fact they had also put raincoats on top of their uniforms which made them abnormally bulky and by halfway they were red-faced and clearly overheating.

For a moment Sebastian thought he should call it off and get out at the next station, after all he had endured, he had sampled the service. But then of course he had to get to London anyway, he was expected to meet an ambassador or something. He could hardly phone ahead and explain he was caught in a second class carriage and it was so stifling that he felt he had to get off and catch the next train, so would the ambassador mind waiting please? No! He would just have to stick it out.

His co-passengers were getting grumpy too, he could feel it. Instead of bodies swaying with the coach as it squealed and lurched its way around a sharp curve, there was resistance, a sort of 'Come on I'm tired too, just stand straight will you! Stop pushing! Carry your own weight!' People who tried to get in were pushed back, anyone losing their footing and accidentally standing on someone else's foot would now justify a withering look and a sharp intake of breath.

At last the train stopped, the doors slid open and the passengers disgorged as if everyone had been given 5 seconds to evacuate the coach. The place was littered with debris, mostly torn newspapers many of them the Freebie newspaper offered at Brighton, and here and there an empty plastic bottle of pop, bits of sandwiches, an apple core and a banana skin.

Sebastian and the policemen were the last to get out. The uniformed officers who had been standing just inside the doors checking people coming in, seemed exhausted. Sebastian thanked them, they said nothing in reply, they were clearly unimpressed by the whole episode. Someone had alerted the Press and they rushed towards him as soon as he was through the ticket barrier. He briefly explained he had heard this was the most over-packed line and that he had come to sample what that was like. "Well" they asked "What was it like?" Sebastian replied "Bloody awful!"

Sebastian went out onto the roadway and was immediately picked up by a waiting official car and taken to No 10 in ample time to receive the ambassador.

On the way he picked up a call in the car from the Minister of Transport. Sebastian asked why it was that this line was so persistently overcrowded. After 10 minutes of explanation, Sebastian still was not convinced. "Well we will just have to pass an act which says standing passengers pay half the rate compared with seated ones".

"You couldn't do that Prime Minister, the franchisee would go bust!"

"Well maybe they'll stick on a few more trains then?"

"Do you want me to suggest that?"

"Nope, that'll come later. Look please nip on over here and let's run through some things!"

"What, now?"

"In a couple of hours please and bring the oversight chappy with you please and the guy who wrote the 15 to 20 year plan, see you in half an hour!"

He swept through the gates at No 10 just in time to receive the ambassador.

A few minutes later his son Rupert called him, he invited his father over to Friday dinner at his Unity college, Camford University, "There are some interesting people I would like you to meet Dad!"

Simon Gibson MP the Transport Minister arrived shortly afterwards, he had only been in post a few weeks. Sebastian noticed that he left the two experts outside.

"Ah Simon!" Sebastian remembered him from three years before when they had both been in the Whip's office, Then he had tried to help Sebastian who was trying to come to terms with the arcane intricacies of the unwritten hierarchy of the place. Sebastian had been having a tussle with the former Deputy Chief Whip and it was Simon who had pointed out to Sebastian that the problem was one of money rather than rank. Sebastian was being paid a tidy salary for looking after just a few Lib Dem MPs, dislodging the former Conservative who had to look after several hundred Conservative MPs. The latter had, as a consequence, suffered a severe drop in salary. Sebastian felt he 'owed' Simon because of his help then and he began in a very conciliatory manner.

"Simon, the problem is that these people are suffering in a most unpleasant way! So, as you know now, I took the 6.57 am from Brighton and it was packed, jam-packed. Almost everyone in my carriage had to stand the entire trip, that's what, 70 minutes? We were squashed like sardines!"

"Well I know that Sebastian, I mean Prime Minister, and I have just been checking, it's what? 5% overcrowding?"

"No! No! probably nearer 50%!" Sebastian explained. "As far as I can judge that train carried approximately twice the registered Second Class capacity. You see, the figure you are using averages out the overcapacity over a two hour period but at its peak it really is this bad! But it's not only that a spate of strikes, changes to timetables, cancellations of services and lack of drivers have left these people in desperation! Some even have to give up their London jobs. To cap it all the parent company Go-Ahead, you know it owns 65% of Govia which in turn owns Southern, has just declared increasing profits and a higher dividend!"

"Well I have just been told that they are buying new rolling stock and that will help surely?"

"No! it's not going to scratch the service, these people have been forgotten! Do you know what the key phrase on the company's web site is 'Focussed on every Journey!' I have just read the statistical reports, do you know that 155,000 people every day have to stand at peak hour travelling into London by train? The problem is that they have all gotten so used to it that they, Govia and the Ministry of Transport believe it's normal!"

"But we have these massive projects the HS2 and improvement to railways in the North. – we have to fund those as well!"

"Look Simon it just will not do! I have sampled the trip and I think you should too! It's just unacceptable! We are treating these people worse than cattle! Can't we do something? The current franchise lasts till 2021 I think? The Mayor of London is clamouring to get rid of them altogether! As I understand it there's a major problem at East Croydon? I am not sure that I understood it, but it seems to be a major bottleneck and has been so for decades. You realise that these people, Govia provide 35% of all rail journeys in the UK? What example is that to them if we do nothing?"

"Well I'll have a look Prime Minister and see if I can come up with anything!"

"As I see it we can either assist Govia, like giving them training grants to set on more drivers than strictly they need, so that this is never an excuse, or we can improve the rolling stock or charge less for standing, or double up the services, one train, following immediately behind another, or use double decker trains. I know it's not all their fault, most infrastructure projects were savaged between 2010 and 2017, but I am sure even a small investment in rail bottlenecks will yield a good return! Please do what you can will you?"

Simon left and within minutes the Deputy PM phoned demanding a meeting. She appeared a few seconds later, obviously very angry, with a grim face. She verbally launched at Sebastian. "Is this how you mean to go on?" she demanded, throwing the early evening edition of the London Gazette across the table. The headlines roared "BLOODY AWFUL" over a picture of Sebastian emerging from the London station. "I should have known you would do this, use your position for Party political ends," She almost spat out those words. "We are running the country not the Brighton Liberal Constituency Association!"

Sebastian fought back, "Well it's true, it is bloody awful and unless something is done one of these days there will be a riot, or more likely they will all swing to UKIP, do you want that?"

"Something must be done!" he insisted

That threat seemed to halt her tirade. Sebastian decided to try to mollify her with a partial apology. "Well alright, I suppose I could have handled it better, I might have forewarned the Minister for Transport of what I was intending to do and then I suppose I might have raised it with you, since he is a Conservative Minister, and we could have seen him together?"

That seemed to do the trick and Sebastian immediately gathered that the procedure was what primarily concerned her, she did not want any Conservative Minister being ticked off in that way by a Lib Dem whoever he was. It would no doubt have reduced her authority within the Tory side of the Cabinet, so to make matters clear he underlined it. "It won't happen again!"

She than appeared to change character completely, she fished out of a file a new layout for a standing only coach. "You see," she said "we could quickly introduce these, in a matter of months by just stripping out the existing carriage furniture and replacing it with more hanging straps and leaning pads, I've spoken to Sir ..." she paused realising that she had probably revealed too much "The Chairman of the Transport Vetting Group? You know they have oversight of the franchise? and he thinks it's a runner!"

Sebastian was amazed "But Simon was only here 10 minutes ago? How did you do all that?"

Pamela touched the side of her nose "The MPS!"

"The MPS? You mean the Ministerial Protection Squad? Good Heavens! But what do they know about this? I hadn't taken them as train experts!"

"Well the leader of the squad was so annoyed at you putting yourself in a position of such high risk from which, if anything went wrong, they could not possible protect you, and for which they would certainly be blamed. He was so furious that he called me and asked me to intercede with you to stop your little jaunt. Of course I refused, but I have been working on this all morning!"

"Hah!" Sebastian burst out laughing "So you knew there was a potential disaster ahead unless you found a solution, you knew those passengers were at breaking point!"

'Well how cunning can you get?' thought Sebastian, 'I really had better watch her!'

She added quickly "Yes but we had already made the point to the rail company several times and they had brushed the problem aside, always saying that capacity would be increased next year. So it really needed a catalyst, a threat to get it moving!"

"Hah!" said Sebastian "So you needed me after all!"

"Hm maybe, Simon repeated to them that you wanted to reduce prices for standing passengers, that seemed to loosen them up a bit! They realised they would lose millions right across the services they run. Then we managed to get funding from one of the City Infrastructure Funds, they saw the newspaper article as well, it's a new package, this way there will be more places but no reduction in prices".

But she said there is a downside to all this: - "Your MPS group has resign in protest, en bloc, they thought the experience was what did you say Ah! Yes! BLOODY AWFUL too!"

Sebastian reminded himself to try to put pressure on this overcrowding when the next transport review came up.

The following day Sebastian called in the Leader of the Lib Dems Dan Stirling and John Thorne that Chair of the Lib Dem executive committee, Bill and Madge were there as well. "They went over the events of yesterday and the outcome. But look we are missing out on something here. I raise a wave and nothing links in to the constituencies and branches, who are still, if you don't mind me saying so, still more intent on finding potholes to report." Bill who Sebastian knew was an ardent user of the Lib Dem 'Focus' newsletter put up his finger as a friendly warning to Sebastian. "Ok so I am overdoing it a bit" Sebastian continued "but none of you have got used to linking in with what I do. We need on every issue of 'Focus' wherever in the country a 'national campaign' so can we have please, on all 'Focus' on the South Coast, a 'train watch group' identifying and summarising lateness and overcrowding, next can we ask for rail travellers to buy shares in the Rail holding company, lets bolster up and co-ordinate a protest group".

They agreed there and then that the Executive Committee would email chairs of all Lib Dem Constituency parties to begin a campaign on inadequate rail performance and begin the connect between these 'interventions' of mine and the members.

It came to me when Pamela Tressider was assailing me for carrying out the 'stunt' for party political purposes that I hadn't thought in those terms, so let's do it! Call it Spinning Down?"

Chapter TWENTY-FOUR – Interventions ONE – Religion

One of the more bizarre and unexpected duties of the Prime Minister, Sebastian learned, soon after his appointment, was in assisting in the selection of the next Archbishop of Canterbury. The previous Archbishop had died in office in early December and there was a certain haste in finding a replacement. Of course the Archbishop of York stood in for him over Christmas but he was rather frail and really didn't want further responsibilities.

Sebastian studied the file. Then struggled to remember what he had promised to do on entering politics.

When taking his seat in Parliament he was offered different formats for the swearing in process. He had chosen the affirmation. He still remembered the words, or at least most of them 'I declare and confirm that I will bear allegiance to the Queen and her successor'. He thought at the time it was rather strange; there was nothing about including any moral code or, indeed, anything to do with the UK Constitution, or justice, or bearing in mind past history, or responsibility to the future, or indeed about the welfare of the people he was trying to serve, just a statement of allegiance to the Queen.

He had also assented to some oath when he had become a Privy Councillor on being made Secretary of State of the Foreign and Commonwealth Office, but he didn't remember the details.

Due to the procedures to allow anyone following any Christian denomination to take up the various options for oaths, Sebastian supposed that had probably dealt with the need of the Government to follow any particular moral code in any senior Ministerial position. Of course there was the Ministerial Code book and exhortations to do their job properly. Sebastian had read that bit OK. 'Ministers of the Crown are expected to behave in a way that upholds the highest standards of propriety, including ensuring that no conflict arises between their public duties and private interests, to comply with the law, including international law, uphold the administration of justice and protect the integrity of public life. All ministers are expected to observe the Seven principles of Public Life; selflessness, integrity, objectivity, accountability, openness, honest and leadership.'

Yet here he was trying to do something to the process of selection of the Archbishop.

Sebastian had indeed never professed to anyone that he was 'religious'. Indeed the only contact that he had had with anyone who was religious was his friend who was a Parochial Church Councillor in Northumberland. When there, usually at Easter, he would go with Douglas and his wife Anna-Lisa to one of the village churches. They had together marvelled at the increase in Easter church attendances that had occurred under a female vicar but later there had been a disagreement with some of the village lay people over the introduction of a modern prayer book, which Sebastian had not understood particularly since prayers were mostly read by the vicar, anyhow. As a result the excellent vicar had decided to move on! Sebastian loved to sing some of the hymns, in fact he knew that this had derived directly from his time at boarding school with his chum Douglas, they had both been in the choir together. This was just at the end of the era of 'muscular' Christianity which had been exported throughout the Empire. But lusty singing was what Sebastian did well. He managed to avoid saying the creed, since he knew he really didn't believe in what he considered to be the 'hocus pocus' of the religion. But he knew perfectly well, although he could leave religion aside, his whole upbringing and education was impregnated and permeated with its themes, which had modified into a more liberal format, and he knew it was impossible for him to escape its influence. So he didn't try. He always went to church on Christmas Day whenever he could, partly to get himself out of the house whilst his wife prepared the traditional Christmas lunch, which it had taken him years to persuade her to attempt and, partly because he was always interested to hear the sermons. These had ranged from the very impassioned pleas for ending the wars in which the UK became involved to, on one occasion, the Vicar merely reading out the contents of his Christmas cards, which Sebastian thought was a very silly idea since the comments were either so general as to be banal, after all he had never seen any card saying 'Have an average Xmas' or 'Wash your hands after going to the toilet'; or then they were so specific as to be once-a-year personal notes.

Anyhow with all that cumulative religious knowledge and experience, which, as Sebastian admitted to himself, didn't amount to a row of beans, he was now supposed to help elect a leader for the Church of England, never having previously met with any of the initial contenders nor having the faintest idea of the exact problems faced by the Church, nor which of the contenders would be best at resolving them.

Oh yes he was well aware of the basic statistics. The file said so. The attendance of Anglicans at church had fallen by nearly 50% over the last 25 years, from 1990 when 1,259,800 attended to 2015 when 660,000 did so. It was a pattern similar to that of all Christian groups in England, so attendance was now below 5%.

He could see for himself the effects of the rapid decline in attendance. The country was littered with the evidence of the Church attempting to downsize. Reducing congregations meant empty churches, many needing repair or restoration work, so they were deconsecrated then sold off. Many reopened as private homes or bars or restaurants

He was well aware too that the Church of England had been obsessed by four interlocking problems; first had been the ordination of women, which seemed to be over, though he didn't know if the position of Archbishop could be female? There was nothing in his notes about that! Next was the problem recognising homosexual relations within the clergy, he had no idea what a celibate homosexual relationship was, after all he reasoned if the two actually did nothing, why didn't they just call themselves friends, or indeed he didn't know much about marriages between same sex partners and whether these should be allowed or officiated at or even encouraged by the Church and then, finally; the international schism between what one might call progressives and traditionalists which threatened to tear Anglicanism apart. He didn't know what the repercussions of that might be.

All this he had learnt simply by reading the papers and seeing TV and listening to the early morning Radio News of which he was a fan.

Sebastian himself believed that these obsessions had diverted the Church's energy away from doing their 'proper job' in favour of their 'navel gazing' which had not appeared to halt the decline of the 'members'.

He saw it as much the same problem as faced by all political parties today, the people you need to get through to and persuade to vote for you are the ones who are not now members, otherwise just getting back to the same declining group of adherents runs the risk of re-enforcing the mind-set of the declining few and militates against change, which might be exactly what was needed to turn the ship around.

Of course everyone said 'well religion will come back you'll see.' In some areas it had done so, particularly in some inner-city churches. Sebastian saw that as an insider's self-delusion, the Christian trend was inexorably downwards, but he knew he wasn't close enough to the problem to offer any solution.

Margaret Thatcher had, apparently, refused to endorse one of the names presented to her due to his perceived left wing views – "Hmm that would obviously have been a great risk! A leftie Archbishop, me oh my, what will they think of next?" Sebastian smiled to himself!

Sebastian noted that Gordon Brown after becoming PM in 2007, had proposed that just a single name be put forward to the PM for onward transmission to the Queen. After all there was an extremely high powered board which had had time to study the details and it seems that this rule is now in force 'unless of course the PM chooses to change it'.

Sebastian decided that he wouldn't look at the name, just ticked the file and wrote 'Do it!' in the margin.

But Sebastian did not at all agree that the Archbishop was the 'Chaplin to the nation'. That notion had been out of date for decades. The declining importance of Western religion, the rise of Islam, other religions building their own prayer halls and then the persistence in the UK of Judaism, meant that there could be no exclusive unique moral leadership.

That was not what concerned Sebastian. The Church of England primarily for historical reasons was one of the essential parts of the glue that had held the Nation together for centuries, whether anyone in the UK liked it or not, much of the social structure of the UK, its treatment of the poor and needy, its ability to bounce back after both world wars, the need for the pensions, free schooling and the NHS had been moulded by people with a high moral ideal. Whether or not successful it was through all of their efforts that we are what we are now. Even now most of the food banks, free food packages, were done through the churches. The Salvation Army dealt with thousands of homeless. Think of the world-wide charities tramping over deserts to feed the poor and needy. It would be frankly impossible to suggest that the Church of England and the many other Christian sects had not massively contributed to that development. If only by a process of permeation of its moral code.

But what happens now? Sebastian had read Richard Dawkins 'The God Delusion' but he failed to find in it any guidelines as to how people should behave. In the post-God world, by what stars should we sail?

Sebastian called the BBC, explained his position and his dilemma. The retreat of the Churches from a position of importance had, surely, left behind a vacuum. What if anything should be encouraged to fill it and give a lead on modern morality?

He said he wanted as PM to pose the nation some questions, 'By what code should we live? What ought we to aspire to ourselves? And how can we distinguish between right and wrong behaviour?'

'How do we compare perhaps; a man in a hum-drum job who tries his best throughout his life to work hard, helps nurture a family and ends up volunteering, and giving his time for free to help others; compare this with a man who pushes his way up the employment ladder, reaches the top, having been not too careful on whom he trod on the way up, but expands, the company makes a huge profit, and pays heavy taxes, which of course gets recycled into new hospitals; or the man or woman who is ready to abuse anyone but makes a fortune on cleverly buying a house, selling it at a profit, then buying another and so on every two years and in this way amasses considerable wealth, largely due to the rise of house prices beyond inflation, but salts it away in foreign bank accounts, only finally paying death duties but she uses health services virtually every day?

If we lack a moral code how do we communicate a sense of belonging and behaviour to people when they come here, immigrants, who, maybe mistakenly, believe that we have no moral compass at all?

The matter was aired on BBC radio and yielded a huge mail. Sebastian suggested that after key speakers had been invited to have their say, a competition should be launched by the BBC for the best Moral Code with a maximum of 750 words or one page of A4.

The BBC's lines were blocked for days.

The problem was that no-one wanted to take the lead and evolve a new moral code.

As before Sebastian met with Dan Stirling and John Thorne. "Let's Spin Down on this? Can someone prepare a fairly straight forward Questionnaire on the subject, test it out in one ward thoroughly then launch the result through 'Focus' then decide if it warrants supporting a Bill?"

Chapter TWENTY-FIVE – Muslin area, Community & ethnic Schools

Lib Dem Headquarters and Sebastian's personal staff worked hard to make contact with the Muslim community.

They built up a visit for late Thursday so as not to interfere with Friday Prayers, Sebastian also took with him Mohammed Rahmam a Lib Dem District Councillor for Middleton whom he had known for several years.

Sebastian realised that as Mohammed intended standing for the East Midlands Regional Assembly, Sebastian was probably going to be constrained in what he could say on the spot to, as it were, the Muslim Community, since if he said something that he could not justify, then it would likely he held against Mohammed and he would lose votes. But he didn't want either to give the impression that he agreed with everything only later to deliver a public speech in which he was critical of certain aspects that he had not dared to mention in this visit.

However Sebastian had a good reputation for honesty in relations with Muslim residents of Middleton, for example although Sebastian had followed other leaders in calling the Charlie Hebdo killings in France 'dreadful' and 'appalling' and 'with no justification' he did not feel able to jump on the bandwagon and campaign on the street for 'Je suis Charley!' He felt then that it would simply glory a small and scurrilous political satirist group, who it seems, had been intent on provoking and antagonising the Muslim community. To come out onto the streets "Je suis Charley" and expect Muslims to do the same would sound as if the public were being called on to heroise the satirists. He did not believe that was right and said so, earning him a rebuke from Lib Dem Head office.

Also it was Mohammed who had saved the day when Middleton Lib Dems had run out of funds in the constituency, but before accepting the money Sebastian had insisted that Mohammed had been aware of Sebastian's wife's charity which provided a 'safe house' for Asian, usually Muslim women escaping arranged marriages and in fear of 'honour' retribution. He had also insisted that before Mohammed had become a Councillor, that the local Chairman, had explained that FMG Female Genital Mutilation was absolutely banned under Lib Dem policies.

So his track record was clear and uncompromising, he was for all 'modern muslims'.

They had decided to spend most of their time visiting Schools, in or near Nottingham; one was to be a Mixed Community Junior School, another was a Girls Muslim school, there was to have been a third school but it had recently been downgraded, or as the local paper suggested, 'slammed' by Ofsted, the school had pulled out of the visits but Sebastian wanted to follow this up with community leaders.

The four of them, Sebastian, Madge, Bill and Mohammed first visited the community school. It was located in one of the Nottingham inner suburbs which had originally been a slum area until knocked down and entirely rebuilt in the 1970s located between the railway Station and the River Trent.

They were introduced by the Head Teacher to the children as they were about to finish for the day. The School had had 210 children up to grade 6, around 75% of them were from minority ethnic backgrounds, the main group being Pakistani Muslims.

It had been rated by Ofsted as 'Outstanding' also it had been awarded 'Best school in Nottingham' by the local paper.

The staff explained that 28 languages were spoken within the school, "Central to all that the school does is a celebration of its multi-ethnicity".

They came away very impressed.

They then visited Long Midgely, Islam Girls High School. It was a voluntary aided school and its premises were owned by the Mosque, taking girls from Indian and Pakistani heritage. They were again taken round by the Head Teacher and popped into certain classes, it was apparent that the girls were attentive and interested and in one session the girls asked the Prime Minister some leading questions like 'Is it difficult to run a Coalition?'

They could see that the schools GCSE results as far back as 2006 were far above the average nationally and they were, for a senior school, top of the authorities list of schools on all measures. The school prided itself on being 'at the forefront in new ways of working and learning'.

There were areas however where the Ofsted report suggested it could do better particularly music and design technology which did not fulfil the National Curriculum in Key Stage 3

It continued that although at this stage it lacked a canteen and a library 'but the school is resourceful in overcoming limitations for example in obtaining funding for refurbished science laboratories'.

Again they all came away thoroughly impressed by what they had seen.

He then walked over to the largest Mosque where they met with several Councillors all elected under Labour and several local imam khatib or priests.

After introductions, where Sebastian expressed himself pleased with what he had seen, but now he wanted some explanation of the other ethnic school which had been 'slammed'.

But one of the Labour Councillors – a County Councillor called Shahid Hussein, seemed keen to avoid that but to engage directly in a rather combative style.

"So, Mr Edwards, we would like to ask you directly do you believe in faith schools?"

"No, in most circumstances No!" answered Sebastian, "Do you want to know why?" He didn't wait for a reply.

"In my younger days, I worked in Northern Ireland, I felt 'look I am a Brit whatever you two sides Republican and Loyalist, have between you just keep me out of it!

Of course they didn't.." he was about to continue when Shahid interrupted, "but come on! what this got to do with faith schools? We are busy people, we just need to know if you'll support a new faith school here?"

Sebastian turned to the Imams "Is this what you want? Confrontation?" Sebastian could see out of the corner of his eye that Mohammed was getting worried.

Sebastian turned on Shahid and shouted at him "Because I believe it caused the death of 3568 people, NOW DO YOU UNDERSTAND THAT?" He shouted at him again.

Shahid was for a moment stunned, people don't often shout right into your face, especially if they are Prime Minister.

Some of the Imams could not speak English well and there was some muttering as Sebastian's words were translated, but the lead Imam had got the gist of it and put up a finger in front of Shahid and said "No!"

One of the Imams then led Sebastian and his small cohort through into a room at the side of the main chamber. It was full of low slung, light-brown, leather chairs ranged around a large patterned carpet. He motioned everyone to sit. He indicated to Sebastian that he had the floor to explain.

Sebastian related the problem of the 1920's settlement in Northern Ireland, how Lord Londonderry had hoped to make all schools non-denominational, neither Catholic or Protestant. First one side, the Catholics became annoyed because already smarting from failure to create an All-Ireland Parliament, they didn't want any Government interference, they just wanted to be in charge of the Catholic Schools and appoint Catholic Teachers if they wished. Similarly Protestants objected, they insisted that Bible teaching should be brought into the curriculum, and they wanted to select their own teachers too!

As a result neither side were prepared to accept the proposals and from then on until the 1970's most education was dominated by the Churches. Generally also the Protestants sides with the Crown, the Catholics wanted an all-Ireland solution.

So there grew up two totally separate parallel school systems.

An old fellow in Greece called Aristotle said "Give me the child till he's seven and I'll show you the man" meaning that if you inculcated a child up to seven then that will form his life as a man! So it's basically wrong to segregate children at that age, they need to know they live in a multi-ethnic world and celebrate that, not allow them to grow up in a monoculture believing that represents the world!

Both sides in Northern Ireland continued to hate each other. Protestants fearful of being usurped from their position of control, manipulated democracy to ensure that whatever was going they, the Protestants, would always win, if it was money or power or anything.

Slowly this self-justified separation became a wall, Catholics were thrown out of their jobs in engineering and were replaced with Protestants. Protestants owned the best land and had the best jobs.

As each sides social lives were centred on their Churches Social Centres or in case of Protestants – their Orange Order clubs, both sides could live parallel lives without meeting each other, for a time each side had their own Hospitals and Teacher Training Colleges and of course Cemeteries.

Eventually the Catholics had had enough. By then it was an US and THEM situation, We were always right in everything we did. They were the enemy, they don't care about US, if THEY damage or threaten US, we will fight.

They did. Over 30 years some 3568 people died in a terrible bloodbath until some sense was restored in 1999.

In my opinion this killing spree was caused by the educational divide, each side was right, each side would sneer and shout abuse at the other. 'Taiges' or 'Brits' or just 'bastards' and 'shits'.

The hatred was unbelievable, imagine I and Councillor Hussein we have been at school together for 5 years, in the same class, sometimes I would help him with his homework, sometimes he would shout a warning 'teacher's coming' so I could scuttle back to my desk. Do you think if someone gave me £5000 and a gun and told me "Kill Him!" do you think I would?

All the evidence is that rational people don't kill, but if they belong to a different tribe which threatens them then they will.

If you are creating here an US and THEM, situation then No! I'll fight tooth and nail to prevent another 3568 deaths."

"So", the Imam listened intently and spoke in perfect English "The US and THEM is the only problem?"

"No it's the main problem but not the only one. I don't like the subservience of women which is often peddled in your literature. Here everyone is born equal, entitled to equal opportunity, equal schooling, equally entitled to choose their partner, equally entitled to a job, to hospital services, to dentists, to be served in a shop. At present you seem determined to allow only the man to work, that's ridiculous, Pakistanis already earn a lower rate per hour as they don't invest in education and training, getting low paid jobs, this is then compounded by their partner sitting at home, whereas in the normal community the wife would be earning too and the family would be wealthier! The result of this poverty is there for all to see, higher crime rate and circle of depravity starts again. Do you realise that 25% of all taxi drivers in Leicester are Muslim, is that what you want? Or are these peasants in a foreign country?

If so they will rapidly feel they are losing out, they are a poor disregarded people, a minority in a rich world they cannot reach. This is the base of the unfairness they see and it makes them easy prey for jihadists who tell them they should not put up with it, it's the western way of keeping the Muslim down, so get up and do something about it!

I want Muslims to grow up Healthy and Wealthy , being Generals, Professors, leading entrepreneurs, Judges, MPs. Teachers, doctors, dentists, nurses, bus drivers, train drivers. We want you to allow the children to be whatever they can be, to achieve their potential, for the benefit of the world, this country, this region and here in their family.

That's your job Holy Men to ensure that the next generation is always better than the last.

But in some areas I hear that girls are being prevented from going to get jobs, from going to University from attaining their potential. Ethnic boys' schools are deliberately cutting off elements of the school curriculum,

I will not have that!" Sebastian stopped suddenly, aware now that he had almost certainly gone too far, so he ended "Many ethnic schools try to mix your religion with schooling, allowing the religious element to dominate the rest. It doesn't work except in rare cases such as those we saw today, the quality of teaching is often poor and it's likely the school will be closed down! As was the one we were due to see today! And I will agree with that!"

There is of course a way round this?" Sebastian was not sure they had heard him, so he repeated it!

Then he said 'paired schools'. "You match an ethnic school with a matching school either mixed ethnic or mostly white British, 75% of all classes would be taught together, maths, science, geography, economics, politics, history, sports would be taken together, hobbies would be done together. A paired school. You keep your religious studies separate. But no US and no THEM, do you understand this?

 I will be happy to help you, it would come out of a special PM fund that I have and can use."

Sebastian sat back and waited, Councillor Shahid Hussein looked embarrassed.

"Of course it would need money, a lot of money to get it started, the schools have to be close together with complimentary facilities like for sports and libraries but we are anxious to do this rather than have several ethnic schools, many of which would up as failures, which does the Muslim image no good, so we can treat this as a pilot scheme, happy to help you!"

Sebastian continued "But no arranged marriages either? They sound innocuous enough but seem to end up as promises, get entrenched and in the end if there is a break up some think it's justification for settling it as matter of honour. That's no good!"

Sebastian muttered to Mohammed on the way out "Was that successful do you think?"

"Well to be frank" Sebastian "I thought when you told Councillor Hussein to shut up, I thought we were finished, but of course as you indicated he was rather rude and you had the edge on him, I am not so sure they liked the lecture, but they know on a paired system it has a much greater chance of success, failure would costs hundreds of £ thousands, from the Mosque funds or supporters! They know you mean what you say. Perhaps, they know they have to modernise, you have given them a reason for arguing with those few extreme parents, who cannot see any objection to pure ethnic schooling!"

Sebastian sent a note suggesting this be 'spinned down'. What was the reaction to paired schooling instead of dedicated ethnic schools?

Chapter TWENTY-SIX – Interventions TWO - Return of The Elgin Marbles

On 11th July 2016 a group of cross party MPs led by a Lib Dem MP Mark Williams, had launched a bid to return the Elgin Marbles on the 200th anniversary of the their purchase by the British Government.

Subsequently there was considerable discussion as to whether Lord Elgin had indeed written approval to buy them, to take them down and sell them to the British Government, and if indeed the Ottoman rulers could be considered to have the moral authority, in any case to sell objects, which clearly belonged to another culture, without consulting the descendants of the objects' inspirators and creators.

Sebastian was well aware that successive Greek Government had sought their return. They viewed them as icons of a former glorious epoch. The requests grew more impatient as Greece suffered at the hands of the troika of institutions that pulverised the Greek's admitted rather half-hearted attempts, to restructure their way of life following the rather basic demand for financial rectitude. Greek politicians thought that the return of The Marbles would inspire the Greek people and help them to transition to a more mechanical, mathematical and financial prudent EU order.

Sebastian picked up a brochure on the subject. It said '*These are defined as being of two types first the metopes or square panels placed on the outside of the building; a continuous frieze running around the outside of the interior; and the pedimental sculptures in the gables at either end. The subject of the East Pediment was the birth of Athena from the head of Zeus in the presence of all the other gods.*' It added somewhat matter-of-factly '*The style of the Parthenon sculptures exhibits a combination of truth to nature with grandeur of conception which has never been excelled.*'

'Humph. Wow! NEVER been excelled.' Sebastian murmured to himself, 'one word which all politicians regarded as 'taboo' was 'never' meaning to eternity and that's a very, very long time and could cover a whole range of differing scenarios and conditions'.

Also he knew that there was another sculpture that was of particular interest. He read.

'*Alongside the Parthenon was a very much smaller temple also dedicated to Athena, called the Erechtheum. Its roof had been held up by six women, they were called Caryatids. Only one was taken and brought to the UK*'.

Unhappily the second reading of the Bill which was presented on 20th January 2017 had failed. The Directors of all the UK museums had run a deliberate campaign hoping to damn the whole thing by using the simplest of all arguments – by extension. "First it's the Elgin Marbles and then what, perhaps 25% of all artefacts in the UK Museums were obtained from abroad, should these be returned as well? What about the Koh-in-noor jewel in the Imperial Crown used for all recent coronations? Should we replace them perhaps with paste copies!? We could of course send the Greeks life sized plaster casts!"

Other more serious comments were used. It was pointed out that keeping hold of the Caryatid had actually saved it. The others that remained, due to the increasing levels of acid in the air in Greece had been badly damaged, their faces were almost completely obliterated. The one in the British Museum was, however, in almost perfect condition. This argument continued, that it would never be possible to put the one in the British Museum back in place on the Acropolis for fear that it would also rapidly melt away. So it could only be shown in a museum anyway and what better place than the place where it had been so carefully preserved? The same applied to the Pediment sculptures.

But the primary case for not returning them was that in the British Museum the Elgin Marbles could be appreciated for what they were in the context of development of art and, as such, they could be seen in historical context. They surely belonged to the world and that transcended any nation 'owning them'.

A straw poll at the time suggested that 69% of those that were familiar with the issue were in favour of their return and only 13% were hostile to the idea.

Sebastian decided to revive the idea. He asked for the Bill to be changed in a number of ways, firstly so that the actual items to be returned be listed and numbered, rather than allowing the Secretary of State to determine what was to be included. There could then be no later disagreement or prevarication; secondly on condition that the Greek Government housed them appropriately, thirdly that all UK citizens presenting their passports to the Museum in Greece would be allowed free entry, fourthly that every four years the Greek Government would provide, on temporary 4 month loan to the British Museum, a selection of its best antiquities, whose costs would be paid for by the British Government; fifthly that the Greek Government would permit further excavations paid for by the British Government where 33% of the removable finds would be made available to the British Museum under a temporary loan basis.

Sebastian believed that these new conditions would facilitate a positive vote.

The Bill was approved by the Cabinet.

The first reading of the new Bill would be held in mid-February and a possible date for the more important second reading would be the end of June 2021.

Sebastian decided that he himself would take part in the debate, he had already written his little speech "This isn't about history or about art or about theft, this is a Treasure that everyone acknowledges rightly belongs to the Greeks. Greeks have been publicly eviscerated over the bail-outs however much it may have been their fault, they did not deserve to be treated like that! Let's help them restore their Soul. Please support the return of their marbles."

He saw that the Greek Ambassador, sitting in the gallery above, nodded approvingly at the Prime Minister's speech.

Sebastian contacted Dan Stirling and John Thorne. "Let's spin this down, can we do a questionnaire over 100 constituencies please?"

Chapter TWENTY-SEVEN – Interventions THREE – Whose right to die?

The Prime Minister Sebastian Edwards. in his Friday press release, called for a cross party group to get together with interested parties to formulate a new Private Members' Bill for assisted suicide. In fact his staff had research this matter over several weeks.

 He then gave an interview expressing his personal views. It was an 'exclusive' with the features editor, Rob Murphy, who had helped him earlier and encouraged Sebastian to come forward with new ideas.

"Let's put the matter starkly, it is now a criminal offence to give assistance to those wishing to commit suicide",Sebastian led off, "Since the failure of the Bill 'Assisted Dying', introduced by Lord Falconer, which did not progress beyond the Committee Stage in the Lords in 2015, the problem has not gone away!"

However we now have had several euthanasia systems running for several years, so we can take take advantage of a comparison between them. Holland, Belgium, Switzerland and Oregon USA all had similar types of systems for several years, and as they they are from similar cultural backgrounds we should now be able to learn from their reports, identify any problems and see if it might be possible to launch a system in the UK. This might then take account of their experiences and suggested improvements. Euthanasia was even for a very brief time in 1996 permitted in the Northern Territory of Australia before being overturned by the Federal Australian Chamber.

UK opinion polls taken in 2015 already suggested that perhaps 80% of the population might agree to some form of assisted suicide, only around 6% were strongly opposed, though some religions, like Muslims 45%, were strongly opposed.

The Courts in the UK are apparently not interested in using individual cases to change the law to permit assisted suicide.

In my opinion they are quite correct not to be drawn into casting what is a moral judgement. That might open the flood gates for dozens of other cases, without there being any fundamental structure in place to monitor and control what goes on, that could result in chaos. An individual case cannot set up a complete system and that is what is needed.

Most Judges appear to believe that this is a legislative issue not a legal interpretation matter under article 8 of the European Convention on Human Rights.

We now need a full debate on the issues of what is a most controversial and sensitive matter.

It's a minefield of paradoxes and questions.

What right does the individual have to choose the time and manner of his going? But what right does the State have to keep alive an individual who is suffering daily, intolerable pain and indignity, against his express wishes?

What place do our own General Practitioners have in this? They are taught in their earliest training to preserve life. Is it reasonable now to suggest that we want to enlist their help in ending life? All the cases will have an element of judgement, yet the decision is binary. Yes/No! So who is going to draw the lines and where should they be?

Is the NHS also to be asked to host any suicides agreed? Or should the state refuse to be involved and allow private groups to carry out the actual work? What is the position concerning nursing homes, would they be licenced? In the same way is the patient to be allowed to die at home? Under supervision? If so whose?

We, as individuals, can rationalise whether we think something is intolerable, but we are not in that position ourselves, so how is it possible to judge whether one level of intolerability is accepted and another is not? But pain is very real to the patient.

If we are trying to ease pain then there are drugs that can do that, morphine can reduce the pain, palliative care can ease suffering, so what place does it have in the scheme? Who judges if that is an alternative?

Most people recognise that someone who, through illness or accident, is suffering may yet be still able to rationalise their position and make a 'sensible decision' , however there are many people who are psychologically unstable, or are even physically incapable of speaking; how are their views to be taken into account?

To what extent should a living will be accepted as the patient's decision in cases where he/she is unable to verbally make the case? Does it have to be renewed, or would a ten year old one signed under different circumstances, be acceptable?

There may be cases where advances in medical treatment overtake and partly control diseases, what account is taken of that?

How can the public be assured that once started euthanasia doesn't becomes a 'slippery slope'? Slowly the cases taken might be widened to also include those who are simply 'tired of life'? A view with which very few people had sympathy.

How is it possible to prevent the patient from feeling induced by relatives and medical staff to proceed with Assisted Suicide on the grounds that staying alive wastes their money or their inheritance or that public money is better spent elsewhere on the NHS, or simply that people might be bullied to end, in the other's view, a worthless life?

If anyone could apply, then should a prisoner on multiple life sentences be permitted to apply? If the State believes he is irredeemable, and will never be released, should he too not be entitled to Assisted Suicide? It would after all save the State maybe £250,000 to £500,000 over a lifetime? Or is it part of the ritual that there is to be no escape for such persons?

Several models of how individual countries have come to terms with many of these problems are now available. In fact they are generally of a similar pattern but with important differences.

It is possible even now to draw together minimum requirements that any UK system is likely to adopt. These might be.

1. The patient should be aware of his/her condition, aged 18 years or older and express a continued interest in ending life not just a spasmodic interest. The patient him/her/self has to make the formal request.
2. The patient should be suffering a terminal illness or is in an intractable intolerable condition as a result of illnesses or accident, for which there is no cure.
3. Where the patient is suffering from psychological problems, such as clinical depression, experts will be needed to evaluate if the patient is capable of making a rational decision.
4. Where the patient is incapable of making a formal request, due to a stroke/speech impairment, then an up to date living Will may be considered as evidence of consistency of thought, but even then some evidence of assent may be required.
5. The patient must be assessed as being free from any external pressure that would otherwise induce him/her to make a specific decision
6. All other options would have to be considered e.g., palliative care, new treatments, explored and rejected by the patient.

7. The patient's own physician would need to discuss with him/her the likely outcome of the existing illness and what options there are available to the patient.
8. Assessment should be undertaken over a period of time, (at least 14 days in cases of terminal illnesses) involving in-depth discussions with trained medical suicide staff.
9. Close friends or relatives should be consulted, they may have originally struggled to keep him/her alive and fought for medical attention, it's likely they may hold differing views from those of the patient, but the views of the patient would be paramount.
10. A second opinion is always required by physician before assisted suicide is accepted.
11. If there is any difference of opinion within the medical experts, reference will be made to a panel of ethical experts for consideration, consisting of medical staff, ethics consultant and two others.
12. When all these procedures have been carried out, a prescription for the chosen killing agent should be issued and given to the patient for self-administration, or in cases where the patient is unable to carry out that function some other method has to be found which did not transfer guilt or legal responsibility to others..
13. The patient even at this late stage may abort the process and choose to die naturally.
14. Death should take between 10 and 40 minutes.
15. Medical staff must always be in attendance and report any product or equipment malfunction.
16. After death a full report will be prepared and submitted to the coroner where the assessment will be made that all procedures have been carried out properly.
17. If correct procedures were not used then the matter would be passed back to the Ethics Panel, who may pass the file over for possible criminal proceedings.

In practice, although not many existing reports suggest as much, the medical profession is now well aware not only of the types of cancer and other debilitating diseases and their outcome but many also use staging, which identifies the progress of the disease or other assessment of severity and can be cross-related to similar cases. In addition some of the effects of these illnesses cause debilities such as bowel and bladder incontinence, reliance on breathing machines, needing care all the time, having to be fed, gradual restrictions on swallowing, sight and feeling reduction. It could better evaluate their physical and mental torture as they see it. It's likely then that a body of gradations will evolve from cases handled, which will lessen the area of judgement in assessment and reduce the stress on patients applying.

For a start an agreed system might start with a narrow range of illnesses/accidents and broaden this in stages as public confidence grows in the cumulative judgements made. So the range might be progressively widened.

As an example evidence from 10 years application in Oregon to 341 patients, suggested the most patients treated were between 55 and 84 years old, 97% were white, and 45% were married, most had cancer, 82% and most were enrolled in hospice 85.8%. Information suggested that primary end of life concern was 'losing autonomy', some 93% died at home. In 35% of cases the lethal prescription was never actually used, possibly a natural death overtook the case or that the patient decided against its use.

One of the main gains of this formalising procedure would be to remove pressure from the doctor who was often the patient's GP, to respond to the wishes of the relatives, distraught at the suffering of the patient to oversupply drugs or withhold water. This undoubtedly is currently happening, right at the end.

Of course the reason why this matter was referred again to the Commons was the changing nature of our society. Not only the State but the churches also refused, in many countries, to accept suicide as a patient's right to die, this was partly because pain and suffering was, earlier seen as part of God's will. But the decline in church attendances is witness to the changing views of society which is now more than ever are attuned to reducing pain and suffering wherever possible.

Sebastian received many letters in support from such patients some demanded to know why they would have to spend £5,000 to £10,000 for the trip to Switzerland. Others were cases which Sebastian and his staff had difficulty reading beyond the first paragraph, many of them heartrending. Madge was considerably affected by the description of their suffering. There were many examples cited. An outdoor fanatic from Derby went over the handlebars, broke his neck, and had no movement anywhere in his body, he needed 24 hour attention, he was unable to settle to anything, could not adjust to a life so limited. Another former GP with Multiple Sclerosis forced to retire early, unable to go to any events because of his violent body movements, had to witness his own gradual decline and loss of control and a humiliating end. It was not surprising then that the suicide rate is higher than average with MS sufferers.

Sebastian was asked, "So what's your view?"

"I think it's arrogant to deny Assisted Suicide to those we know to be in extreme pain or whose quality of life has fallen so low as to be permanently degrading. Modern techniques in assessing staging can reliably grade the severity so it would be possible to draw up a library of likely cases, to prevent abuse of the system. The picture changes daily, increasingly new drugs can give hope to some sufferers and improvements to palliative care can reduce pain. Ultimately you have to put yourself in the sufferer's position, most of us, in reality are not very brave, we rush to the dentist if a toothache lasts for longer than a few hours, what would you do with a pain 10 times greater, all day, every day, for years and years?

Basically I am a coward, I couldn't put up with that. I wouldn't have the courage to face it every day! We have to change the Law!"

Again the Lib Dem team were called in and the item was 'spun down' a brief questionnaire was created and sent out to 100 constituencies to test the public's response.

Chapter TWENTY-EIGHT – Interventions FOUR - CEO pay and Performance

Sebastian was invited to attend the annual meeting of the largest Employers' organisation.

The modern hall was located in the centre of London, it was three-quarters full.

The Meeting's objective was announced from a plastic banner which spread across the curtains at the back 'MAKING BRITAIN GREAT AGAIN!'

Sebastian was seated centre stage but towards the rear alongside 3 other 'panel' members.

The front row some four feet below the level of the stage in the auditorium was, so Sebastian was told, to be made up of the CEOs of the largest UK Companies.

The watching TV and Press were assembled at the extreme left and right of the audience seats.

The Chairman, himself a former FTSE100 Company Chairman, was seated at a table near the front of the stage towards the right.

The lectern, a modern metal version had glass sides enabling the speaker to read notes and look to left and right, was centre stage at the front.

The Chairman spent a few moments introducing the audience to the speakers and reminded the members and Press that CEOs of "something like 10% of the UK's GDP was here present." This drew a generous applause from the audience.

Sebastian moved to the Lectern.

For the first five minutes of his speech he had expressly praised British Industry for its pioneering work he particularly mentioned IT Companies for software development, and Pharmaceutical Companies for the development of new drugs, suggesting that these were shining examples of companies, training staff, creating jobs and spinning off new products.

Indeed many of the older hands were looking at the programme for the day and their watches seemingly thinking perhaps 'OK another 20 minutes of this is just bearable, I suppose we had to ask the old fruit, should have been the Tory PM but he'd have to do instead!' and settled back, they could, after all, cope with adulation.

But then the audience detected a change of pace, at first it must have sounded pretty innocuous. "I have been meaning to raise this matter publicly for some time".

Sebastian standing on the rostrum, hesitated, there was a pause, they waited. Was he ill? Had he lost his notes? He looked at the Chairman, he surveyed the audience. He spotted a number of CEO's whom he knew by name. They were looking at him expectantly. He calmly took out of his pocket what looked like another speech. The total time elapsed would have been less than fifteen seconds. But it had an electrifying effect.

"I can find no direct evidence that substantial bonuses paid to CEOs of large FTSE100 companies have any direct effect on the performances of the companies which employ them."

TV crews had been alerted by the silence, took notice, they crowded towards the platform, they knew that this was inflammatory stuff. The stewards tried to hold them back but they formed a semicircle in front of Sebastian, the Chairman looked concerned.

"On the contrary I find that they exaggerate the importance of short term profits at the expense of longer term development.

The bosses think no-one is watching them. They are wrong.

I find that, high salaries and bonuses are massively divisive in terms of the sense of fairness in companies as between their earnings and those of the bottom of these companies.

The bosses think this does not matter. They are wrong.

I find that, despite what had been hoped and expected, the major institutional investors failed to haul back excessive pay deals, primarily because they too are wedded to the same short term objectives.

The major pension funds think we don't notice, they are wrong.

I find that overall this attention to the short term has had a dramatic and undesired effect on capital investment and productivity throughout the UK such that, we here are hopelessly behind our main competitors of France and Germany.

Bosses seem to think no-one notices. They are wrong.

I find that the odium that attaches to bosses being paid bonuses whilst their companies make losses is substantially justified.

These bosses seem to image no-one notices. They are wrong.

In my opinion these bonuses are no longer 'fit for purpose'. Nor will it be possible simply to add the bonus to the salary and hope that no-one will notice. I notice.

The only shred of evidence that has ever been put forward in support of such excessive pay, is that the companies have to compete with the USA and Globally in order to get the best CEOs.

But that's where we came in a few moments ago. Isn't it? If high paid CEOs actually were able to translate that into high company performance with high investment, high product and patent development and high productivity then I would not be here.

The former Tory Prime Minister tried to persuade CEOs to subject themselves to the decision of the shareholders, that didn't help as the other Directors who are there defer to any strong CEO, there was also an attempt to have some employee say in fixing the CEO's pay but that didn't happen either, did it?

Accordingly Mr Chairman I draw to your attention my intention of only allowing any pay including bonuses of more than 50 times the average salary and paid to board members as tax deductible provided only they can be justified as adding value for the company - a linkage proved in terms of improved results in figures, and be fully audited.

What could be fairer that that? What would you have to fear from that?

Thank you Mr Chairman for the opportunity for me to come here and express my views.

I will be here to answer any questions you or other individuals may have."

With that he turned and left the lectern and returned to his seat alongside the other panel members who were yet to speak.

There was a general booing and shouting "Get out!" from the audience. There was immediate pandemonium, some stood up, arms shot up to speak from around the room. A few made for the exits.

The other three remaining panel speakers looked extremely uncomfortable, presumably not only would this ruin the timetable so they wouldn't know if they would be given a reduced time to speak, nor if the audience would be in receptive mood, nor if there were going to be any audience left to listen to what they had to say.

The front row of seats in the hall conferred amongst themselves in little groups. One of them stood up to speak.

The Chairman managed to get the stewards to usher away the TV lights crews and Press who also demanded to be able to speak. He then stood up and appealed for calm. He assured the members of the audience that the Prime Minister had high-jacked his spot and it was not the speech that he had been sent by email just that morning. "But as he is here you may as well get him to justify his outrageous statements!"

Sebastian moved back to the lectern "With your permission Mr Chairman, I would like a link from the PC I have here to the screen? And I would like to bring on my files".

The Chairman nodded the, in-house IT man connected Sebastian's PC, Sebastian scrolled down to 'CEO's Pay'. Bill and Madge appeared wheeling an open wired trolley which must have had 20 or 30 differently coloured files. Bill, like a conjurer seeking to prove that the files really did exist, picked up one of those files and held it up. It read 'BUILDO-FLEX' 'Housebuilder' He placed it up against the side of the trolley so that all could see. He did the same with five other files. They were all large UK FTSE100 companies. Companies whom Sebastian knew would be there.

There was an angry reaction from the front row of CEOs "This is private information – how did you get hold of that? It's outrageous it must be a breach of the Data Protection Act!" They turned one to another "He must have our Tax Returns too, he cannot do that!"

Sebastian again turned to the Chairman "With your permission Sir?"

The Chairman realised that he had no option now but to allow him to continue, so waved his hand "But Mr Edwards I am going to limit this to 20 minutes, these other panel members have been very patent so far!"

Sebastian clapped his hands and two smartly suited men appeared whom he introduced. "This is Mr Clive Woodthorpe a senior partner in the second tier firm of accountants. This is James Strongworthy we asked him to buy £200 of shares in each of the top FTSE100 companies and to use, if necessary, the Freedom of Information Act to obtain details of CEOs earnings, he is also a Director of the 'Highest paid CEO Unit' a consultancy."

"Now let me refresh you with the main problems associated with these huge payments, then perhaps one of the CEOs of as FTSE100 company would like to challenge me?" – Sebastian paused then continued, "All the following have been fully checked through" he proceeded to run through the bullet points quickly

1.   Linkage. Sebastian explained "It is extraordinarily difficult to cross link any individual CEO with any event or decision that he alone makes and then track this to a conclusion. This is because these sized companies have several layers of committees and managers each struggling to put forward ideas, request funds, develop new products, recommend buying new companies or selling others. Most FTSE100 companies have a complex structure and a strategic plan already in place. It's very unlikely that with a good quality board a new CEO will achieve much if anything in the first year. Thereafter at best it's likely to have been a team effort."

2.   His action likely to be opportunistic. "If he overrules the board it will likely be of the destructive or opportunistic kind. Typically a CEO's pay will be at least partly profit related. So he can look around for easy pickings to improve results, it's not usually that difficult. The monthly list of operating results will give him a hint, if he can cut out a few red numbers he thinks he'll be doing fine! Moreover the Financial Press will praise him as a 'man of action' shares will recover a couple of % and everyone hopes that it will temporarily take the pressure off the company to do something.. You will all remember the Boston Consulting Group categorisation of a company's products into, stars, dogs, cash cows and question marks. On the basis of Market Share and Market Growth. Unfortunately these are subjective depending on how tightly you define the terms (in a district, town or whole country and competitors' products don't always exactly match do they?) An incoming CEO might well assign a particular product to be a 'dog' whilst others still think it will come good and assign it a 'question mark'. Witness the simplest case of all, Marks and Spencer tried at least twice to establish its self in France, Paris particularly. Every time M & S hit bad times, whoof, Paris gets the chop! The Financial Press are jubilant! Something has been done! The shares go up. Probably a bit more bonus for the new CEO! But wait a moment don't the French wear clothes? Of course they do! There is certainly a market there, but the CEO gives up and sacrifices huge start up and redundancy costs, most of which have been already

reserved. He takes the easy way out. So everyone around the boardroom mutters 'sunk costs' which makes it all apparently OK."

3.   Drafting of the Bonus Rules. "Of course it just depends how tightly the bonus rules are drawn up., they will have to try to exclude matters arising from outside the company, like exchange rates, interest rates, employment legislation and accounting re-classifications. They should also exclude windfall profits generated by the previous CEO. The Rules could be based on dubious criteria, how do you unlock the effect of a take-over? If the bonus is based on Earnings per Share then do you allow the CEO to gain from share buyback? So the company buys its own shares, so there are fewer shares in the market for the same profit, so of course the share price goes up but does it have anything to do with the CEO, probably not, all FTSE100 companies are plagued by brokers offering advice, but, frankly, it's not much more complex than hailing an ice cream van."

4.   Use of Ratios. "Ratios are now the modern magic to use as the basis of a bonus but they can all be easily manipulated like return on capital, other payment system like, stock options and deferred payments just make the calculation more complex and even less related to performance. So if most of the ratios are fine but the company makes a huge loss what does that mean?"

5.   Lack of Objectivity. "So who fixes these crazily high payments, well the remuneration committee, who are however you look at it up to their eyes in conflicts of interest over a third of them are themselves directors.   And as little fleas on the back of bigger fleas their own extraordinarily high fees would be affected. Those that are external frankly will have no idea exactly what makes the company tick better. Do Shareholders help? But they have also got their hands on the same loot! It's possible I may be missing a conversation or two, maybe the largest institutional investor is phoning the CEO before the AGM, 'Come on Bill you have had a poor year, cut the crap and reduce your bonus to nil!" That's not what seems to happen but the last thing any Institutional investor wants is open war. He knows perfectly well if he accuses the company of grossly overpaying either he will be totally ignored by the CEO or that the City does take notice and the share price drops and he may just have lost his pensioner clients £40 or £50 Million in share value".

6.   Multiples. "The resulting multiples, the number of average earners that can be contained in the CEOs earnings show utter contempt for the average person in your company. It creates a sense of injustice"

Sebastian continued "You know I am losing interest in this discussion, I have a hundred better things to do.

There is little discernible link between directors' pay and corporate success.

The pay the CEOs get does not do what I want, or your country needs, higher investment, improved productivity, increased R & D, patents, better training, more apprentices, retaining skills, developing new products, strengthening brands and generally getting added value for the company. Nor does it recognise the efforts of those within the company, indeed they will naturally ask, why can't I have a bonus system too and soon like bankers a certain level of bonus becomes a 'right'.

A specialist consultancy has worked out that 'bonus payments increased at roughly double the rate of EPS and company profits between 2000 and 2013' The FTSE100 CEO Total Remuneration received as a multiple of average employee earnings rose from 69.81 in 2002 to 149.58 in 2014.

Nor do I buy the idea that you have to receive ridiculous salaries and bonuses to keep globally competitive, evidence suggests that fewer than 1% of top companies hired CEOs from competitors, some 80% were recruited internally. That's what boards should be doing training up their own talent, expanding their tasks until ready to take over. Evidence we have suggests internal promotion is better for the company too.

There is simply no doubt at all that CEOs pay has increased at a faster rate than performance. One analyst suggested that just 1.3% of the change in annual bonuses can be explained by the change in pre-tax profits.

The whole system is bunkum. Complete BUNKUM"

Sebastian paused and looked at those on the front row.

He now began the challenge "OK so who wants to go through their files in Public?? Come on now those who shouted loudest must surely have a point?"

You Sir are you not the CEO of BUILDO-FLEX' 'Housebuilder'?"

Sebastian motioned to Bill to pass him the file! The CEO got up and walked out.

Sebastian motioned to his PC "We can flip through the key points again if you wish? – Right any Questions?"

A silence gripped the audience, most began packing up their papers.

Sebastian leaned over the Lectern "Don't look so worried Ladies and Gentlemen nothing will happen this tide, not with this wind. But we have the measure of you, soon and not too long now, we know exactly what we have to do.

Chairman its time you got to work, haul them in one by one and sort them out!"

With that Sebastian's team left, on the way out he apologised to the other panel members still sitting there waiting for the call to speak.

On returning to Lib Dem HQ Sebastian asked Dan Stirling and John Thorne to 'spin down'.

Of course bits of this seminar leaked out to the Financial Press particularly **'Bunkum'**

On the following day, all the Financial Press were "Outraged at Political Interference – stating the CEOs were lining up to move their Headquarters out of the UK"

Sebastian briefly responded "Well I hope that these moves are widely reported allowing the UK public to find alternative home products! If the FTSE100 companies don't come to their senses – then we will legislate and that will be part of any future New Coalition deal."

Chapter TWENTY-NINE – Interventions FIVE – UK version of Pousada or Parador?

In another of his Friday afternoon Press Releases, Sebastian Edwards floated the possibility of launching a new use for some Stately Homes or other important buildings which were run down but which could not be adequately either transformed into other uses or were not acceptable to the UK National Trusts.

There are often suitable cases which are neither furnished to the acceptable level nor had a large enough endowment to be able to provide for future maintenance costs, which the National Trusts often demand where possible, that's because they try to make each unit cover its own costs and cannot take on those which continually leak money..

This idea is to create a chain of luxury hotels across the UK , using and at the same time preserving the buildings.

"Like many other UK residents, I have taken short breaks in Pousadas de Portugal or Paradores de Espana and have been impressed by their ability to convert or adapt castles, palaces, fortresses, convents, or what we would call stately homes, into hotels.

Here, instead of allowing any remaining historic buildings to be demolished or essentially sold off for private use we ought to borrow a page from these groups in Spain and Portugal to see if we can make better use of these, often iconic, buildings and get them into public use.

They are important for three reasons, firstly that they might be useful in increasing tourism, particularly of foreigners wishing to take in the genuine flavour of our past and, secondly they provide an opportunity for any UK citizen to 'Live the Life of a Lord'. It's most unlikely that new houses of this kind will ever be permitted to be built in the locations ever again. They are often in the countryside, or in cities where they have become part of the fabric of the place. They therefore present opportunities to allow anyone to indulge for a time in a different age, for which perhaps their ancestors needed to pay homage. Thirdly it provides an opportunity to protect, long term buildings, often representative tiny period of our history but of considerable importance.

In Spain the system was started in 1928 and there are now nearly 100 Paradors. It is still Sate run. Pousada in Portugal were started in 1941, the idea was to create hotels that were both rustic and genuinely Portuguese, there are some 44 installed in historic buildings. In Portugal the operation was initially run by the State but latterly, in 2003, the business was partly privatised.

In its application to the UK a company, once established, might consider all types of legal structures. For example, one of those that might be suitable would have been Wentworth Woodhouse, the so-called largest private house in the country, with 365 rooms. It was built from 1743 to 1810 by the Fitzwilliam family and its development became notorious in a political battle where senior Labour Cabinet Ministers insisted that coal mining be carried out right up to the doors of the place, in a show of class hatred that few others thought was sensible. There are several other structures throughout the UK which could be bought by the State, converted and then run as a group by private catering or hotel companies.

It's likely that this format might also fit many existing visitor sites which are not ideally suitable for day visitors because of nearby competitors or because of their location. There the family owners could live on in a separate wing.

It's an opportunity for ordinary people to be able to live the life of a Lord. It should add another layer of interest for foreign tourists. As we move into the age of meritocracy future generations can wonder at the huge private wealth spent in this way and the massive inequality which pervaded those times."

The idea featured in the centre pages of Sunday papers. Considerable interest was aroused in guessing which properties might be suitable. The Old Queen Elizabeth's Castle of Mey in Scotland was first choice! Many minor Dukes still grappling with trying to pay heavy maintenance costs came forward. Several hotel groups expressed interest.

Chapter THIRTY – Interventions SIX - Productivity is Everything

Sebastian spoke to some invited Financial Press reporters.

"We need your help to find out what's going wrong with the UK's productivity. It seems to be a mystery that no-one can resolve.

It was Paul Krugman who famously said 'Productivity isn't everything, but in the long run it is almost everything.'

Nobody seems able to explain what's going wrong, but unless we do find out and address it as a problem, we are going to suffer. The most likely result is a steadily falling £ as we have to find a way of discounting our poor productivity compared to our competitors, so if a Frenchman produces 27% more per hour than an English worker, then sooner or later our products will become overpriced and uncompetitive obliging us to, in effect, devalue!

So what's the measure of the problem?

Productivity and living standards have stalled since 2007, that is since the recession began. In international comparisons we are some 30% behind Germany, France and the USA. and behind Italy and Canada, of the G7 countries, only Japan is behind us.

We, in the UK, can only obtain faster growth and increase GDP through increased productivity or other creative initiatives. Without an increase of productivity the UK is going to suffer long-term. Workers need to produce more to earn higher wages.

Another associated worry is that when the £ exchange rate drops, as it has done from time to time often for months at a time, there is virtually no immediate and sustained increase in trade as you might expect, instead Manufacturers appear to take the extra profit from a drop in sterling.

There are of course 'trade-offs'. For example, French labour laws encourage companies to invest in capital instead of hiring workers who are correspondingly more difficult to get rid of than in the UK but this may be one reason why the unemployment rate there at 10.5% is almost double that in the UK. So, the more flexible UK's employment laws, might be encouraging lower investment and lower productivity.

Of all the regions only London stands out above the poor average. Northern Ireland and Wales are the worst and only just above them is the West Midlands, once the workshop of the world, remember that? The West Midlands was a centre for industry during the 19th century, leading the world in industrial design and innovation. As a result, the region was dubbed the 'Workshop of the World'. Well it's not that now!

There have been many possible reasons put forward; these include, a) a low rate of investment in plant and equipment over several years, b) a low rate of lending during the financial crisis 2007-2014 to the most efficient firms, c) once profitable industries are now in decline, d) slowing rates of design, innovation and creativity, e) the working population is getting older and slower at work and taking more time off, f) companies are holding on to skilled labour even though work has declined because they cannot afford to train new staff; g) bankers being unwilling to pull the plug on 'zombie businesses' which would crystallise their losses, h) entrepreneurial zeal is lacking, or technical skills are missing at management level to recognise opportunities, i) it's also possible that our employment figures are overstated as self-employment has blurred the issue, j) certain industries like banking and airports are more closely regulated, needing more hours for the same output reducing our productivity, k) lop-sided training providing more degrees, some of which cannot be used, rather than vocation skills that can, l) low rates of research and development leading to a lack of production changes using new technology, m) foreign firms coming in are using the UK for 'slave' factories. At these foreign-owned plants, manning levels, skills, pay, capital required and output are mostly determined abroad so improvements occur at the behest of their engineering directors, senior grade work is often not carried out locally.

However if we imagine that most foreign owned firms are also major exporters into the larger EU market place, they probably are competitive, since any long term fall off in productivity would affect their sales. By deduction this must mean that the average smaller UK owned firms selling predominantly into the home market have probably even lower productivity and are even less able to compete on the open market.

We know that productivity is poor across very nearly all sectors.

Until we know the reason for our low productivity, we cannot tell what we, the government, can do to try to fix it. Of course we have some ideas which most agree with, like developing digital and transport infrastructures and there is as always the crying need for an increase in vocational training which would also increase wages among the lower paid. But we need to identify causes, then to produce an improvement plan, Ultimately this was one of the reasons for creating the Regions. Regional Assemblies have to become the drivers of efficiency, attracting new industries and tying in the vocational training needed, having surveyed the needs of employers with colleges or private training suppliers".

The Press reacted immediately.

As Sebastian had expected they honed in of the words 'slave factories' and tried to assess their productivity.

A Productivity Plan had been published by the government in 2015 but appeared to have stalled. George Osborne's comments as Chancellor of the Exchequer, earlier that year, were remembered 'We don't export enough; we don't train enough; we don't save enough; we don't manufacture enough; we certainly don't build enough and far too much of our activity in our nation is concentrated here in the centre of London!'

Several of the more weighty columnists interviewed both the major employers groups and the major unions.

Several firms of consultants eagerly fell on the raised interest to set up seminars on 'productivity'.

Leading figures in the regions began to understand that they now had much greater powers than previously under the LEPS to increase the creation rate of new jobs and businesses.

In response to the increasing demand for an explanation, several ministries applied pressure on the Business Development Ministry to hold a High Level Task Force, made up of business sector groups, MDs of selected companies, training organisations and academics to review the causes and make specific recommendations.

Chapter THIRTY-ONE – Interventions SEVEN, and spinning on

At the following Friday Lib Dem meeting, Sebastian pointed out that the 'spin down' of topics appeared to have worked so the next thing to do was to co-ordinate it and set it up on a professional basis.

"Here's what we can do,

We know now that it's best either for a Cabinet Member or prominent Lib Dem to pick a topic and give it some public airing or to pluck one from a number of views and opinions which pass before us from the Press or TV

We should then research the topic, write a brief paper on it as back-up and see if it is suitable for spinning.

We then prepare a very short list of questions, options or strong/weak opinions. We test these out in one Focus in one lead area, review the answers to see if the questions are clear or ambiguous, refine the questions.

Then ask a minimum of 100 constituencies (based on the pre STV areas) to run the item, an exact copy of that prepared or amended in the lead area.

The results must be easy to copy across to a summary sheet for the constituency, but it is better if done by the recipient on line, where he can access the briefing paper and register directly.

The gist of the topic must not be directly hostile to the government eg 'This Govt has been woefully deficient in doing X hasn't it? Y/N' but positive and possibly graded 'Do you believe that Student fees should be reduced for those degrees like engineering where the numbers need to double? Grade importance Low 1-2-3-4-5 High.

There are several purposes behind this first to lift Focus from a street type political sheet; to aim to capture interest across wider fields and topics, to link in with national Lib Dem campaigns, to make sure we are seen not just as Political but interested in people's views.

It should also work the other way around, any listed constituency that believes it has found a particular matter of interest and has done its own questionnaire, can suggest that this be taken up nationally, so that this also becomes driven to respond to public demand. We should then single out which of these should gain Lib Dem and possibly Coalition support.

There are many peripheral matters of interest that might be developed for example:

Flags and Anthems, are these due for a makeover, maybe 'God Save the Queen' should be used only when the monarch or family are there? Should 'Danny Boy' be officially used in Northern Ireland? Should new UK 'faith flags' be encouraged a mixture of the Union Jack in one quadrant with Star of David hanging free, or Green Crescent etc. for other faiths, perhaps we need to adapt to being British AND Muslim etc? This might allow minority groups to feel more connected, after all to many of these groups the Union Jack represents an imperial past.

Union of the Unemployed. Recently Job Centres have become much more rigorous in assessing if enough effort has been made to find a job, if he or she is deemed not to have tried, the applicant can be sanctioned and loose benefits. The unemployed are being increasingly being challenged. In one case a woman was in danger of being sanctioned if she turned the job down or worse losing the children to an aggressive social services if she accepted. Can Job Centres operate as both helpers and supporters and job seeker pushers and enforcers? Some think not! Do we need a Union of the Employed to look after the interests of those out of work and to put pressure on all levels of government to bring in more work to that area and maybe, provide better training?

Touring Culture Hubs. Our Museums and Galleries are overwhelmingly based in London. Should we oblige all such London institutions to have a permanent touring culture hub so that art, and items are brought to the regions? Each region could provide rent free an open building near main Motorway intersections, to be filled by continuous exhibits or visits from Key London based items like Ballet and Opera.

Dissolution Honours. Now that there are going to be no more peerages created, then how does an outgoing Prime Minister thank his long suffering and probably underpaid staff a) not at all there's no need – pay them more b) award an entirely new decoration 'for political services' or use an existing award like O.B.E? Are we giving away too many knighthoods too quickly to sports, but how many top scientists are awarded, how many that really make us great in first or world class businesses

Family Courts. Should family courts be open to the public? We can still protect the names and retain humanity in disclosure. What other public safeguard is there that "Justice is seen to be done" Perhaps initially just the press should be admitted? How do we know that social services are taking a balanced view when taking children into care. Here the press has a valuable part to play. How do we know that later care is adequate? Why do these courts justify separate treatment?

Legalising certain drugs. What's the public reaction to Legalising Cannabis and Prostitution. Here we have to be careful to distinguish short term benefits, like elimination of the needs for thefts to buy the drugs, until that is they find another drug to use and steal for, against the long term effects on the individual and steady decline into perhaps mental chaos. And if you are in favour of licensed brothels, can I set one up next door to YOU? We don't want NIMBYs, it is OK provided it's not in my back-yard. Where would you put them? How do we ensure that prostitutes are not imported against their will? Who ensures that dirty money does not increase drug gangs? Who inspects?

Link in to Lib Dem TV ad. Often Lib Dems at the top have only vague indicators of things going wrong, we mention that in our political advert but we need to sustain interest and drill down. So is mental Health provision improving or not, collections of real case studies can make a point, so maybe Focuses should ask 'Do you know of cases where parent or patients are seriously concerned by poor services? Waiting months for treatment? Treated more than 70 miles from home? Desperate situations of risks to others and the patient? Or maybe it's a failing Ambulance service, but the real reason is a couple of A & E are blocked solid and ambulances are waiting for hours unable to get away. To get action we need chapter and verse. Please get the Constituencies working on these!

For these Questionnaires to work and be co-ordinated and for the results to be useable, we probably need a minimum of 50,000 respondents and we need to classify them in 4 ways, 1. Lib Dem activists, 2. members, 3. those signed up to Focus Research Groups (not members) and Finally 4. random members of the public.

Basically Lib Dem members are likely to vote in sympathy with the Party, but the Research Groups and the Public are not – so it's their voice we listen to first of all.

See how much more powerful it is to say 'Look we have the research, 40,000 people think this is a good idea!' It isn't quite instant politics but it is catching the interest, show we relate to their concerns and will try to work on it! Look we have incredible advantage being in Government and we are the party of innovation but it's no use just arguing in the Quad, those are mostly Tory proposals we try to halt, we have to be more proactive!

What I want is an upgraded and enlivened 'Focus' dealing with proper issues of the time, showing the public Lib Dems are interested in their problems."

Dan Stirling, the Party Leader agreed to take over this personally, it meant moving away from Conference resolutions defining Party Policy, although they could still be used in conjunction with the new system.

It was agreed to put it before the Executive Committee who agreed to let it proceed on an experimental basis. They began to collect a list of possible suitable Spin Up and Spin Down topics. They in turn would put it to the Spring Conference in early March which would then mean that all Constituencies would become involved.

"It would be a huge benefit for us if we could have in effect our own polling group, it could also give indications of where we could do better and areas to avoid! But the central idea should not be overlooked, to retain a central position we have to also nurture radical change, whether or not Lib Dems are in Government." Sebastian emphasised.

By Mid-March the e-mail systems were positively humming with ideas and questionnaires. Sebastian hoped that it would continue long after he ended his term as PM.

Chapter THIRTY-TWO - Royal Commission Banking & Financial Services

Sebastian had always worried that the Royal Commission would get shelved pushed out of the way. He expected that the Banks would pay heavily to avoiding its tentacles, there was real concern from the Bankers that many directors and managers would be named for their part in the debacle, shamed and excluded from similar work by the FCA, the Financial Conduct Authority.

In 2020 many unnamed people, with no doubt more than a little guilty conscience in the horrendous collapse of the banking system, paid for a full page advert in the Financial Times which deplored the whole idea of such a Commission, asking all bankers to 'reveal nothing because there is nothing to reveal' and even offering a help line to any individuals who thought they might be accused of serious crimes, to guide them to the best and fastest legal brains and so avoid prosecution.

Another similar advert offered to those bankers, worried by the Royal Commission, job opportunities in France, Germany and the USA.

Sebastian read the report handed to him. It made grim reading. The Bankers were in revolt. There was little doubt from reading the Press that, tactically, they had, as a group, decided to face out the Coalition Government relying on the known preference of the dominant Tories in the Cabinet to do as little as possible to change the situation. The Bankers regarded any change as restrictive and as a restraint of their right to trade in an open market, what's past was gone, it was their responsibility to their shareholders to optimise their profits.

The members of the Commission had started off on a positive note suggesting that, by cleaning up the City and gaining the stamp of approval of the Royal Commission, they would likely pick up more new business for the City. Of particular concern was the notion that sooner or later the Eurozone group might exclude the UK Financial Services sector from their privileged status which the UK negotiators had previously won for them in 2017. The Eurozone needed transfer of capital from surplus to deficit countries and one of the ways of doing so was to encourage companies from the fastest growing fringes of the EC where new products could be financed and launched with the City's help.

But the major Banks refused to permit the intrusive questions which the Commission had prepared. So the Commission changed direction and just used the information of which they were aware, particularly the Parliamentary

Commission on Banking Standards 2013 as a building block and moved ahead from there.

The commission reviewed what they thought the finance sector was supposed to do and concluded that it was as follows; 1) It operates the payments systems without which most transactions could not occur 2) It channels funds from individual savers to larger companies so they can expand. 3) It creates other products such as investment funds that spread the investments and spread savers risks, 4) It provides liquidity to the market by encouraging the sale of assets and indeed companies themselves 5) It helps the individuals and companies to manage their risk and also to even out future cash flows and foreign currency.

The Commission concluded that some of these objectives were not being performed very well.

The Commission then reviewed the major problems that had occurred partly because of the financial crisis and shortfalls of the sector revealed by many critics. They prepared detailed lists of the apparent anomalies that had taken place.

The main problem, they concluded, had been that in 2008 the structure of the UK Banking system was fragile and that 'entrepreneurial' as some would say or 'greedy' as others would have it senior Directors, simply took advantage of the weak and fragmented regulatory systems in order to increase their profitability. The responsibility for review and control was divided between the Treasury, the Bank of England and the Financial Services Authority.

The real cause was not difficult to unearth. Chat rooms comments in the USA had abounded with gossip that Morgan Stanley employees had called the dollop of toxic assets that it sold as variously 'Subprime meltdown' or just 'Shitbag', the sellers were amazed that professional buyers would fall for it without subjecting it to any kind of due diligence. It was just madness unlimited.

Whilst the financial services sector had been comparatively small in the 1980's by 2000 it had surged to 8% of GDP roughly double that of France and Germany and yet again it had increased to 12% by 2012. So the share of UK GDP was then 5 times that of the USA. There had been a huge expansion in the UK and it was insecurely based, as the control regime was not yet in position, to monitor the behaviour of the banks or to protect the customers.

Most larger Banks had decided on a feast of absorbing ever larger companies, often using the strength of their Balance Sheets to create more shares which required ever higher dividends to feed their share prices. Managers were being paid huge bonuses for doing what everyone else saw was just the same old job. But in fact it was a culture that took hold, the directors insisted that they needed to make more profits because that's what the shareholders wanted and expected. They had to pay Bonuses just to keep their staff who were free to move to the highest bidder. Indeed even when bust they still insisted on paying and for 2015 all UK Banks had indeed paid out £5 bn in bonuses

It became almost a parallel economy to the rest of the UK. But it was sucking in the brightest brains to the detriment of, say, manufacturing, and leading the huge increase in London House prices, all the while walking the financial tightrope as the banks were undercapitalised. Also extensive new derivatives systems were created to the detriment of other high productive investments. Although, after the 2008 crisis, steps were taken to strengthen the Banks reserves and to make them more resilient to withstand future shocks, in most cases this had been by some Banks simply capitalising the money given it by the government to use to increase funding for businesses, or paying this out in dividends, so, much of it was never passed on as lending to businesses. This meant that the financial recovery in the UK had lasted longer than it might have as expanding companies were unable to secure the finance needed.

The most radical proposal had always been to separate out the 'retail' normal branch banking, from the 'casino' banking which was a mountain of risks. Those risks had never really been explained to shareholders. Eventually it was considered too radical a step and under the Vickers Commission it was agreed to ring fence certain operations hoping that there would be no cross contamination. The Structural reforms to take effect to this change took place in 2017. The Royal Commission confirmed that position.

It was noted that the government had felt obliged to set up a 'British Business Bank plc' to plug the gap with the larger banks had conspicuously failed to do in targeting funding for companies with a turnover of up to £25 M. This had been established by the Lib Dem Secretary of State for Business Innovation and Skills, in 2014. Other competitors lamely tried to claim it had created unfair competition!

The more difficult problems came with personal responsibility. For judging on past banking misbehaviour if ring fencing was truly important, it had turned out to be about as much good as one layer of chicken fencing would be against a determined and clever fox.

These misbehaviours seemed to happen in isolation to anyone and everything else around them. That was because the Corporate Banking culture was corrupted by the huge bonuses and it seemed that the actions of individuals were scarcely supervised. At least the few cases that came to court that was what both the managers and the individuals charged appeared to be saying such as with the forex rigging and 'libor' rigging episodes. There was corporate amnesia and corporate distancing from the messes revealed.

The European intervention did not appear to help much, it simply stated that only a certain portion of earnings could be paid in bonuses. The reaction of most UK Bankers had been to hugely increase the fixed salary proportion of the staff earnings; this, it was pointed out tirelessly by all bankers whenever challenged on bonuses, simply increased fixed costs so that when troubled times were encountered there was less 'fat' that could be squeezed from the earnings figure. Overall this made it more, not less, difficult for British Banks more to cope with financial adversity.

The Royal Commission was specifically requested to name names, identifying the initiators of all the problems. These included those who had managed or rather abused the so called asymmetric knowledge. This meant a banks client being confronted by a bank manager suggesting that other Bank products might be suitable. But it was generally agreed that the client could not evaluate fairly the costs and benefits; on some occasions the obtaining of a loan was dependent on taking these Bank products for which the Bank manager would himself gain a bonus. If it wasn't a condition then it was clearly indicated that it might influence the granting of the loan because similar products would be required..

The list included miss-selling of PPI, credit default swaps, Libor and Forex scandals, bonus driven trading of derivatives, crushing of smaller businesses so the bank first ensured its own money was secured irrespective of the needs of the business clients or its creditors. There were implications of a stitch up between Banks and Liquidators particularly over the former owners buy back in, where the latter had to curiously raise the funds needed to pay off the bank and of course the liquidators.

They attempted to track down responsibility to individual Bank employees but the banking fraternity held solid and refused to reveal exact responsibility zones. However the Royal Commission was able to state that 'in all probability' the named positions which they had extracted were those responsible for the asymmetry problem and indeed the buying of rubbish bonds. They left the FCA to carry out checks and assess whether this amounted to breeches of the rules and to assess if laws had been broken and perhaps to prosecution through the CPS. Some 100 positions were identified in the draft of the Royal Commissions report which was known to circulate in November 2019.

This was immediately hit by the fury of the large Banking Corporations which, including the fringe financial operations, numbered some 250 separate businesses in total. As a group they threatened to sue on behalf of all and every mention of the positions and names. The Royal Commission, lacking direct evidence of wrongdoing and proof of culpability, had no alternative but to withdraw the list.

With that died any hopes of gaining any worthwhile convictions for those that had caused the banking meltdown.

The Royal Commission had however expected that response and sought new ways of hitting at the bedrock of the 'culture of greed' as they so aptly put it. They targeted 'personal responsibility' they wanted to subject bankers to the same sort of code of ethics which applied to all professions.

First, of these were to insist that each Bank or other Financial operation, nail definitively the organisational structure, post by post defining the scope of authority of the individual, and the responsibilities and checks required at every level so that managers in charge of individuals could not simply ignore infringements which sometimes caused £ Millions in losses.

Second, was to state categorically exactly how the bonus was to be applied, who would share in the sums awarded and exactly why this level of skill was over and above what was normally to be expected to be that of an ordinary salaried employee. The bank must state what additional profit was earned and why and how this related to the bonus proposed.

Third, was that any bonuses must be paid evenly over 5 years and must be more than 50% paid in shares. Undrawn bonuses were to stand as surety for the good behaviour of the individual and any breach of the rules should carry a penalty against such moneys.

Fourth, every bank was to carry out not only a yearly performance review of every person above a certain amount earned, together with a job evaluation which should describe the role and the level of competence required.

Fifth, all CEOs bonuses was to include the 'mal' clause, to the effect that if the Bank suffered losses, then shareholders would have the right to claim back any bonuses paid or even under certain circumstances to claim back a proportion of the loss.

Sixth, every banker achieving manager status or receiving a payment of £100 K plus has to undergo training by an outside group and at the end of which should sign an ethical undertaking – A code of Conduct of the following kind.

1. Treating all customers, colleagues and counterparties with respect and acting with integrity;
2. Developing and maintaining their professional knowledge and acting with due skill, care and diligence; considering the risks and implications of their actions and advice, and holding themselves accountable for them and their impact;
3. Being open and cooperative with the regulators; complying with all current regulatory and legal requirements;
4. Paying due regard to the interests of customers and treating them fairly;
5. Observing and demonstrating proper standards of market conduct at all times;
6. Acting in an honest and trustworthy manner, being alert to and managing potential conflicts of interest; and
7. Treating information with appropriate confidentiality and sensitivity.

This is to be mandatory and breaches of these rule when reported to the authority will mean that the individual may be prevented from carrying out any work in the UK Banking Sector.

Seventh, that only real employees should be permitted to operate on behalf of and for customers, those operating from within shell companies must be clearly indicated as not working for any other company.

Eighth, records should be kept of all bonuses earned by the individual and the basis and criteria, any failures which result in reworking the calculation shall be recoverable for 5 years.

Ninth, that although procedures already existing to prevent the City being used as a money laundering hub, this had not been applied sufficiently diligently suggesting a significant flow of dirty money into London and thereafter into the London Property market. Proposals were made to tighten all these procedures.

Other non-Banking Financial Services were also reviewed and that included, Fund Management Companies, Investment Managers, Fringe Banking operations, Mortgage Brokers and Accountants, Actuaries and particularly Solicitors.

All professional bodies involved in Financial Services such as take-overs were very heavily criticised for failure to quote for work properly for example on major mergers, or work on first application for Stock Exchange listing. Particular examples of charging high fees included; overcharging using 10 hours for an 8 hour day and often substituting junior staff for more costly senior staff. Sleight of hand practices included abstracting a fee from funds raised for a floatation without the clear approval of the client. It is often unclear how much of the floatation goes to pay off the previous owner who scampers away and how much if left to the company's use.

All work quotes should be clear and precisely valued, all time sheets must be available to the client on request to justify any bills supplied.

The Royal Commission expressed the view that the failure of most Banks to co-operate suggested that the Banking Culture, which had partly lead to all the various failings exposed, had not in fact been overcome and should therefore be legally enforced, particularly personal legal responsibility for the actions of every person involved in the Financial Services sector and that of their subordinates.

The report hit the Cabinet Table with an almighty political crash which threatened the Coalition immediately.

The Lib Dems chorused their disapproval of the Bankers failure to reform, for the most part the Tories accused the Lib Dems of attempting to carry out a witch hunt over events that had taken place over a decade ago and that they were destroying the only hugely profitable and highly productive UK business sector. Lib Dems counted by stating that all Euro Countries knew of the weaknesses of the UK banking system and without it being properly cleaned up the Eurozone would likely withdraw the City's privileged position and the UK Financial Services sector would in any case collapse as its failings were widely published.

Sebastian felt he had no alternative but to wave the traditional rules of Cabinet joint responsibility so both parties agreed that the debate or discussion should take place openly.

John Wires MP the Lib Dem former Business Minister who had previously negotiated some tightening of the previous rules resulting in a voluntary agreement was asked to negotiate a settlement, as otherwise it was clear that the split would eliminate any hopes of forming an agreed policy on the matter and with that the Coalition could flounder.

Most of the Cabinet were aware that it was Sebastian's initial intervention that had specifically included the Royal Commission in the Coalition Agreement.

But he was also aware that the Banking revolt had made it impossible to name names.

He announced to the astonished Cabinet that he would insist on the re-introduction of the Banking Levy to be fixed at 0.50% as of March 31st 2021.

The levy had been previously raised was an annual tax on the value of most of the debts of the UK banks (including money deposited with the banks), The purpose originally had been to discourage banks from relying on risky forms of borrowing, which were blamed for making the 2008 crisis much more dangerous, in effect it amounted to insurance against the bank's collapse and an indication of the huge funds the government had had to invest to save the system.

Incidentally of course the tax would also raise a lot of money for the government. Over £1 bn

Sebastian, as Prime Minister, later sought to mitigate the abruptness of the additional levy by making it a minimum tax to be recovered from any other corporate taxes paid by the companies. In effect this left exposed all those businesses in the Banking sector that evaded paying tax by deft manipulation and transfer of costs across different tax regimes.

During the following week's Prime Minister's Question time, he was harassed by the leader of the opposition John Dabbs who asked progressively more difficult and probing questions.

"Would the Prime Minister agree with me that the attempt by the Royal Commission on Banking to finally clean up the sector and reveal the culprits who had been responsible for ruining the lives of countless workers, has been nullified by the arrogance of the large Banks?"

There were shouts across the Chamber as Labour MPs waved their order papers and shouted, "Justice! Justice!"

Sebastian simply responded "Conclusions of the Royal Commission are there for all to see and there are many recommendations that would be useful to introduce."

"Does the Prime Minister intend to accept that banks are now not only taught to believe that many are too big to fail but also now that they are too big to be held accountable and too important to finally clear up the mess they have left behind?"

A chorus of 'Here Here!' resounded throughout the chamber as MPs of all parties including Lib Dems shouting support.

Sebastian replied "I have proposed to my honourable friend the Chancellor of the Exchequer that the Banking levy should be reimposed to make clear that unless and until the Banking sector agrees to accept that it will never be clean until the notion of 'personal responsibility' is accepted by every manager, and that as part of the package every banker has to sign a code of conduct which is enforceable at law".

"Is the Prime Minister aware of the traumas caused by Banks to many small businesses across the UK even after measures were put in place to refinance the Banking system by the Government such that exiting from recession was longer and more painful than might otherwise have been the case?"

Sebastian stated "The events of the past cannot be changed, it is my concern that we try to ensure that we have a banking system fit for the future. Accordingly I plan to introduce a Bill calling for mandatory 'personal responsibility' throughout the financial services sector."

There was considerable frisson caused by this statement, Tories were in huddled groups around the chamber and those in the Cabinet on the front bench looked glum and angry.

John Wires made strenuous efforts over the following days to try to reach a compromise, but the Banks were unwilling to expose any of the guilty parties.

One the other hand they appeared to accept the principle of personal responsibility and other matters relating to future conduct such as job evaluation and retention of 50% of the bonuses for at least 5 years and every individual signing up to a new code of conduct. They could not however accept the reasoning behind the 'mal' clause, nor that the bonus system was to be changed in any way.

Sebastian was however unwilling to relent on the whole of the Bank Levy but stated that he expected the Chancellor to include in his next budget a revised figure of 0.025%.

Most of the larger banks seemed to have reluctantly accepted this, although Sebastian noted that he received a much more hostile and aggressive treatment than usual in the financial press.

He hit back ferociously, attacking immediately:

"The European Banking Authority has revealed that in the UK about 2086 Bankers in 2013 earned more than Euro 1 M. that's twice as many as in the rest of the Europe put together. I can understand why the EC, instead of seeing the City as a valuable asset assisting financing across the EC, sees it instead as carrying with it a 'British Bonus disease' with which they might be steadily contaminated and whose corrosive influence will likely destroy trust in the Banks together with grossly inflated pay scales arising principally from the period of low regulation prior to the meltdown which few of us wish to repeat".

Sebastian was now in direct conflict with the Banks, several of whose directors signed an open letter to the Financial Times, stating that unless the Government rescinded its aggressive attack on the sector banks would shift Headquarters and Operations to other Countries.

Sebastian responded that he would, if one of those Banks moved, refer the matter to the EC in order to place a special tax on any bankers earning more than an assessed value of their job and that this would then operate throughout the EC. "You would still of course all work in the USA!"

Sebastian was so incensed that he had actually planned to buy hundreds of cheap airline tickets to the USA and offer them free to any Banker earning over Euro 1 M.

As soon as he heard of this latest proposal Dan Stirling the Party Leader called on Sebastian and said that the arguments had gone far enough, that the Cabinet and Coalition would collapse unless there was an end to it. The Banking Unions, although representing the lower ranks and mostly in retail banking, were becoming increasingly worried about the daily insults hurled at them by otherwise innocuous customers. The Labour Party was thus driven to warn that further arguments would damage all employees and called for all sides to cool off.

John Wires meanwhile was attempting to negotiate a settlement.

This was to the effect that:

1. There would be no further witch hunts of those whose actions caused or contributed to the meltdown.
2. There would be a cap on pay of all senior managers earning over Euro 1 M employed in the Financial Services sector this would last for 5 years. This would be after an independent assessment of those jobs of which they already had details against other similar jobs outside the sector. All Banks had agreed to accept the findings.
3. Individual bonuses had to be justified in financial terms and related only to additional profits derived over and above that expected from a normal salary, in other words outstanding performance had to be proven.
4. There would be accepted the principle of personal responsibility with outside training and ethical basis and long term barring for breaches of conduct.
5. Money laundering procedures were to be tightened, especially for funds aimed at the London Property market.
6. The Banking levy was to be further halved but was not to be removed, it would be used first on re-training staff and then on paying for the independent assessments and finally in setting up operations in other EU countries so as to offer funding to expanding companies in the post 2000 enlargement countries; for example in Bulgaria and Romania, which had poor existing funding arrangements in place.

The Banks had hoped to delay any agreement till after Sebastian handed over his role as Prime Minister at the end of March, but John Wires had stuck to a target which he had initially agreed with the Bankers as 4 weeks.

There still remained the problem as to how this could be encapsulated in a Bill when most of the Cabinet appeared hostile to such a change.

In the end the Financial Press did the work for them, Sebastian had thought to mollify the Bankers and expressed the view that 95% of Bankers were doing a good job for the Country and Society and it was unfortunate that the 5% rotten apples had taken advantage of loose regulation, but that period was now ended and he hoped that the Banking sector would regain its proper position in the commercial life of the Country. The Financial Press then appeared to accept that as an apology, or at least as near as they were going to get, and dropped all further antagonistic attacks on the changes instead seeing them as a new dawn to extend the reach of the City to every Capital City of the EU.

At the following Cabinet meeting there was no opposition to the reforms proposed.

Sebastian wondered if he had 'gone over the top' he knew he had gone as near as dared to threatening the whole coalition. He also knew that it had drawn the Tories together in Cabinet to oppose him, it had reactivated a moribund 1922 committee. He could not risk a similar confrontation.

However he had gained a victory of sorts which would enhance his standing in the EC, and this he could and would use to effect.

Chapter THIRTY-THREE - The Visit to Poland – Military & Health

The Foreign Office received an urgent request from the Polish Government – from the Polish President Tomasc Woda. 'Would the UK Government be willing please to assist the Polish Government in the defence of the Northern Front'.

Michael Morgan, the Conservative Secretary of State for Defence who had been a firm Brexiteer until the second UK Referendum, visited Sebastian on the same matter. He advised strongly against carrying the matter any further. "Sebastian I know that we will just get sucked into another round of 'Euro Army' chats that end nowhere. The UK's stated policy is to support NATO whole heartedly and not to encourage a Euro Army which would simply weaken NATO. It is NATO that has been our lynchpin for peace and we don't want to offer any alternative that might change that position".

But Sebastian had other reasons for wishing to visit Warsaw. In the winter of 2016/17 Sebastian had been a junior minister of Health and as part of that he had wanted to get an idea of the UK's services compared with similar sized Countries in the EU. One of the Countries he had visited was Poland, others being France and Germany, whilst in Poland he had put forward the idea of a Joint Venture with the Polish Health Ministry. This was for the supply of Locums for the UK, temporary Medical appointments until a permanent replacement could be found. These Locum fees were costing the NHS a huge amount and the premiums paid reflected the shortage of qualified technical staff. On the other hand there were frequent moves of Polish doctors to the UK although the language barrier prevented some moves. When a Polish doctor moved to the UK the Polish Health Service had to wave goodbye to the very extensive training costs they had invested in each doctor they had trained.

Sebastian's idea had been to set up a small real UK Hospital Ward in Poland with virtual NHS systems, in effect an NHS training base there. All interested Polish medical staff' and those in nearby countries could take a four week 'submersion course' in both NHS practices and procedures as well as in English specifically as used in medical circles such as related to CT Scans, pharmacy, IT systems, surgical procedures. They would then be placed on a register which would be matched with UK vacancies as they became known. When sent to the UK the Polish staff would gain the UK pay and conditions with the Polish Health Service received an engagement fee.

This was to replace the fees paid to agencies in the UK which could be several times the average salary plus the agency fee.

By agreement, no pressure would be applied in the UK to suggest that Locum's position was permanent, but if that were to happen the UK would pay the Polish Health Service a Capitation fee in compensation for the Polish training costs in proportion to a declining scale reflecting the years already served in Poland.

The benefit to the NHS would be access to a pool of trained medical staff, where their past performance could be checked and who were immediately transportable into particular vacancies and at a substantial saving on the current exorbitant locum staff costs.

The benefit to Poland was that their staff would have access to more modern practices and technical equipment than the Polish Health Service as able to deploy and their staff would be able to take such career temporary secondments to refresh their own careers yet be available in view of short term placements for example to married staff who might not otherwise have such an opportunity.

Sebastian had proposed this at the end of his report to NHS but it had never got off the ground, he now wanted to chase this up.

His third reason was to meet up with the 'insider' whom Sebastian had been led to believe would help him in his mission to strengthen the UK's position in the EU. This was Payunk Wask a former Prime Minister of Poland known to be pro-British but had ended his career before the current, more right wing, Polish Government had been elected. He then prospered in the EC as one of the Presidents from which post he had recently retired.

Sebastian managed to persuade the Cabinet of the importance to responding to the request of the Polish President. The visit was agreed. A number of high ranking UK individuals stepped onto the tarmac at Warsaw Airport. It was 10 am and they hoped to make it back in the day.

The group consisted of Sebastian himself, his PPC Bill Bennett, the Junior Minister of Health, and then the Head of NHS England Walter Jefferies. The Defence Secretary Michael Morgan, the Head of the General Staff General Sir Charles Winterbotham, and finally the permanent Secretary to the Foreign and Colonial Office Keith Williams, who had been on their last Warsaw visit dealing with a problem in Belarus. Accompanying them was a Security Advisor was Colonel Simon from NATO headquarters in Brussels

They were warmly welcomed by the President at a brief buffet in the Presidential Palace. One of the guests paid their host a compliment and remarked that it was good to see such an old building still in use. The President loudly responded, "It isn't old it was built in 1951 the entire old part of Warsaw was demolished by the Germans in revenge for the Warsaw Uprising everything above door height was blown up - completely destroyed! We were as determined to rebuild that as were to rebuild our Country."

The Party then split into two, Health and Military. The Health group went to visit a nearby hospital.

The President then led the other group into the ornate meeting room on the first floor. He spoke through an interpreter, although his English was passable he did not want to risk being misunderstood.

"You know we think of you British as our allies and we were much offended over the first UK referendum because there was much we had in common and we hoped together we might reform the EU. We also think back to the Second War years understanding that you were the only one that could help us free ourselves of the Nazis. I think many of our soldiers fought alongside you. Unhappily we had hoped after the war to return to our independence and had hoped for your support. But we realise now that it simply would not have been possible to persuade Stalin to leave us alone. So we had to endure nearly 45 years of torment within the embrace of the Russian Bear. We think we know the Bear well!

Something that may surprise you was Mrs Thatcher's friendship with Lech Walesa. Shortly after he was elected he visited her in London and expressed great concern that the Polish Currency would not be able to take the strain of the transition that Poland had to carry out moving from the 'Command' to the 'Demand' economy. She immediately called in your Chancellor and together they offered Lech a £300 M reserve, to be used if the Polish Zloty collapsed. It never did but we were always grateful for the idea that you would support us, and to this day we are not in the Euro.

You may think it strange that I, as President, am personally involved in requesting your assistance. I decided to do what I could to support my Prime Minister and together we suggested that I should do this.

You will all know that I met up with your Prime Minister who was then Foreign Minister last year. He faced off the Russians for us who had done some clever sabre rattling and had set off a story about Belarus being occupied by Russian troops on the death of Belarus' leader.

Thanks to that prompt action for a few months Russian interest in the area subsided but late last Autumn it started again. Again NATO sent in troops to temporarily boost defences in the Baltic States. But it's a Russian move which now seems permanent. It's not clear exactly what they are trying to do, most likely it is to draw in NATO towards the frontier areas which it can then claim is a NATO offensive move which entitles it to take action. Both ourselves and the Baltic states are wide open to any land attack as there are no natural geographic features to protect us but NATO refuses to be drawn in. The result is that the Polish population in the Eastern provinces are in perpetual fear of a Russian advance. Will it happen? I don't think so but many of these people are old enough to remember that when Russians come in they are almost impossible to get out – just see Ukraine for that? The same is true of the Baltic States, they have even fewer troops and hardly any modern equipment.

Now I am well aware of the argument over a Euro Army, indeed it was your determination not to see NATO subordinated in any way which scuppered it! But at the same time the USA rails about NATO Countries not paying their share of costs in terms of 2% of GDP. So we do not feel we are effectively protected by just by this shield which none of us believe could be operational in time for any direct Russian attack!

I have asked the Leaders of the Baltic States to come tomorrow morning to explain to you in person before you fly back to the UK, I hope you will listen to them?"

The Defence Minister, Michael Morgan, cut in "Mr President we are of course willing to discuss these things with you but you must understand that formally speaking, our Strategic Review suggests we have a global role to play, we are happy that in Europe NATO should be the bedrock of our policy and if NATO will not move forward because it does not want to provoke the Russians then we will have to go along with that!"

The President dug in his heels "Yes exactly that's the position but we cannot and will not accept it. If you cannot bend that ruling, then if the UK will not help, then we shall have to turn directly to Germany or France. No matter what you say soon, very soon, moves will be underway with or without you support to provide military cover. You don't seem to understand that is what the people here want, evidence on the ground of a willingness to protect us as our Defence Minister said what we want is 'presence, presence, presence'. I am not sure exactly how you would react if half of the UK felt threatened in the way we do? What would you say 'No I don't agree. You are perfectly OK. There's a shield 500 miles away, you'll be OK, we cannot and will not do anymore!'

You see this is where your strategic view collapses; the people will not have it!

You see what none of us can understand is WHY there isn't a way to allow a hybrid structure, local troops at the front and in the case of attack then bring in NATO?"

The Defence Secretary had apparently no desire to respond. Sebastian wanted to test an alternative route but the General Sir Charles Winterbotham jumped in.

"Do you mean Mr President if there were a formal army here facing Russia that, for example the Baltic States would increase their spend to 2% of GDP and re-equip?"

"Yes that's exactly what I am saying, but without evidence why should they? What they want is troops on the ground, permanent troops and proper co-ordination between what I will call the Northern Armies and other allied groups like Sweden and Finland. They need airbases and people to help train up some of their own, they need tanks and aircraft to encourage them to build their own defences. They know they cannot do it on their own. It requires leadership, Mr Edwards, leadership!

You do not need me to tell you that the UK is still known in Brussels as the 'opt out' champions of the EC. Frankly we don't want the Germans to take a lead. If it's not the Russians it's the Germans who charge across our land and chop it into pieces. But if we have to go with them we will, I don't think the French will bother they have their hands full with Southern Europe!"

"So" Sebastian sought clarification. "What you seem to be saying is that you are offering the UK as if you like command of what we might call the armies of North Europe coming under and being directly responsible to NATO forming the first line defence from where? Finland to Hungary? and having within it responsibility for arming, training and equipping all those Countries armed forces."

"Yes that's it almost exactly" the President replied "although as in most EC things, it has to be co-operative, you will have to persuade, cajole and argue rather than order or command!"

"And what about arming them? Sebastian asked. "Few of the Baltic States have much weaponry no tanks or modern aircraft, even Poland uses many former Russian T tanks?"

"Well we use the Leopard as the main battle tank but we are well aware of the new Russian main battle Tank and would be happy to co-operate in jointly developing with you a successor to Leopard and your Challenger 2 Tank ready for 2030. You could keep the Germans in the frame by buying armoured vehicles from them so gradually reducing the varieties of military equipment in the EC. Higher volumes equals lower prices and better products perhaps?"

Keith Williams had been silent in the background but now raised his voice, '..but how would all this be structured, how would it be possible to assure NATO which means the USA that the UK command would be effective and not rush away out of control blundering into a war no-one wants because of a mistaken view of a threat, leaving the US to pick up the pieces?"

Sebastian replied, "Well we would have to evolve control mechanisms, but you understand the logic? Ask yourselves is there any good reason why the EC should not bear more of its own costs of defence? If your answer is No! then we have to find the mechanisms to achieve what we want!"

Colonel Simon Collingham commented "One way that NATO might be happy is to embed USA military representatives in each major army group, with instructions as to reporting direct to NATO HQ as well as prior notification of all military manoeuvres of any kind!"

Sebastian delved deeper "Where might such bases be?"

The President clapped his hands and various maps were presented. "We have several former Soviet bases which could be refurbished or we could build new. We would prefer to save 'real' money for creating better defensive structures. If there is an attack of course any bases will be immediately hit in a massive bombardment; so protection underground of equipment, tactical headquarters, supplies and personnel is very important. We would prefer to spend money there rather than in nice houses, personnel accommodation?"

"So you are looking for army, aircraft and naval support?" Asked Sebastian

"Eventually perhaps yes, but in the short term we would take just the beginnings, allowing ours' and the Baltic States' own trained up forces to fill the gaps?"

"What sort or equipment orders might be placed?"

"Well it's not clear perhaps 80 main battle tanks, 100 artillery pieces and 30 aircraft probably Tornados to tie in with Germany."

Sebastian asked if any of his team had any further questions but there were none. Sebastian thanked the President reminded him that he, Sebastian was a temporary PM, but that he would put before the Cabinet a faithful record of the meeting for consideration.

It was then scarcely 2 pm.

The Polish military in attendance suggested they make a quick trip to see a possible base 300 miles east of Warsaw and most of the Military peeled off for that flight to be back in time for evening meal scheduled for 8.30 pm in Warsaw.

Sebastian himself went back to the British Embassy with Keith Williams head of the FCO. There he called Payunk Wask as arranged and they met in the British Embassy at 6 pm.

Sebastian suggested to Keith that he was about to unveil his Plan for the EC, he Keith should not be surprised at the content but that Sebastian felt it was the right time to update him and hopefully gain Foreign Office support.

Payunk was a large man broad-shouldered and with a big pudgy face his receding hairline managed to emphasise the large toby jug ears by which he was known throughout the EC. He had an open and welcoming nature.

They sat in the ambassador's almost regal main meeting room, with white painted furniture and blue and white striped furnishings.

Sebastian introduced Keith who was the epitome of Foreign Office staff, well turned out indeed immaculate in his dark suit and yellowish tie, as always his bronzed skin suggested he had probably recently spent a couple of weeks in the Caribbean, his tall and wiry figure sunk into one of the armchairs.

Sebastian quickly launched into his view of the Euro and of Britain's likely reduced role, likely being excluded by QMV as the Euro centric behaviour became taken for granted and eventually took hold, side-lining any country not wishing to join the Euro. Sebastian said "It's sure that the first moves, will and must be to rescue the Euro! So I cannot object to them tightening financial control mechanisms within the Euro Group."

Payunk and Keith listened intently then Sebastian launched his vision of a modern EC. First it should sign up to the original 2020 proposals identifying economic targets to achieve. "The EC is at its strongest where it attempts to achieve what people want, more jobs, more money and more ways to spend it; at its worst when it gets tangled up in politics and demands riles, more rules!.

Then it should be spread over three concentric circles, in the inner circle will be the Euro Countries which must eventually move to a quasi-Federal State.

The next circle was of those countries like the UK unwilling for economic or cultural reasons to move that far but wanting to remain in the EC as a looser knit group within the customs union and enjoying the full benefits of the single market.

Finally a grouping of other EC neighbours whom the EC should encourage and offer reductions in duties to help them build up their economies, such as Turkey."

Payunk interrupted and put down his glass of Vodka. "But if you in the UK are not to get side-lined you will need to form a special group, an 'Enhanced Co-operation group', but in order to legally register that and obtain rights which you can enforce, you will need 9 members, There are currently 37 EU members 28 in the Euro that would mean that you would have to register every one of the others, but I know that is not practical as there are certainly one or two still anxious to join the Euro but have been told to hold off until the problems with the Euro are resolved. So where will you get your support from?"

Sebastian responded, "In principle you are correct, but you will have noticed that Greece had a major problem, it's possible they might have done better exiting the Euro but remaining within the EC. I understand that legally that option was never open to them. The Euro is no revolving door, once in you are trapped and have to face that or total rejection by the EC which hardly any country could accept because of the chaos it would cause. Accordingly I believe that there are several Euro members that might welcome membership of the wider group if only as a reserve measure. The EC rules appear to allow this since all such groups of 9 must not be exclusive but open to all EC members. However I would not necessarily pin my hopes on that, but there are three countries Norway Switzerland and little Lichtenstein who are not in the EU and others like Iceland and Greenland who might reconsider joining under certain conditions and allowing 'opt outs' but currently they all have to agree to abide by the EC's provisions now and into the future. In most cases unless they are EC members they have absolutely no rights to have a say in how the rules that are deemed to apply to them are constructed. They must worry that sooner or later they will be drawn ever deeper into assenting to measures they might wish to object to but with no voice they can do nothing except be a spectator in the actions that might squeeze the independence out of them! The benefit of the new arrangement for the EC is that they would have no need to rush any applicant through to the Euro, with such a fall-back position in place, countries could move ahead at a less hectic pace".

"So" Payunk needed clarification " you mean to what? Encourage these other countries to what? Join the EC?"

"Yes that's right. That's exactly what I mean!" Sebastian blurted out. He was desperately hoping for a positive response, Payunk knew the EC constitution inside and out. If he should damn the idea totally Sebastian was, as it were, up the Rhine without a paddle! He had no plan 'B' . He thought that the lure of a real united Europe but swimming at different speeds might be one that Payunk might go for. Sebastian knew that for one, the French believed that there were already too many in the Euro Group. This made it much more difficult to obtain accord and bring them all to decisions at the same time, a new level of membership could indeed provide the Euro Group with the flexibility they and the EC needed.

Keith remained frozen to his seat it was the first he had heard of such an ambitious plan, he sat open mouthed as Sebastian's brief had unfolded. He could tell that it would be a ground-breaking change within the EU.

Payunk, pulled his large body out of his chair and walked backwards and forwards across the carpet as if working through a list of obstacles. Sebastian nervously twiddled the signet ring on his little finger.

"Hmmh" He said in a voice which betrayed not a hint of his Polish background, partly because as Sebastian knew. he had spent his earlier years in the USA where his parents had taken him as a young child. He had risen to be a Professor of economics before returning to the land of his birth. "Yes, it might work! So what do you want me to do?"

"To help me prepare the case, sell it into the EC and circulate around the counties involved persuading them to join!" Sebastian thought there was no point in going for half measures.

"Hummph" Payunk said again and turning to Keith asked "So what do you think? We have great admiration for this Sebastian Chappy, but he is only going to be PM for another few weeks. Do you really think he can pull it off?"

Sebastian was worried about this question he and Keith had crossed swords on several occasions and they had not always seen eye to eye. He consider the matter then spoke slowly and deliberately "Well frankly I have no idea, but if I had to back anyone to do the job it would be him, and there's no-one else in the

UK who would even stand a chance!" – much to Sebastian's amazement he continued "Tonight is the first time I heard of the plan, but it fits in every way with what the UK's vision of the EC ought to be!"

"Ok I'll help" Payunk advanced towards Sebastian and they both shook hands. They spent some minutes discussing the next steps. Payunk left them, he considered the current Polish Government too right wing and did not want to attend the formal dinner..

By then it was time to return to the President's Palace and join up with the others.

On the drive to the Palace only a few streets away, Sebastian turned to Keith and thanked him for his support. Keith responded "That's OK you deserved it! Next time tell me earlier?"

They had an excellent evening for the President was a fine host and they were liberally supplied with 'vodka' and encouraged to stand and give a toast and a brief speech, one after another. The UK party tried gamely to tackle some of the local delicacies such as 'Golonka' which were pigs trotters and 'Flaczki' pronounced flach-kee or tripe as the interpreter kindly translated. As the evening wore on the hands holding the glasses became increasingly unsteady, the speeches more hesitant, full of gaps and regaining a seat appeared to require an increasingly gingerly manoeuvre, one or two of the partly seemed to get lost in the loos, either by luck or design to avoid the next toast.

The party dispersed after singing a Polish song ' Sto Lat'. The British interpreter suggested to Sebastian that it was a birthday song, literally translated it means 100 years, may you live a 100 years! but no-one could work out whose birthday it was and nor by then did anyone much care.

The met up with the military Heads and Prime Ministers of the three Baltic States the following morning and each of them repeated almost word for word what the Polish President had told them the previous day, they all looked at possible military sites and compared lists of equipment of all kinds. The Baltic States were emphatic if there were forces on the ground they would lift their spend to 2% of GDP as quickly as they could and they would be prepared to buy British equipment if the UK troops stayed to to train them and form the 'presence presence, presence' that they all required.

The UK NHS Group then reported favourable on the possible Health Service Locum Agreement, even expressing the hope of setting up a buying unit to acquire hospital light equipment from Poland and neighbouring countries.

They flew back to the UK in the early afternoon.

During the return flight Sebastian, and the Defence Secretary, Michael Morgan, who was supported by the General, locked horns over any possible such deal.

"Mr Edwards, Prime Minister" Michael started "Are you fully aware of the Berlin Plus agreement signed nearly 20 years ago in 2002? This was an agreement between NATO and the EC, it was comprehensive involving security arrangements, the exchange of classified information, access to NATO planning capabilities, availability of NATO assets in crises conditions. The procedure was that use of NATO assets by the EU is subject to 'the right of first refusal' by NATO and then that EC use has to be agreed by all NATO States. The current state of NATO is just not compatible with the hybrid role that you are suggesting. What you appear to be saying to NATO is 'We in the UK want to take over command of the Northern Armies of NATO, excluding the USA Troops, and that we are responsible for that zone to NATO and the Countries within that area."

"Yes that's right!" Sebastian agreed. "But I am also adding that USA Troops can in time be reduced in that sector as the local armies come up to speed. There are 38,000 USA troops in Europe each soldier costs between $10,000 and $40,000 per annum more than it would if in the USA. Who pays for that, you? Me? The Poles? No not a penny. Michael you have to grow up! At any time those troops could be withdrawn and likely posted to the Pacific where China could pose a huge threat to the USA's mercantile interests." The General tried to interject but Sebastian was not finished "The problem Michael, is that unfortunately we never have a full review of the wars we have fought – Oh I grant you at the behest of the USA, most of them yes – they have been mostly unmitigated disasters.

Sir Charles Winterbotham pushed in "Look I wouldn't say that, we did what we were asked to do! You know!!"

"But that's the problem, the Strategic Defence Review allows you to operate anywhere in the world when you are asked 'in defence of the UK interests'! But that's bunkum! We had no interests in Afghanistan or Iraq or in Libya yet any Prime Minister who comes along and says "Hey let's invade so and so, off you go ever ready to oblige on the back of USA coat-tails, the result is you are not part of the planning system or structure, you have no idea of the long term objectives or how to get out once you are in and you never have enough of the right equipment because we don't have the money for these jaunts which suck us in for years! Look I could go on but it just makes me angry and you military play the game. A world-wide presence needs aircraft carriers from which to attack, but one might break down so we have to have two and because you can't send a carrier on its own, it has to have up to 5 escort boats and a repair unit and a couple of platoons of marines. So Yes Sir! Choose between a UK wandering world-wide almost spoiling for a fight it never wins, at the request of some dotty Prime Minister – choose between that and the request from the Prime Ministers of four Countries begging for your support. And of course you are conditioned to go for the old Imperial view! Those days are gone don't you understand? Gone!"

The General was not to be fobbed off "So if we go your way we would have given up the Falklands and let the Argies all over us!"

"Wrong! Wrong! Wrong! I would have made sure through diplomatic means that we came to terms with the other parties, if I thought for a moment the Falklands were important to the national interest, then I would have defended it properly, what exactly did you expect the 30 odd marines to do when invaded! It was silly, stupid, senseless!

Listen – if you don't accept this offer of leadership, then you might as well leave Europe for good and in my opinion the British Army will never fight another war. We have the lowest number of troops for centuries and you will not get another opportunity to spend money. The best that you can expect is that on any USA led foreign escapades, you will end up working directly to USA field staff, as a unit within an American Army, you will never again come anywhere near any independent command structure. Do you understand me?

Look, as opportunities go, this is the best you will get, command of allied armies in Northern Europe with willing supporters, dull boring perhaps and you have to get used to the Vodka and Golonkas and Flechki but it's a role that's there and needs doing!"

Sebastian calmed down and turned to Michael Morgan again, "I take your point about NATO's structure but we will see if we can change it to bring it into line with current needs! I assume that if NATO were to accept a modified structure then you would have no objection to the role that I have suggested?"

"No Prime Minister you cannot assume that, I will have to tie in with my Conservative Party colleagues, you will appreciate that our opposition to a Euro Army has been on the basis of it weakening the role and position of NATO but if the UK forces, as frankly one of the only two battle trained forces in the EC, are to play a lead role then it puts a different aspect to the whole thing! But would the French wear it do you think?"

To the General Sebastian suggested "From my reading the 20th Armoured Infantry Brigade is still hanging about in Germany, we could switch them to Poland. See if that would work, will you? Get back to me tomorrow please!" Sir Charles took a note and sat a couple of rows further back on the plane.

Sebastian sank back into his seat 'bugger' he thought 'it means another trip to France! And I'll have to get hold of the USA defence Secretary, to see if I can swing the changes to NATO on the promise of him being able to return another 5,000 troops home and getting the 2% of GDP from all northern EC countries?'

They arrived back into Northolt and it was already dusk

He was driven back to No. 10.

Sebastian fell into bed and was sound asleep in minutes.

He was awoken the following morning by a persistent ringing in his ear, he lifted the phone on the private line he had no idea who put the call through. There was an immediate bellowing which he at first thought was a crossed line and that someone was calling to object.

It took him a minute or two to take possession of his surroundings.

The angry voice said that he had apparently been spotted coming off the plane at Northolt wearing a crumpled suite.

The Sebastian realised that it was the CEO of S & G, Lord Israel Jacobs. He was on it like a flash "Look there's really no point in me spending a fortune taking photos of you splashing them on bill boards throughout the country and launching the new product range; only for you to mess it all up arriving back in the UK in the most screwed up suit I have ever seen! And having that on the front of every single paper! Now pull your socks up or I'll have you off the 1500 posters. OK? I'll send you around a crease resistant suit – it'll cost you £250, you can send me a cheque!" Then in a calmer mood "by the way have you thought of a charity yet?"

"Yes, for 'looked after kids'!" There was no confirmation at the other end so Sebastian made it clear "I mean children in care, whose lives are in effect taken over by the state. I think they have a rough deal. This is to help add something to their lives, special training, extra holidays abroad, sports aptitude assessment, grants for those that get to Universit…"

Before he could finish the word the line went dead and he fell back into bed fast asleep!

Chapter THIRTY-FOUR – Cabinet meeting, Sebastian's EU Policy exposed

During the Monday afternoon Sebastian met up with his Lib Dem Cabinet colleagues and updated them with them with the results of the trip to Poland and also other considerations. He explained that he felt he had now no alternative to share his views with the whole Cabinet if they wanted to move the whole EU project further on. If it was delayed beyond his Premiership he had no doubt that no decisions would be made and that the UK would gradually slip out of the EC after being placed in an impossible situation.

Sebastian asked the Cabinet Secretary to arrange for the normal Tuesday's Cabinet meeting to start the following morning at 8.00 am and for the Ministers not to be expected to be released till 1.00 pm, apart from some ongoing matters it was all to be devoted to Europe.

There was a frisson in the air at the start of the meeting and it did not help that it was snowing outside, snow settling on frozen ground spelt, possible traffic disruption and rail and airline hold ups, so they all kept looking at the lawn outside.

Sebastian spent an hour summarising his view of the position.

a)   The continuing failure of the UK to monitor or contain the immigration, threw into doubt the temporary hold over the freedom of movement of people, that had been won from the EC and formed the basis of the second referendum. Sebastian said he would ask the Home Secretary to explain this later.

b)   The need within the EuroGroup to put in place stronger measures that would correct some of the design faults of a currency with no state. Such measures would inevitably sooner or later lead to QMV on a range of issues and Sebastian was strongly of the view that the UK, despite assurances, would be left behind and outside that Group.

c)   Sebastian's view was that there was still time, before the 4 years' temporary review was up, to try to change the EC structurally so that it would be possible to develop the EU into something to which everyone would feel happy to accept. In other words a two speed EU but in order to achieve that and secure our position long term the UK would have to lodge an 'enhanced group' which could then define the right of the UK's position within EU Law.

d)   Sebastian explained that this approach needed a group of 9 members there are 28 in the EC just 19 in the EuroGroup that means every other member not aligned to the Euro unless other members could be found to support this Group.

e) Sebastian then went over the trip to Poland and the request of the Prime Ministers or Poland, Lithuania, Latvia and Estonia to accept the UKs leadership in a Northern Army's alliance, within NATO. Sebastian expected that might exert some pressure to help him and join the 'enhanced group, he price he would extract would be their membership of the 'Enhanced Group'. Sebastian also felt that Norway and Switzerland might be tempted to join in this outer membership of the EC since they would gain some ability to have a say in the rules to which they were subjected which, as it currently stood might squeeze the independence out of them.

f) Finally there would be an outer-outer ring made up of neighbours who would be awarded trading and customs duty exemptions but would not be eligible to join the EC because their culture and backgrounds were too different, this would include Turkey.

g) The objective then is to protect the UK's position in the EC in perpetuity and it's right to membership of the Customs Union and the Single Market, without being compelled either to join the Euro or to allow totally free movement of people, perhaps a modified movement might be possible, from the EC into the UK.

There was a tense pause. The Home Secretary responsible for immigration started to explain.

"Well we thought the opt out would allow up to put in place our own control systems, we tried an Australia type system which was a failure for a number of reasons, we tried to revert to our old systems too but these proved too slow to match jobs with available people. Latterly the increasing GDP has meant us taking in large numbers of people, partly from the states investing here and partly from the EU. As a result our immigration is pretty indistinguishable from the times before we had the opt out. But the opt out remains a highly emotive concession that we won, any open admission that it is withdrawn might again lead to the rise of UKIP and calls for another referendum from my right wing colleagues who are still smarting from our denial of the 'will of the people' in the first EU Referendum. There is a way to re-install a border control system but only at the expense of curbing our own freedoms – that is it having a UK wide Identity Card. This option was discarded some years ago.

As you know after March Sebastian is to switch to the Home Office and I expect that he will study this in greater detail and see if he can find a solution."

There was a pause, the Conservative Cabinet members heads drooped at such abject failure.

Sebastian was subject to some robust questioning. "Was this the reason for your aggressive stance over the Royal Commission on Banking?" Sebastian replied that part of the reason for his fury was the basic injustice – a desperate man fiddles his benefits for £1000 and goes to prison, Bankers cause billions of damage and go unpunished – but the other part yes! It is related directly to the EC's perception of UK Bankers' earnings, given any opportunity and as you see we are giving them ample grounds, they will gladly end the passporting arrangement which currently gives UK bankers free licence to trade within the EC!"

The Health Minister burst in "I suppose that's the reason too for the deal setting up a virtual NHS training unit in Poland?" He explained to the Cabinet the basis of the deal they had been discussing last weekend. Sebastian responded "I first proposed that several years ago because it made commercial sense to both sides but as it happens Yes! It would clearly help make our case as to how an agreement between UK and the EC on a limited freedom of movement of people might work!"

Another asked "So part of the cost of your scheme to curry favour within the EC is to do what we said we would never do, encourage the creation of a Euro Army, it will replace NATO you know?"

Brexiteers remaining in the Cabinet turned to Michael Morgan to explain. He appeared to have had something of a conversion over the weekend and suggested that there could be large orders for UK military Equipment, tanks, guns and aircraft. But he suggested that the Northern Armies plan still needed NATO assent.

Several junior Cabinet Ministers were annoyed and about to walk out stating that this represented a major change from the Coalition Agreement and the matter should be left till after March when the Tories could deal with it themselves.

Other older Conservative, members urged caution indicating that Sebastian had at least warned them of the impending trouble and had found a possible way out of the difficulty. He should be allowed to continue, check with NATO, confirm the military split of Europe with France and Germany and see if he could set up the 'Enhanced Group'.

Sebastian also discussed the possibility of a joint base with France in Northern Nigeria covering the Lake Chad area and following up the Boko Haram there. "Not all my work has been self-serving you see!"

Sebastian then disclosed that he hoped that Payunk Wask a former President of the EU had agreed to help, because, as Sebastian stated 'Frankly it's a terribly complex world within the EC.'

This was greeted with some relief around the table, Payunk Wask was well liked in the UK.

Although there were clearly considerable misgivings when a vote was taken there was a 2/3 , 1/3 split to proceed. One Cabinet Minister belatedly suggested that the return of the Elgin Marbles was also part of the plan. Sebastian said "No! I always thought they should be returned but Yes! I was also well aware of the benefit that it would do us when push came to shove – we are going to need every possible help we can get to sort this out, you know, besides the Greeks have had a terrible time and they deserve some encouragement surely?"

The Cabinet meeting finished at noon.

Sebastian was exhausted and went to the flat upstairs cut himself a slice of bread, toasted it, ate it standing up in the middle of the kitchen with a glass of ice cold milk.

He cancelled all afternoon meetings, he received calls from Bill and Madge congratulating him on succeeding.

They told him also that the Tories were in the middle of their Leadership Election, there were three contenders, the Chancellor Stephen White, the Home Secretary Pamela Tressider and finally the Defence Secretary Michael Morgan, of these only two should go forward to the final run off. Bill suggested that this state of tension in the Tory party had found them in an uncertain situation, none of them wanted to be outflanked, they were hesitant, as Bill said "They didn't want to endorse your EU proposal but they had nothing to put in its place, they each knew that the first to praise it or damn it would be torn apart by the others, but Sebastian, you are making credible proposals, so it's a warning that sooner or later the 1922 Committee, the right wing group of Tory MPs, will try to bring you down, as they did to Lloyd George's Liberal Coalition in 1922."

Sebastian went into the bedroom walked past the two suitcases which he still hadn't unpacked and still lay opened on the floor, and collapsed onto the bed.

He again had a terrible nightmare as he had had during his 'bumpy ride' just weeks before.

He was in a large building in Brussels on one side ornate with gold fringed stonework, on the other a huge picture window looking out over the 'Bois de Brussels'. He was standing to present his case, Payunk Wask was by his side, but he had had to go, Sebastian did not know why, his team consisted of Keith Williams, who was dressed in a Caribbean coloured shirt and Bermuda shorts and another person who seemed to be John Denny the police inspector. They were trying to restrain him, several European Heads of State were shouting at him, REMOVE PASSPORTING and NO ENHANCEMENT others were yelling in French he thought something about LIBRE MOVEMENT but the interpreter told him he had to speak German, he was suddenly surrounded by Generals each stamped NATO on their foreheads, they demanded that he choose a tank, 'Leopard, Challenger!' shouting 'NOW, NOW!' He was instantly removed to a large army artillery firing base, it was on an open moor somewhere, there was a large green signpost, he struggled but he couldn't get it into focus to read it, it seemed to be in Russian. There were explosions going off all around him, he was then in a field hospital he could read the letters clearly N – H - S, there were masses of doctors demanding jobs, Jobs JOBS, then he was back in the Commons and the Speaker, who was dressed in black with a mask as an Executioner was reading a Bill called the 'Last rites of the Coalition' from an old brown coloured mediaeval scroll. There were shouts from all sides 'resign, Resign RESIGN!', the Tories on the front bench sat glum and several of them began to rip off his jacket, but soon everyone was on their feet waving green order papers. A few of his supporters from Middleton who had managed somehow to gain access, were trying to force their way through to him, he could just see Bill Bennet's bald head shining in the TV lights, but it was useless and the crowd surged. Then he was in a train but it was moving over Westminster Bridge ramming into some traffic light flashing on amber, those around him were shouting 'Overcrowding SEE!' He was pushed to the floor with a bump, and thought he was suffocating, there was a dreadful smell and the crowd swarmed on out of the Commons carrying the Golden Mace the symbol of legality in the Commons, before them down the Mall carrying EU flags with stars, towards Buckingham Palace shouting 'Down with Lords'.

Sebastian awoke with a start, he was wringing with sweat, he had fallen out of bed and he was lying face down in one of his two open suitcases, containing his dirty socks!

It was still only 10.00 pm. Sebastian knew he could not carry on like this for much longer, the tension was horrific, so far he knew he had been lucky. Any one Cabinet Minister this morning openly rebelling would have been catastrophic, it would have sabotaged everything. He had no fall-back plan.

He carefully began to count down the days to the end of March, then FREEDOM again, he imagined walking with his friend Douglas in Northumberland on a long walk through a large wood, and then being at home again, sitting in his favourite chair with the world held at bay at the front door.

He called home which he had not been able to do whilst away. He updated Sylvia on the past week-ends events, he tried not to show the strain he was under and asked about the charity and her family. She evidently picked up the vibes and said "I am coming to London this weekend shall we see a show?"

He awoke refreshed the following day and cooked himself a hearty breakfast.

Bill and Madge called in at 9.00 am asking if he was OK and discussing the diary for the following week.

As luck would have it they explained that Cedric Elsworthy, the USA Secretary of State was in London and they managed to book an hour with him later that day at the USA Embassy in London.

Chapter THIRTY-FIVE – Sebastian NATO reforms with USA Sec of State

Bill Bennett had put together a paper on Sebastian's proposal for a reformed NATO in Europe.   The same team as in Warsaw, Sebastian, the Defence Secretary Michael Morgan and the General with their NATO adviser Colonel Collingham visited the Embassy in London as arranged and met with the Secretary of State.

It was the first time that Sebastian had visited the new US Embassy which had reportedly cost of £620 M but was credited at the time with livening up the whole Nine Elms area. The huge cube finally opening in 2018, the building had triangular features breaking up the otherwise stern appearance. Sebastian was told that the small moat on one side is actually a security feature. It looks out over a bend in the Thames. It is situated near to the revamped Battersea Power Station, now a gallery. The UK party trooped in along a huge glass sided corridor up another level with floor to ceiling large picture windows and so into the Ambassadors main meeting room.

Sebastian and his party were duly welcomed by Cedric Elsworthy the USA's Secretary of state and generally reckoned to be the third most powerful figure in the USA. He was a small rather pudgy individual but he was known to be a quick decision taker and a good judge of people.

Sebastian immediately set about describing the proposal based on the prepared paper;

This is a proposal for reforming NATO. In effect it splits the command under Brussels into two, the Northern Armies commanded by a British General based in Berlin and the Southern Armies commanded by a French General based in Paris.

This includes Armies, Navies and Airforce as shall be described in detail to be attached.

Every unit of both armies was to have an imbedded officer from the USA or from Canada for the French Armies. All military moves or manoeuvres were to be signed off by NATO in Brussels 24 hours before taking place, no movement would be permitted without NATO consent.

The Commanders or the Northern and Southern Armies were to be responsible for ensuring that the 2% of GDP would be met by every country in their orbit.

Each of the Commanders was to be responsible for liaison with other neutral Countries in their area to ensure that those countries also were properly equipped in case of a major war.

Over a period of 20 years equipment suppliers for tanks, ships and aircraft were to be halved reducing cost and standardising for ease of use.

Within 5 years it was estimated that the USA troops based in Europe could be reduced by 10,000 men saving some $20 Billion per annum.

Europe is eternally grateful to the USA for the economic and military help since 1945 which has helped to keep the area free and now economically wealthy. We wish to take over greater responsibility for European Defence. We still see the USA as the keystone of our defence but we see this as a necessary and natural development of NATO. We ourselves in the UK have been a consistent supporter of NATO throughout its history and have played a part in many of USA's foreign ventures unstintingly. We have discussed this with four countries within the Northern Command and they have assented to this proposal. Although the French have had a more ambivalent relationship with NATO we believe that they are the only other EC Country whose troops are battle-trained that could undertake the Southern Command, they are also the only other EC country apart from ourselves with a nuclear deterrent and we believe that still to be an important factor in the defence structure.

The Secretary of State was sitting at one side of the large boat shaped table. He looked at the document carefully and passed it to his military advisers, Senior Generals standing on either side of him.

"Have you tried this on Germany and France yet?" he asked.

Sebastian replied "No! not as yet, as you know the Euro Army project has had a controversial life and I wanted first to put a proposal to you then, with your approval work down through the various National military and political entities!"

Cedric asked an aid "What d'e say?"

The General replied "The Brits blocked the proposal originally but they hope to get this though the various governments!"

Cedric asked his staff "Could it save that much?" pointing at the figure mentioned.

The same General his face almost completely obscured by his military hat which he still wore bent down to the Secretary of State "Probably more!"

"No runnin' off and starting a war for us?" He asked Sebastian.

"No all military movements approved through NATO in Brussels!"

"All?" Cedric Elsworthy queried

Sebastian replied "Yes All! but if all means too much red tape then you tell us what all means!"

"Hummph! And you Sebason Edwards, you are, I understand, just in the role temporarily? What happens after you go?" then without waiting for a reply, pointed at Michael Morgan "Are you the Defence Secretary?" Michael nodded "What do'ye say?"

Michael Morgan was slow to react, he was clearing his throat "Well Mr Edwards rather sprung it on us and we are going along with the idea to see if it has legs!"

Cedric turned to the same General again "Was' 'e mean – legs"

"He means he doesn't know, he's sitting on the fence till he sees which way the wind blows!"

"Ah one of those, we have plenty of those in the Pentagon don't we General?"

"Yessir!" They laughed.

Michael Morgan was about to respond but Cedric cut him off, the British General Sir Charles Winterbotham burst in "You know we still have an infantry Brigade based in Germany – we could move those directly!" Michael Morgan flung a 'what the hell did you say that for?' look at him.

Cedric looked at Sebastian "You a gambler?"

"Yes! I have to be, I have to back my judgement, it's the right time to do this!"

Cedric stood up and formed a close circle with the US Generals, there was a nodding of heads!

"I agree! So go do it!" Cedric was emphatic.

Michael Morgan stuttered "You – you want us to organise this?"

"No, YOU go do it Mr Defence Secretary! You do it!" Cedric was insistent.

"Your boss has taken the risk of coming here, he stuck his neck out, you would have cut it off, you would have let him down. Now it's up to YOU Defense Secretary! Your turn to walk the high wire, I think!"

"Good-day Mr Sebamus Edwards and good luck!"

Colonel Simon Collingham was the only one to congratulate Sebastian on the roadway outside the Embassy "So the long walk was worth it! Well done!"

"Yes" Sebastian replied, "I see you are still limping a bit!"

"Can't complain!" was the rejoinder "It earned me a couple of months R & R"

"Not in Loughborough though I guess!" Joked Sebastian.

"No! not Loughborough!" They parted company.

At the following week's Cabinet meeting, Sebastian reported on his NATO Proposal.

Michael Morgan tried to explain, but the other senior Tory Cabinet Ministers, interjected "But Michael you seemed to have ended up putting the proposal into practice? Didn't you say anything about it weakening NATO and formulating a Euro Army?"

"No I didn't, Cedric Elsworthy, is quite right though, it's time for us to stop messing about and get stuck in!" and turning to Sebastian "I think you did well Prime Minister, very well."

Sebastian, always worried that any adulation aimed at him was sure to be followed by a request for him to do something, said "Well, I'll come with you to all these Countries! Next is France I think, then Germany, that's a tricky one because they don't have nuclear weapons, and only a small navy, so they spend comparably more on land and air forces than we do!"

With that all talk of rebellion over NATO and Euro Army was finished, nobody seemed willing to challenge the Defence Secretary further.

Sebastian realised that was definitely not the answer the EU Elite in Brussels had in mind, they wanted an independent Army which would in time be able to operate in its own right and like the nearly Federal state it was, it had long sought an EU Foreign Office and an EU Defence Establishment.

But Sebastian sensed that most of the former Eastern European states had no doubt about it at all, a European Army unconnected with the USA was not worth anything, by the time any EU country had been invaded it would take weeks to pass through the various committees and the crisis would have been over before any action was agreed. This was the 'sales chat' that Sebastian worked out with Michael Morgan to convince the smaller countries, so all they had to do now was to convince the French and Germans. That was not going to be easy.

Sebastian reported back to Payunk Wask that the first stage of the NATO proposal had been successful.

Sebastian called Colonel Simon Collingham, "Look I need you to do a special job for me, could you trot around later please?" They were spotted together outside No 10 deep in conversation. Simon Collingham nodded his head and said "OK" then left.

Chapter THIRTY-SIX - The NATO plan moves ahead

Sebastian and Michael Morgan together with Simon Collingham arranged the visit to Paris to meet the French President; this time it was a formal visit at 10.00 am.

Sebastian wanted to do the double, drop in at Berlin on the same day so they had booked a flight from Paris to Berlin at 2.00 pm. But he wanted to allow the French time to absorb his proposals. Unlike the Americans, Sebastian expected some ruffled feathers as the USA appeared to have gone along with a UK Plan, that was quite enough to raise French hackles and throw it out from the start. Any UK/USA plan so the French always reckoned was bound to be an Anglo-Saxon plot that would put the French at a disadvantage. So Sebastian had earlier realised that he needed something to mollify French sensibilities. He hoped that Simon's homework would be worth it!"

The UK team were driven into the Elysee Palace just off the Champs-Elysee. The French President advanced down the steps to meet them. A red carpet had been rolled out and a troop of Republican Guard were duly inspected by Sebastian.

The President told them something of the place, it was basically started in 1722 in what could be called the French Classical style. It was sold in 1803 to the Emperor and it was here that on 22nd of July 1815 that he signed his abdication. In 1853 Napoleon 111 made significant architectural modifications. It was in 1873 that it became the official presidential residence. There are considerable gardens attached. The French President led them from the vestibule d'honneur, the meeting and greeting are straight into the Salon des Ambassadeurs the small reception area for foreign dignitaries. There was an imposing chandelier and large mirrors on one side. Several period chairs with blue furnishings on the chair uprights and gilded wood were ranged around in a semicircle.

After normal pleasantries Sebastian started. He aimed to begin where he had ended the previous conversation.

"Mr President, have you had any further thought about the Joint UK/France African military base near Lake Chad? I have received expressions of interest from the Nigerian government!"

The French President was non-committal "Well." At that moment one of the French Generals leant over and whispered something in his ear. "That Oh Yes I remember, yes it's on our OK list but not yet at the top of the file!"

"Well, I have been doing some research and I think we have found the perfect leader, a man of exceptional talent, who I would like to propose to you?"

The French President was playing with a pencil on his jotter, he said nothing but waved Sebastian on, he was clearly prepared to be bored with details of a no-doubt well tested British General whom he had never met, and probably never would!

"Yes its Colonel Jacques Moulin! You will know him of course! Our research shows that he did exceptional work in Mali a couple of years ago, a linguist and former foreign Legionnaire, I think? He is well acquainted with the tribes in the area!"

The French President looked up "Qui? Who?" He repeated in English.

"Colonel Jacques Moulin!" Sebastian repeated. Michael Morgan began to worry that Sebastian must have got his wires crossed somehow and was about to as he thought intervene to save Sebastian. But Sebastian waved him away.

The French asked for a couple of minutes and formed a group at the other end of the room.

The President returned almost transformed.

"You say you want this man to lead the Joint Group?"

"Yes that's it! That's it exactly!"

"But he is French!"

"Naturally with a name like that it's unlikely he could be anything else! My research suggests he's the best man for the job!"

The President disappeared again amongst the military personnel. He returned "Yes we can do that!"

"Good thank you Mr President, now I want to get to the main matter in hand!"

The French President interrupted him "You know Mr Edwards you come up with the strangest things and we don't know whether to laugh or cry. You remember some time ago you were talking about sharing Nuclear Weapons do you remember?"

Sebastian shot a 'Ok wait till I tell you' nod at Michael Morgan who clearly had heard nothing about it.

The President continued "..and all that came to nothing, we spent hours ready for a briefing to your Military but nothing happened. So what have you got for us in your bag today?"

Sebastian handed out, across the elegant table, copies in French of the letter he had given to Cedric Elsworthy.

Again the French disappeared as a group!

The French President returned scratching his head. "You mean to split NATO into two, you take one half and we take the other?"

"Yes that's it roughly, of course the USA troops won't fall under either command! You will see that we did endorse you for this role?"

"Where would the line run?" asked one of the French Generals.

Michael Morgan sprang to life and responded, "North of the French frontier UK, Holland, Belgium, Luxembourg, Germany, Norway, Czech, Slovakia, Hungary and the Baltic States. UK also deals with neutral states Ireland, Sweden, Finland, Iceland. It would call for a naval presence in the Baltic. And several new airfields probably in Poland and several early warning station probably in the Baltic states.

The South is to you to organise; Spain, Portugal, Italy, all the Balkan states, Romania, Bulgaria, Greece, Cyprus, Malta all you. Also you probably dealing with Austria and Switzerland. Monaco, Lichtenstein and so on, even neutral countries need to be updated. It would call for a naval presence in the Mediterranean. It would need probably several airfields in Greece and early warning stations on the perimeters? But that is up to you?.

I must confess I have not yet added up the populations in each zone, nor the GDP and we would have to try to equalise things as much as we can, but I guess we could do that? Also some countries on the peripheries might prefer one zone or the other, we would try to accommodate that!"

"But, but" the French President was still hesitant "Will the USA agree?"

Michael Morgan again "It seems so! The lure for them of course is twofold, first both North and South commands bringing countries up to the 2% of GDP which the USA has tried to do but failed completely and second saving perhaps $20 Billion per annum through reduced USA military costs in Europe!"

"Yes Yes I can see that!" The French President still hesitated. "Would the other Countries agree? Would Germany?"

Michael Morgan clearly warming to his task, "Well Poland and the Baltic States are in! You see up there they believe that Russia is a constant threat, the politicians there don't think it will come to that, but the people have long memories they will do this to get 'presence, presence, presence' of troops on the ground, that's what the people feel they want, but they also want to retain NATO and not run a parallel army! That's roughly how we got here!"

"So no Euro Army!" Asked the President.

"No none at all! – everything would be done in and through NATO."

"Hmmh" the French President seemed to like it "Brussels will not like it!"

"No I know they will not, but if you like, this is partly payback to you for the years that you have spent developing your nuclear shield under which most of these other states in the South have now found protection!"

"By the way, one of these days when National sensitivities are a bit less aggressive, I firmly believe that it will be possible to have a joint nuclear deterrent., It would save up both Billions. Some day! But not today not yet awhile!"

The French President nodded gravely. "Ok what's next?" he added.

"Well are you in?" asked Michael Morgan,

"Probably, let you know tomorrow! It has to be referred to Cabinet, it would just be an outline assent of course?" came the reply. "So what are you doing now?" the French President asked. "We have guests' quarters you know the Hotel de Marigny nearby. You would be welcomed to stay and this afternoon I could have you shown the impressive Portrait room here, it's a snapshot of all the European Heads of State of Napoleon 111's time?".

"Going to Berlin" replied Sebastian, "want to finish key NATO members today - flight leaves in an hour!"

"Good Luck! Then and bonne chance!"

"Thank you and don't forget Colonel Jacques Moulin!" Sebastian shouted to the President as they turned to leave.

"Who? Qui!" he shouted back , they both laughed, as he waved farewell. "A demain! Till too-morr-ow".

They scratched a few sandwiches at the airport and took a normal commercial flight to Berlin.

They arrived 90 minutes later and were driven direct to the Bundeskanzleramt the German Federal Chancellery and met with the Secretary of State Peter Eldernaier, who greeted them on arrival, he gave the UK party a brief description of the building "It's made entirely from concrete and glass in what is called postmodern style, though some people refer to it as the Kohlosseum from Kohl and Colosseum, because of its huge size. It's the largest government HQ in the world". He then took them to the Chancellors personal offices to meet the Prime Minister, Frau Angela Schwerdtfeger.

There were taken to a modern suite of offices up several flights into some plush air-conditioned meeting room fully carpeted and with light brown leather chairs.

Sebastian introduced the topic and Michael Morgan as before launched into his project. It was apparent that they must somehow have been pre-warned because the German group had appeared to stop listening soon after the start, but continued to read the paper given them, pointing out to each other certain clauses.

Their questions were much more direct.

"So Mr Edwards what makes you think you should take a lead?

Simon had been briefed to answer this and he gave a long list of UK's military involvement in the last 20 years. Michael Morgan described in some detail their nuclear deterrent.

"So what role do you expect us to play in this?"

Sebastian thought there were two levels of interest. "First there would naturally be some several senior command posts available. Initially it's my view that the Senior General would be British, thereafter he or she would be chosen on merit!"

German eyebrows shot up and Sebastian knew he had their interest. Michael Morgan continued.

"The other thing that might be of interest is that part of our mission is to ensure that all EC countries in this sector and even neutral countries should spend the full 2% of their GDP that means additional equipment. Aircraft, Tanks, Armoured Vehicles, Headquarters, Communications, listening posts, perhaps landing craft, submarines and intelligence networks. So we would be looking to you to supply alongside us and naturally the other NATO countries compatible with their skills. For example probably standardising on Typhoon Aircraft, which your country and ours have in great numbers. Naturally we would expect double jigs and tools so that in the event of any invasion the same production would be available from different countries beyond enemy reach, dispersed!"

"What would the value of this equipment be?" One General asked.

Michael Morgan replied "We don't know yet" he continued "We envisage the Northern Command being Headquartered here in Berlin because it's easier for land movements".

"You should understand that all troops in all these Armies come directly under NATO, so we are not weakening but strengthening NATO. We will not move without their agreement!"

One of the German Generals was more belligerent "We always knew there was some reason for you holding back from the Euro Army concept we simply could not understand why you tried to deliberately screw it up all the time! But I suppose here we have the answer you were waiting for the USA to want to reduce spending in Europe and seeing an opportunity jumped in to seize leadership which according to your available land forces you do not deserve!"

"General you are totally and completely wrong, despite your past, hardly any of your troops have seen active battlefield duty".

"Well some of your battlefield experience recently has not been that great!" The General interrupted again.

Sebastian would have none of it "Frankly you have nobody yet fit to command your own troops never mind any other countries. One other Country told us bluntly they would prefer not to have your troops at all, but it's a case for them of needs must! So you can take that head on General you would be a 'needs must' commander. You may be aware that the UK has in the past on occasions been asked to take command of a naval operations taking charge of British and US and French warships, this is an extension of that, being under the leadership of one country should ensure speedy decision-making something that would be likely to outperform a committee run Euro Army.".

Michael Morgan nudged Sebastian and whispered in his ear "you are going too far" .

Sebastian continued unrepentant "My colleague here is reprimanding me for being too tough on you General but I do not think so at all! What you and I are saying is exactly what the troops will be saying lower down, so we may as well engage directly right now! Ultimately of course the USA might want to reduce its nuclear forces from Europe, if it did so then however much you deride our Nuclear Forces they would be your shield too, you are lacking that arm, I think!"

The German General wished to relent, Sebastian said "There's no need, I much prefer that you say such things to my face than behind my back, those are the sorts of robust comments we have to live with and I am glad that we can start in an open and honest fashion!"

The Prime Minister had no further questions they thanked the UK delegation and told them that they would discuss this in Cabinet and with their coalition colleagues and give their first response on the following day. "It's not" their Defence Minister suggested "quite the thing we had been expecting, but on the whole we welcome the UK's renewed interest in defending Europe which we believed you had long given up to concentrate on a 'global' capability!"

The meeting ended and they all flew back to London that night.

Sebastian felt the strength draining out of him during that last engagement with the German General, he felt weak on the way back to the embassy car which had come to collect them.

Sebastian felt tired, he put it down to a lack of drink during the day, but it was obvious to the others he was wobbling putting out his hand to steady himself on every handrail for support. On arrival at the airport he fainted.

When he came around there was a yellow oxygen mask over his face and a white coated Medic was peering at him anxiously. They had to rest in a special Government reception centre for a few minutes before he could board.

Colonel Simon Collingham told Michael that he, Simon, would handle him and see him on the plane "We have done this before Sir, him and I"

"Oh really?" said Michael Morgan with some surprise.

Simon pulled up his trouser leg to reveal some nasty scars across his lower leg. "Five years ago this person helped drag me down a lane out of Russia into

Ukraine, I can tell you as sure as I know anything, that had he not done so I would now be in goal in Moscow facing a further 10 years in prison!"

"When was that?" asked Michael.

"Oh in 2015!"

"That's before he became an MP?"

"That's right, he and I we go back a long way, we were in business in Russia!"

"Ah that was it, I had heard some vague rumours about how he got his O.B.E.!"

Simon very gently put his arm under Sebastian's and they moved towards the plane and he murmured to Sebastian "Just like on the old trail, one step at a time, can you make it? When we get to the foot of the steps, the staff will want to see you walk up unaided, if you can't we might have to take the next flight. Sir, can you do that for me? You won't fall I'll be right behind you!"

"Yes that's OK Jeffery thanks, I'll manage now! Thank you" Sebastian croaked rather weakly.

So they boarded the plane and headed home.

As he later explained to cabinet colleagues, it was clear to Michael Morgan as he saw Sebastian helped onto the plane, that it would now be up to him to complete the changes proposed.

During the flight Sebastian discussed it with him. Michael Morgan would have to visit every one of the NATO member countries, there would be no change until and unless every country agreed. Sebastian asked him straight out "Can you do it Michael?"

"I'll have to make sure my Tory colleagues agree but given that YES! I will!"

They shook hands, then they each went home.

Sebastian again did not sleep well. Bill and Madge alerted Sylvia to Sebastian's worrying condition. Sylvia understood that immediately when she saw him the following day. She installed herself in No. 10 and immediately took control. From Friday lunchtime she banned him from all meetings, she gave him some of the pills that Sebastian's Doctor had given him in December the previous year.

He slept like a log that night and on the following night.

He briefly called Payunk Wask the following day to the effect that the second and third items of the NATO proposals were now underway, he signalled to Payunk that he should start the preliminaries for the UK EC Project. Sebastian asked him to come to the Cabinet meeting the following Tuesday.

Meanwhile a brief press release suggested that the 'Prime Minister was confined to bed with a severe head cold!' Sylvia told Sebastian "I am staying here now, in London, until your Premiership is finished! Do you understand?"

Bill Bennett and Madge knew that booking any future meetings had to be routed through Sebastian's wife.

Over the next two days both Germany and France assented to the NATO plan in principle. The news soon leaked out.

The EU elite was furious, they knew they would not now get an independent Euro Army.

Michael Morgan later told Sebastian that, after a tussle with fellow Tory Cabinet Ministers, they agreed to change Defence policy and ordered a new Strategic Review, the commitment to NATO (North) was to be made clear and urgent steps were to be taken to locate two suitable permanent military UK bases one in the Baltics and one in East Poland. The bases in Cyprus were to be vacated, the gap in the Mediterranean was to be covered by one of the new aircraft carriers in the Eastern Mediterranean. France was to cover the Western Mediterranean and the South Atlantic with its Subs and Carriers.

Chapter THIRTY-SEVEN – Consolidated Constitutional Bill – final passage

Sebastian had received a warning message from the Chief Whips office. It just stated baldly 'Forty to fifty defections likely on Devolution Bill!"

For the following Tuesday's Cabinet meeting Sebastian again warned the Cabinet Secretary that they meeting should start at 8.00 am and that cabinet members should not rely on finishing before 12.30 pm.

After a brief updating on the NATO restructuring, Sebastian passed to matter to Michael Morgan for more details. He confirmed that both Paris and Berlin had agreed in principle, although they may be a re-arrangement of one or two countries to shift from North to South as although the populations in each zone were about equal at 250 Million people. The GDP favoured the North on the current suggested split. He said he was now visiting each of the capitals of countries associated with NATO as well as all the theoretical neutral states.

Theoretical he said "because if there is a real conflagration it's unthinkable that those who are members of the EC and gain advantage from it, would see co-member EC states being attacked and overpowered. So whilst we have to accept their current stance on neutrality, it's unreasonable to imagine that if all hell broke loose they could or would just stand by. Otherwise they might themselves just be overwhelmed as was Belgium in the First World War and Holland in the Second. Accordingly all neutral states within the EC will be pressurised to re-equip themselves adequately to ensure that they might not be the weak links in the chain through which member states might be attacked.

So far I have visited a further 9 countries and expect to cover the remainder within two or three weeks. Then I will be in a position to make a fuller report.

Thus far the response has been positive, the exact command structure will need creating together with a plan for the deployment of troops, airfields and naval bases and a programme of re-equipping will have to be put in place.

There are going to be difficulties, we know that. Bulgaria, although a member of NATO, has historically been much more favourable to Russia than any other EC Country. This is because Russia came to their aid in the nineteenth century to free them from Turkish rule. Indeed after the Second World war they were the only country in the Soviet bloc which Stalin decreed did not require USSR occupying soldiers. So maybe we have to treat them like a neutral state. I am liaising with the French Government almost daily on matters such as these!"

Sebastian praised the Defence Secretary for his prompt taking over of the issue.

Sebastian then moved towards a review of the Consolidated Constitutional Enabling Bill whose third and final reading was scheduled to start the following Monday. He reminded the Cabinet that this was one of the planks of the Coalition Agreement. He asked the Chief Whip to comment on the likely voting patterns.

Instead of his normal parade ground confident and strong voice, the Chief Whip's voice was barely audible; Sebastian asked him to speak up. He repeated more loudly, "Well. Sir, All Lib Dems would be voting for, of course, as well as most of the Tories."

"Most? How many absences or defections are expected?" asked Sebastian.

"Forty-five, Sir!"

Sebastian appeared not to have heard what was said merely saying "And?"

"Of the opposition, it appears that the SNP will probably vote against, the Labour Party do not appear to have made up their minds yet, but the view is they might also oppose. The position of the Northern Ireland MPs is unclear!"

"So your prognosis Sir John?"

"A likely defeat, Sir."

"Are there any of those around this table who have intimated they intend to vote against, Sir John?" asked Sebastian.

"Yes! Sir, three."

"Come out now please – who are you?"

Slowly hands were raised, first one, then a couple and another and then later another still – 5 in all.

Sebastian turned to Pamela Tressider the interim Tory Leader. "You realise that this was one of the Coalition key points! Accordingly I want to hear from you by tomorrow noon that a three line whip will be deployed and that those who fail to vote in accordance with the Coalition will have the Whip removed! – Can you confirm that you intend to do that?"

Pamela Tressider demurred, hesitated for a split second too long.

"So I have to take matters into my own hands, I see." He continued,

"Let me be clear that unless I have on my desk no later than noon tomorrow a letter from each of you five confirming that you will vote with the Coalition on this matter, I will have no alternative but to suspend you from the Cabinet!"

There was a muttered protest "You surely cannot do that!"

"I am well aware that under the agreement it is for the Tory Leader to specify which Tory should be in which Government post. So I will not be changing the posts. However we do have a precedent for what I am now proposing. Each of you five will lose your Cabinet ranking, you will report direct to me in respect to your Ministries on a daily basis. This information will be made Public at 1.00 pm tomorrow. Cabinet Secretary will you please now draw up the necessary papers.

In view of this, I will, this afternoon, engage directly with the SNP and with the Labour Party, hoping to engage their support.

As you will remember I have been involved with all Parliamentary parties on this matter right from the start over two years ago. I therefore know exactly what the price will be for each of them.

Let me tell you all what it will be.

The SNP will ask me to guarantee that any future Lib Dems in Government will introduce a Bill for a new Scottish Referendum to be taken as and when the SNP, or if you like the Scottish Parliament, thinks fit. You will all understand that polls on the matter regularly go up and down, so it would be a considerable advantage to them to be able to pull the trigger on the starting gun, when they choose. Subject to my Party's agreement, I am minded to accept this. Such that any reformed Coalition in this or any other future parliament of which we are a part, will carry this bag and baggage.

Will you, Sir John, please make clear to all who intend to vote against or abstain, that I will do this. I don't want to, but if I have to, I will. Each of those on your list will be the direct cause of a likely break-up of the UK. Make sure they understand this please!

I will also discuss the matter with the leader of the Labour Party. Their remaining doubts over it are as follows;

Firstly they object to the 70 'selected experts' who are included in the reformed second chamber, in order to add depth and expertise to the debates and ensure that any laws are both practical and necessary. They want these 'experts' to have no right to vote, nor indeed, in their view, should the 10 religious appointees. Their argument has always been that these people will tend to be older and richer and more likely to back a Conservative, rather than a Labour Government. In order to mollify them I could introduce some sort of independent judicial review of the issues, so these 'cross benchers' could only vote on matters which were not threatening to the Government of the day. I would and could agree to that but it would introduce a legal framework, unnecessarily in my view, and diminish the independence of these 'experts'.

Their second objection is that since NHS has been devolved administratively to the Regions, they want to ensure that those Assemblies can in effect block all attempts by outside parties to quote for and obtain portions of NHS work. Currently they have, under this Legislation, only powers after an outside quote has been obtained to allow the NHS Unit concerned, or even any other NHS Unit, a period or 90 days in which to re-organise itself internally to equal or better the outside quote. You can understand this is a point of principle, currently time is allowed to improve the internal service, under Labour's requirements there would be no further ability to open any areas up to outside competition in regions where they control or dominate those assemblies. This is their so-called 'privatisation' of the NHS. Both I, and the NHS CEO, believe it will not be to the long term advantage of the NHS to do this, since it would protect the NHS from any kind of competition and encourage staff to object to internal changes to make them more efficient. However in order to obtain the support of the Unions and The Labour Party, I would, if I must, agree to their changes.

Would you therefore Sir John, as Chief Whip, make known these trade-offs that I am prepared to do.

Ladies and Gentlemen this Bill will pass with or without your consent. Cast your minds back if you will to Trident. None of us Lib Dems at the time believed that you Conservatives had tried to review alternatives as you said you would. Never-the-less, it was in the Agreement so we felt obliged to allow it. You now face a similar challenge. Are you able to carry through your commitment?

Just consider for a moment the value of any undertaking in future given by your leaders on behalf of all your MP's!"

There was silence around the table.

"Ok then we meet here noon tomorrow". Sebastian announced quietly, he was however twisting the signet ring on his little finger and looked drawn.

"Now whilst I am on the subject there are a couple of amendments on which I would like to seek your agreement.

Many MP's previously got themselves into incredible trouble over expenses and I would not like to see a repeat of that, it brings all politicians into bad odour. Accordingly I have asked the Cabinet Secretary to locate a couple of hotels to accommodate 200 people and to acquire them for the purpose of allowing all 'Senators' to stay there. If, of course, they chose another place then that place would not be eligible as an expense!

Currently there is too little debate in Parliament of either ongoing EU laws, this is important so that MEPs are properly briefed on the views of Members of Parliament; nor indeed is there adequate review of the Ombudsmens' reports, these too are important since they allow Members of Parliament to plug the gaps where flaws in our laws are exposed. To that end I intend to ensure that at least two days a month are left in the Parliamentary programme for proper televised debates. It will be mandatory on all MEPs and Ombudsmen to attend.

I hope you will agree with these changes?"

One Cabinet member asked if it was indeed legal to compel MEPs to attend.

"No it isn't, not yet!" there was a pause, "But I intend to put the matter to the EU, they are well aware of the gap between National Parliaments and the EP."

The meeting finished with no votes taken.

The Cabinet Secretary hung back and caught Sebastian's eye.

"Are you sure that you wish me to draft the necessary papers, PM?" His eyebrows shot up in obvious alarm.

"Yes please do so immediately and also draft the Press Release just the changes no explanation and please get the amendments to the Bill agreed with the Minister Sarah Driscoll!"

There was a pause. Sebastian considered for a minute.

"Now please get me the Leader of the SNP! And please Cabinet Secretary pick up a feed-in line, but on no account speak OK?"

A few minutes later the phone was pressed into Sebastian's hand.

"Ah hello there, I wanted to invite you to make a presentation to the Cabinet, you know I think it's very useful to make direct contact. The Cabinet Secretary will be contacting you shortly as far as dates are concerned. Now there's another matter coming up. I am most concerned that whilst we are in a 'United Kingdom' we should ensure that you are properly consulted. In effect this left representation of Wales, Northern Ireland and Scotland to be further defined, however I now think it would be best to carry those changes out at the same time. Tell me! Were you intending to support the Bill next week?"

There was silence for a moment.

"Well Prime Minister, that omission was one of the reasons we had intended to vote against, we couldn't see anything in it for us, we were just ignored, but if you intend to put the amendment in then we might reconsider!"

Sebastian pushed further "Well what I had in mind was to permit you as of right to attend a Cabinet meeting in London every month to discuss the effect of ongoing legislation and also to allow you to yourself to press for changes in our legislative programme affecting the whole of the UK?"

"Well Yes! To give us a statutory right to meet the Cabinet on a regular basis might be something we would value, but as you know, there's only one thing we really want from you, that's the ability to call the independence referendum at a time of our choosing!"

Sebastian paused, "Now you know the Conservatives would never permit that?" he said admonishingly."

"Oh well, it was just a hope! – Anyhow I'll think of the point you raised and I'll discuss it here!"

"Oh! yes and there is another point, following changes to NATO it's likely we can relocate Trident to another Port. That's what you wanted I think? There will be some redundancies though!"

"Well, we are not as keen on that as we were. Unemployment in Glasgow could rise!"

Sebastian responded "Well it's your call, we are all ready to move on this!"

"Thanks" responded Sebastian "I am trying to plan ahead here, could you give me a call back tomorrow AM. There may be some Conservative abstentions on the Constitution Bill, I would be grateful if you could see your way to supporting it, after all the Regions here are being belatedly offered the sort of powers you had several years ago! It would be a pity if you were castigated as unable to see their point of view? Opposing everything from Westminster doesn't endear your case to anyone here you know!"

"OK, I'll bear it in mind!"

The Cabinet Secretary had been listening intently on the separate line. "Hmmh" he murmured "where do you think that leaves us?"

"I don't know" Sebastian replied, but please get your constitution group to first draft amendments for each of the three country Leaders to attend a Cabinet meeting as of right, say once a month!"

There was another pause as Sebastian considered what points he could make to the Labour leader.

"Now let's have the Leader of the Labour Party – same basis as before – listen in carefully please".

"Here he is Sir" and the phone was passed over to Sebastian

"Hello, look! Sebastian here, I was just calling to check up on you reaction to the NATO proposals. I know the matters might have leaked out, but if you have a few moments, I'd like to run you through what we are doing? Good? OK."

Sebastian ran through the proposal in outline. "There are two things that might be of interest; first in order to increase NATO spend up to 2% of GDP, many countries will have to re-equip and that could well mean buying British Aircraft, Tanks and Communications hubs. The other is that playing alongside rather than against France as far as nuclear arms is concerned, it then gives us huge opportunity to develop joint Nuclear defence systems, reducing substantially the stock of nuclear warheads."

"Well both of those sound interesting Sebastian, let me know how they are proceeding please.."

He was about to hang up when Sebastian stopped him, "There's just another point. Have you made up your mind as to whether you are prepared to support the Constitutional Bill. There may be a few Conservative abstentions so it'll be tight!"

"Abstentions are the least of your problems, I hear that 50 will vote against and several Cabinet Ministers too or haven't you heard? An ex-Whip like you? I would be very surprised! You know how it works, so you know all that already?"

"Well yes, I spent today fire-fighting – it would be a pity to see the Bill die?"

"There is one thing that might help us swing it in your favour though Sebastian!"

"Ok I am listening."

"The Regions should have enough powers OK, but they won't have enough Capital to help young thrusting firms in the Region to expand. It was thought that our current UK big banks would help and set up a sort of 3iii replacement. You know in the 1950's the UK big banks created an independent unit specifically to invest in smaller companies. Sadly like everything else in the deregulation period they too became very posh and won't go anywhere near the small fry; £250 K is far too small for them. Is it possible to have a fund? There's the British Business Bank couldn't that be created for each Region? – I think that would help our decision making! That and of course this NHS competition rules thing, but I guess you will not change that!"

"You are right, it hits at the basis of what we are doing which is to increase competition at all levels, but the Bank idea is a good one. I'll work on that! I'll call you tomorrow!"

Sebastian put the phone down and gave a big sigh of relief. Then to the Cabinet Secretary, "Please get me John Wires, you know? He was Business Secretary in the 2010/15 coalition".

They met a twenty minutes later. "John, I need a small business bank in each of the Regions, what can you do for me?"

"Handelsbanken, that's what you need Svenska Handelsbanken!"

They spend the next two hours working out doing some research, seeing if it were possible to set up look-a-like Banks in the UK. They called the UK's Head Office of Handelsbanken.

At the end of that time they were far from sure that they had the right answer. The Handelsbanken had indeed a very considerable reputation. It really was your friendly local bank and it had already penetrated the UK market, as it said 'We serve more than 60 communities in the UK' it was a brand likely to expand further. It had received awards for its Business Model, for being ethically correct, driven by internal growth that was higher than competitors, having exceptional customer orientation despite a lower cost, with lower loan write-offs, and to boot a wide range of financial products and a procedure which left decisions in the hands of the local bank manager. The latter was a practice which, in the UK, had almost completely died out decades before, UK Bank managers had absolutely no commercial powers, they were mere paper pusher. So it appeared to tick all the boxes!

The problem was that it didn't enter the Equity Market, It didn't invest in a local firm as part of that company's equity. Basically it leant on the basis of assets, like buildings, land, equipment, or on sale invoices sent out for which it would provide money up front, it would also support export operations or indeed buying foreign materials. So it was ideal for established businesses looking to expand.

But it didn't lend unsecured and as almost all start-ups lacked any assets, they were battling to find cash for opening expenses.

They looked deeper into why the Handelsbanken model had not been taken up by other countries. A study had been carried out in 2014 by the Danish Banking sector hoping to use that model for their own medium sized banks, however they had reached the conclusion that the Danish banks would be subject to stricter regulation on decentralisation as the Danish comparator bank's default risk was much higher, also that Handelsbankens' 'cultural control systems' and the more 'trust-based and output oriented style of leadership' could not be adopted easily by other existing banks.

It was clear that once the system was in the UK as one of its 'Home Markets' it would and indeed had expanded at its own rate with which it felt comfortable, but it was not a model that could be copied or forced into other UK banks. So whilst its presence would be welcomed, it would not be an answer to their immediate problem.

Britain's past attempts to create Funds and subsidise capital injections into the SME market had been a dramatic failure. In a scheme launched by Labour called Regional Venture Capital Funds, £137 M was raised from private investors, plus £80 M from the Government and a further £53 M from the EU. The Government even stated that in the event of trouble the government's portion of any investment would be the first forfeited, so private investors had less to loose. A research report suggested that the scheme 'had had no impact on employment' and that the taxpayers stake by 2010 had fallen by 93%.

A further attempt by the 2010 coalition investing £200 M in 'Enterprise Capital Funds' failed to lock into the Regions and the vast majority was eventually run from the Oxford-Cambridge-London hub, so that too wasn't a track to follow.

At a higher level the £3.2 Bn Regional Growth Fund launched in 2010 seems to have become hi-jacked into making loans to larger firms, basically try to save well known iconic companies, but they were not interested in the smaller fry.

They knew that the British Business Bank, which John Wires himself had a hand in setting up, does not invest directly but through and alongside intermediate groups or other venture funds, often labelled, 'Catapults'. It did not seem sensible to restructure that, investment connections often take years to develop and on balance it might do more harm than good disrupting those carefully constructed networks of contacts.

John Wires said "If it has to be based on a Regional basis and I agree that if it has to fit in with the new Assemblies to give them depth, they they will have to invest across a whole range of industries, they would be likely too few to specialise in any one industry, but generalist investors suffer worse results as they have to try and understand each industry sector they invest in, even when that happens, that knowledge cannot be used further unless there are following investment in that sector".

They stood back baffled. Sebastian was twisting the ring on his little finger again.

Sebastian picked up the positives. "Look in these Regions there are many large and medium sized successful businesses, some companies from USA, Germany and Japan, there are likely to be Business Schools, a pool of Legal and Accounting professional talent. Universities are keen to get in on the game to capitalise on their IP, which often means they have the ability to spin off new developments. Also now there is the added desire to create businesses, for the Region of which they are part. So there is or will be something new Political Will and Regional Pride!"

"Meaning?" asked John Wires.

"Why can't we throw it at them!"

"What? At them at the Regional Assemblies you mean?" Asked John still mystified.

"The Challenge! The whole point of Regionalisation is to allow the Regions to bloom and do their own thing. Hey you out there! Get together, formulate a plan, use the talents you have there. We have ballsed it up from London – it's your territory, come on think!"

"Well all good rhetoric, I am sure Sebastian, but we cannot exactly put that into law can we?"

"OK let's start at the beginning" Sebastian was not giving in. "why don't we ask the firms there that are already successful to nurture a new business each, you know, chip off the old block? They have already inside knowledge of a particular sector and they themselves have proven ability so could form a subsidiary or associate with outsiders and then spin if off if successful! Look one of the companies I am think of is in the North, one of the few remaining IT companies. First they must have hundreds of Software proposals coming to them every year, most they will reject and it isn't in their specialism not in their field for existing customers who are accounting based but what happens to those ideas? Then that IT company has masses of IT engineers and designers, if they have good ideas unconnected with their mainstream products what happens to those?"

"Well" John Wires was thinking "you mean Corporate Venturing that's what it's called, of course you would have to be careful that the large company didn't nick the ideas or just get distracted if they had their own problems, but Yes it's a different approach!

As I remember it the concept of Corporate Venturing has existed for many years in the US where many of the top companies have a venture capital fund or offer strategic alliances. You know '3M' is often quoted as an example? While the number of companies involved is much smaller in this country, it has existed for many years and in many sectors but it has never been officially supported or encouraged. Let me do some checking I'll be back shortly!"

Sebastian was still nervous he needed something to 'sell' something to show that he wasn't just mouthing words which he had no intention of fulfilling. The idea had to have 'legs' or in his book it would not be worth doing. Of course there were the £2.0 BN 'Innovation and Productivity Grants, but these were operated from London and decisions were made there, he needed something with a Regional immediacy.

John Wires returned within minutes "Yes we can do something, good old HMRC, the taxman actually prepared a separate tax structure so that companies investing in smaller offshoots with third parties could gain tax relief so the structure is there already. The bad news is that the CVS scheme lasted from 2000 to 2010 and due to low uptake was never renewed. But the idea of Corporate Venturing has been successful and several large companies such as; Intel, Unilever, ARM, Reed Elsevier and BP have developed models of their own which apparently work. What I like about the idea, Sebastian, is that it should encourage the largest businesses in the regions to think laterally, to think how can they add businesses either eventually for themselves or to help develop the region. Too often we see large companies plonk themselves down in an area but yet are not part of it and they lack the wider responsibility for their town! So maybe a Japanese Car Company can set up a unit making small car parts here or developing skills it uses in its sophisticated paint shops to apply say to white goods manufacturers. It's something that the British Business Bank could invest in too. It's a way of getting spin offs from such companies and maybe as you say a UK IT developer thinks of a new APP and the IT company helps review it!

Ok Let's go for it! I'll ask the chancellor to re-open the CVS scheme and see it we can pump prime it by dropping in £100 M for each Region!"

Sebastian was relieved, sometimes he thought perhaps his own rhetoric overwhelmed the practicalities of his ideas.

"Ok thanks John, can you come back tomorrow noon and let me know if it is 'doable'? I have a feeling that we will need such things if we are to succeed on the Constitutional thing, otherwise the whole beast will crash down again! You will remember that we won the second EU referendum, we imagined that it was largely due to us gaining exemption from 'Free Movement of Labour', but maybe it wasn't that, maybe that under this devolution Bill the people see themselves as being able to influence important matters in their Region?"

John Wires left with a smile and a wave, unwilling to waste time ruminating over the past.

Sebastian was left alone, he set to thinking of the Constitution overall, he was deeply concerned over the issue of how the semi-independent smaller countries in the UK were to be governed and represented in Government decisions.

He remembered that in December 2017 one of his Cabinet colleagues had asked immediately after the constitutional referendum 'OK , Sebastian, I suppose this new constitution finally answers the question as to where and how matters involving these smaller Countries will be settled?' He had brushed off the question, then, but it was coming back to haunt him now. He felt a deep unease that Northern Ireland and Scotland were drifting away and that Wales would do the same maybe later. Until the 1970's or so Conservatives were linked in with the main Unionist Party in Ulster and Labour had at least a relationship with SDLP, similarly in Scotland all three main English parties were until the rise of the SNP strongly embedded there. But the Unionist Parties changed in Northern Ireland and there was now a separate power sharing agreement, and in Scotland all English parties took a severe drubbing in 2015! The Cabinet, Sebastian considered is no longer representative of those areas.

Sebastian mused 'So we work with this fiction that the UK Prime Minister appoints a Secretary of State FOR Northern Ireland and Scotland, these Ministers represent those peoples but they are not OF those peoples. In effect we run an English Cabinet passing laws in what might be called very much a Colonial spirit, of course as I found out, Cabinet Ministers don't often debate outside their ministerial remit, even when asked, but the Scottish and Northern Ireland aren't even given the right to challenge!

It would appear to be relatively simple to change matters. Just get the representative leaders of those Countries to join the Cabinet. Job done and they could drop in their penny-work as any other Cabinet Minister. But under current convention it's not possible. The Cabinet works as a unit. It alone gives instructions to the UK Civil Service, convention dictates that all the cabinet have joint responsibility for all decisions. Even if individual Cabinet members disagree they are never-the-less bound by that decision, unless the PM specifically states that for a particular matter that rule does not apply. But the SNP disagreed with austerity in principle and in practice and since cut backs affected most departments, it would have been completely impracticable to allow the SNP either to be steamrollered at every meeting 'I know you don't agree with austerity but...' or alternatively that SNP would question every decision. So it seems that estrangement of Scotland and Northern Ireland is inevitable. There would even be a way around that creating a sort of UK Cabinet over an English Cabinet, but then almost however it were arranged the numbers in each unit would be totally unequal – asymmetric, as they say. If you allocated points to countries on populations or GDP or gave say 2 points to a smaller country and 10 points to a larger country it still wouldn't make a workable arrangement. It would have to be so biased, like 1 vote to each country, to allow each country equal weighting to give the smaller countries a sense of relevance, but it would be so patently daft, with possible populations of 7 Million, outvoting England with 53 Million, that it would be just bloody daft.

Sebastian wandered up and down the Cabinet room circling the huge table; thinking out loud.

'So we are left with what is, substantially, an English Cabinet spewing out Laws which these Countries might not like. Previously of course Labour followed Tory which followed Labour etc., so opponents of one Act had simply to wait and when their time came simply overturn it or at least modify it, but someone in the SNP cannot reply on that bobbin's turn, they might never get the opportunity to over-turn it. They will' thought Sebastian 'get increasingly disgruntled or disaffected. The invisible threads which had connected Edinburgh and Belfast to Westminster for generations have been stretched over the years and were nearly broken'.

Sebastian had no solution, 'Maybe it's better to release Scotland now? But it wouldn't be possible to do the same with Northern Ireland, all the Protestants would immediately feel let down – and with some justice'.

Sebastian saw that he could take it no further, he had run out of ideas 'Even though we might be on the brink of the biggest constitutional rearrangement in the UK for 100 years, my plan is far from perfect, it is incomplete.'

He retired upstairs to the flat, deep in thought.

He saw that Sylvia, his wife, was getting worried again about his condition again.

Chapter THIRTY-EIGHT – Constitutional knock-about goes to the wire

The Cabinet assembled on the following day at noon.

Sebastian asked the five which way they intended to vote. Four of them said that after consideration they had agreed to allow the Bill through and had been persuaded to vote in favour. The Fifth said he was unable to change his view, he felt strongly that the House of Lords had worked effectively and there was no need for change, therefore he had intended to vote against but in deference to the interim leader of the Conservatives he had decided to abstain.

Sebastian turned to Pamela Tressider. "What do you intend to do now, replace him with another person in that role or just leave the matter there?"

"Well I had hoped that his abstention would be enough?" She appeared to be hoping the Tory minister could stay.

Sebastian rose to his feet and pointed a finger at the nervous Minister across the table.

"You are fired from this Cabinet!"

There were horrified glances around the table, no one could remember that any Cabinet Minister had ever been treated in that way, dismissed in front of colleagues was totally usual. Several Tories objected vocally and were about to walk out but were told by Pamela Tressider to "Sit Down!"

Sebastian took no notice but merely said, "May I thank you for your services as a Minister but I am unable to accept your ambivalent position. You lose your cabinet ranking and report through me on a daily basis".

Then turning to the Cabinet Secretary "Now Cabinet Secretary please remove him immediately and please have the Press Release issued as agreed at 1.00 pm".

A copy of the brief, three line press release was handed around the table. There were angry faces and grumbling around the table and several raised their hands asking to speak but Sebastian brushed them aside.

Sebastian then turned to the chief Whip. "Did you talk with those who told you previously they intended to vote against?"

"I did Sir!"

"and the result..?" asked Sebastian.

"There are still ten who will not change their mind!"

"Well thank you Chief Whip you have, I imagine, done considerable work there!"

Sebastian turned to Pamela Tressider again "Are you now minded to adopt a three line whip for this Bill and if so, can you state what punishment you intend to enforce?"

She replied hesitantly "Yes a three line whip will be issued but no I have not yet decided what further penalty to apply, that is surely a matter for myself, the Chief Whip and the individuals concerned?"

"No I am afraid it is not! There will be other slight amendments which I will inform you of tomorrow. May we meet again at noon tomorrow!"

"Pamela" Sebastian rarely called coalition colleagues by their first names, he was trying he believed to show empathy. "Do you wish for a further day to try to draw in those who disagree, in my younger and more idealistic days, I would probably have been in their shoes too on other similar matters. But I have devoted nearly 3 years of my life to this and its key to the Coalition. Please ask them again! If they have any coherent suggested changes I will still listen at this late hour of the Bill's life. It is not my intent to humiliate any Cabinet Minister but they should all know, that if I have to be the enforcer then I will."

"Yes an extra day might help" Pamela said.

The meeting finished.

Two days later at noon they met again.

Everyone could see immediately that Sebastian was in a much more positive mood. He had in fact just received information which suggested that those Northern Ireland MPs who normally attended Westminster, that means without Sinn Fein who had never entered the House of Commons, would likely vote in support as would the Greens. But everyone knew neither of these small blocks of votes could be relied upon.

Sebastian immediately went through the additional amendments.

Well I intend to permit two MPs each from the Assemblies in Northern Ireland, Wales and Scotland to attend a Cabinet meeting in London every month, as of right, to discuss the effect on their areas of ongoing UK legislation and also to allow them to propose changes in our legislative programme affecting the whole of the UK.

Next in order to make the workings of the new Senate House more efficient, the Government will be granted 8 and the opposition 4 further members from those elected to act as Ministers to take a lead in proposing or opposing the Government Legislation. I have been convinced that the small pool of Senators may not be sufficient to produce the leaders required. These will also serve as the Whips would in making sure the parliamentary work is completed. They will be able to speak but will not be also able to vote. They will be replaced as Senators by the next named individual on the regional lists.

A sub-committee is already to be established to adjudicate on conflicts between the House of Commons and the Senate House. If after a first attempt there is no resolution then the matter will be passed to the three senior Law Lords for decision.

Next there should be funding for the Regions so that they can develop their own growth. Past regional funds set up to invest SMEs which these days require a minimum of £250 K have been disasters and I see no reason why the same pattern would not be repeated if we were just to put in another £250 M in the same way. Accordingly I intend that a Corporate Venturing Scheme will be established supported by £100 M in each region and Country. The purpose of this is to link in those already successful businesses in those regions to use their skills to encourage or create new businesses either for themselves or for ideas generated in the region to which they can add their skill and technical expertise."

"Is that all?" Pamela asked in some confusion, she had obviously expected some larger bribes to be involved to ensure the passage of the Bill.

"Yes that's it! for now, other points are still ongoing!" Sebastian replied. "What is the score now Chief Whip?"

"Five, Sir, just five – most from the Oxfordshire area. It's to do with the new Region they wanted 'Heart of England'."

"So nothing ideological then!"

"Nothing!"

There was a sense of relief around the table, but no-one could be sure that the number would hold till next Tuesday. The meeting ended.

Sebastian went upstairs to the No. 10 flat and cancelled two meetings, he was plainly washed out.

Sylvia tried to jolly him along and eventually called his son Rupert and suggested that they nip over and see him on Friday as his college Unity in Camford, have dinner there and then spend the weekend at home.

Rupert being glad to host his father at his college, introduced the tired Sebastian to the 'masters' there at the top table. He was sitting next to one of them who happened to have a PhD in Operation Research on the other side of him was a Behavioural Scientist. They had both seen the TV clip of him arriving off the Brighton train, and one of them immediately asked question about the numbers of people, number of stops, drives absentee frequency and train speeds, the other one asked about alternative modes of transport like buses, car speeds, house costs and, what difference there was between sitting and standing and relative costs. That was all given at least as far as Sebastian could remember by the time the soup was finished. He ate his main course of roast beef in silence, the two experts scribbling away on either side of him. By the pudding, which was Jam Sponge covered in thick custard, they were ready with the answers.

"Well it's clear, if you cannot lengthen the train? Or increase its height to a double decker? Then you have to use trains following each other two minutes apart, forget trying to get rid of the guard, instead place him in the rear coach with backwards warning distance radar!"

"That's it" asked Sebastian amazed.

"Yes, that's it, at least from what you gave me?"

"So no taking seats out and using a bare carriage with sit-upons" As Sebastian which was his favoured option.

"No! No! Waste of time, all that will do at your preferred lower passenger price, would encourage more people to travel by train, as you say the roads are also clogged. The Rail franchise loses money and the passengers are as crammed as before. Running a following train will not necessarily increase the passengers by much, as other people that want to get to London, somehow do so anyhow. So it's likely passengers will shuffle themselves around between the peak time trains! If as you say the standard delay between trains is 5 minutes then you can only use that time before you would disrupt the whole time-table!"

Sebastian was amazed and was soon in discussion with them on other possible similar blockages he had come across, he made a mental note to return perhaps another Friday to test out other problems, he realised he had become too tied up in a little world of three or four major projects to the exclusion of everything else.

He thanked Rupert for giving him a diverting evening. He noticed his wife echo that thanks. He glanced at her, she smiled, Rupert smiled. Sebastian realised that they had done it as a ploy to get him away from his worries, 'Well' he thought as he 'turned in' at their guest accommodation in college 'they succeeded!"

Chapter THIRTY-NINE - The Damn Bill – Dead Bill or Live Act?

Sebastian awoke early on the Tuesday, they had had a calm week-end at home with no visitors and no surprises.

He was ready for the fray!

'Come what may' he thought 'this is the end of the Bill, after the final vote it will be either a dead Bill or an Act.'

The debate was ably lead off by Sarah Driscoll, she had clearly been through the material well and Sebastian had told her the bits she hadn't picked up. She had spent days preparing, she was going to do her brilliant best.

She did, she recounted the earlier failed bills and quoted the various leaders' comments, she informed, she implored, she used the logic of local interest, she challenged the people in the regions to wake up because they really were in control of huge budgets.

If hospital beds were not available for A & E patients and it was caused by bed blocking – We'll sort it out!

If traffic stood for 2 hours every day in a traffic jam in Tint whistle – We'll sort it out!

If there was a shortage of HGV Drivers or Brickies – We'll sort it out!

By the time she had finished going down the list "If there's a problem with…" the house didn't hear the end of the line, the supporting MPs shouted back "WE'LL, SORT IT OUT!"

SNP had decided to turn the other cheek which Westminster had never seen before, the cheek offering help and advice. The SNP promised to offer advice on setting up committees, working out targets, pay for their civil servants; they almost appeared to adopt the Regions from birth. Northern Ireland MPs offered advice on working together if parties were equally balanced on committees.

At last the Labour leader weighed in, claiming that he had been consulted at an early stage and he was glad to see that some of his (unnamed) proposals had born fruit and hoped that this would lead to the revival of the long-forgotten regions. He said "At long last the treatment of the elderly can be fully integrated under one administration 'bed blockers' in hospital can be transferred to monitored accommodation perhaps staffed partly by volunteers, this will help patients and hospitals alike."

Several of the Northern Conservative MPs were enthusiastic as were those from Birmingham.

Some Conservative and a few Labour MP's within the once-proposed new 'Heart of England' region were hostile saying they were losing one 'master' for another, and that it was a golden opportunity missed. Their referendum to create the new Region had passed but without reaching the the minimum turnout required, so it was deemed not legal.

There was a backlash from some MPs who had found that the force fit of Unitary Councils had unfortunately push dissimilar areas together. They were promised a review in 5 years.

When eventually the vote was taken there were in fact few against, some twenty in total. MPs of the main parties realised that voting against would send a very bad message to the voters in the areas whom they would then have to pump up and reinvigorate to get the same voters to support their candidates in just a few months' time.

The Bill was passed.

The Lib Dems biggest Constitutional gamble had come off, with virtually no support they had won through.

As Sebastian retreated upstairs for lunch, he immediately called Pamela Tressider and thanked her for her support, suggesting that no-one should be punished and the lone Minister should be restored to his full Cabinet role.

He had asked in the event of a victory that all the House of Lords Whips both Government, Cross Benchers and Opposition to meet with him that afternoon at No. 10, he requested the Garters Kings of Arms to attend as well, together with the Law Lords and the Lord Chancellor.

They met in the formal dining room at No 10 and the ever growing list of important members of the legislature parading down Downing Street drew reporters and the TV crews.

Sebastian read out a formal prepared speech which was also handed out to the waiting Press.

He said that now the Bill was passed, there will be a brief transition period, "... indeed some of the Lords might become senators in the new house, we hope they will put forward their names since many of them have skills as experts which are likely to be in short supply in the new House!"

He thanked all those present and past Members of the Lords for their Service to the State highlighting the number of famous members of the aristocracy and how they had developed along with the constitution from Stuart times through to the Victorian era. "Many must have felt that the House of Lords would have been been written out in the 1905 voting reforms, but they still survived and found a new purpose in life as excellent law reviewers".

Here he was able to quote some comic examples given him by the Clerk of how last minute adjustments by the Lords had inadvertently perhaps 'saved' a number of Bills, by eliminating errors left by the Commons.

He thanked the Life Peers for their interest and quoted examples of how their expertise had been of use.

He thanked the Lords Spiritual for their constant moral support of the socially deprived.

He then ended with the reason for calling them all together. "I want to make sure that we send you off with all the due pomp and circumstance that your past has earned you. Accordingly I hope to arrange a full ceremonial procession from the House of Lords to Westminster Abbey for a service of thanksgiving. I hope that it will be the week before Easter in 6 weeks' time. I have requested this because many of you, I know, will wish to retire soon and I would like for as many of you to attend as wish to do so.

Also I have for some weeks been secretly negotiating with the Kings of Arms to make a presentation to you of a plate either in Porcelain or in Silver, it will have your name and titles inscribed and carry a brief poem by the Poet Laureate in gracious thanks for your service.

The details you may find out through your Whips Office.

May I thank you once again for allowing through this Bill in one final act of Loyalty to the State. Please pass this message on; 'Thank you for your service to the State!' "

There was a buzz of approval and many thanked Sebastian for this unexpected courtesy.

Sebastian moved upstairs to the flat. He was exhausted but relieved, exclaiming. "Two main tasks completed!   One more to go! Ah March 31st! It cannot come too soon!"

Chapter FORTY - Tory Tricker or Defector?

After these particularly gruelling cabinet meetings, Sebastian saw Simon Gibson hanging back, he appeared to want to speak with him.

It was a trifle unusual as Tory Cabinet Ministers tended to go out together in a group. Sebastian of course knew Simon from years ago when they had both worked in the Whips Office and he had done Sebastian a favour. Of course they had recently worked on the overcrowded trains problem too, so when he saw Simon making a bee-line for him after the others had gone, he stood there waiting for the approach.

Simon stated falteringly ' Er Sebastian, I mean Prime Minister, I am getting increasingly worried about the infighting in the Cabinet today and I am seriously annoyed about the huge sums about to be spent on HS2, to the detriment of other routes for example do you know that one of the three routes from Sheffield to Manchester has been regularly clogged at TinTwistle for 10 years, traffic there often stands in a queue for two hours every day! Do you know that?

I tried to dissuade the Midlands Tories but it's quite impossible. Also I am very much in favour of the regionalisation and setting up of the Assemblies that you are promoting. Indeed I find myself wanting to support your stance on many many issues!"

"Well I am glad to hear it!" Sebastian replied and was about to move on out of the room when Simon blurted out "I think I would like to join the Lib Dems."

At first Sebastian did not appear to take in the words and was about to mouth the words, he started "Well that's good you want to.......!" but did not complete the sentence he had intended. He turned round to face Simon, pulled back one of the Cabinet chairs and said quietly, "You what?"

Simon amplified "Yes that's right, I have thought about it for a long time and finally made my mind up last night!"

"Well of course that's great" Sebastian warbled "Are you sure? Crossing over isn't easy you know and there are those on either side who will distrust you for ever! You know that?" Sebastian could see by the look on Simon's face that he was in some mental anguish.

'Well if you are sure then meet me in my old flat that I share with Bill Bennett he is my trusty and I value his input on such occasions. See you tomorrow night at 8.30 pm? OK"

As soon as Simon left Sebastian called Bill Bennett and arranged for both him and Madge to be there the following night at half an hour before the appointed time.

They met as agreed at Sebastian's old flat well away from any prying eyes. Sebastian quickly brought them both up to scratch including Sebastian's former contacts with him in the Whips' Office and the train incident.

Bill Bennet started taking the rational angle; Where was his constituency? Would he likely win as an LD if he switched – did he carry weight? In the large STV constituency what was the political make up? What was his voting record on all issues? What was his track record in his constituency, was he active and engaged? Was he well regarded within his Party or had he committed some policy infringements?

Madge looked at it through the personal behaviour prism; What would motivate a guy who clearly has his first foot on the ministerial ladder to jump ship as it were? Lib Dems had no power to increase their share of seats in the Cabinet, so had he thought he would lose that role and substantial income? Was he married or otherwise in a relationship and if so what were his partner's views? Was there something more fundamental that he was concerned about?

Sebastian argued that they had to be careful, it seemed unlikely but possible that he was a plant to discover 'our plans on voting through the EU measures for example', if he was able to gather information on Lib Dem intentions that would be worth its weight in gold to Tory Ministers! It might give them an early warning of the collapse of the Coalition if any Lib Dem walk-out was planned! – "not that we have any of course at this stage." He added quickly.

There was a knock on the door and Simon popped his head around the door walked in and shook hands confidently all around. Sebastian explained that he wanted Madge and Bill to ask him a few question before they made plans as to how to affect the transition.

They questioned him for a good hour as to his track record in parliament and about his constituency and indeed about his home life.

He withstood their questioning in good spirit saying that he did not like the straight jacket that was the Tory party. He then asked some hesitant questions about how the Coalition would be proceeding on various upcoming votes. Bill and Madge were non-committal feigning ignorance of Lib Dem ongoing tactics.

After about a couple of hours, of mostly light hearted chat and banter, Sebastian said that he would report this to the Party leader and he should expect to hear back in about a week's time. The Party would have to go through matters like; it's effect on the existing ranking of parliamentary candidates; but for himself he would happily see Simon Gibson come over and join the Lib Dems.

A week passed, at the following week's cabinet meeting as the Chief Whip was leaving he passed a note to Bill Bennett. After the meeting Bill pointed out the letter to Sebastian and they opened the envelope it simply said 'Whips don't cross the floor – ever!'

Sebastian, Bill and Madge met up with Dan Stirling the Party Leader as well as John Corn, the chief of staff. Bill Bennett summarised the meeting a week earlier, Sebastian chipped in about their time together in the Whips' Office and his work as a Junior Transport Minister. The others were silent then each in turn looked at the hand written message.

They deduced that unless it was a very strange co-incidence that the Chief Tory Whip Sir John Hopkins knew all about it – But about what?.

So what was Sir John trying to do? Perhaps warn Lib Dems that Simon Gibson was a plant or at least that he wasn't sincere in his views? But why would he do that? All that Sir John had agreed with Sebastian was to the effect that he saw it as his responsibility to protect the Coalition Government. Indeed he had been remarkably accurate about the advance notice he had given Sebastian concerning defections over the Devolution Bill. But would a junior Minister changing sides affect the Coalition? None of them could see how it related. Maybe Sir John knew something of Simon Gibson's past, maybe that if, whatever it was came out in public, then all Lib Dems would look very foolish? Maybe Sir John was merely trying to protect the Tories from becoming destabilised?

There were dozens of questions and no answers. Of course the most obvious thing would have been to call to Sir John and have it out with him. But they felt they couldn't do that, it would be tantamount to them interfering into internal Conservative matters, in any case if he had wanted to, Sir John could have made it clear why he had said what he did!

They all agreed to let it go for a further week.

During that time a sharp-eyed newspaper reviewer in Lib Dem HQ spotted a tiny report. 'Conservative MP discloses he is Gay!' It went on to reveal a sequence which was all too familiar. An MP with a wife and family in the country 100 miles away, goes to a gay club. Meets someone and begins a gay relationship. Sooner or later he knows it will come out and leading a double life involves a huge personal pressure. In desperation he looks around for safe havens. He eventually comes out before being exposed. There will be months of embarrassing meetings with family, friends, constituents before he will know whether he can continue in his chosen profession or has to retire discretely, if he can, from the public glare and forge a new life.

The information was quickly passed to Sebastian, Bill and Madge. They met briefly, they agreed to proceed to the next stage, though, as Bill pointed out, he had not come clean at the meetings and they would have to discover somehow if his meeting with them was co-incidental or if it was part of a rescue plan. If it was the latter was he simply trying to escape what he expected might be Tory chauvinism or was he, as he had suggested to them trying to find a party which was more aligned to his personal views of life?

Sebastian suggested that he should meet Simon with just Bill as a witness. They agreed he should confront Simon with the newspaper clipping.

A few days later they met in Sebastian's flat that he had shared with Bill.

Sebastian reported to Madge, Dan Stirling and John Corn on what happened next.

"He was obviously distraught, alternately trying to explain his failure to disclose background information to Sebastian by saying that he had not then decided to come out but that a local paper had threatened to expose him, so he had no alternative. He tried to explain how it had all happened, a deep feeling earlier on that his relationships were not the same as others, but that his family and work friends, he had earlier worked in the City as a broker, simply pulled him along the track and he went along with it for years and years.

We asked him what the reaction had been from within the Conservative Parliamentary Party and his own local constituency.

He said that he had been surprised, 'Of course one or two had objected, but basically it was OK.'

I then asked him the leading question. Did he still want to be considered transferring to Lib Dems?

He had replied 'Yes, I think so. Please!'

I then thought about it and asked him to wait whilst I chatted to Bill outside the room.

We came back into the room and I told him the results of our findings; we told him that the next few months would be difficult for him to negotiate and that he would need all his friends' support to survive, but good friends would pull him through it. If he left the Tories it's likely it would cause further disruption to that support system. Many Tory friends would turn against him. Whilst his gay status would be no problem to joining the Lib Dems, it would not mean he would be accepted without a fair degree of scepticism and questioning nor could he take it for granted that he would necessarily be selected as candidate, with the new STV system in operation the constituencies were far larger and existing time served Lib Dems would demand the top spot on any ballot paper.

'We cannot, I am afraid, guarantee you an easy ride! On the other hand there is nothing that actually identifies you as a lib Dem by conscience. We are also inconsistent on HS/2. You are essentially a nice guy who would fit into either party quite happily. But the answer is at the moment No! Our recommendation is that you plough your furrow within the Tory party, I am thinking they will not try to excommunicate you in any way. You have had the courage to come out but let us hope that you will not be badly treated. You are a Cabinet Minister already, you might well go further. Good Luck to you Simon.'

With that we stood up and shook hands. He thanked us kindly for our time, but he did in fact look highly relieved and he smiled easily as he left.

Simon knew he had helped me earlier and he must have known that I would listen. Perhaps it had been after all a desperate search for understanding, looking around for friendly faces. Anyhow let's hope that helped him, he knows now what he has to do."

"Pity" Dan Stirling said "A defection of that kind would have done us a world of good with the pollsters!

Chapter FORTY-ONE – Into the Lions' Den – the 1922 Committee

Sebastian knew that he had to pull his speech to the EC together, only he could do that!

Sebastian knew that this EU presentation would be the defining moment of his career. If he gave just a standard low-key speech which all the previous rotating Presidents had done, then he would be formally thanked by the EC Elite would would breathe an enormous sigh of relief and consign the speech to the bin.

Payunk Wask updated Sebastian on the EC's view of him. They knew of Sebastian only by reputation and from press reports. They had of course seen him at several events whilst the Foreign Minister over the previous year. There was open admiration for the ease with which he appeared to have delivered the UK's major constitutional change with only 30 or so MPs. They knew all about Sebastian's suggested changes to NATO which would place the UK right back as a key leader in Europe, they didn't like his proposal because that effectively squashed their own proposal for an EC Army, but the Brussels Elite realised that Sebastian's plan had the support of both the USA and many former Communist States for whom Russia was a threat. They had tried to block it but had failed and gave up trying, learning to live with its consequences instead. There was anyhow now a much more effective structure than before.

They comforted themselves that Sebastian had only a few weeks left of his 'reign' and that he had appeared to be in poor health. The last thing they needed in Brussels was something that would over-turn or at least upstage their urgent work of making the Euro safe. With luck and to save embarrassment on both sides, the 20 Elite Civil Servants who were the eminence grise of the EC, hoped, as they met over coffee the week before the meeting, that Sebastian Edwards might not even make the meeting! It would, they convinced themselves, anyhow be unusual for any one country, apart from Germany of course, to actually shift anything of importance. Certainly from a 30 minute speech. So the EU elite encouraged his appearance, getting whatever Sebastian had to say out in the open would allow some of their former Presidents to crush the ideas immediately before they could gain any political traction.

Sebastian was in the No 10 flat and he pondered the options. He could of course just speak about the UK's place in the EC and what UK's hopes and fears were. He could confine himself to matters excluding the Euro, go down as an improvement on all former 'opt out' UK leaders, but not by much. He could as he really wanted to, to rip both the construction of the Euro and its management to shreds, he had enough ammunition to do so. By favouring some

Euro members he might try to encourage a split in their ranks, but that might rebound on him with negative interest. He might take up the case of one or two states who Sebastian knew felt particularly abused and offer support but he had no means of helping them if not in the EuroGroup. He could support malcontents and wind up those countries with large anti-EC voters and wave the flag of open rebellion, it would certainly give him a hero status in a few EU countries, for a time, for a very short time, whilst he himself would be forever ignored by the Elite, he would be finished in Brussels – for good.

 He pondered, he even reminded himself of the Eurobar polls, his chance of making a major impact on 'Voters at home' were limited at best. Polls showed there never had been a massive Europhile wing in the UK, as a proud nation by and large the British resented EU interference, even should he double the Europhiles in the UK and they all voted Lib Dem that would still not remotely give Lib Dems any return for his massive personal investment.

However, Sebastian sensed it, he was on a roll, the pollsters said he had risen massively in the popularity rankings when asked 'Is the Prime Minister doing a good Job?'

'90 % - it was unheard of but then just about every poll appeared incapable of predicting the correct outcome any outcome, the betting odds were probably more accurate. But even if it were so, how long would his popularity last? Two months? Three months maybe!'

However he could detect amongst his Lib Dem colleagues signs of increased deference to him. He had thought that one or two of the Lib Dem Cabinet might turn on him, after their failure to support him in his 'bumpy ride'. Apart from Sarah Driscoll, he didn't altogether trust many of them – except Bill and Madge whom he relied upon completely, he did what they asked and they appeared to know how far they could stretch him. He knew that without them and Sylvia he would not even have got that far. Even they were saying that he had struck a chord with many different Groups. The Press had learned not to harass him for being a Lib Dem, when they did they received sacksful of angry letters back, as one editor remarked to Bill, who quickly passed it on to Sebastian.

No! Sebastian didn't really believe all that. It's true he was often confused attending events by loud clapping, he assumed there was a film star somewhere behind him in the line waiting to be introduced. He rarely appeared on TV except where the interviewer agreed to keep to a script of questions. He distrusted adulation , it made him immediately uncomfortable.

But then he received a letter out of the blue. He could see that it was very brief, as he opened it a cheque fell on the floor.

'Here's the cheque for the first £ million. I hope it's made out to the right charity, 'Looked after Children' we cannot find it listed? My people say can you smile a bit more often please!'

'Jacob Joseph'

He didn't know how many suits or jackets it amounted to.. but this wasn't a poll, it was reality.

Quick as a flash he knew what he must do.

He called the Chief Whip asking for a favour. Would he please contact the 1922 committee, the bunch of orthodox Tories who believed they held the ultimate right to influence Tory policy, they either did it covertly through associated Cabinet Ministers or overtly by inviting as many Cabinet Ministers as they could get to their regular meetings and discussions.

To Sebastian's surprise and Dan Stirling's horror they agreed to meet.

They met in one of the large committee rooms in the House of Commons, There was seats for about 60 but MP's and SPADS were standing lined up against the walls as well, there must have been well over 120 packed in. The Chairman of the 1922 Committee introduced Sebastian to this 'extraordinary event' and after a few lines of welcome took up a seat at the far end of the table to the right.

Sebastian sat at the main table in the middle with Bill and Madge on either side of him.

Bill passed around blank A4 sheets of paper which caused some amusement.

Sebastian rose to speak, "I come here as it were into the Lions' den. I just hope that you will have the courage to give me 30 minutes of your time to listen what I have to say, please try to be open minded. I want you please to write down why you dislike, me the Lib Dems and the Coalition, I have asked one of your number to collect them, he will not release them to me!"

A few MPs did as requested and passed the sheet over. Most didn't comply, they just looked amused and embarrassed.

After a couple of minutes, Sebastian explained, "Well there was just a hope that you could leave your bag and baggage aside for just a few minutes!" They laughed!

Sebastian carefully took them through the changes proposed to NATO, the Great Consolidation Bill then stopped "Next is the EU!"

He outlined what he saw as the huge risk that the UK would now be side-lined.

Several of the audience shouted out "So why did you argue that we should remain. You are a hypocrite now asking for our support."

Sebastian counted "No! – I am not asking for support – I am trying to explain what it is that I will have to do next week when I will use the Presidency to make a speech in Brussels.

There is one last ploy left that I believe that I can use. If I cannot, then our cause is sunk. And we probably will be squeezed out or even ejected from the EU. It's because of that risk that I am speaking to you now. On most things we may never agree but one thing I ask you to do is never to question my loyalty to this country any more that I question yours!"

He then elaborated how the failure of the Euro had been partly due to its construct, partly to the people running it and partly due to circumstance. Most MP's were astonished mostly because, Sebastian supposed, if you are actually against something there's no point in memorising a lot of detail for repairing something beyond sense anyhow, more useful to remember better things.

Sebastian told them of his amazement at the treatment of Greece, yes they were clearly foolish but to be publicly eviscerated? That did not make sense.

He re-iterated his view that the ideal of joining Europe together was still there, it was a noble ideal and that UK outside the EU would, in his opinion, not stand a chance, he listed twenty reasons justifying this.

They began boing at this!

"What I am going to try to do, is push the whole thing back on course."

"Impossible!" some shouted.

Sebastian retorted." Maybe but I am going to try, I owe it to all of you supporters or not!"

Sebastian then stood up and spoke "I am not going to allow these people to throw the UK out or to side-line us or to run rings around us". Then he shouted at the audience "I AM NOT, NEVER, NEVER, NEVER!"

The audience was hushed, they had picked up the vibes he had intended. It wasn't about left or right but the UK's standing into the future, whether they were Brexiteers or Remainers had lost all significance, they could all see that Sebastian, who had clearly struggled as no other minister recently to push the UK's role to its rightful position in the EC, was at his whit's end. He was signalling that he might be defeated with terrible consequences.

"If I should fail and I hope that I will not, then it might be that the nasty side – the vindictive side of the EC appears again and that this time they will ask for article 50 within 4 weeks or begin some spiteful deliberate slowing down of trade, like blocking the channel ports, which the French could easily avoid responsibility for, by claiming it was a Union Dispute. We are, I am afraid, hopelessly vulnerable.

Accordingly I intend on my return from Brussels to introduce an Emergency Bill to strengthen the UK's position. I hope that you will in due time support that Bill."

There was an immediate buzz of conversation. The Chairman of the 1922 committee, who stood up at the far end of the table, tried to regain some control. The hubbub was intense. He shouted towards Sebastian "er Mr Edwards do you have time for questions?"

"No!, none at all!" He then walked towards the door with Bill and Madge in tow behind.

Sebastian hoped that some of his anger and determination would leak out.

He learned later that one of the few remaining Tory MEPs had been there and, seeking to enhance his position at the EP in Brussels retold the story, word for word to other MEPs, or as many as would listen to his 'news'.

Sebastian meanwhile had decided what position he would adopt. He disclosed this to Bill and Madge the following day.

"I know perfectly well, how I shall do it, there's no point in me playacting, the only way I can play it is to be myself and to use my integrity as my greatest weapon."

In the meantime he had a brief secret meeting with the Head of the Security Services, loud voices were heard coming from a room next to the Cabinet Room and protestation "No! I cannot do that, its surely illegal"

Sebastian's voice was heard equally loudly "Well you know what they have done!"

"I don't care! What you ask for is illegal" the other voice repeated louder "illegal".

Sebastian was then heard shouting "Do it or you are fired! DO YOU UNDERSTAND!"

....
.....

Within 24 hours there was a tiny article in the Financial UK Press copied from Europa News.

LUXEMBURG SAFE BURGLED – OR NOT?

"The safe in the office of the Luxemburg Finance Minister had been burgled but the Ministry had refused to say if anything was missing, but at first view, it appeared not.

Chapter FORTY-TWO – Sebastian's elaborate speech preparations

Sebastian had tussled with writing his speech and was worried about it either being too strident or too passive. His speech writers had offered to help but he had spurned them, it was something with which he, himself, must feel happy. He wrote and then ripped it up five times getting even more agitated, before he found the right mode. Eventually he teamed up with Payunk Wask and they spent days locked up together writing and refining it.

By the time he arrived at the Embassy in Brussels early the day before Sebastian had rehearsed every word, every pause, every different level of voice, every action, every gesture. He would speak to no-one except Payunk.

At noon he called in Colonel Simon Collingham and John Voss, for whom he had great respect following their Palestine encounter where he had shown a firm, cool direction.

Sebastian revealed that he thought it very likely that at certain points in his speech, the EU who really could not handle either openness or criticism who attempt to simply shut off his speech. He would of course still have handouts which he had already had prepared for Press but that was not enough.

He pointed to his speech. He had marked on it the gestures he would use and where he would stand or pause and shout. He described each in detail. "I am making damning statements so that they will, they have to react! Here, here and here. Their reaction will be as I said to close me down. Your job is to keep me on line alive until I have finished, that's all! OK?

Simon, I think you were given the plans of the place as part of our security?"

"Yes that's right! Basically there are two things we have to worry about Sir, The supply system for incoming power to the audio is situated in a box fixed into the wall right opposite from where you are speaking that would need a key, we actually found a spare one would you believe hanging near it! A cable from this runs directly above into the translation box which hangs out over the hall. There is a master translator position which switches on all translations simultaneously. John will take stance at the box down below and will be on shortwave to me, I have a couple of back-up people outside. I will be in the Translation Box for which I have wangled a pass. John and I will carry red dot lights, military type. If we are prevented then we will point these, right at your microphone, at first an alert suggesting you speed up then continuous if we cannot hold out! I hope that's OK?"

"Sounds really impressive, I shall sleep well tonight! You guys I am sure understand that when making a speech everything, just everything goes into it, The slightest distraction can lose contact with the audience and can throw me off course, I am not a natural or talented orator everything has to be contrived".

He walked in on time to a room bubbling with curiosity, it was full, backed outside by a huge number of press swamping the roadway, tipped off that something was about to happen.

Sebastian had sent an outline of the speech to the trio, he strode in, avoiding personal contacts and walked straight to his chair, flanked by Bill and Madge, with the bulky figure of Payunk Wask a few feet behind. Stacks of translations of the speech were to one side.

Chapter FORTY-THREE – The EU Speech as President – The Hegemon

He stood when introduced and after a brief pause ensuring he had the rooms attention he started.

Initially he paid homage to the founding fathers; of their desire to end conflict and their ideals of working together. He used one or two quotes.

He pointed out that he was here because of a double chance, he was the UK's 'unintended steward', he wasn't even the leader of a minority party, but he was thrown into this position by a chance accident of which they all knew the circumstances.

Because of that he had had little direct involvement in the EU process. He had never been involved directly in internal EU decisions. As a European idealist he had spent his time trying to ensure that the UK remained in, but latterly as the UK's Foreign Minister he had begun to be aware of the turmoil within the Euro Group and the general despondency within the EU.

The temporary nature of his current position and his distance from the inner workings made him perhaps the most independent and objective reviewer of the position, he said

"All I have is my honesty, openness and integrity.

I have to say that I am saddened and disappointed by the current position, which has moved so far from the ideals of the founding fathers. They would surely be ashamed.

I come to the Euro. It's a sad story. As UK PM, I was able to catch up on the discussion and minutes of the Council, which you seek to hide from view. It shows clearly that there was a build up over 10 years in trying to establish convergence between the DM and FF. There can be no shadow of doubt at all, that for those reasons, let alone the large number of new members the Euro would have been under intense pressure for the start.

Monitoring and controls were so rudimentary that in my opinion they were 'designed to fail! At the first shock. Yes (Shouts) 'designed to fail'

It is now in retrospect possible to see why and how that happened.

During the launch of the Euro all German politicians gave a solemn promise to the mythical 'Swabian housewife' that their beloved DM in the form of the Euro would not be used to fund the fickle southern European states.

From the very start, then there was no trust, no empathy, no equality, no co-operation.

To the surprise of everyone the system appeared to hold but the overspending Greek were caught in the headlights.

There was to be no compromise as the troika and Teutonic Star-chamber were installed.

The public evisceration of Greece was necessary for the Germans to prove they had kept the Swabian promise, that the agreement copied the defects of a Versailles agreement was overlooked.

The result of the Teutonic Star-chamber was the devastating 'one size fits all' criterion which almost at a stroke plunged the Euro into a second recession when GDP reduced by 7%.

During this havoc the Euro was under-priced and Germany's exports bolted ahead, the south remaining impoverished.

The huge gains by the German Hegemon, which is now the only state able to underwrite the Euro, and it's Helot state Holland were not reprocessed to the south.

The result is a dreadful stand off as the Hegemon state determines the fate of the rest.

This is unacceptable and is contrary to all the hopes of co-operation on which Europe was based.

The Hegemon must go! (Shouts) Or the Hegemon must pay the price.

They have to decide if they are US or THEM, they must learn the responsibility of leadership or Go!

In 1947 just two years after German forces had been trying to kill, murder rape and pillage, there way across Europe. General Marshall instigated one of the most generous acts of financial friendship ever recorded over 216 BN $ was injected back into Europe and right into the heart of their former enemies, why? Because it was needed for Europe to survive.

How does that lie with the Swabian promise?

Germany must review the errors of its recent past, if it wishes to regain trust!

For the UK now, the moment of the public evisceration of Greece was a moment of decision too, very much all in the UK were horrified and it's as if a sliding door had closed, it was a defining moment. That was that never would the UK submit to that Troika or Teutonic Star-chamber. Never is not tomorrow, not next month, not next year, NEVER (shouts).

Bearing in mind the increasingly vindictive stance taken within the EC to those who speak out, we have had no alternative but to engage with others to form an 'Enhanced Group. Within the EC where we will with 8 others agree on a less demanding and more agreeable arrangement, we will welcome others who wish to withdraw from the Euro and who wish to pursue their own priorities in their own way. This will formally launch multispeed Europe.

We will provide a compromise on freedom of movement of people. We will demand you continue to open up the fourth Services to open competition which you have each protected.

The UK is part of Europe, none of you 'own' Europe we will not be despatched, we are here! (Shouts)

As far as the wider roll of Europe is concerned. (Sebastian stands and holds up his right hand) I now state that the UK now vetoes the applications of Turkey, Belarus and Ukraine, they will never become members of the EU, instead a new way must be found to spread the wealth of the EU by trade agreements encouraging setting up new industries and employment there but recognising the limits of this organisation cannot be continuously extended.

But I am not quite finished yet…"

Sebastian could see his people now being pushed and shoved, "More than anything we in the UK have been disgusted by the people you have to guide you. You all know who I mean, the Luxembourger the biggest legal corporate tax thief in the EU! Did none of you notice their GDP is twice the US? Its money stolen from you all! (Sebastian detects movement, waved instructions from the floor to shit off proceedings)

We will not accept that, nor that your budgets increase whilst we at home suffer recession, accordingly we will only, pay in accordance with a 1% tariff on increased trade between us.

Those are the reforms of the UK Government which I ask this council to consider without delay!"

Sebastian turned around and left the premises immediately, Bill and Madge clearing a passage for him as he walked quickly to the waiting cars.

Chapter FORTY-FOUR – Repercussion from the EURO Speech

Sebastian stayed for the remainder of the two day event but was holed up in the British Embassy for the remainder of the first day. Foreign office juniors constantly reported back for any EU Press interviews they could reach . All the Brussels Embassy staff were drawn in to a little network and this was supplement by specific transfers of key staff from London, Sebastian needed to know urgently what the reaction was to his speech.

UK Civil Servants, MPs and MEPs were asked to call their contacts, any contacts, Foreign Ministers, Finance Ministers and Members of the European Parliament, right across the spectrum, EC supporters and opponents. All remaining London staff were to peruse all main and regional newspapers right across the EU.

It was clear that the impact had been huge.

In certain countries it was clear that he had unleashed huge support and that there was a groundswell of interest in his proposal. The important difference between Sebastian's comments and anti EU politicians usual rants, we that he was perceived as a mainstream EU supporter so the speech came as a bit of a shock, this was one of the elite attacking the elite.

The reaction of the German Press and the quotes picked up from their leading politicians, was massively hostile. 'ANOTHER BREXIT LOOMS !' shouted one paper 'WE SHOULD NEVER HAVE ALLOWED THEM BACK IN!' suggested another. 'Let the UK GO!' wailed a third.

The French Press, already aware of Sebastian's help over the NATO re-arrangements was muted but their leader writers in the main daily papers analysed the speech calling it 'Interesting' and 'Factually correct.'

The Dutch press were furious "HELOT STATE - RUBBISH' and then started to analyse how many times they had actually diverged from the German view and whether indeed they had been party to the HEGEMON.

Political TV commentators across the EU, seized on the speech and immediately tried to draw in live comments in TV Studio analysis. Panels and audiences from a wide range of political views in their countries were asked for their views.

Behind the scenes in the actual meeting of the Heads of States there was turmoil as Germany sought to pull in past favours in their bloc, the 'helot states' as

Sebastian had called them, to make a public announcement refuting the logic of the speech. But many industrialists thought it was common sense getting back nearer to their blessed D-Mark – a minor proposal.

Those Heads of States normally supportive of Germany demurred and sought the view of their governments back home.

Late on the second day Sebastian gathered all the helpers together in the British Embassy in Brussels and thanked them for their work.

The information was summarised by Keith Williams the Permanent Secretary of the Foreign Office. "Some shift – but not enough" he paused adding hopefully "Maybe more will agree with you when they have had an opportunity to discuss it in depth".

On his return to London that evening, he called Michael Morgan, the Defence Secretary and asked him to be at No 10, for 9.00 am the following day.

He retired to bed exhausted.

Michael Morgan was shown into one of the smaller rooms, he was clearly surprised to see there already just Sebastian, looking very grave and the Head of the Civil Service and Cabinet Secretary Sir James Knotwood.

Sebastian was too busy with his own thoughts to notice Sir James' eyebrows seemed to have become stuck up very near to his hairline, perhaps in permanent surprise and confusion.

"Thank you both for coming Michael, Sir James." At this point Sebastian began pacing the carpet speaking as if from a memorised script. "Michael, I have asked you here to act as a witness to the proceedings – I know you to be an honest person, I have no power to prevent you disclosing what I am going to say, but I hope that you keep it to yourself until I am no longer Prime Minister, then you must do as you think fit!"

"I would, Prime Minister, if I knew what all this is about but I cannot give you a blank guarantee or open promise on what you have said so far!"

"OK let's start from the beginning. Please take a seat. I would prefer if neither of you took notes!"

Sebastian also sat down and pointed to a file in front of him.

"This is a summarised reaction to my speech of two days ago." He handed them each a copy of Keith Williams Summary. "Look if you will at the last line!, 'Some Shift - but not enough!', See it?"

Both Michael Morgan and Sir James Knotwood nodded.

Sebastian continued "You both know of me as an ardent Europhile and I think neither of you could fault my actions over the last two and a half months to re-integrate the UK into the soul of the EU?" Sebastian paused, staring into the distance. "But what I have said might be taken so badly that not only do we fail to make the changes to the EU that I had hoped and so end up with a better 'Reformed EU' but that one particular group of Euro Member States might try, deliberately to oust the UK or make our position so unbearable that we are obliged to exit.

For example this might mean interfering with the operation of the City against our wishes, the Euro Group could theoretically at least remove passporting from all non-Euro based banks. There is, in the EU, a certain vindictiveness which was exposed after the first UK EU referendum do you remember that Michael? Words to the effect, 'We are not going to give you an easy time over Brexit'. 'Remember we, the EU have time on our side, we can slow the discussions down and leave you two years after you have operated Clause 50 with no agreement at all!' You cannot expect an easy deal which might encourage others to leave!' To me that sort of smells of the old mafia sayings like 'corse you can leave our gang – in a box!'

Sebastian paused.

"I didn't like the sound of that then and I hoped never to hear it again, there's no case for a vindictive approach if the parties really don't fit! But remember what happened to Greece – they were publicly eviscerated, the Greeks may have been foolish but you don't treat nations like that do you? Any more than you would if you saw a man in front of you being punched and kicked to near death, as if by thugs. It doesn't matter what he said or did before that does it. We simply do not tolerate battering a guy to within an inch of his life, do we?

"We don't do that – on the other hand there's plenty who do? Do you agree Michael?"

Michael Morgan nodded.

"The trouble is that it's difficult to beat off a dozen of them? – If the EU, as a result of my speech, turns vindictive, then it will have been my fault and, as the one responsible, I want to put in place some form of protection for the UK."

Sir James who already appeared to be thinking ahead asked, "And what would that be? Sir"

"Well give me some ideas!" challenged Sebastian. "Here are some things I have been thinking about; l first we will fight every legal way we can to stay in, we will shred every EU article to find out what we can do, what case we can make! Sir James make sure that the legal boys are up to speed, I want to hear if the EU do try to exclude us from meetings or information or squeeze us out that we will fight back legally automatically. Is that clear?"

"Yes Sir!" Sir James assented.

"Now if it does go the whole hog and we are excluded we will need more bigger guns and ammunition, because we are very vulnerable!"

"If they threaten to kick us out of the single market and the customs union, they might get really aggressive like lift tariffs on cars to say 10%, then what answer do we have? You can say that they will not do that because that would kill the production of cars made in German Plants here in the UK, but they could within that two year time frame switch all the UK production they need to their other European Plants, leaving say just the Mini here. Some German Car Makers could simply switch sales from the UK to China or even Russia, nothing obliges Mercedes to sell into the UK does it?

They have so much the whip hand that, just thinking about it, makes me feel ill.

I brought you in Michael because I thought you, as one of the original Brexit team in 2016 must, surely, have been worried in the same way?"

Michael Morgan paused. "Well we did look at everything to try to dissuade them from bullying us, we even went so far as to wipe the dust from the old Second World War files, you know 'Sequestrations of enemy assets' and "Trading with the enemy Acts.' But we realised that we could do nothing. The EU wasn't designated an 'enemy' and doing anything like using those powers, which by the way are still on the statute book, would immediately land us in huge legal complications with all the world trade bodies and apart from massive fines imposed on us, those bodies would surely kick us out, making our position much worse, as we would lose all the minimum tariffs that we would automatically enjoy!"

Sebastian was glum "Well is there any way of getting advance warning of what they are doing, like switching manufacture away from the UK".

"Well we could, I suppose," Michael Morgan coughed discretely "Set some of our own intelligence people on it?"

"You mean infiltrate the workforce of EU owned larger companies with managers, bin cleaners, that sort of thing?" asked Sebastian.

"Yes, something like that!"

"Do you have any comment Sir James?"

"No not really. But I would strongly advise against the sequestration route, the consequences for the UK could be devastating, if anyone even over-heard we were thinking about it! What I can do is to check whether there are any remaining bilateral treaties with any of these countries, but I doubt it as almost all new treaties came within the EU framework. As Mr Morgan suggests the next best option is for you to operate our own secret service and frankly the less I know about that the better! Is that all Sir?"

"Yes and No! Sir James, just in case would you please dig out the provisions used in the First and Second World Wars concerning 'Trading with the Enemy' and 'Sequestration of Assets'?

"You cannot be serious!" eyebrows leaping up. Michael Morgan put a restraining arm on Sir James hand. "Just a moment, hear him out!"

"Well what I was thinking was a two stage action plan:-

First draft the emergency laws to cover basically three main eventualities

A, taking over the Direct Supervision of EU owned Companies that is taking over the whole operation, ejecting their managers replace them with our own and run the operations of UK plants from here – full bloodied sequestration.

B, Forming a new Supervisory Board replacing the foreign owners. But it's much more likely that we would simply take control by that I mean simply to ensure that they carry on trading as before and for example don't shift money, equipment or brands away from the UK and keep on buying parts necessary to make what they assemble, i.e. not to take anything away just to ensure that they continue as before.

C, Forming a 'Virtual Board' just monitoring everything that's going on in the company but nor directly intervening at all.

It is much more serious where we eject their managers and run it from the UK as in case A. But in case B, we would simply tell them to work to the instructions of a new supervisory board, in effect replacing their German HQ. In case 'C' we just hover, hoping that we will never have to act.

However before we do anything at all we need to carry out detailed research into exactly how many EU based companies there are and their size and complexity and effect on UK life.

I would stress that either case A or B would be a last resort and would have to be approved by Parliament, but we have to try to protect the UK and it might just prevent the EU from trying to eviscerate the UK as they did Greece, which is something that haunts me!"

Sebastian slumped into a chair, clearly exhausted.

"Hmmh!" Michael thought for a moment "Who else have you told this to? Has any other person got a gist of your proposal? Prime Minister."

"No – no-one, no one at all!"

Michael turned to Sir James, "What do you think of this?"

Sir James' reaction was instantaneous and damning " Its rubbish, total rubbish, we are not at war with anyone, these matters should be treated like any other contract negotiations between countries, I mean if anything like this were to leak out we would severely damage our international standing and reputation. Any Foreign Investor in the future would be wary if his country falls out with ours that we might jump in and 'nick his company' for reasons he cannot understand! You cannot launch a pre-emptive strike in the way you are suggesting, it's completely outrageous!"

There was a pause.

Sebastian insisted "Well we should at least carry out research to see exactly what is at risk and, frankly none of us here know the extent to which our own industries would be damaged if the Germans and French left? How many parts and services do they buy in the UK? What would the effect of their pull out be? Who provides the power trains for our own plants like Jaguar Landrover? I think we have to infiltrate large EU owned foreign plants just to find out the risks! After all it will take months to get a network operational, we need to 'be prepared".

Michael replied "Yes I think you are right, it is outrageous and it's probably illegal in several ways to actually take over foreign owned plants, on the other hand would I like to have known on the first referendum that I had at least some power or even knowledge of what exactly was at stake in reserve? It would have been much more comforting!"

Turning to Sebastian "I agree it's something we should have in our tool-box! Let's do it, Research and Infiltration, I don't think we need to do anything else right now? But nothing must leak out as Sir James said, it might do us immense damage!"

Sebastian was relieved "Thank you Michael!"

"I think you are being too pessimistic, PM, don't panic! My understanding is that your speech went down well. I think it hit home exactly as intended. You were courageously magnificent. Things I was minded to say myself for years. Will it bring change? I don't know! But as always PM you did stick it on them!

But there are other things which we can do! When you get into the Home Office role you are going to be our key man putting our case continuing or adapting our temporary derogation on 'Free movement of people'. It's like many other cases, we are often too honest for our own good, somebody asks a question and we reply, often others just don't put their hands up or don't bother giving us support; there's several refusing to take immigrants who, once in the EC can move, so how do they use that 'freedom', other Countries like Romania realise they have be devastated by those departing, leaving a huge empty gap behind them, now recently the Netherlands are calling for work permits.

We need to get all and every one of the quotes of those 'backsliders' and be prepared to use them!"

"Yes thanks Michael. That's a good point, can you set up a system for that Sir James?"

"But there is something else, "Michael continued "All the while we were told there are 4 freedoms, Yes? But the one they never develop in any detail is 'Services', there is supposed to be a single market in goods AND SERVICES. So Germany does fine with its cars across frontiers because the GOODS are sorted out but not SERVICES where the UK is likely to be a winner as we have a double advantage, the language which most people speak, even is as a second language, and our lead in IT, but the EC has never delivered! This was one of the things that rankled me about the EC they are very selective.

So what I think we ought to do is get hold of a dozen different UK companies explain the position and ask them to try and make 'sales of services' in other EU countries. When they are fobbed off we take them to their own EU Court and dispute it, in that way highlighting our complaint against them! It'll take months of course, but if we don't start it will take even longer, won't it?"

"OK sounds alright to me" said Sebastian, can we get the Chancellor to get some of the City guys working on that?"

"I've already tried him on that one, he will not do it without your say so!" Michael admitted.

Sebastian reached for the phone and called Stephen White, who by chance being just next door, popped in.

Sebastian updated him on the whole conversation, lastly picking up Michael Morgan's points. Stephen explained that he would himself not authorise anything like that because all EU matters were to go through the PM, but he thoroughly supported such action and would begin preparing suitable cases immediately, but then added;

"Yes PM you are being too pessimistic, the currency markets have indeed reacted, mostly due to currency speculators taking up forward positions, so the ECB and EU Institutions are bound to comment soon, you can usually tell it only takes a few minutes to construct a put down, but they have been at this for several days, it's probably then going to be a considered response, which is what you wanted! You did OK PM!"

Sebastian was slumped deep in his chair, twiddling the ring on his finger, he appeared not to have heard, Sebastian carried on.

"One final thing, the information that I obtained from Luxembourg, it shows their deal with one USA company, it gives them a massively discounted corporation tax rate provided all profits of their European Operations come to Luxembourg. In effect they have robbed the original 6 EU countries, their neighbours, of billions of $. Of course there are dozens more like that! I want that leaked to the press if they come out fighting. Is that understood?"

"But where did you get that, Prime Minister, there's a rumour it was stolen?" Sir James asked.

"Look, Sir James, I don't give a shit about your morals, I am fighting here for the UK. DO YOU UNDERSTAND" He shouted at him.

Sebastian turned to Michael Morgan, "Michael, at the first sign of them playing silly buggers, you will discuss the matter with Stephen, if I am not here you will instruct Sir James to leak that, if he should fail to do that then sack him, if we get into a dirty war of words, there's no good being nice, you'll have to dig the boot in hard! Do you understand me? Michael? Stephen?"

Michael started to reply, "Look Sebastian are we not becoming a little paranoid here?"

The last exchange appeared to have drained all the energy out of him but he replied, "Yes, Yes perhaps we are" He turned to Sir James "Look I am sorry, I do apologise I should never have shouted at you. Yes, perhaps I am being too gloomy, but I hope you all admit, we need to have a plan to defend ourselves. We had nothing in 2016, did we on Brexit, not the faintest clue how to extract or defend ourselves or even understanding the risks?".

"I am sorry, I've just panicked but Sir James, please set up a Brexit Risk Assessment Committee as a Cabinet Sub-Committee, put these points to them and ask them to evolve a defence plan? OK? Would you do that please?"

He slumped in his chair and didn't move.

Michael was concerned. "Are you OK Prime Minister?" passing him a glass of water, which he persuaded him to sip. Michael quickly quietly related to Stephen, the problems after their visit to Germany. They exchanged glances.

"Yes, yes I am OK thanks, just a bit tired – counting the days you know!"

They called to the flat above, in a trice Sylvia was downstairs, she shook her head sadly at the near lifeless cramped body in the chair.

"Come on now Sebby, just a few more days and we will be free!"

Michael Morgan, propped him up one side whilst Sebastian hung onto the handrail on the other so he was delivered upstairs despite his protestations "It was very hot in there, the glass of water did me fine, I'll be OK in a few minutes, you'll see!"

Chapter FORTY-FIVE - Calmer reflections on possible Brexit plans

Sebastian recovered quickly from his state of near paranoia, but that didn't stop his mind whirring although this time without a sense of personal guilt, they had agreed to set up a 'Brexit' sub-committee, just in case.

He pondered now what outline instructions he might give.

First of all who and what should be the priorities

The first consideration must be for those areas which had voted to remain.

Scotland. Was it fair to suck those down with the ship if things were going to get really bad, as far as Scotland was concerned it would give ever more grounds for a break up. He knew that a break up after Clause 50 would lead to years of worry for Scotland as they were laboriously driven through the acquis taking maybe years.

Instead he would, if it were left to him, give Scotland an opportunity to vote again.

The question would be "**Do you wish to separate from the UK and simultaneously apply to continue membership of the EC**"

Sebastian thought that such a momentous vote, not only separating but in effect casting off would demand a clear cut decision. One that was overwhelming.

Sebastian thought that clear cut would be 75/25 but there should be a minimum nothing below 66% would do. Between the two it would be left to parliament to interpret and decide the results. For example if areas strongly were against separation but which technically might still be administered from the UK, then that could be evaluated, so Orkneys, Shetland and the Western Isles might be disaggregated on the basis of a later referendum. Clearly the southern-most areas of Scotland could without difficulty be added to England. Any such areas would need to oppose by at least 66/33

This might then recast those percentages. Judgement given might include the solidity of perhaps the diaspora vote, should it be allowed to affect the different categories, since they had in all probability escaped the country and would not necessarily therefore have to live with the results?

In order to prevent the dreadful quality of the previous referendum, each side would present Two economic cases, one of their own choosing and another selected by them from a list of independent economic experts arguing their case, This would include any currency problem. Each side would then be allowed time to rebut the others case. This would be in a three hour long TV presentation.

Another three hour long presentation would contain all other issues, cultural, educational justice, policing. again their own cases and selected independent cases. The purpose of the independent's experts view would be to prevent, outrageous statements being made, since these should be neutralised. This could be open to a balanced panel of questioners.

A third three hour long session should be a joint one between the two sides and would be devoted entirely to the relations between the parties post referendum. This would cover particularly relationships with Military and any other UK institutions, tax offices and what, if anything would be the UK's fade out financial support, what would Scotland's position be on future oil revenues and would there be any compensation for earlier massive royalties when the price of oil was higher? if so should additional past major funding given to Scotland also be taken into account? If an agreed dateline were drawn when would that be? It seemed probable that a hard boundary with crossing points would be required. Where would they be? Parties should also agree who should vote, all Scottish residents which might include EC citizens, or only those with some sort of connection? and would the diaspora be able to vote in foreign embassies on the basis of the stated place of birth on the passport?

The UK government should then agree to withhold delivery of Clause 50 until the referendum had been held which could be organised quickly.

The European Courts of Justice would be pre-warned and would be requested to give an immediate response, though it would appear extremely logical if one part of a country should wish to remain by a clear majority, and become independent before clause 50 were applied, then there would appear to be a very strong case which the UK should agree to support. If it's going to happen the UK should use it best endeavours to help it. We would like to establish a best neighbour approach?

Northern Ireland. The same basic rules should be applied to Northern Ireland although the picture is made more complex because of the cultural, religious and nationality divide, so each county should have at least 50% and the question should relate instead **"Do you wish to separate from the UK and simultaneously apply to continue membership of the EC, within the existing State of Ireland"**

This then becomes a referendum which cuts across 'the divide' which has been so carefully covered in a democratic way, The same rules would apply those counties with massive majorities to separate should be allowed to do so. In original reports in the 1920s justifying the boundaries in Northern Ireland, virtually the only real argument was that a even smaller province could not survive. It was of course nonsense, but there is no logical reason why two or three counties might not be shifted 'south'. The remaining Unionists might feel safer in a smaller area where their majority is more solid. That would have to be part of the debate there?

London. This is the third main area for remain based on the first referendum data in 2016.

Without defined borders of course, it would be difficult to see how London could be offered an opportunity as Scotland or Northern Ireland which were in many areas semi-independent already. There might be a way somehow of making London there but not there as far as EC rules were concerned a huge 'Freeport' of some kind. But for a number of reasons the City is very unpopular in the EC. The primary issue concerns 'passporting', the right of any existing registered EC bank to apply its business anywhere within the EC. Any Clause 50 deal would almost certainly break that right. But it would be quite possible prior to Clause 50 to transfer the Headquarters of all UK Branks and peripheral associated operations to Scotland if by then its EU status was clarified or to Dublin in Ireland, this could nullify Brexit shocks as the EC operations could continue from Dublin whilst the world-wide operation continue from London, that might save those EC operations but not necessarily the staff, if freedom of movement of people into the EC from London were later denied.

But Sebastian thought that it was an option that MUST be considered.

By starting with these consistently REMAIN areas, Sebastian thought that it would release internal tensions, he had no wish to deliberately compel any party against their will, best to lance the boil and indicate a willingness to be open and fair from the start, those who saw Brexit as a Titanic sinking have a right to escape, a fair country would take that for granted.

Then what of the rest the huge remaining bulk? What reference points should be applied here? Sebastian thought there were probably five basic categories of type.

First were EC owned businesses, unless the UK took arbitrary control in some way, there was little that the UK could do to control matters, however one must assume that these would go for any deal that simulates how they now trade, tariff free within the customs union and products capable of being EU authenticated in some way so that trade in parts or finished goods could proceed as usual, back and forward. This authentication would be important as would the reach of patent rights. Any such company would be desperate to avoid all goods going through customs stations involving possible weeks delays making impossible any advanced 'just in time operations' which would be fatally compromised due to uncertainty of stock arrivals.

It did not seem unreasonable to ask the EC that these specific companies should be specifically exempted perhaps using some adaptation of 'Freeport status' for larger operations, there seems no reason to punish them particularly, as the end owner in the EC would be damaged too.

To this group might be added Defence and Aircraft associated products, no doubt that sooner or later the French would seek to end Airbus UK operations, take it over and transfer it into France. The UK having stupidly sold its shares would not have a leg to stand on, but until then they almost might operate under some 'Freeport status'

Next were the large UK owned companies which regularly traded with EC countries. Most of these will already have subsidiaries within the EC and could transfer staff to enhanced operations there. Their likely problem was exclusion from UK produced items and being subject to a tariff and customs delays if outside the customs union.

In Sebastian's view this would be best overcome by the use of one standard low tariff rate say 1% applied each way, the income would be huge and would offset the eventual loss of the UKs huge support for the EC budget, it would be senseless to expect no cost that would be unrealistic. A 1% tariff should be easily found, indeed it might give at last a reason for many firms to improve their productivity, which the government has long been shouting at industry and commerce to very little effect.

The quid pro quo would be avoidance of customs exclusion.

A bigger problem however was how to get around the EC insistence that the EC was the sole controller of quality and standards of what was allowed as goods approved in the EC. All UK producers would be compelled to use every new rule passed down, not only in their own factory but in every supplier factory they used, which might cover hundreds of smaller plants, some who might have no idea that the eventual use of their supply was within a product sent to the EC. If that applied then virtually the whole of UK manufacturing sector would still be covered by these rules. The EC might demand thousands of certificated supplier conformity documents with every item exported. The problem might easily erupt, for example if the UK when now outside the EC tried to reduce the expensive labour rights agreed whilst earlier being in the EC, the EC might then claim this effectively gives the UK a 2% cost advantage, demanding an extra 2% being added to the into EC tariff. If the EC in future loaded even more social costs onto companies then they could similarly demand a blanket increase in tariff or obliging the UK to carry out identical changes in social costs.

Without a voice at the negotiating table the UK would be obliged to submit as Norway does.

Some co-partnering deal might be constructed as suggested by the Breughel paper but it might take years to construct and apply and there could be little pressure that the UK might apply to encourage it, most of the EU countries in fact hardly traded with the UK at all and probably couldn't care about the consequences for the UK.

Third were the occasional suppliers to the EC or regular supplier of one line of products. Sebastian thought that most of these would be impossible to 'save' in the sense that only a general ruling would mitigate their plight.

This is where into the future it would be almost impossible for a smaller UK company to trade with the EC, the paperwork trails, the authentication, the possible different tariffs would be beyond the smaller company, many traders would instantly stop trying any export anywhere, since the competitor markets were mostly on their doorstep other lesser markets were thousands of miles away and lay in a different business culture. Long term Sebastian thought there would be no export trade at all from this group.

Haulage firms would be directly affected by any change in customs rules, they would be unlikely to accept EU lorries steaming in and out, whilst their own loads were 'Stuck in Customs'.

Sebastian had no idea how UK based pharmaceutical suppliers would be affected, probably he thought they would be passported through a friendly country like Ireland for a price whilst all design and development costs would continue to be carried in the UK. Pills are made up of chemicals traded worldwide so the actual derivation would be almost impossible to trace.

Fourth came the general mass of UK businesses which had little or no interest in the EC These were the solid inward looking, 'what's the EC ever done for me?'. Even many large retailers were like that, oblivious to the fact that their idea of shooting out to the Far East for subcontract, destroying acres of

UK manufacturing, would come home to roost in a falling £ and squeezed profits. They would simply ignore the problem and continue as before, start-ups would avoid the UK just in case their product might be scalable for the EC. Highly specialist product makers like university spin offs would clamour for a much better informed export Chamber of Commerce to help them promote abroad for a fee in return for market intelligence. Probably import trade with the Far East and India would increase. If the UK general public believed the EC was deliberately 'getting at them' then substantial numbers of their products would be avoided as 'being British and loyal' would again hold sway, for a time, till everyone saw, as before, the 'T' shirts were made in Taiwan!.

These would be the most vociferous in demanding reduction in the, mostly mythical, reduction in EC demanded paperwork, much of it was no more than replacing one form with another; the cost of going back to the original and updating it for the few rules that were jettisoned would be huge. Of course politicians would promise to do something, but it would soon drop to the work-in-progress tray then into the bin. It seems almost certain that the 'roll back' of existing employment rules would not even bear mention whilst the two years of Clause 50 worked through.

Fifth would be Foreign-Owned but not EU-owned larger companies settled here because of easy EC access. These are the non EU FDI Foreign Direct Investment, their purpose is generally to trade into the whole of the EC. Any curtailment of their market which is a considerable but unknown value of UK exports, would be met, judging from patterns which emerged after the first referendum in 2016, for request by them for the UK underwriting any additional costs. This was rather stupidly and clumsily assented to at the time. If the deal achieved was a poor one, and their exports were threatened, they would immediately attempt to re-site operations within the other EC states, leaving perhaps the truncated UK factory to deal only with the UK. This would shut off UK's exports.

The other choice would be to await an opportune moment, in a business cycle either demanding a subsidy from the UK government, holding them to ransom, or else move the factory lock stock and barrel assuming the site was of no value. They would do this if they concluded that the UK market itself was deteriorating. It could easily become a rout. Cleverest companies, would stop production, let the UK operation go into liquidation in its own right, reducing taxes by setting off current profits against closure costs after taking out all cash, patents etc. and avoiding pension costs. Several of these happening at the same time could destroy whole areas very quickly

General affect, but Car number plates would have to change, as would drivers' licences and passports, costing each person perhaps £250 but in view of the vast numbers it would take years to do, probably itself restricting travel to the EC 'awaiting documents'. All airports would have to be reconfigured.

UK/EC Resident or Citizens Position. Perhaps most important is what happens to the UK people stuck in the EU as residents, and what would we do with those here with settled residential rights? First must be to establish pension transfer and healthcare rights but of course their cases were totally different. Those coming here from the EU would tend to be younger, mostly of working age and paying taxes, it would be important to get rid of those with police records, courts should be immediately instructed to send all offenders home, otherwise extradition might be affected by Clause 50 leaving hundreds of former EC residents in prison here. UK residents in the EU would tend to be older and likely be big users of foreign health services, but they had chosen that life, they should be given no guarantees. All foreign office literature, from even now, should advise all UK subjects living in the EC to seek EU Citizenship as a safety measure whilst they are still able. Even should no Brexit occur the matter of these people should be clarified with specific dates from which residency and citizenship run and exactly when termination dates, apply eg from Clause 50 date or end of negotiations

But there should of course be some opportunities some gains? Where should we look?

Well there are some, but they are fairly well hidden

First there are possible gains in foodstuff imports. The EC's Common Agricultural Policy was calculated by one set of experts to actually change most peoples' expectation of a gain from EC membership into a loss. CAP was estimated to have cost 0.5% of UK GDP.

It's not exactly clear to most if that meant in taxes paid into the EU for CAP or that, in any cases resulting prices paid for products were higher here than world-wide. It's something that could be very easily tested.

Huge quantities of beef and lamb could be imported probably more cheaply using long term contracts with ranches in Australia, New Zealand, Argentina and Brazil. There would be no obvious reason why such enquiries might not start right now.

Other staple items like various sorts of USA or Canadian Grain or Pork could be reviewed. It could mean that we have to change our eating habits. Would more

Caribbean sugar help? It would be possible to carry out wholesale switching of wines to Australia, NZ, and places like Chile, all of these now much improved in quality. Dairy products in the UK could expand into products that have been more quickly exploited by the French in particular, Yoghurts and Cheeses, special grants might be needed to launch replacements.

Any well experienced Agriculturist would reveal all this within days.

Then there is future developments of shorter life items apples and other soft fruit, of course, but greens, lettuce, chicory, radishes, onions, cabbages, celery, kale, sprouts, potatoes , could possibly be grown elsewhere but in the EC. African equatorial countries could use sunlight to growth crops better and cheaper and funded from the UK, this would also provide meaningful employment in joint venture operations maybe partly funded by DfID of infrastructure to get the products to airports. There is even now a healthy trade in flowers from Kenya to Holland. This is a huge opportunity, which might also drive more exports to those countries who become wealthier because of the trade. Unlike the French we have tended to avoid trade with former African colonies. We would have to seriously work at it!

Next there are huge opportunities in IT expansion.

It's well known that the UK started early learning to use and apply IT, initially we actually started its development in the dark days of the war, even produced some of the best known equipment until any UK product preferment was ignored and such advantage as we had was lost, a careless and stupid oversight. IBM forged ahead partly on the back of huge sales of their perforated cards which were used under licence to more easily track down those of Jewish origin for selection for the Holocaust. For a time IBM in Europe WAS computerisation.

Never the less for a time IBM were everywhere triumphant the proud little acknowledgement 'managers don't get sacked buying IBM' the reason being that it was IBM that decided if they would let you buy one! With the PC came the IT revolution, again in the UK there were small but visible attempts to get into the market but again IBM with its massive fire power dominated. A legal breakthrough separated, in effect, hardware from software. Apple's genius was to transform something he had 'nicked from somebody else into the early Apple machines linking mouse to screen to computer. But IBM still dominated realising that software sells hardware and produced many dedicated applications. But the rival Apple soon allowed software companies themselves to become more powerful. IBM lookalikes appeared as if by magic, software flooded onto the market as the price of chips and PCs cascaded.

Somewhere in all that the UK became very adept at creating bespoke software and in building games on the back of the X-box, that became almost a cottage industry. If a good IT man could be persuaded to initially accept a low wage, the company could earn megabucks. Dedicated software for accountancy practices caught on, in fact often making small firms of accountants 20% more efficient in staff usage.

As far as EU is concerned UK was an 'early adapter' and still has a significant creative advantage. As its applications are practically borderless it could yet lead to a massive global presence, unaffected by what happens in the EC but with India particularly catching up at 25% of the costs such an advantage has to be targeted and supported. More IT trainees will be needed in the UK is to keep ahead.

Chip related derivatives have to be looked for and driven forward, that means applying principles to every piece of working equipment, designing it for longer, more efficient, life then thrown away, as better cheaper more efficient products takes its place.

For this we need to produce more and more of the types of trainees needed to make this surge possible, more creative geniuses, lend them money and them them make their products fly around the world.

So we have to clamp down on the obsession with ever more costly housing, we must get used to financing companies to expand and export.

At home we must prioritise companies that add value in the UK, using a steadily more skilled workforce at all levels to improve performance and develop, patent and create whilst slowly offloading work that can never be upgraded to external suppliers.

Such creative explosion must cover all areas of the UK Hospitals, railways, schools, farming, electricity generation. We have to pull ourselves up by our bootstraps as if the devil were behind us. We have to learn better ways of making life comfortable too, if we want a better NHS doing better with the same money we have to rethink the model. Maybe every person retiring earlier than 65 should be asked to be part of a National Volunteer Service, retrain as a hospital porter and work for half pay saving the NHS a fortune, or a home care assistant at a between-home allowing more efficient use of Hospitals.

Under the shock of Brexit nothing should be over-looked, all avenues must be explored.

If we cannot or will not export, then we cannot import, that means not buying foreign goods or going on foreign holidays. If the pound sinks all imports cost more, this must be rammed home.

We export or we go bust. Under Brexit nobody owes us a living – we have to earn it

If the worst comes to the worst perhaps war time conditions should be implied and direction of labour taken seriously for a period of 5 years to halt immigration whilst people somewhere still on the dole are redirected as the 'Bevan' boys were to the coal mines.

All our natural resources should be looked at again, we will have to consider every sort of energy, wind, solar, tidal, wave, gas, oil, fracking and even coal. To be safe we will have to become energy independent, that rather than Climate Change will have to become the priority.

All Banking off-shore operations should be closed or subject to open scrutiny to prevent the rich from soaking away money, there should be zero gain, all that means 100% of moneys treated as fleeing the Taxman should be taken, for social cohesion in tough times, no CEO should take more than 50 times his lowest paid employee. Self-Companies should be abolished. The rather silly tax opt outs for ISAS or whatever should be ended, they are a middle and upper class tax hideaways, another way of tax evasion this time legally, a thoroughly bad example to set to all the other evasion schemes.

There are dozens of ways to exploit the best in us, we have always responded to national need, we need to capture that feeling.

But to ensure maximum support as many of these matters require almost war-time redirection, requires a unified populace shown that we really are equally and together sharing the burdens and eventual gains.

With a still sharply divided Brexit and REMAINers groups that unified status is yet miles away, if we are not prepared to undertake national re-direction to maximise the use of our skills then we will simply become two people, one insistent that Brexit destroyed our good life, the other that Brexit failed to give them any real hope for the future!

Chapter FORTY-SIX – The European problem is transformed

In the following days Sebastian was told, the UK received plenty of comments from other Heads of State, variously thanking him or abusing him, for the content but none of them denied Sebastian's right to speak as he had.

Surprisingly Luxembourg initiated a discussion in the Council of Ministers on how to move the EU and the Euro forward.

Everyone waited for a detailed response from Germany.

Sebastian was plainly wilting under the pressure, Sylvia was plainly baffled by his mood changes, he was at times brilliantly analytical, at others increasingly paranoid. All the Cabinet became concerned. "This man has the Nuclear button – for God's sake" but the public and press were generally unaware of the problem, he seemed suddenly the man of the moment able to resolve any nasty problem and they would listen to nothing else.

His standing rose in the country which seemed to take utterly to his David and Goliath battle, the UK Press were completely in support, but as his physical and mental ability appeared to shrink.

Nobody was prepared to wield the knife.

Payunk Wask had, in their detailed preparation appraised Sebastian of what he thought was the basis of the 'German Character', he had disclosed this to Sebastian over several sessions they had together.

The need for honesty at the top was fundament to German integrity. Their integrity and the rule of law was really what distinguished then from the 1930's.

Germans would always try to work from a basis of best principles; technical evaluation and logic re-enforced this, the concept of justice was something they knew had been disastrously abused during the Nazi era. They knew that the structure of their state, with its division of power between their home states gave devolved power, restricted its ability act impetuously as it called for endless internal negotiations, and then the creation of the independent Bundesbank meant that whatever politicians said, the Bank would not budge, its rules were sacrosanct and were never politically over-ridden except in the moment of passion, re-unifying Germany. For that every rule was broken, all risks were acceptable.

But Sebastian had openly challenged them.

Their supposed reluctance at dominating the Euro through the European Bank he had exposed as Germany bullying.

The thing, just about the only thing, that Germans hated was being singled out, exposed with uncomfortable parallels to their past treatment in the 1930's of smaller states. If ever all those states ganged up on Germany, and German integrity were exposed as self-serving dominance, they felt that the German behaviour pattern built up so carefully over decades, would sustain a knock which would shock every level of German society.

Germans now pretended to be the 'Good Germans' they were different and better, they had learned from the past, they were not the same people as stormed across Europe trampling nations under foot, thieving, robbing, killing at will.

It was this that had formed the basis of Sebastian's' speech, this was his trigger to force the changes needed both for the Euro and EU. That and the challenge that the technically structured Germans had failed to put in place controls, 'designed to fail' doesn't really translate into German at all

The Germans knew that Payunk Wask had become a close confidant of Sebastian. They invited him to visit them three days after the speech.

The Germans asked Payunk Wask to explain. They question him about Sebastian's' motivation why did he say this and that, what was behind him proposing this or that. Why did he target Germany? Was it all a ploy to stay in power in the UK? Was he hoping for a surprise general election? If he was so ill what was he doing putting himself under such huge stress for such slight gain?

Payunk Wask simply said, "Well that's what he thinks, he says what he thinks, he trusts his own judgement, he does what he thinks is right, right for his country and indeed for other countries too, he was deeply ashamed of the treatment of the Greeks, he has total integrity and no-one that I know has ever questioned that. He is an old Liberal but he is more radical than Liberal and initially was reprimanded for his slightly unorthodox views over integration, he does not hold back and seems reckless to the point stupidity, challenging long held views on Banks and CEOs , battles which he knows he cannot win. He is an overdog who speaks for the underdogs. He knows if he stayed long in the PM role, he could never sustain the anger over the near obliteration of the Lib Dems which drove him politically.

He is what you see nothing more nothing less, he has no guile he is not vindictive but hates those who are with a passion that would surprise you.

He is a Comet, a lone agent, he has no clique, trusts implicitly barely half a dozen people, he has no influential friends, he seeks no reward.

And finally he is by some long measure a simply brilliant evaluator of what it is possible to do, an outstanding person, I knew immediately that he meant every word that he said. Nobody but nobody does that.

In your reply don't try to be trite, or clever or dominating or question his motives or destination. I myself won't stand for that, my country's past will not allow me to hear you denigrate him in that way and I shall visit every EC country and tell then exactly what I have told you today.

If you want to answer the charges do so.

Remember he challenges you on one key issue are you US and the rest THEM or are all Euro members now part of WE, until you answer that you will not know what you must do next. To be WE means that you have to take on trust those you have bullied and abused and financial implications flow from that.

Have you really made the grade to being a mature and responsible leader. The decision is uniquely YOURS.!"

He kept to his word and the gist of his talk soon became public knowledge.

German reactions to this were hard to discover, according to one person there, at the meeting, nobody said anything for ten minutes as they each scuffed and then threw away the notes indicating their possible lines of attack, but the person would reveal nothing more of the process.

The announcement went it came was ridiculously brief and to the point.

It was followed minutes later by another.

The German Government will underwrite general Eurobonds, guaranteeing the Euro!

The German Government accepts responsibility for recycling a portion of its surplus into Capital Joint Venture Projects in countries likely to be in deficit, given certain assurances, to assist those countries in their economic development.

Then even later the same day clearly to placate French fears of being permanently side-lined; that the next head of the EuroGroup was to be a Frenchman

And finally

That Germany would accept the 'Enhanced Group' proposed by the UK and accepted a multispeed Europe.

However the press releases each noted that the deal was subject to ratification Germany was to go to the polls in two months' time.

The change of direction would need the ringing endorsement of the German electorate.

Sebastian noted they never did respond directly to his challenge.

Not many could work out how much of Sebastian's speech and resulting change had been due to Sebastian Edwards and how much to Payunk Wask's support of it to the Germans.

Had one prompted the other? Was Sebastian the voice box for Payunk who smarted over years listening to arguments rammed home and witnessing the Germans' overbearing attitude on the Euro? Or was Sebastian the originator, using Payunk Wask simply to provide him with a suitable angle, and filling in the joined up case that Sebastian was in any case, seeking.

Was there a puppet master and a puppet or was it simple a remarkable co-incidence of views?

They were never interviewed together and neither responded to questions designed to find out the truth. After one such enquiry much later, on BBC Radio London, Sebastian merely chuckled and refused to reply.

Payunk Wasks's response had been identical.

Of course the Brexit planning papers were never used.

Two months later the numbers required for the 'Enhanced Group' were achieved, as the natural leader of the group the UK was permitted to attend all other EU meetings to assure themselves that there was no attempt to side-line them. In this role the UK began to question rules which appeared to be unnecessary at the European level, much was delegated to National Governments. The UK challenged changes to the Euro rules themselves, if they thought them farfetched or intrusive. Small individual Euro Countries would use the UK to help them make their cases. Similarly the UK delegate was often asked by the Euro Group to advise on differences of opinion as to whether rules had been breached on not. Because it was not itself a Member of the Euro Group, the UK's objectivity was trusted. Soon tensions eased

It was a sort of incremental accumulation of useful tasks and the UK had finally found its role at the heart of the EU.

This of course took months to develop and was only revealed in the following year, Sebastian himself was only dimly aware of the changes as he was no longer responsible for Europe for which the new Prime Minister had taken personal charge. It was all of course public knowledge.

But Sebastian, was way ahead on the next project, unscrambling immigration and how to prepare a suitable case to the EU.

Chapter FORTY-SEVEN – Secret meeting with the Russians

Sebastian was by now back to his normal self though not as positive about matters as previously.

However the Cabinet greeted the change of German position as a victory and the UK press were unanimously in support of his victory.

Sebastian recovered his need for work to occupy him for the last weeks of his tenure.

A message was received through unusual channels, for the UK Prime Minister to call Sergey Kramrenko who would be in London at the Mayfair Hotel.

Sebastian did as requested. He was however worried that it could be a hoax, after all any guttural Russian accented voice is much like any other, so he asked as validation that Sergey recount their last meeting, the name of the building and the name of the Belarussian Police Chief whose statue remained in the main park.

Sergey did this.

"So how can I help Sergey?"

"President Medvedev is on a State visit to Sweden today, he must to see you there tomorrow, please!"

"Is that all?"

"Yes must be secret!"

"Sergey I remember well that four years ago we had a great discussion about ending the stand-off with Russia, holding referenda in the Ukraine and regularising relations, finishing sanctions but then what? Russia gets tangled up in Syria, the unwinnable war, and so the deal I helped to put together with you went nowhere! Although it appeared that there would be normalisation, nothing happened."

"Yes correct, but we have to keep to try, Yes?"

"Yes I suppose so." Sebastian sounded reluctant "What's it about?"

"NATO and a deal!"

"OK about noon tomorrow? How long two hours? The Russian Embassy?"

Sebastian spoke to Michael Morgan "Tomorrow Stockholm, 8 am start, please organise an RAF flight to Oslo, then break off to Stockholm, say it's a delivery of equipment parts for urgent delivery. It'll take 2 hours 40 mins each way – I have to be back by 4.00 pm. You me and security that's all."

Sebastian later that day called his wife that he needed to meet his team earlier the following day, at 8.00 to discuss difficult Prime Ministers Questions. He simultaneously left a message for Pamela Tressider to take over as he was feeling unwell.

Sebastian and Michael Morgan were taken to the nearest RAF base, they were joined there by a the Permanent Secretary of the FCO, David Andrews and Colonel Simon Collingham.

When they were in the air, Sebastian let rip.

Sebastian asked "How the hell did you know this was going on, Andrew?"

"Well of course we monitor all Russian Diplomatic Personnel, especially those who DON'T stay at the embassy in London. I thought that this time I could possibly help!"

"Oh! And how so! – you appreciate this is supposed to be a secret meeting, but it doesn't already sound too good, security-wise does it? I mean how many more know about the 'secret meeting'?"

"Nobody I assure you apart from the listening centre and I ordered those recordings to be destroyed"

They were delayed in Bergen where Oslo air traffic control ordered them to land as the passenger list they had not been filed.

After a few rather embarrassing moments requiring them to explain a bit about a security meeting with the Swedes, they were released.

As soon as they were in the air again Sebastian turned to Andrew again.

"OK Andrew, let's have it, what's your info!"

"Medvedev has been made President again, so that Putin can carry on with the myth, that he doesn't serve more than two terms, so Medvedev stands in for him. As such Medvedev has little power but he is titular head of the armed forces and also titular head of their Foreign Office. He is sent away on State Visits like this, so that Putin can get on with the real work of governing. Of course when their positions are reversed then its Medvedev the Prime Minister who does all the State Visits. So, in effect, Putin is always in control. Medvedev is a much lesser character and was chosen by Putin because he thought he could be manipulated. It is Putin the popular, Putin for the people and so on.

Putin's foreign policies have been an internal disaster, sanctions meant a falling rouble but also Putin has decided to refurbish the army, so a huge amount of the budget goes to one particular sector, the military equipment businesses. The disastrous war in Syria sucked in Russian forces ostensibly to win a friend there and even though they mostly won most of the country back but also built bridges with Iran, also a Syria supporter. But he cannot win the peace there. The Syrian president Bashar al-Assad is an Alawite which is a subsect of Shia but 70% of Syrians are Sunni. Putin is trying but failing to build a governing coalition there but it's like making mud bricks in the rain. If he ditches the Alawite most of the rest of the country are hostile, if he continues to support the Alawite, then nobody will deal with Putin.

So all that he has achieved so far apart from a show of force, is getting onside with Erdogan who seems well on the way to abolishing democracy anyhow and must be regarded as a long term liability. Oh! And of course getting on well with Hezbollah, who control about one third of Lebanon.

It's easy to see the downsides Saudi is Sunni as is Jordan as is 40% of Iraq, all these are now deadly enemies.

Of course, because of Putin's support for the Syrian regime and their dropping lots of nasty stuff, makes them potentially supporting a War Criminal, so the West is switching off Putin big style. The fact that he has a Donald Trump style effect on Russians, who believe that he is almost a re-incarnation of Soviet Power, makes him pretty invincible.

Except that is for his chums and acolytes in the ruling elite. They know that Russia has lost half its GDP following these crazy policies, the poor are worse off, the businessmen are worse off, city councils up and down the land are worse off.

It seems that Medvedev might be thinking the unthinkable!"

"Oh Ah! Yes I see! So what's your role?" Sebastian asked.

"Just to Watch and Listen! If I know half of what is going on, he will want to sum you up, check you out, see if he can trust you, see if there is any continuity in the Coalition Government for your views, they know who I am, they know if I had doubts about what you are saying, Kramrenkov will pick it up instantly."

Medvedev will not say anything much, if he got found out it would be certain death. He knows he is playing for really high stakes, literally for the future of Russia. He probably needs some sort of evidence from you to sell to his supporters, to persuade them onside."

"And my role?" asked Michael Morgan.

"In my opinion" Sebastian started "he will start questioning us on the New NATO format, is it all just about public knowledge?"

"Pretty well, we have had a good response and of course our man supporters are Poland and the Baltic States, Norway is 100% behind us, the only worry are the Germans, they say yes, but one gets the feeling that, they will need a pacifier, like equipment orders and us taking on board some of their top Generals into the command structure. We can do that but I will not make that public until I know they support it. So yes we can talk about it in general terms but not specifics. OK!" Michael Morgan spoke with an air of authority which was unmistakably more confident than the tone he had used visiting the Germans.

'Blast' thought Sebastian' looking at his watch 'that only leaves a couple of hours chat and then back home'.

They met up in comfortable but not overpowering rooms in the Russian Embassy, with music so loud it was often difficult to hear.

Sebastian remarked how in fact they had met several years before, for a presentation in the Kremlin. Medvedev looked at his file on Sebastian and said "Yes I remember now, the Englishman and the Mad Dog or was it the Mad Englishman and the Doc". But he had the photo of Sebastian with the Russian Policeman surrounded by the dead dogs, he held it up for everyone to see.

It broke the ice.

Sebastian talked of the great unused mineral wealth in Russia and the poverty of the people.

Medvedev asked questions about the new NATO structure, Sebastian introduced Michael Morgan to answer.

"The problem was entirely caused by your silly tactics, sabre rattling, constant needless patrols of Russian submarines, military exercises right up to the borders of the Baltic States and Poland, constant overflying by the latest MIG jets over areas where the States below don't have a single jet fighter to even engage if you did decide to attack. For our part we responded to the needs of these countries and seeing the USA being unwilling to continue to pay the huge subsidy, we intervened and took for ourselves the sort of role we always ought to have had!"

Medvedev seemed impressed, they then discussed Ukraine and Sebastian introduced David Andrews who explained that the deal with Ukraine was as before, wrecked only by Russia's earlier pulling away. On Syria that the UK and USA stand willing to try to negotiate a proper peace through the UN, and that if that was successful all sanctions against Russia should be withdrawn. But also we hope for changes within the EU" and he passed the conversation to Sebastian.

We are trying to reconfigure the EU apart from the Balkans no new potential states will be admitted, instead we aim to introduce a special 'associated status' To countries like Belarus, Ukraine, Turkey and I would hope Russia, this would encourage lower tariffs and investment transfers!"

Sebastian stopped adding quickly that the proposal to the EU only went in and was made public quite recently and we have a lot of work to do to make it 'fly'.

His choice of word 'fly' had the translators confused at first, think it was some new plane, but then they laughed.

Medvedev chatted in Russian with Sergei Kramrenkov.

Sebastian asked several leading questions about the Russian military in the Baltic States frontiers, asking for a reduction in intensity and about Ukraine and Syria, the replies were non-committal and seemingly deliberately confusing, largely made up of slabs of Russian Foreign office propaganda all the UK people had heard many times before. It was clear that the Russians were under orders to reveal nothing at all.

Sergei Kramrenkov clearly did not agree with his boss and sought once or twice to intervene, but Medvedev held up his hand to cut him off. Medvedev spoke in faltering English "Sergei – he like too much the English!"

Sebastian threw a wave at Sergei, they had in fact met several times and a friendship and respect had grown between them.

The meeting over and the job done, the UK party returned home.

As soon as Sebastian and party got back into Number 10, he realised something was wrong, there were papers books, shoes and clothes all over the floor of the lobby. Sylvia charged downstairs like a banshee alternatively abusing and shouting endearments at him.

"How could you Sebby, how could you! Where have you been? Are you OK? We couldn't find you! We thought you had gone missing! Well you told me you were preparing for PMQ. So, unusually, I turned on the BBC but you weren't there, I called Bill and Madge and demanded to know what they had done with you, the deal is they are not to let you out of their sight! So then security called in and said you were in Norway or Sweden. I told them that cannot be. But they said it was so! Where have you been? What have to been doing? I have been going frantic with worry!"

Michael Morgan was standing just inside the door "It's OK Mrs Edwards, he has been OK today, the meeting lasted just over two hours, we all took sandwiches, we have met in secret with some very important people. I have been keeping an eye on him as has Simon Collingham, he's the chap your husband smuggled out of Russia remember? Everyone is OK I assure you, Mrs Edwards."

Simon began collecting up all the material strewn on the floor and stairs and taking it back upstairs under Mrs Edwards instruction. "So it was you in Ukraine?"

Sebastian shouted up the stairs "Thanks Simon!" he replied quick and to the point "Sir I think you did brilliantly!"

Bill and Madge, crept out of one of the neighbouring rooms, they seemed to have taken a serious verbal beating and were thoroughly relieved at Sebastian's reappearance. He apologised to them for not dropping them an email telling them he would be away and them having to face such an onslaught.

"I am afraid it was Top Secret!" he said rather lamely. He admitted that he had never heard that his wife had ever watched PMQ and they had over-run their time by a good two hours due to the stop in Bergen, it was quickly sorted out but it had taken extra time. It was, he agreed a rotten plan!"

"But was it successful?" Bill and Madge asked almost in a chorus

"I think so! A couple of months will show"

Peace at last descended on Downing Street.

Chapter FORTY-EIGHT – The Chancellor's Spring Statement

Sebastian recovered that evening but he realised that he was becoming increasingly argumentative, aggressive and forgetful. In short bursts he could cope OK, but during longer sessions, he was more easily distracted. Every other day now he felt exhausted by 5.00 pm and did not appear much before 10.00 am unless for special meetings, he had himself arranged.

His departure was only the matter of a few weeks away. He should surely be winding down, but he was irritated that his legacy would not be representative of his views.

These big things, Constitutional Reform, NATO and possibly even the EU were just as it were something he had bumped into along the road, he never thought that he would be involved in or able to take a key role in, all of them, but he had become so wrapped up in them that it left little time for anything else!

So the Coalition's agreement on the future Finance Act, which was previewed in the Spring Statement, appeared to him to be an ideal way to correct that 'legacy balance'. Accordingly he asked Dan Stirling the leader of Lib Dem MPs, if on this occasion he, Sebastian, could sign off the ongoing finance policies expected to be enacted in November to apply from the following 5th April. Dan Stirling agreed handing Sebastian a list of his suggestions.

Sebastian met with his Chancellor of the Exchequer Stephen White just a few days before the new Leader of the Conservative Party was due to be announced, it seemed that he was well ahead in all indicative polls. 'Perhaps it was this', thought Sebastian as he read the first draft, 'which made him want to put out such an extraordinarily biased Spring Statement, he seemed to want to say 'Well here at last I am!?'

The Meeting started off calmly enough as Sebastian passed back across the table the written statement with his suggestions and amendment marked in red.

Anyhow Legacy fading out or Legacy storming in, there was not much agreement.

The Tories top lists items were; Lower Top rate of Tax – too high for too long, eradicate Inheritance Tax, Increase Pension Life-time limit – needs more flexibility, Reduce top vehicle tax of Chelsea Tractors, Fund new Grammar Schools in experimental areas.

The Lib Dem list he had been given was; Increase age at which Working Parents can get grants for Children during Holidays, Allow councils to borrow more to build more affordable homes, Improve the employment prospects of no hopers, with no exam passes. Get more applicants for Engineering Degrees which is what the country needs!

Sebastian launched out on his favourite topic and he tried to do some bargaining. "Despite what Sarah Driscoll is doing building affordable homes, we still need more. We have to prevent the housing market overheating again.

We have to cure the British obsession with Housing, we here suffer from rising demand and constricted supply, we are still not building enough of cheaper housing for those in need, and yet did you know that 7 million owner occupied houses have two or more spare bedrooms and 25 million have one spare, increasing the inheritance tax threshold further will just make matters worse. Rich owners will just sit in their houses till they die, but we need those spare rooms brought into use. So No! I will not agree to raising the IHT threshold, but what I will do is to agree with you that older people downsizing their homes three years or more before death will be allowed to halve the rate of IHT applied on a like amount of money old house-minus new house, in their wills, size will be defined by reducing the Council Tax band of old and new houses, also trebling the £3000 annual in-life gifts IHT free and reducing IHT on gifts made from the 7 years clawback to 5 years.

But I will also need you to understand that second homes are destroying some areas so that local council taxes may be trebled in specific areas within the powers of the New Regional Assemblies – I would exclude from that timesharing or multiple ownership of properties.

Also to complete the picture lets remove VAT from listed buildings modified for accommodation and more grants for conversion of second floor space over shops into flats!

Millions of private tenants are being priced out. However our obsession with housing is impacting the economy, provision of housing dominates private budgets and because there has been a huge increase in the return on buy to let in the last 20 years to 16% per annum, and that far outstrips the gain from shares of just 6.5%. So instead of investing in private growing companies which would help our economy grow and increase jobs, we invest in houses!

We have to bring into use every available room!

About 50% of our Bank lending is for mortgages it sucks money away from funding SMEs. So we need you to fund an additional £500 K for new Council housing. Many Council houses built in the 1950s and 1960s have plots twice the size of modern-day plots. I would like those areas where at least 60% are still in public ownership could apply for funds to compulsory purchase the lot then knock down and rebuild moving up from 2 to 3 stories high, aiming to double units on each estate. We could use modern Prefabs they are much better designed and constructed now!"

OK Prime Minister, I get the message, let me think about that I'll get back to you!"

Sebastian launched off again "No we don't want to get into Grammar Schools again we will not support that, it's not a problem of teaching brighter pupils better, it's a question entirely that the remainder become no hopers, second class citizens. If you can address that problem then I'll discuss it with you but you never do, selection must mean what happens to the unselected! But we could fund 'paired schools' so that each ethnic school is matched with an ordinary secondary school, so no ethic pupils grow up just in their own isolated silo. If I have to choose between Grammar or Paired schools then it's the latter every time, segregated on ethnicity is much worse long term for social cohesion. Right now that's the problem here!

Don't you realise the distorted expectations we have of University people, but we have a desperate need of Builders, Plumbers, Plasterers, Electricians, Joiners. We are always caught out, on the rare occasions that housebuilding is charging ahead, we come to a grinding halt because of a lack of people to do the work. The training for these people is often rudimentary and yet the aura we give to getting a 'good degree' is astonishing, these people in comparison are treated like yobs. I want to see a full year's residential course for 'Master builders' with some entry qualification but lifting this set of skills in the eyes of the public. I want to see the Press lauding this set of skills, I want to present it as a desirable attainment to those who don't want to go to university and struggle with theoretical subjects but who want to develop intensively practical skills. There must be an old RAF base somewhere that you could convert, quickly, you know before the next housing boom??

"Ok Prime Minister I'll work on it!"

Sebastian continued "This leads me into our standard topic. I see Universities doing two completely different things. First allowing as many people as wider choice of subjects as they want – that's to make self-realisation work, do what you want to do, become what you want.. Second however what they are supposed to do is to train enough people in those degrees that we, the country needs, to support our commercial and manufacturing operations. You have forgotten the second, Stephen. It's not working!. There's a huge mismatch!".

"No I had not forgotten they just don't want to be Engineers and Biophysicists and Chemists." Stephen retorted.

"Exactly, but we need them, this country needs them! I have a report right here, we need 87,000 Engineers graduates a year but we are only producing 46,000 a year. Manufacturing makes up 54% of our exports and we lag far behind when it comes to spending on Research & Development, but there is a multiplier effect too. So for every £1 in Gross Value Added from an engineering job, £1.45 is generated elsewhere within the UK economy, that's why Engineering is a much better investment than in Retailing where the add on jobs are much fewer! What do you want us to do? Buy in Engineers from the EC because we cannot be bothered to enthuse our own?"

"What do you want Prime Minister?" Asked the Chancellor.

"Free Tutorial fees for selected subjects! Take Engineering first plus as you said other priority degrees, then the modern languages we need to compete commercially in this world! Start off with French, German, Russia and Chinese." Sebastian shot back.

"Hmmh that's a horny old Lib Dem item eh? Ok, OK! I'll look at it!"

"Yes but it's the bit that's worth it!!" retorted Sebastian "and one final thing please 50% grants for childcare for working parents up to the age of 10, that means school holiday provision. I know there is some provision already but it needs improving and updating! It should be an opportunity for the kids to develop in their worst subject, a catch up process perhaps. See if you can do something on that?"

"and then? Prime Minister and then?" Stephen was obviously determined to get something for his side!"

"OK reduce top tax bracket by 10% for earned income, that is earned as an employee, not Directors who often switch between Salary and Dividends, nor anything for Service Companies, you know the Ltd Cos who employ just themselves or possibly the wife and charge costs for this, cars getting to work, entertaining expenses, training and that against the earnings of their company, as a result paying hugely reduced taxes as they in any case use pay the lower Corporate Tax" Sebastian had finished.

"I'll see what I can do Prime Minister. Frankly you haven't done us bad, we don't all hate you, you know!"

Sebastian exhausted from the recent days tensions, said nothing, looking down at his papers, he said "Stephen, I am just all washed up, I tried to do too much too quickly, I am counting the days till I leave, as is my wife."

"Prime Minister, don't be alarmed, we mean you no harm, but I think we can help you there!"

Sebastian looked at him calmly, "Anyhow Stephen thank you for your support!!

Chapter FORTY-NINE - Sebastian's Ides of March, despatched?

Two weeks after the momentous EC Speech and a just days after the tussle with Stephen White over the Spring Statement, the matter of the Conservative Leadership was finally resolved. All elements of the Tory Party were united in the view that Conservatives had become distracted by their own leadership hustings, with the two front runners often being missing from Cabinet meetings and neither of them being able, openly, to confront Sebastian for fear of interfactional rivalry interfering with the workings of the Cabinet. Accordingly they had agreed to suspend hostilities within the Cabinet. Their party contest had been quiet but bruising.

Michael Morgan originally also stood for leader but was soon eliminated so he was the most senior non leadership candidate, he had comprehensively backed Sebastian's NATO position so there were in effect three blocks of Tories, Those supporting the Chancellor, Stephen White, those supporting the interim Leader and Home Secretary Pamela Tressider and the majority of the Tory ministers following the lead of Michael Morgan who was happy, to do nothing, to let time play out. He had agreed to support the new leader whomsoever it was.

However the announcement that Stephen White had won the members vote by 60/40 had immediate repercussions.

The 1922 Committee, which had almost unanimously supported the Chancellor, immediately sought to bring Sebastian's reign as Prime Minister to an end. The overwhelming view of the MPs as a couple of members later admitted to Bill Bennet, was that Sebastian's very success had driven them to act. Huge centre spreads in respected Sunday Papers were unanimous in their praise for Sebastian and his great 'European Speech' which was endlessly quoted and analysed line by line. They felt they had to put a stop to his seemingly inexorable rise in the approvals rating of the voters before it turned into a clamour to extend Sebastian's period as Prime Minister.

Sir John, the Chief Whip managed to get a cryptic note passed to Sebastian a couple of weeks before. 'Beware the Ides of March, though they want your position not your life.'

Sebastian knew that Sir John would mean exactly what he said. Sebastian discussed the matter with senior Lib Dem Cabinet and senior officers. Many of them thought that the Tories would be extremely unwise to break their agreement for the sake of a couple of weeks, it might even wreck the Coalition and the Tories were still nowhere near in the polls to taking a majority if there were a General Election. So the warning was dismissed. However Sebastian became calmer as the date drew nearer. He believed Sir John.

When the strike came at the following weeks Cabinet they were all amazed, but surprisingly Sebastian himself seemed quite unruffled.

A sharp eyed Conservative party worker had noticed a discrepancy in the dates of the agreement over the Lib Dems initial take over and therefore also the hand back. Some emails said 'Ninety Days' others 'Thirteen weeks' but the date of Sebastian taking over as Prime Minister was several days before Christmas, whilst everyone had been working to March 31st as a convenient date. The new Tory Leader simply stated that in accordance with the agreement he, Stephen White, would be taking over as Prime Minister as of the following Cabinet meeting. He supported his statement with copies of emails giving the various dates.

There was no doubt, Stephen appeared to be right, if counting the week before Christmas then 90 days from that was next week, not three weeks' time. Sebastian and his Lib Dem colleagues looked at the papers, Sebastian called over Bill and Madge. Sebastian suggested a 20 minute 'time out' of the Cabinet meeting which was agreed.

He immediately summoned senior Party Staff and Lib Dem Cabinet members to the room next door. Key was the Cabinet Secretary's minute dated December 22nd, it stated three months. They all agreed, the Lib Dems didn't have a leg to stand on, they could not end the Coalition, there were insufficient grounds, no rules had been broken. The ninety days had been sublimated by March 31st, a tidy fixed date. The reaction was muted.. One member said "That puts paid to you, Sebastian, representing the Government for the formal and magnificent procession of thanksgiving for the Lords agreeing to the standing down of their own chamber which we know you had insisted on". They trooped back in.

Sebastian stood up and quietly announced that Lib Dems would not contest the request, the new Conservative Leader would take over as Prime Minister at the start of the next Cabinet meeting. He himself would be advising the Queen at the regular Thursday meeting that Stephen White should be the next Prime Minister. He thanked all the Cabinet members for their assistance over the past thirteen weeks.

There was relief around the table seemingly no-one wanted a verbal fist fight.

So all the Conservative Cabinet Ministers stood and applauded Sebastian, after some hesitancy the Lib Dem Cabinet Ministers did the same. Sebastian had not moved but sat solid in his chair.

Stephen White in response, reminded the Cabinet of Sebastian's determination to continue with the Former Tory PM's policies as he had pledged to Robin Turnbull he would. And he thanked the Prime Minister for keeping to his word. In accordance with that spirit he Stephen White would maintain the wording of the Spring Statement which he had just yesterday agreed after hours of discussion with Sebastian, also that he would continue as far as he was able with policies agreed by the Cabinet on the Constitution, NATO and the reform of the EU.

This appeared to satisfy all the Lib Dem members of the Cabinet and the handover proceeded without further problems.

Stephen White then summarised the intended Spring Statement without relating details.

The following day they all assembled on the front benches in the House of Commons, squeezing themselves uncomfortably for the full Spring Statement. The House was packed, this was living history.

After commenting at length on financial and economic forecasts, the lesser items were revealed.

1) Free Student University Tutorial fees for selected classes – first would come Engineering, Chemistry and Biology this September, then some leading foreign languages would follow next year. This was to reflect the degrees that the country needed

2) Setting up a residential college to specifically launch 'Master builders' to help with the hoped for surge in house-building

3) Agreement for Regional Assemblies to charge up to three times Council Tax for second homes.

4) £500 M Special Grant to knock down and rebuild council houses nearest London.

5) A 50% increase in Child Care grants for older children of working families.

6) Reduction of some IHT taxes by those who effectively downsized to smaller properties before death, and other reductions making it easier to give money away.

7) New Venture Capital Trusts to be licenced to operate in Greece, Bulgaria and Romania subject to finalising the details, this would give British Taxpayers advantages as if it was invested in the UK

There appeared to be cross party support for most of the items.

Immediately after the Spring Statement Sebastian rose to make the announcement that he would be standing down at the start of the next Cabinet meeting, somewhat earlier than scheduled. "In the meantime I congratulate the Right Honourable Stephen White on his election as Leader of the Conservatives and reassure this House that I will later today recommend that in 4 days' time Her Majesty should call on Stephen White to be the next Prime Minister. I would add that both he and I have been working to achieve an easy hand-over – I think we have succeeded here. I would like to thank my Tory colleagues in the Cabinet for listening to my proposals.".

There was a huge buzz across the floor of the House.

Sylvia was listening from the visitor's gallery above and could not conceal her delight to the amazement of conservative back-benchers.

However in TV interviews later that day, Tory back-benchers quickly realised that the price the Chancellor had seemingly had to pay to remove the PM early, as they had requested, had seriously badly backfired on them.

Chapter FIFTY - Those who cannot live together should live apart

Sebastian had, of course, to remove his belongings from No.10 the same day that he resigned. He was seen loading their suitcases into a taxi, he appeared to be quite happy and made no speech from a prepared lectern in Downing Street. He just walked over to the waiting press and TV lines, saying nothing but posing for photos and offering to sign anything presented to him. He just waved and waved.

He temporarily moved back in with Bill, then luckily the Opposition gave him an easy pairing, he need not attend Westminster that week, so Sebastian and Sylvia, for a few days moved into a Hotel near Rupert's lodgings, Sebastian slept solidly for the first 24 hours there.

But his mind did not switch off.

Sebastian now saw no need to constrain himself politically – he was out of office because with Tory disruptions, the agreement had said 13 weeks and that's what they had kept him to. Nobody had thought to be that precise at the time, in fact technically although he had agreed with the Queen to form a Government. He wasn't at all clear if that actually would run from the date when the actual Cabinet first agreed and what if anything his powers had been before the House reassembled in January.

The 1922 committee has seized on it so there it was. The same agreement stated that he was to take over as Home Secretary after Easter which was in the first week in April.

He had handed over the seals of office, as it were of PM they day he left office, but had not yet signed back in as a Minister as the Home office, so there was a gap when he held no Ministerial position.

As Prime Minister he had eventually conceded that his various 'interventions' as he called them, had to be shown to Cabinet before publishing to prevent embarrassment. All Ministers of the Crown were, of course, bound by convention to send any pronouncements they might make to the Prime Minister for approval before release.

Sebastian realised that as he was not a Minister, he was not prevented from stating exactly what he wanted and that no-one could stop him, even the Lib Dem whip could only act retrospectively.

For the first time in years he was unconstrained! He meant to use that freedom!

He was in fact grateful to Stephen White, who had allowed him some considerable 'legacy projects' as the price for his not contesting the muddle over the start and end dates of his appointment. In fact they were more generously inclined to Lib Dems than even he had thought possible. Frankly he confessed to himself he did not know how he could have survived those two last weeks anyhow. The strain of standing throughout the elaborate ceremony witnessing the passing of the old order, the House of Lords, and bringing in the new, the Regional Assemblies, had begun to haunt him   What if he collapsed half way through the ceremony? Then shaking hands with endless lines of Celebrity Peers who would no doubt be steered towards him, whose names, for the most part, he could not recall?

Stephen had pointed out to Sebastian that one of the last things he personally needed was to ignore the 1922 Committee who had been his followers from the start of his Leadership Campaign. Well he had delivered what they wanted. He told Dan Stirling that he thought it was a sensible price to pay to start of a good coalition working relationship.

For his own part, Sebastian had had enough of the gruelling work and constant tensions. Every week off his time of going was like 'live another day!'

Stephen White's offer had been too good to miss but when he previously thought that he was going to be kicked out and on receiving the 'Ides of March' note; he had, in fury, called his old friend Rob Murphy the features editor of the largest Sunday Broadsheet.

He had promised him something 'explosive about the Middle East'. He decided that now instead of a very aggressive article which he had planned, it would be instead, advisory and avuncular.

The gist of it would be the same 'Those who cannot live together, should live apart', he decided that he did not have to take his anger out on the world from being deceived by the Tories, he seemed to have miraculously and thankfully escaped the 'chop'.

The anger and righteous self-induced justification which he had expected to be mirrored in his article had gone. He had ended up with a bonus!

His case was now much simpler, aimed rather more at explaining what he might have done next on the World Stage rather than criticising UK or USA or EU foreign policy

It could be read just as a discussion paper, ideas not criticisms.

The nub of his paper to the features editor Rob Murphy was that after the seizure of Aleppo by the Regime several years ago, there had been a cease-fire, which was intermittently broken then re-arranged. After years of trying at conference after conference there was still no peace.

One of the main problems being that the non-regime Syrians were no longer there, they had been the majority but they had fled, all records had been destroyed so there was no voter registration database. So it was impossible to identify who was or was not eligible to vote. It would take, so they all agreed, about two years to re-create the lists, but no-one organisation was prepared to do it and people anyhow were shy of being identified. So various groups pronounced themselves as the legitimate heirs to those in the diaspora, some had fought as rebels, others seemed to possibly be terrorists aiming to create chaos, but none could claim a legitimacy which the other parties would accept.

The regime refused to allow elections within its area. Turkey and the Kurds who held pieces of Syria, were only interested in seizing bits of land, either to create a buffer zone in Turkey's case, or to incorporate Kurdish Syrian areas into Kurdish home territory. Whatever Turks wanted Kurds refused because part was culturally Kurdish, whatever Kurds wanted Turks refused on security grounds. Iraq opposed Kurdish plans because they thought that by legitimising claims over parts of Syria, that would open the way to Iraqi Kurdistan breaking away.

Iran and Hezbollah thought as they had fought they too should have a stake in the peace.

The real victor in terms of its direction of the war in support of the regime, appeared to be Russia, which had at last proven to all Russians that the Russian Military were still a force in the world. But they were baffled by the peace. It soon showed that Putin had only one gear, quick forward and he was hopeless at listening to others or compromising. The tangled chatter at the peace conferences became embroiled in minutiae, he soon handed over to his Foreign Minister. The latter knew if they unseated the Syrian President, the rest of the Alawites would object and as the only strongmen were from that sect, who were Shia, replacing him by another Syrian General might not help, it would not deflect accusations of War Crimes as these lower generals were in all probability those who had actual proposed and used the weapons, but what it would do would be to anger the majority who were Sunni as were ISIL whose remnants remained somewhere about. That was why when Allepo eventually fell even the normal residents tried to get away, they were Sunni!

In fact the problem spread wider than that, Saudis were 85 % committed to Sunni and theirs was a very strict form, so they had supported the rebels in Syria. Iran supported the Syrian Regime because they too were Shia as were the majority 60% of Iraqi and Hezbollah, Even further way a tribe in Yemen called the Houthi Shia had annoyed the Sunni Saudis enough to provoke a little war of their own. There was also trouble brewing in Bahrain where the poorer Sunni majority were ruled by Shia."

The main centrepiece of the Sunday Newspaper showed the Sunni Shia split, together with Sebastian's opinion that anyone who tried to put together a Syrian Peace Plan had to acknowledge the deep religious fissures that ran throughout the Middle East.

But Sebastian also acknowledged the UK's part as the Imperial Power in the 1920s and 1930s in creating this chaos, indeed it was that which had encouraged Sebastian to 'come clean' "The truth is" he said, "that at the end of the First World War, British Forces had done enough to claim victors' spoils throughout that area, despite Laurence of Arabia's protests he too was party to the massive deception, Britain gave a way a chunk of that area, Lebanon and Syria, to France but they manipulated all the boundaries not on the basis of religious affiliation. Back then, it is true, the differences between Shia and Sunni were not so marked. Nor on tribal patterns like Turkic, Arab or Kurdish. Some boundaries they chose on the basis of the old Turkish Empire provinces. For other boundaries like Iraq and Iran, they sought to either protect and own the main waterways like Iraq or to control the oil in Iran".

Sebastian suggested that some Kingdoms had originally been artificially created in the 1920s and 30s, like those offered to Saudi and Jordan, which then appeared to be empty deserts and they were just lines drawn. Also Iraq was treated in the same way with a Hashemite ruler to keep them happy for their assistance to the British in the war against the Turks. Indeed it helped the British that these rulers might have to depend on British troops to maintain the power, in their own countries. Later on, British protection in return for British commercial interests, must have seemed to the British a reasonable deal. If the Shah of Persia thought to seek alternative support, he was duly replaced, if there was even a scant hope of a sort of Independent Democracy in Mossadec, then he too must be replaced by a more pliant Shah.

Sebastian admitted, "The unpalatable truth we, British, have to confess to, was that British public opinion then was of the view that the 'Arabs couldn't rule themselves' the last thing the British Empire needed was a massive new ungovernable joined up Arab State. So virtually all the boundaries were created for the UK's convenience. At that time in the whole area there were no delineated states. We drew the lines in the sand to our order.

The result has in about the 1970s when the religious divide re-started, there was a massive asymmetric problem, peoples that were shoe-horned into these new states, were often ruled by a King-family with total powers or sometimes by Dictators. Many of these Dictators were from minority sects like Saddam Husein a Sunni or Basharat Hassan a minority Alawite, affiliated to Shia in a land with a Sunni majority. It seems very clear why they would become Dictators; reaching high office already, but not yet at the top, as a thrusting representative of the minority, such people would be vulnerable and open to any representative of a unified majority grouping. They must have thought it was either 'sit and wait' to be kicked out at best, or at, worst to be killed or to himself 'take control' Once there, of course, he would have the support of all his tribe and maintain control over the majority by giving his tribe 'accelerated promotions' and thereon continue by force..

Under those conditions there would be no point in open elections, token parliament giving him total support would be fine, but open elections, why so? Why risk the power that you have? All you might do holding election would be to lose power and that would involve retribution for those families whom the Dictator had disposed of securing his own power base.

So the weird nonsensical lines in the sand did more than create pockets of minorities in strange lands, it ultimately lead to a rash of Dictators, as each side Sunni and Shia became more aggressive, democracy proved a dead governing format. Witness Iraq where it is said the Shia majority caused the rift with Shia that lead to ISIL, the West had blissfully imagined that all one had to do was to arrange a Coalition of all three Shia, Sunni and Kurd and 'bob's your uncle'. Hey democracy wins OK! No-one party has a majority – fine! Good, now we have moved them from Dictator to Democracy, that's shown them!

But the Sunni/Shia car bombs and mosque degradation did not stop, the result was the rise of the political militia and that was the effective end of Iraq!

So it's all our fault, Yes? or No? Of course we were not to have known that rivalries became hatreds became wars.

The whole of the Middle East, the whole of Islam has been witness to this murderous devastation, this monstrous, useless loss of life, the destruction of homes and wealth which ought to be enjoyed by the whole area. There is indeed wealth enough for all!

I therefore call on all Sunni and Shia in every country world-wide to put pressure on all governments to end this alienation. It must not continue. I respectfully suggest that a Grand Council of political and religious leaders representing Islam should meet and to try to arrange a means of living together.

If they do not do so, then the UN should begin the search for peace based on one simple message, 'those who cannot live together, must live apart'. There is so much danger and devastation that all countries boundaries should be based on simple referenda. All religious minorities should be allowed to leave or boundaries redrawn to reflect the religious divide. Oil revenues from output within the whole area should be shared on a per capital basis.

The reason why this makes sense now is because the massive Syrian diaspora has left an empty country, so there is plenty of space to arrange population swaps, there will never ever be such an opportunity again to correct the mistakes of the past..

Maybe then in 100 years' time when tempers have become less frayed, Shia Muslim might again call Sunni Muslin 'brother' and vice versa and moreover mean it!"

Sebastian Edwards.

There were of course many other contributors to the piece, and some who flatly contradicted Sebastian's opinion. There were former ambassadors, military personal who had been in the wards there, professors of some Universities there and so on most saying it was 'rubbish', 'wrong interpretation of history' 'totally impracticable'. 'UK was not to blame'.

In the countries where Shia and Sunni lived in peace it was greeted more enthusiastically, particularly amongst the minorities.

The Editor told Sebastian later that he had received several unpleasant letters and emails. Some death threats warning Sebastian Edwards to stay out of Muslim affairs, some threatened a Fatwa on him.

The death threats he had passed immediately to the Ministerial Protection Squad.

Chapter FIFTY-ONE – Travelling North – free at last!

Back in January 2021, Sebastian promised himself that, as a reward to himself for lasting out the 12 weeks since his accession, he would escape to his friend's house in Northumberland for a few days of mental recovery. It was a sort of ritual, a cleansing of the spirit, he had visited his old school friend Douglas almost every year at Easter for over 25 years. In the years he couldn't make it, he always felt as if something was missing which his body clock or brain seemed to need.

For a few days he was there, it was as if he was transported to a different world entirely.

Douglas Finlay was a countryman at heart and his wife was artistic, a talented amateur painter. These were worlds far removed from Sebastian's normal life, accountancy, business, then politics. The format of the visit didn't vary much and to Sebastian that was its attraction.

On Saturday he would arrive somewhere between 12.00 and 5.00 pm depending on his workload and when he could get away.

Saturday evening dinner was prepared by Anna-Lisa, Douglas' wife, this was followed by topical discussion and an update of what was happening in the countryside. They would then briefly plan the following day, Easter Sunday, which invariably included a trip to one of the nearby village churches where Douglas had been a parochial church councillor. Then off somewhere for a walk, and there were literally dozens of good spots or trails to take; or maybe a trip to the bookshop at Alnwick, where Sebastian now had an account, and probably a picnic lunch. In the evening either a meal at home or at a local restaurant, then home to watch TV, and catch up on common friends and then to bed.

On Monday perhaps a short walk into the village to buy papers at the all-purpose shop the 'Border Reiver' a name which harkened back to the Tudor times when lawlessness was common in the border area between England and Scotland and cattle were regularly stolen and found their way across the then border just a few miles away. Then maybe a local trip, lunch at a small restaurant somewhere; the 'Otterburn Mill' was a favourite. Somehow this woollen mill had survived for decades and when, it was finally closed, it was turned into a restaurant with some of the original machinery still on show in the entrance lobby.

Sebastian usually left in the afternoon and enjoyed travelling back listening to the '100 best tunes' on Radio Classic, he never worked out the winner and although he had often called as directed had never won any of the guessing prizes. Still it was a relaxation; he normally never felt he had the time otherwise to sit and listen to music. He was often stuck in traffic but it didn't matter that much if he was listening.

Sylvia was always happy with Sebastian's Easter trips as she told him 'I know you are in good hands!' She herself usually used the opportunity to get closer to her own family and always stayed the night with one of her sisters. On this occasion it was the sister married to Ahmed. In 2021 Ahmed's whole family has been banned from the Edwards' house following the incident. So this time Sheila was to stay away at her sister's house.

On this occasion they had been delayed leaving Camford and had travelled home to Middleton for lunch. The MPS handover was usually by county in the now well-rehearsed 'chain reaction' system. One county police force, would hand over to another, constantly shadowing Sebastian till he got home.

He had begun to relax after the most arduous period in his life and fell asleep at home in Middleton. Sylvia thought the rest would do him good so went shopping leaving a note for Sebastian with some pots of marmalade to take north which Sylvia adored but which she also made annually for Douglas' wife.

Sebastian awoke with a start, he had slipped off his favourite chair and slumped to the ground, the TV was blaring and the Rugby game he had been watching was long finished.

It was now 4.00 pm and it would take him maybe three and a half hours to get up there. Leaving a bit of time for traffic congestion, he thought he might arrive at 8.00 pm. He called Douglas to apologise for the late arrival. Douglas said that, in that case he would go to a friend's for a party, to which he had been invited with his wife. He expected they would be back at around 8.30 pm, their house-key would be in the usual place under the log near the front door, Sebastian was to make himself at home and pour himself a glass of sherry.

Picking up his weekend bag which Sylvia had prepared for him and put by the door Sebastian rushed out of the house and jumped into the car accelerating away trying to make up for lost time.

He had gone more than 10 miles when he realised that he had left his mobile phone behind. 'Blast' he thought 'I'll borrow Douglas' phone when I get there'.

As he knew it would be getting dark when he arrived he decided against using the 'scenic route, as he called it, the A 68 north of Scotch Corner, which had delightful switchbacks as the road looped over various hills and valleys. It ran basically along the spine of hills and cut off the industrialised North East. He decided he wouldn't see much so determined instead to follow the A 1 (M) and then take the A 696 to Jedburgh. As he was no longer PM he thought he was free of any restraint. The feeling of relief was euphoric, every hour of freedom from responsibility felt as if another stone had been lifted from the haversack on his back which had threatened to crush him.

His Toyota Auris was rolling along happily just below the legal limit. Sebastian decided to wear a baseball cap which he pulled down to cover the top of his face, that way he seemed to have escaped most recognition. He didn't want people either making rude gestures at him or attempting 'high fives'; mostly those that did recognise him appeared immediately to try to use their mobiles, probable to call a friend 'Hey look who I am driving alongside', and aim the phone camera at Sebastian. At times he had had to accelerate away then dodge in front of a heavy lorry on the inside lane. Anyone who tried to run parallel in the middle lane quickly got blasted off by overtaking vehicles.

After about 50 miles a police car drew alongside him and motioned him to pull into the hard shoulder, the police vehicle stopped behind. Sebastian noted it was just before A1.M Junction 62.

A weary policeman stretched his legs as he walked up to the driver's side, Sebastian lowered the window. "Are you Mr Sebastian Edwards Sir?"

"Yes! How can I help?" It was only then that he made the connection. For so long every physical movement he made, every ride he took, every visit he made anywhere to anyone had been made under the scrutiny of the MPS. But he had imagined that, being no longer the PM, he could now resort to his former less important status. He had not had the time to check with Superintendent Denny. As he was late setting off, he had not bothered to call into the police house on his way out of the cul-de-sac to check on his new status under police rules..

"Well Sir! You have run us a merry dance. When the Nottingham lot realised you had 'done a runner' as it were, Sir, your wife was interviewed, she said you had left your phone behind so could not be contacted but that she noticed you normally use the A 68 and cut across country as it were. But you didn't do that Sir! Did you? Nottingham Superintendent, John Denny was most upset, he was! Because you are still under the MPS for at least the next 6 months – Just so as you know Sir! Now can you confirm that you are spending the next two nights at your friend's house, let us know please if you intend to change you plans Sir!

Easter is a pretty busy time for us Sir, catching criminals is our main line of business you know Sir, so anything you can do to help?"

It seemed to Sebastian that after this wigging off but he replied "Yes I am". The policeman appeared to turn away to return to his own car.

So Sebastian started the motor, disengaged the brake, drove off and re-joined the Motorway.

He thought he saw the officer waving to him so Sebastian acknowledge it by winking his lights, he continued on his way.

His thoughts then drifted to the walks they would take tomorrow and he wondered what Douglas had lined up for him.

He wasn't quite sure how the MPS 'chain link' system of surveillance would work up here. He couldn't see any trailing police car.

He pressed the accelerator and the Toyota Auris speeded up a bit, it was already 7.00 pm and it was getting darker outside.

By the time he arrived at his friend's house at 7.45 pm, it was pretty dark and as he got out of the car dragging out the single small travel case, he paused and looked over to his right. The final rays of the sun were hitting some lone clouds in the sky. Then the sun was diving down towards the skyline

He had hoped that his friends would have been back before he arrived, but there was no light on.

Douglas' house was hidden behind a small hill, which to some extent protected it from the northerly winds, on the other side of hill was the MOD firing range. Sebastian knew he had to move quickly as within minutes it would be very dark. The final rays of daylight were disappearing fast, within minutes he would be in total darkness in the shadow of the hill. He parked the car in its usual position on the grassy patch across the road opposite to the five bar, white gate. There was no point in pulling into the driveway because that's where his friend usually parked.

He slipped open the gate and moved down a path and turned left to the front door which was within a small porch. It was now very dark. 'Now where did he say the key was? Ah Yes, under a log to the left of the white door', he fumbled around and could just see a dark shape, he lifted it up scrabbled around with his fingers and touched something metal. He grabbed it and lifted it up. Good! That was the key, the rest should be easy!'

He turned the key in the lock and within a few seconds he was in and fumbled around for the hall light which he couldn't find. "Damn and blast!" He cried out "Damn!" as he bumped into the open kitchen door.

He knew the layout, the house was a bungalow built of limestone blocks with curious spots of iron imbedded in the iron-stone. To the left was a large lounge, ahead was a galley type kitchen with an Aga cooker which they kept on almost permanently, he could feel the heat from it already. His bedroom was the first door on the right, so he felt his way along the wall. He opened the door with relief, he turned on a light paused for a moment stunned by the intensity of the light. He put his case on the bed nearest the window, that's where they invariably put him.

He turned around towards the front door, he had remembered that there were some important papers in the car and that he must bring inside. The was some light from the bedroom which he had left open.

As he approached the front door, he noticed that he seemed to have left it ajar, 'That's funny, could have sworn I had closed it?'

The next moment he was shocked as an almighty thump on his back sent him headlong into the door which slammed shut as he tried to protect himself from the fall. He felt a heavy weight pushing him into the ground.

There was an excited chatter in a foreign language interspersed with English which he couldn't follow. His arms were lifted up and he was dragged into the darkened lounge, blood was pouring over his eyes from a cut on his head which he thought he must have banged on the sill of the front door. He kept wiping the blood from his eyes.

They pulled him onto an armchair in the lounge. There was an excited chatter as before. One of them began to wipe Sebastian's face on a table cloth he had yanked from a side table.

He shouted to the other in perfect English "That's him, that's him! Do it do it now! Now. He's the bastard that's ruined my life, he's a devious fucking bastard. Do it. Do it NOW." screaming at the top of his voice.

Sebastian was still dazed, had a banging headache and didn't move. He saw that they both wore ill-fitting dark coloured balaclavas. The first man was hopping from foot to foot in an agitated state

The other man calmly told Sebastian "Here hold this" and he jammed a cushion to his chest. Sebastian meekly did as he was told. Then the other man brought out a handgun and pressed it to the cushion but said to the first one 'Hey! Just a minute, turn the bloody light on will you!"

"Why?" said the first one "Just do it!" "What do you want a bloody light for?" the first man argued "just aim at the bloody cushion, it'll muffle the sound! Do it and let's get out!"

"No! The light – NOW" and aimed the gun at the first man "Do it NOW" he shouted.

The first man did so and the second man looked at Sebastian "It's him, the man, the Prime Minister". and promptly rounded on the first one, "What game are you playing, you little shit, you said he was someone who let you down and it was a matter of honour as he had broken his word to you! You are mad, you know that? MAD, totally fucking mad! Come on! Let's get out, the place will be swarming with police!"

The first man lunged for the gun "Give it me, if you cannot do it give it me and I'll finish him off!"

"No!" they struggled, both men appeared to locked together. There was a deafening roar, a shout and a scream.

The first man fell to the floor, the second man raced past Sebastian for the front door, he could not have been more than a foot beyond it when, a searchlight illuminated him and a loud hailer called out "STOP, HALT, THROW DOWN YOUR WEAPON", but the man kept on running and firing the hand run wildly. A single shot rang out. It was out of Sebastian's line of sight.

He must have fainted.

He regained consciousness as a policeman was wiping his face with water and another was giving him emergency artificial respiration.

He heard the groans of a man outside and Sebastian concluded that the second man must have survived.

Sebastian saw in the background Douglas and his wife Anna-Lisa. He waved at them and must have fainted again.

He next awoke when he realised that he was being bodily lifted from a table onto a trolley and moved outside into an ambulance.

They arrived at a hospital and Sebastian's wound was dressed. He was moved to a ward. The consultant suggested to Sebastian that he should stay in hospital for a couple of days just to check that he had suffered no further ill effects.

Sebastian fell sound asleep without eating and did not awake till noon the following day, Sunday, when the police made contact.

By then the wounded intruder had decided to 'spill the beans.' The police said he was 'singing like a canary'.

They disclosed that the dead man was indeed Ahmed. The police had managed to piece together the story and they wished to publish the main elements to prevent the notion that this had been a terrorist attack.

Apparently after the incident on Sebastian's driveway Ahmed had been enraged at Sebastian's demand that he sign the letter which would reveal him as a thief. He then had devised a plan to get himself into prison so that he could meet with a hit-man, whom the gang for which he worked had identified, and pay for him to 'take out' Sebastian. He had therefore assaulted another officer and luckily was sent to the same local prison, remanded on bail with his case due to be heard in two weeks' time. He had convinced the hitman that he had been badly let-down by the target and the hitman had believed that the target was a man of Pakistani origin from the same village as Ahmed. He had paid over half of what Sebastian had given him with the balance to be paid on successful completion of the task.

The police officers who had stopped Sebastian on the A1 M had in fact received the information that Ahmed had escaped just as Sebastian had driven off, but they were not aware of the significance of the news. They were unwilling to chase Sebastian because the next turnoff would have been beyond the Durham County boundary and they decided not to try to catch up with him. However the MPS had received the information that a man of Pakistani origin was threatening to kill Sebastian and alerted the local police. It was these who had raced to the house in Northumberland and had arrived in the nick of time.

The second man, the hit-man, had recovered quickly, luckily the bullet had passed straight through a muscle in his arm.

The MPS were there in the debriefing sessions and passed all this information to London.

Sebastian insisted on being released that evening, Sunday, and he was taken back to Douglas' home.

The TV channels by now alerted to the story of the initial attack, parked their cars and vans on a layby on the main A 696 near the site of the attack. So it was a struggle to get passed them up the narrow lane. The TV News had initially described it as a 'probable' terrorist attack. On Monday the Press thought was a direct result of Sebastian's dramatic proposals for the Middle East which had been published the previous morning, although this was corrected when it was realised the dates did not tie up.

The Government was determined too to correct the impression of a terrorist which they realised would create considerable alarm. The new Prime Minister, fearing a backlash, went on air to state that it seemed it was a private matter, but that didn't clarify much.

No 10 became more anxious that the media not jump to the conclusion that this was an attempt by terrorists to hit at the heart of government.

Sebastian was informed and agreed. He called Ranjit Singh, the solicitor, to release the letter signed by Ahmed in order to clarify the reason for the motivation for the attack. This was published the following day.

Sebastian was undeterred over the incident and seemed cheerful occasionally rubbing his sore head. He did not appear to remember the detail of the event when Douglas asked him to recall it. "I can remember putting the overnight bag in the room on the bed and then going back to the door as I had left important papers in the car, then I heard a movement behind me and woke up in the ambulance!"

Anyhow he seemed alright although nervy and unable to keep still, he kept on pacing the carpet. He suggested that they continue as planned and drop in tomorrow for lunch at the Otterburn Mill before he left to return to Middleton.

He went to bed early and fell asleep and again did not awake till noon the following day.

Sebastian drove them the few miles to the restaurant.

He assured them that he felt fine.

They went straight to the table nearest the window overlooking the fields. Sebastian insisted on wearing his old baseball cap partly, to disguise himself and partly to cover the wound on his head. He also pulled up the collar of his coat, it was still quite cold and he was, he felt, indistinguishable from the other visitors.

Sebastian was about to order his snack from the menu when he saw one of the service staff dressed in black advancing towards them holding sets of cutlery, each wrapped in a black serviette.

Sebastian sat rooted to his chair but shouted "No! No! not again" and hid his head in his hands sobbing uncontrollably. His cap fell off and people at the surrounding tables recognised his as the former Prime Minister. Staff noticing the commotion were drawn to the table. Douglas and Anna Lisa were trying to comfort Sebastian.

An off-duty nurse offered help and Anna Lisa explained that Sebastian had been attacked the previous evening. "Shock it's probably delayed shock!" She immediately took charge and asked the staff to close that particular room and laid Sebastian on a bench seat, taking his pulse. Some blankets were found and were placed around Sebastian. A local GP was called from Bellingham and arrived about 20 minutes later, he confirmed the diagnosis. "Mr Edwards I have called an Ambulance."

Sebastian, who, by now had partially recovered, tried to object. The doctor was insistant.

"I have to advise you to treat this seriously, each person's body reacts differently to shock. They will probably tell you that you will need to stay overnight under observation."

An ambulance arrived and Sebastian was taken under protest to Newcastle Hospital once again.

The police sealed off the lane from the main road to the Douglas' house, as a 'crime scene'.

The local Press alerted to the incident in the Otterburn Mill by members of the public remained outside the Newcastle Hospital determined to catch a glimpse of the former Prime Minister or any celebrities visiting him. The TV Crews eventually made their way there.

The National Press' response had been muted as few papers had yet received the full story and this second incident they thought might be a continuation of the first. The full story was not shown until the Tuesday with reference to Sebastian's later collapse.

Chapter FIFTY-TWO - Convalescing

The same consultant he had seen before, visited him again later that day.

"Mr Edwards, I did advise previously that you were not ready to leave. You dismissed the cut on your head as 'nothing really'. Let me tell you what the problem is.

Minor jarring of the intracranial contents may cause concussion and a clinical state of transient loss of consciousness due to temporary neuronal dysfunction. You may have suffered this. Retrograde amnesia is common.

It's possible that you temporarily forgot the incidents that led to your loss of consciousness.

These might then have spontaneously been remembered when a similar incident occurred.

We will have to carry out a number of tests on your memory to see if there has been further brain damage. These will be of two kinds, current readily available information in the world at large and your own personal information, probably family knowledge.

We'll have to re-enact exactly how the injuries to your head occurred so that we can see exactly the forces and pressures applied.

With severe injury, a cerebral contusion may occur when the head strikes a stationary object such as when your head struck the ground or was it the door, or was a weapon used? You see the head decelerates abruptly while the brain continues moving forward to the point of impact. The result is a severe contusion in a region opposite the point of impact. A backward fall causes contrecoup contusions at the frontal and temporal poles of the brain, whereas a fall on the side of the head causes contrecoup contusions at the opposite temporal lobe. Generally, a forward fall does not cause contrecoup contusions on the back of the brain because the interior surface of the skull is smooth at this point.

So we will have to carefully go through exactly how you fell as far as you can remember!

But first we shall ask you to undergo several brain scans so that we can see if there is any detectable brain damage.

Meanwhile you will be under observation.

Now on this occasion, I am afraid I will not take 'No' for an answer, with your friends agreement I called your wife and she has agreed, you will stay here for at least a week probably longer."

Sebastian reluctantly agreed.

The TV and Press were told that Sebastian Edwards would be there for several days but would issue a Press Release before he left Hospital.

The Car Parking staff told all the attending media to leave "Goo Gerr orf an doon't cum back 'ere"

At least that's what Sebastian later saw on the TV. It's not known if the press fully understood all that, but they nevertheless departed.

Sebastian was a reluctant patient but kept pacing around the room, later that day a nurse dropped a tray of medical instruments with a crash in the corridor outside his room. As before he shouted out "No No! Not again" and ended up in a huddle on the floor where the staff found him. He realised that a sharp noise was likely to bring on the same reaction. He found it difficult to sleep and was given medication.

Thereafter he submitted himself calmly to the tests and scans.

After a few days without further incident he thought he had proved he was OK. But then a vase was dropped somewhere nearby, setting off a similar reaction, freezing, crouching embryonic position on the floor.

However within two weeks although any loud bang caused reactions, they appeared to lessen in intensity and duration. The consultant experimented making noises behind a curtain, although he visibly winced and hesitated. he no longer had the automatic reactions as he had previously.

But Sebastian knew that he wasn't yet fit to return to work, his concentration which was legendary, appeared to have been affected and he still kept pacing endlessly, backwards and forwards, backwards and forwards. He had no doubt that as soon as it became evident that loud bangs set him off or even made him hesitate and loose his drift in discussion that many MPs would try to distract him in that way.

He occupied his time with two main matters, Letters of Thanks. He wrote personal letters to everyone who had helped him as PM, Cabinet Ministers, Lib

Dem staffers, SPADS, some Civil Servants, and personal staff, thanking them but apologising that he was the first PM who was unable to use the dissolution honours. To selected staff he gave inscribed House of Commons memorabilia.

He persuaded Andrew Laws, his erstwhile Conservative/UKIP opponent, to organise the charity created through the retailer, 'Children in care' alongside Dr Singh Sebastian's GP. They asked if he had any instructions. Sebastian replied 'No I trust you both, just get on with it!',

After three weeks when they had found nothing medically wrong he was discharged, but the Consultant read off a whole list of other underlying problems, raised blood pressure, hardening of the arteries, a weak kidney function. The pressure of office had also taken its toll in other ways.

Madge came up by train to Newcastle and drove him back home to Middleton, at the time announcing that She and Bill were getting married. "It was a messy divorce you know!"

Sebastian confessed that he had never inquired about Bill's marital arrangement and knew nothing about it at all! But he wished them well!" Madge asked if she could take over the flat "Of course" he said still imagining he had No 10 still.

Sylvia was delighted about the marriage plans, but whisked Sebastian upstairs to bed.

His own GP Dr Singh gave Sebastian a full checkup the following day, "I suppose you discharged yourself originally?" he said. "Hmmh thought so, impetuous as usual! Have you been pacing around, and how have you been sleeping? Yes it figures!"

"Sebastian, how long have I known you?"

"I suppose about 10 years."

"Do you remember when you saw me last?"

"Oh it must have been a couple of years back, when I had an attack of Sprue!"

"No it was early December last year! Do you remember that Sebastian?" Asked Dr Singh.

"No surely!"

"Yes it was during your 'bumpy ride' I think you called it Sebastian!"

Sebastian paused "Yes that's right you called around for something, cannot remember what that was!"

"It was about you Sebastian, to be blunt your nerves were shot to pieces, I have no idea how you managed to get back up to London, you really were in no fit state to work, you must have slept it off. Then you were Foreign Minister and I understand you carried the weight as well of the hopes of all the Lib Dems on your shoulders. You have been working frenetically.

Since becoming Prime Minister and trying to put the UK to rights, it has exacted on you a fearful, terrible cost.

I have kept in contact with Sylvia every week since then and she has become increasingly worried about your frenetic work rate, seeing you at the end deteriorating, almost week by week, nightmares and a tendency to paranoia. But you are no longer Prime Minister. Lib Dems will have to find another shining star. Any other period like that again will kill you".

Dr Singh was emphatic.

Sebastian responded "Well as Minster in charge of the Home Office, the work is much reduced, I see no reason why I should not be able to work say" and he thought "well four days a week!"

"Hummh" Dr Singh sighed "Well you made a promise to Sylvia, do you remember that?"

Sebastian reddened "Yes but…"

"this time no buts" Dr Singh interrupted "it's time for you to make a public announcement, you will stand as an MP, because I seriously think if you didn't stand the stress on you would be even worse than standing, but that you would no longer seek high office!"

"OK, you are right, I owe it to Sylvia, I'll do it as I agreed I would at next month's Constituency meeting!"

"Next week!" Dr Singh contradicted him. "I'll see you there."

The following week the press carried the following release;

FORMER PRIME MINISTER TAKES BACK SEAT.

Sebastian Edwards has made clear to his constituents that due largely to the recent attack he does not believe that he would be fit enough to seek high office again at the end of this parliament and, although he still wishes to stand at the next General Election, the number one position of Lib Dem candidates on the ballot paper will be taken over by his colleague Tim Holland.

 This caused a certain frisson in political circles as one complainant wrote in The Times, letters to the Editor.

Dear Sir,

'Retirement indeed, it's a cynical ploy'.

'Are we to believe that Mr. Edwards supposed retirement from High Office is anything but a cynical ploy to gain an extra seat for Lib Dems? At the last General Election Mr. Edwards got in by the skin of his teeth, the sole LD elected from a five seat constituency but of course by positioning himself as number two he merely hopes to increase the number of LD seats won from one to two by giving the Number one person all Lib Dem votes whilst he attempts to gather all the other parties' second preferences, which he hopes he has earned from the publicity drawn from his twelve weeks at the top! It is appalling that this self-promotion also included his adverts for men's suits, surely a most inappropriate method of advertising for a Prime Minister! Should not the value of that free advertising be included as election expenses at full cost?'

Yours etc., Appalled of Golder's Green London.

Few were aware of the reason for his extended absence from Parliament.

Sebastian finally agreed to take a further weeks' holiday with Sylvia on condition that he could return to work if Dr. Singh would give him a clean bill of health, apart, of course from the problems normally associated with a man of his age.

Whilst on holiday he signaled to his office that he thought he would be returning the following week.

Despite protests from Sylvia he returned to work on the following Monday, all his staff were aware however that they were instructed to make sure that at 5.00 pm every Thursday he was seen off in his car back home to Middleton. On the first day of his return to the House of Commons he was greeted with appreciative cheers from all sides of the House.

Sebastian was at home over the weekend but caught on Sky TV the momentous speech from the reviewing stand at the official May Day military parade in Moscow.

President Medvedev announced

"There will be no more intimidation of the Baltic States, we will settle affairs in Ukraine and we will accept a United Nations motion to restart the Syrian Peace talks".

Everyone craned their necks on the reviewing stand searching for the face of Prime Minister Putin, the TV cameras followed, but he was not there.

"Prime Minister Putin resigned yesterday night, there is a case against him of embezzling state funds!"

There was some hissing and booing but the parade continued unchanged.

'Hmmh!' Sebastian warbled to himself 'about time too! Well done Medvedev!'

The following week the Russian TV and Press announced that some thirty of Putin's closest confidants had been arrested on charges of corruption. A new Prime Minister was announced, Sergey Kramrenkov was raised to Deputy Foreign Minister with responsibilities for Europe.

A few days later intelligence reports, from both USA and UK agents, indicated that tank commanders in the Moscow Military Region had all been replaced and the senior most Russian service chiefs were each retired.

Chapter FIFTY-THREE – At the Home Office; Prisons and Immigration

Sebastian had been off for 6 weeks but was bursting to get back to work He could not now quite remember why he had insisted on being overlord of both departments except that there were close linkage between the two and a solution was more likely from an all-round perspective which needed both departments and an ability to cut across boundaries.

He knew that he faced two serious problems.

The Prison Service showed every sign of being in danger of collapsing, In Prison violence rising, more frequent prisoner mutinies, staff leaving but the service unable to replace them quickly, rising prison population, signs of breakdown of controls within prisons caused by easy access to drugs.

Ministers like Michael Gove were said to have had sweeping reform ideas, like rebranding similar to academy schools, but he had been dismissed before they could do anything, succeeding Ministers had been too timid to even try and had spent their time 'fire-fighting'. So Prison Governors' hopes had been raised that something would be done, and then dashed. So as far as Sebastian was concerned action rather than blather was needed to restore staff confidence.

As far as immigration was concerned Sebastian knew he had, in a few months' time, to be able to present a workable case to either amend or continue the derogation of Freedom of Movement of people. Unless he was able to do that there was the likelihood that a minor EU state from Eastern Europe would put in train a legal challenge, if that were successful the UK might face further volumes of immigrants. This would signal that the government was not in control and would inevitably lead to the rise of UKIP once again. He saw his main difficulty that the last Home Secretary had spent years in the post and achieved nothing. Sebastian was expected to be a miracle worker, he had about 15 months to get something working.

All this he had to do in just the 4 days a week as he had agreed with Sylvia, he had to return home to Middleton every Thursday night by 8.00 pm

He started off on the Prison Service but intended to run the review of and Immigration in parallel, devolving much of the work to professional staff.

The now Conservative lead Coalition seemed happy to endorse Sebastian. Tory Cabinet Ministers openly told their Lib Dem colleagues so, this time they thought that as 'just another' Cabinet Minister that if successful they could bathe in his reflected glory as part of the team or find ways or reshuffling if he became an embarrassment, he was now at least 'under control', this they repeated endlessly.

Chapter FIFTY-FOUR - Reform of the Prison Service

As Prime Minister Sebastian had read all the papers, standard reports, ideas, opinions, proposals and suggestions relating to the Prison Service HMPS. He had any missing papers secretly delivered to him at home during his convalescence times to arrive whilst his wife was working at the charity.

He requested and was granted a Conservative Junior Minister and, he it was, whose job was to filter all his work so that only matters of real importance in the Ministry came to Sebastian's attention. They quickly evolved a way of working together, the Conservative Junior Minister would have a huge pile of paper every week. They would sit across the table, the Junior Minister called out the item and they made instant decisions, it would either come to Sebastian or it would be left with the Junior Minister to deal with. There was a 'follow up list' of decisions they had made and a 'work in progress list' of matters they could not resolve, by and large it worked well. The Junior Minister accepted the extra work knowing that he was doing much more, higher level, work that otherwise he would. He grabbed at the opportunity which Sebastian gave him.

This then allowed Sebastian to devote at least 50% of his time, half time to Prison Reform, whilst the rest was, of course, on the Home Office and Immigration.

Although his prison visit of the previous January had been a 'disaster' he realised it had allowed him to focus on one key objective.

Prison was awful, overcrowding made it a living hell! At least 60% of prisons are overcrowded, this damaged any real chance of any effective 'rehabilitation'.

Currently he mused 'Prison simply did not work, we are just recycling criminals and we are training newer inmates to be better criminals, they often had more access to drugs inside than out, useful formal training was virtually non-existent so they were leaving with no better chance of earning than before. The places were choc-a-bloc, leading to pressure on the staff, greater time locked in with the result that the prisoners were more often stir crazy ready for a fight with other inmates or staff or just self-mutilation. – the only thing it did do was keep the same criminals off the same street, but just for a time as a huge number returned.'

Sebastian acted quickly even as he was travelling down to London by car on the first Monday morning, he was giving instructions before he set foot in the place. His chief link was to be a long serving manager Angela Stone.

He asked her to set up a meeting for the following Monday, with a special group, representative of the services yet hand-picked to be open to new ideas.

These were 5 selected Prison Governors chosen as having outstanding performance at least one from a women's', prison and one from a youth offenders institution, a Crime Prosecution Service Director, two Assistant chief Constables, a Director of the Probation Service two Senior Social workers and Security Directors of a prominent retailer and a high vale goods seller, an NHS Director involved in mental health and the senior most Training Service provider and the key man in the Prison Service Legal Department, finally the Inspector of Prisons, plus three from the Prison Service management team..

On the day of his arrival in the Prison Ministry, he quickly prepared lists of open ended questions which he fired off to those attending.

He fixed the timetable, certain of them would be taken first like the Security Directors and the Police, Youth Offenders and Women's prison Governor, not as he explained that they were not important but because the core problem was adult male prisoners who constitute about 80,000 of the 85,000 inmates.

Angela proved a godsend, as Sebastian reported to the Permanent Secretary of the Ministry of Justice. She had rapidly put Sebastian right, when he missed that several acts had been passed of which he was ignorant. She had advised on the best people to get to the meeting and where they were. Sebastian learned that she had been in charge of a women's prison, so she knew at first hand the problems of prison life. Now in her early 50's, at first glance she looked austere, maybe that had been her intention as it would have impressed prisoners, her greying hair was curled in a bun, she was plump but carried it well, she was of average height and wore a dark trouser suit with matching lighter sweater, Sebastian soon found that when amused or interested she had a great smile which seemed to be at odds with her formal personality.

Whilst busy sorting out the agenda, he received a call from Lord Israel Jacobs "Look! I've sent you another Big Cheque, the money certainly surged after the attack, sorry to say but it was good for business! Anyhow hope you are OK?"

Sebastian was about to reply when he realised it was useless, Lord Israel Jacobs did not engage in chatter, he was not asking but telling, the only thing to do was to wait until he stopped talking.

"Well what do you want me to do now call it 'Minister' instead of 'Prime Minister'. No can't do that Eh? Sounds too religious, what about, er I know already, 'Privy Councillor' no that's no good either reminds people of the loo!

Ah! I know 'Minister of State'! Yes that's it exactly, perfect, OK? Might need a new photo from you outside a ministry? Call you later!"

Then he was gone

Sebastian spent the rest of the day with the senior management team explaining what he intended to do and how he thought the meeting should proceed, he asked for a 'figures person' to be available for reference and the Inspector of Prisons to bring along the last 5 years' worth of visit reports.

He quickly established a rapport with Angela Stone, she had told Sebastian that she had been concerned that he was just another politician playing around and had been at first wary of possibly going through just a structural upheaval for the sake of appearances. She made no secret of her hopes that with his intimate knowledge of how the government systems worked he could bring in change for the better, whereas with most other ministers it had been just chatter or often responding to public whims and so, in effect, pushing ever more work onto a service which could not protect itself. She reiterated the mantra that no Governor had the power to say no, if there was room in his prison he had to take an allocation whatever. If there was a prison brawl in Leeds, a wing might have to be emptied there, prisoners would be dispersed to the nearest prisons day or night, if it was within that Prison Governors Useable Operational Capacity, he would have to take them and simply adjust internally. It could disrupt prisons for days. Governors could not control their intake. That was the Governors' nightmare, that and the inevitable sharp rap if any prisoners should escape. Their first job is public security keeping prisoners inside. These two constrain and condition their minds.

On Tuesday Sebastian attended the Cabinet Meeting under Stephen White the Prime Minister, he was warmly greeted from all side. Sebastian gave a summary of his first day back and what he hoped to achieve, no huge change just many small ones. Afterwards he had a brief discussion with Stephen alone and suggested that he might need several small Bills and asked to be allocated enough time in the Commons programme. Stephen White was relieved that there were going to be no sweeping changes to the sentencing rules, because the 'stick them in prison' had been the answer to criminality by the right wing Tories for years and he was reluctant to cross swords with the 1922 committee again so soon after the last confrontation. Stephen asked for frequent updates. He also assured Sebastian that the funds set aside years earlier under David Cameron would be available so he hoped, that was for a massive new prison building programme. Sebastian promised a report following next Monday's meeting. Stephen asked if he was sure he could run both Prison Reform and Immigration in parallel, Sebastian told him how he intended to operate.

Prisons Mondays and Tuesdays, and Immigrations systems on Wednesdays and Thursdays. His assigned Immigration assistant there was Roger Boot.

Sebastian told the Prime Minister that under the rules agreed to by his wife he could work at home on the fifth day. He had argued with Sylvia that he couldn't, wouldn't be under any stress just reading bits of paper! Sylvia conceded, happy, as she said, at least that she could keep an eye on him for three days a week and if necessary block incoming calls or simply pull him out from work as 'sick'.

On Wednesday Sebastian refined the questions for the Monday Meeting

The Prison Review meeting started at 10.00 am on the Monday and lasted all day.

The first item was a general review by Angela of the current background, crime and imprisonment taken from the latest government publications.

Key data on Crime. She took them through key tables: Total Crime (England & Wales) in 2004 was 11,000,000 (itself just over half of the rate it had been in 1994, but in 2014 it was only 7,000,000, but the prison population in 1994 was about 40,000 in 2004 it was about 70,000 and in 2014 it was around 85,000. So apparently crime was reduced to a third over 20 years but prisoners had basically doubled in number.

Sebastian's first question was "Why, if crime was reducing was the number of prisoners increasing?"

Prison numbers and numbers of Crimes don't correlate. Angela explained. "There was an earlier hope that community based sentences might work allowing the prison population to be reduced. However a comprehensive report by the European Prison Observatory seems to have failed to find that such sentences had any impact on prison populations , neither in England and Wales or the rest of the EU countries. In the UK 110,950 community sanctions in 2013 had no apparent impact on lessening the number of prisoners. Although it's possible that it might be working in Scotland where the Social worker actually influences the sentence and the revised structure of the probation services are highly localised.

Basically the problem appears to be that unless linked to a watching social worker, there is no attempt to reform the offender. Perhaps with the introduction of more sophisticated electronic tagging, the individual can be monitored more closely, from for example, home to education, to work and home again. Restorative Justice has not yet taken hold in the UK and there are concerns that it will become another sanction rather than a real alternative."

Sebastian suggested. "Perhaps we should pro-actively seek to improve probation service support, but in view of the apparent disaster in semi-privatising the service in London we cannot guarantee we can do that!"

Angela quoted Kenneth Clarke, as a previous Justice Minister, that there was no correlation that you could assume between the number of crimes and prisoners.

They spent several minutes discussing the conundrum; there had been a drastic reduction in vehicle-related theft, burglary and criminal damage. It was agreed that some of this was related to improved car security, reduced consumption of drugs from the heroin epidemic, improvement in forensic and DNA recording, improved CCTV, improved house and window locking devices and also lower metal theft due to better detection systems, but there were increases too particularly mobile phones, now 538,000, card and other fraud, 5,100,000 incidents, although 70% + obtained some compensation. Then the same old topics which apparently resist improvement, shoplifting, 300,000 offences and bicycle theft, around 375,000 offences.

Scope for further Crime Reduction. Angela introduced the next topic briefly looking at ways to further reduce crime.

There was considerable discussion with the Security Directors, Theft represents about 15% of all offences. Sebastian thought that it was probably time to try to make sure that all high cost items say of £25,000 should be identified in some way by marking for traceability and photographed if a non-standard item like an antique and that this should be a standard requirement in all insurance policies and that all vehicles sold over that should also carry immobilisers. One of the Security Directors mentioned that it would increase costs unless the devices were factory fitted.

They discussed the use of standard software for mobile phones that would locate the stolen items and also download the contents and even disable them using a specific code. As far as bicycles were concerned, the problem is that they were easy to pinch and often left unlocked and unprotected, but here again any new bicycles could be fitted with locators and be registered, after all as Sebastian grumbled "We chip dogs and cats so why not byc's ? The more the reduction in crime the more time the Police have to catch the other criminals".

Finally they discussed shoplifting, Sebastian interrogated the retail Security Director. There were huge numbers in prison for theft, mostly younger and it was the most frequent cause of reimprisonment, reducing opportunities for theft might well reduce the cycle of reoffending.

Sebastian suggested that in most supermarkets the products were so well laid out and so inviting, that they were easy to 'nick'. What was needed was better supervision and more security products to detect theft before the thief leaves the premises and then when caught the thief could be included on a blacklist provided to other retailers. Innovative chipping causing security warnings and more CCTV. The Security Director suggested that the gangs of immigrants were causing the most trouble and they should be thrown out permanently. Sebastian asked for greater efforts from retailers to protect their own goods, otherwise the Government might have to rethink and reclassify all shoplifting as a civil not a criminal matter. The Security Director objected strongly. Sebastian asked him to get in touch with the retailers association and request an outline of future security developments proposed.

Sebastian asked the CPS representative to research then draft new laws on; Items over £25,000 Including all new cars, carrying identification and using locators and immobilisers. Insisting all new mobile phones should carry the AP. Persuading all cycle retailers selling new products to mark and use locators. Insist that all supermarkets improve security possible reclassification of the offence or charging them police time for police assistance. "You shouldn't reply upon police to assist you if you know perfectly well that a crime will be permitted, the retailer should be expected to use his own duty of care!"

"This isn't a total solution, it's just that we have to chip away at criminality every year using better techniques to prevent and then entrap wrongdoers".

Sebastian summarised: "So we have found some reasons anyhow for the Crime Rate reduction but none really explains Prisoner Increases does it? They don't seem to correlate at all. If the prisoner numbers declined at the same rate then the prison population would be much less. The only real supportable suggestion is that over the years we have imprisoned 'the regulars', the 'bad lads' who keep reoffending and returning. This was the idea behind the 'get them behind bars' "

Sebastian then interjected the reason for his presence. He reported on his Christmas Day visit and the effect it had had on him. "My mission Ladies and

Gentlemen is to reduce the prison population, reduce wasted lives, reduce the dreadful effect on the prisoners families, reduce violence in prisons and ultimately reduce costs.

But I am not going to indulge in tricks, like changing sentencing rules, that's a separate point, nor as one Minister suggested simply changing the structure by copying across academy schools to the prison service and in effect privatising them, that in my opinion will do no good!.

Reducing recidivism. Perhaps the first thing is to look at recidivism, unless we can break the cycle in some way we can never really improve much."

He passed over to Angela to introduce the next topic: She identified key tables from Prison Population Statistics and Reoffending Statistics.

She said "There are some compelling statistics, there are several different measures, so for example in 2014 around 488,000 adult and junior offenders were cautioned, received a non-custodial conviction or were released. Around 125,000 of these offenders committed a proven offence within a year or 25.6%, around 399,000 proven re-offenses over the one year follow up on average 3.20 offences each.

Adult offenders with 11 or more previous offences have a higher re-offending rate at 45.2%, Theft offences was the highest category of reoffenders with 42.5%

Confusingly perhaps the proven re-offending rate from those released from custody in 2014 was 45.5%, but those with sentences less than 12 months was a massive 69%"

Sebastian interjected "Unfortunately then, this suggests that the pre-prison warnings are not a very good deterrent but neither is prison itself!"

Angela continued, "Some 26% of prisoners are classified VATP, violence against the person.

So what we have in prison is a core of professional violent serial offenders."

Prison system is failing. Sebastian again interrupted, "As some said the criminal justice system is failing, failing the people who service the system, failing the offenders as it suggests a dose in prison will 'sort them out' whereas it seems to harden them, failing the victims because the same people are out of prison almost waiting to commit new crimes, with distressingly little attempt at rehabilitation.

Common ground in solutions. However there is some common ground amongst politicians as to what might be done to improve matters. Justin Blunt a former justice minister, talked of ending the 'revolving door' suggesting that time in prison should be the opportunity to learn skills getting the offenders back to work.

Lib Dem Justice Minister Simon Hughes suggested amongst many other points that there was a need to 'double existing education'.

Labour's then Shadow Justice Secretary Sadiq Khan suggested in 2014 that 'reforming criminals and reducing re-offending will only be successful if prisoner's time behind bars is put to good use on work education and training'. David Cameron referred to the need 'to help find work on release'.

Almost everyone accepts that we have to change a prisoners behaviour pattern if we are serious about breaking the cycle, of prison, release, reoffending, prison.

I believe that one of the ways of doing that is to commit to education and training as a key element in reform. If a man has a skill as a painter or plumber from which he might in time earn £1000 a week, why would he bother nicking anything then suffer the boring and mind numbing legal process and then imprisonment. But of course most of the people in prison lack even the most basic skills, so getting a job on release is difficult and the pay is poor for the low skilled work they go for, and the ex-con carries the stigma of imprisonment, not surprisingly the job if he gets it doesn't last long and he slips back into his old ways."

A the main findings of a report by Dame Sally Coates was reviewed 'Unlocking Potential – A review of education in Prison'

Sebastian continued, "Right now, in prison learning a new skill comes way down the Governors' priorities. The Nottingham Prison trains cycle maintenance and industrial cleaning. Do you think that will succeed?

We have to carry them to a new level. Give them the opportunities they have missed.

First is to reduce the prison population, to achieve improved training.. But currently the prisons are jam-packed, we cannot do anything until we clear the log-jam. I am myself convinced that overcrowding is the direct cause of so much violence and death in prisons, one side of this is that prisoners may spend 23 hours a day locked up, they emerge 'stir crazy' ready to lash out at anybody.

<u>I believe we have a two stage reform plan</u>.

a)   So we need to clear the decks of any prisoners we can place into different
     surroundings more suitable for their needs
b)   We need to set up a proper number of training prisons specialising in
     providing skills which analysis show are in short supply at the moment
     research suggests these are, Fork Truck Drivers, Heavy Goods Vehicle
     Drivers both of which are not usually paid for by the individual but the
     employer, if the employer has enough trained staff he doesn't train more
     staff, new business cannot get in to start as they cannot find drivers, we can
     train them. We can also train builders, carpenters, painters electricians,
     plumbers. All these earn a higher than average pay and should launch a
     released prisoner onto a much higher life, probably than they could through
     'thieving'.

So I have brought you here to advise on the make-up and implementation of
these plans which have to be costed and approved.

It is only then that prison staff will believe that we are serious about reform,
there has been too much chatter too few deeds.

I am just the amateur. Let's get it moving shortly I am going to pass it over to
you, you are the professionals, you are also 'handpicked' Sebastian said which
brought a smile to some faces but a frown to others.

<u>Prisoners to be excluded</u>. Sebastian continued. "We already know there are two
categories of prisoners who should not be there.

<u>Mental Health.</u> , those with mental health problems so severe that the prison
environment itself will never cure them in fact it might make them worse.
Perhaps 49% of prisoners have some mental health problems. Urgent
discussions are needed with the NHS, to identify early those with such problems
and how these should be treated, whether other more hospital related or
associated facilities would be required

<u>Drug Addiction</u>. Then there are the drug addicts who simply infect the whole
prison and often find it easier to get drugs inside than out..

I would like your suggestions as to how these can best be separated from the
prison structure and use other rehabilitation techniques where they can be
treated apart. There is the work of HOPE to look at a system started off by
Judge Steven Alm. It's called I believe 'Hawaii's Opportunity Probation with
Enforcement'. It's been used mostly for Drug cases, so called tough love. So it

depends for example on randomised and frequent drug tests, if they fail these they are arrested immediately. The process starts with a 'Warning hearing'. Probationers have to call a hotline which tells them when they have to present themselves for testing, they are called six times a month. A violation of the terms results in immediate imprisonment, those with multiple violations are mandated to intensive substance abuse treatment services. Studies have shown that probationers are 72% less likely to use drugs, 55% less likely to be arrested for a new crime and spend 48% fewer days in prison than normal probationers. It is thought likely it will be used in several US States. Should it be tried here, what specialist facilities would be required?

Treatment of Slow Learners. Another such category is what you might call 'slow learners' or 'special needs' where their educational attainment is so poor that they are unable to protect themselves in a prison environment, they should really have training to maximise their abilities and additional education so that they can at least read and write proficiently, it's not going to happen in prison where the best they can expect is to be used by other prisoners perhaps as drug donkeys. If we allocated much greater education resources to them, does it make sense after the classes to put then back in a normal prison routine where we suspect that are often as a dis-advantage and are abused again?

Then there are two other categories we could as it were 'do without' in the current prison set up.

Foreign Prisoners to be extradited. There are a large number of foreigners, around 10,000 people or about 11 to 12% of the population, of these Polish & Lithuanian make up 15% or about 1,400 people. Here I can perhaps help directly. I think I have some favours to call in from those countries and I'll try to make a personal approach, maybe we could even take over one of their empty prisons owned by us, managed by the Poles and Lithuanians, perhaps within the embassy territory ready to transfer to local control on formal extradition.

Many of the prisoners are from those African and Asian countries into which we pour grants from the DfID. 368 prisoners are from Nigeria. Again here I can be of some help, I will try to press hard for the DfID Minister to send back all prisoners to those countries in receipt of our huge grants funding. If they refuse then we will simply halt the aid programme for that particular country.

Finally there is a further category of prisoner that I am very concerned about and that is the plight of thousands of ex-servicemen in prison.

Ex-Military Service. Angela took over "Actually they are difficult to locate because many choose not to identify themselves as ex-military, as, either they become the target of the real hard men who see former military as a threat to their top position, or, these days fear an attack by Islamist extremists. Very often these people accepted the disciplines of military life but as soon as they leave, perhaps to get married and settle down to what seems like a cushy civvy street job, they fall apart and cannot cope, the wife leaves, they start drinking, hit out get arrested and all of a sudden they are on a downward spiral of self-destruction, Some of these may indeed be suffering with traumas from active duty. PTSD issues aren't often revealed while in the serving context because while still in service the individual is being supported by their 'band of brothers/sisters' who understand. "It is only when the individual finds themselves completely alone that they find those issues start to seep out. And that is often how the delay is explained. There are apparently 3,000 ex-military in prison, mostly army mostly over 50 and they are in for mostly VATP"

But early leavers may be more vulnerable to going off the rails because they've signed up to serve Queen and country and they may, for example, be leaving because they've failed a drugs test, suffered a training injury or something has gone wrong".

Sebastian came back, "I think I may have contacts where I can attempt to change the situation, the army has a continuing responsibility for assisting those who have been operating in a war zone, Some of these may be the result of this though never investigated or reviewed. I want to try to assist here.

So now I need you all to help create this two stage plan under Angela's chairmanship.

First reduce crowding, what groups can be taken out, how to define them, where they go to, what facilities are needed?

Next invest in Education and Training, What prisoners should it be aimed at, what courses are needed, what facilities, what costs. Currently 47% of prisoners have no qualifications whatsoever. But 10% of the prison population is in for sentences of less than one year, how much can be done in that limited period to change behaviour patterns?

Other Developments ongoing

There are a couple more points, an interesting development in Scotland, it links families with more distant prisons, it suggests it is a video but seems that it could be adapted like Skype so for example a wife could visit say one prison booking a room and have virtual contact to say a link in Lincoln prison where the husband is imprisoned, this maybe helps in two ways, firstly it reduces physical contact and thus risks of drugs being imported bur secondly perhaps allows more flexibility in locating prisoners to more distant specialist units.

One of the more recent proposals for Prison Reform was to create six pilot reform prisons, these were to be semi-autonomous units run by governors with authority to switch budgets as they think necessary, it's not clear to me what benefits that would bring apart from freeing the Governors from the rule book.

Separation of 'jihadi' prisoners. Finally there seems a need to segregate 'jihadi' terrorists from infecting other muslims in prison. As of March 2016 there were 12,506 Muslim prisoners, that is 14.6% of the prison population. There is evidence that prisons are used as recruiting grounds for radicalisation and so create even more potential terrorists, many younger muslims would be easy prey from older determined activists to whom the younger ones might gravitate for protection, they have time to be re-taught the more aggressive side of Islam using the aggrieved oppressed and disadvantaged minority approach, how should this be handled, there may be 50 to 100 such persons per prison at risk or radicalisation.

So there you are. Angela will keep me informed of progress and I will as promised report direct to the Prime Minister.

We are not trying to totally reform we want as far as possible to make changes which don't require legislation but can be effective as quickly as possible.

Angela it's over to you now!"

Angela discussed and arranged the meeting schedule, basically two days a week for the next eight weeks, each member to be given 'homework' in their particular area of expertise as identified by Angela.

Contact with the Prime Minister. A copy of the minutes and schedule was sent direct to the Prime Minister's office. Nothing of this was to leak out, the last thing Sebastian said he wanted was staffs' hopes being raised then possibly dashed.

Sebastian realised that he would need substantially all of his time supporting this two days a week, he requested in effect a two day pairing with an Opposition MP, for this and another two days for immigration.

<u>Opposition pairing MPs unusually co-opted into the Teams</u>. Sebastian was of course well known and his request immediately caught the attention of two Labour MPs who both had an expertise that might be useful, they asked to see Sebastian one had been a prison visitor for a number of years and the other was an IT expert with a large company of which he was a recently retired director. They both asked if they could be more closely involved, it's much better they suggested than as one put it 'building paper aeroplanes and seeing which of us can fly furthest from the top landing of Portcullis House.'

Sebastian put this unusual request to the PM, stating that he thought it would improve and strengthen the teams. A long term pairing like this was unusual but with he, Sebastian, out of the Chamber would make it easier on his successor he had no intention of intervening but his presence there might allow himself to be drawn in unwittingly even which could cause perturbations.

Reluctantly the PM agreed. It did not appear ever to have been attempted before. They were each brought in as Deputy to Sebastian to ensure continuity and consistency.

Each of the teams was thrown into some confusion. What of security? What of political leaks and embarrassment?, but these matters were ironed out by agreement by the political parties.

It seemed to the teams that Sebastian, once again, had a 'magic touch' that would make things happen, someone who knew the ropes and how to gain from that.

The work in each team seemed to double in intensity and purpose.

<u>Team asks for General Principles to be considered.</u> Within a matter of weeks the team produced a list of principles which they thought should guide their work and asked to approval.

These were as follows;

1. Future Development of prisons to tie in with the new Region Assemblies in order to link in with Probation Services which we under the Regions. The linkage was important
2. Wherever Possible Drug related crime and addiction should wherever possible be treated in separate specialist units, this allows concentration of skills to improve. treatment and prevents contamination to the general prison population.. Is there in prospect the use of the HOPE Scheme

3. Foreign Offenders should be identified prior to sentencing, assessment of potential extradition should be made at the same time. On conviction they should be contained in one holding area, within easy reach of extradition experts to ensure quicker processing.

4. On Admittance to prison all prisoners should be voluntarily screened for military services, these should be reviewed and passed to the military, they should be sifted for, military with exemplary record going off the rails in civvy street, those with action in a war zone and possibly affected by PTSD but which has not been reported which should be passed to experts and to closest prison unit.

5. Skills Practical training is currently restrained by available space, expanding this into more desirable and useful skills, like building trades or vehicular related like Fork Truck or HGV will require considerable space

6. Clarity is needed for facilities needed for Education under the Coates Review, will this mostly be banks of PCs, Can those with 'learning disabilities' be identified before arrival at prison, so they can be segregated, otherwise they become at risk from the general violent street-wise prison population.

7. The use of 'virtual contact' of the prisoner with family particularly in view of relationship of connection with lower re-offending, should be be viewed as a general application throughout the prison service so that all prison units should be linked allowing attendance at any unit with the prisoner at any other. It should be more efficient for the staff as less search is required, easier for the family if the prisoner is moved further away for specialist support, less likely to result in drug importation

8. The segregation of Jihadi prone prisoners, depends on early identification before arrival at prison. Drawing all these together into a bloc might easily lead to unduly high concentration of fanatics, creating a highly dangerous gang culture, requiring additional security to prevent mass escape. It's unclear what process of dejahadisation is suggested.

9. The most persistent reoffenders at youth level is theft, the shorter sentences however rarely permit planned behaviour change or retraining or reskilling, more research is required into suggested treatment regimes.

10. Many of the proposals appear to require specialist segregation to be effective, this will in fact reduce the flexibility available to the the general prison population and will therefore require additional capacity. Consideration should be given to emergency facility back up like a purpose built prison ship to contain wing mutinies causing extensive damage which disrupt nearby prisons obliged to absorb additional numbers.

11. It ought to be possible to mathematically simulate the number of prison officers required for each prison given an number of arrivals, visitors,

hospital visits, assessments, health plans, learning and training plans, lock up procedures supervision, below which no prison should fall, a regional reserve staff capability should be held

12. Improvements to tagging equipment using GPS should be continued with the target of better probation control, use of weekend only prison sentences for those already in a job, removal of prisoners on bail except in cases of VATP.

These points were duly made and responses expected.

Sebastian continues his own homework. Whilst this was proceeding Sebastian set about his own particular tasks with gusto.

These were

1. Using European contacts to speed up repatriation of EC originated prisoners particularly Poland and the Baltics
2. Using DfID contacts to speed up repatriation of prisoners, particularly to those countries in receipt of large grants
3. Reviewing with the Military treatment of possible war zone affected ex-servicemen and possibly rehabilitating any good quality soldiers gone off the rails.

Sebastian's Contact with the Prime Minister. Sebastian appraised the PM with his plan to apply direct pressure on the three groups to speed up the process and with his assent made direct approaches to the Prime Ministers of Poland and the Baltic States who quickly agreed to his requests and a procedure was put in place automatically triggering extradition from the court papers.

DfID agreed to insert into every new contract with any country in direct receipt of DfID grants that, any funding was conditional on facilitating extradition of those countries nationals a maximum response time was agreed and that failure to honour this would lead to automatic suspension of all grants to that country in whatever guise.

Sebastian had a tougher time with the military, that was because the old military 'glass-house' had been closed and in effect throwing military prisoners back into the prison services.

He tried to persuade Michael Morgan "We closed down the Colchester 'Glass House' didn't we, years ago and put our lads within the prison system somewhere, didn't we? I want to reverse the process! I believe that some prisoners who were, in their time, first rate soldiers simply collapsed under the pressures outside, mostly in developing a career outside the army and in being poor at personal relationships. I think they would do better in the rigid discipline of the glasshouse and I believe some could regain their own self-belief and self-confidence in that environment, even perhaps re-joining under special condition. Anyhow I'd like to try."

"You mean send us your military cons?" asked the somewhat bewildered Michael Morgan

"Yes, we seems to fail with them, they keep on coming back, again and again, for most of them it's simply the wrong environment, they feel constantly under threat and soon begin to take instruction from the strong men as if they were the sergeants and then they become mules, either carrying drugs or getting their wives to do so for them, they cannot escape and easily get scapegoated."

"Hmmmh, I don't like the sound of it! But look, because it's from you, I'll consider it, send us over a paper will you?"

"Oh and there's more!" said Sebastian trusting to luck.

"Yes I'd like you to consider setting up, what did they call it? Ah yes that's it a 'Forlorn Hope' battalion. Well these chaps, were the naughty lads in Wellington's Army in the Peninsular Wars, they could redeem their positions by joining this battalion who were given the task of being the first attackers in the most dangerous spots. By and large, I think, they acquitted themselves well and many re-joined their old battalions"

"You mean rather like the 'dirty dozen' in the film" the old cons, but don't they end up all dying?" asked Michael.

"Well that was a film" muttered Sebastian, "what I was thinking about was putting them on patrol in the new camps in East Poland and Baltics. They would all be volunteers, not Press Ganged!"

"Sounds a mad idea, but then I thought your NATO plan was a mad idea, your department would subsidise the military of course?" Michael still sounded doubtful.

"Yes certainly!" Sebastian confirmed. "and finally…"

"There's more? Oh hell! What have I let myself in for now?"

"Well I believe that many ex-military prisoners might be suffering from PTSD but have never been properly analysed or registered, I would like them reviewed and if they are then I would like your guys to take responsibility for their treatment, perhaps running a small unit within your 'Help for Heroes' but in any case using your PTSD experts."

"Ok I'll buy that Sebastian!"

"Oh er I'll need a couple of your guys to do the reviews?"

"OK, OK I get the message write please and tell me exactly what you need and I'll do my best. I am still up to my eyes here, Sebastian, working on this Northern NATO Military Command Structure, the Germans want every damn post going and want us to buy all their equipment too. Huh! I may need you back here to give the Germans another lecture as you did before?"

Chapter FIFTY-FIVE - Michael Morgan explains Sebastian's move

"Well Michael, I would like to help, but as you know in the end it nearly broke me, I still reckon that had you not got me out early I would not have made it to March 31st anyhow!"

"Yes we knew that Sebastian, we couldn't see you collapse, it might have rebounded on the good work you had done, those might have questioned if you were, when negotiating NATO and the EU, in your right mind, we couldn't allow that view to take hold.

You remember that day you wanted to review 'Trading with the Enemy' if you had walked into Downing Street and exhibited that level of paranoia, you would have destroyed all your successes, they would simply have put you down as mad! And thrown out all your ideas.

Stephen and I were wondering what to do when your 'Bill and Margaret'.."

"Madge, you mean Madge?"

"Yes, Madge, came to see us with the possible way out using the dates. So we struck a deal with them, there and then. You could have everything you wanted as legacy, but you had to go!

None of us, Sebastian, could give a bugger about the the 1922 committee at the time, we just used it as an excuse to move you before you fell over!"

"Yes I guessed that something was going on – it seemed a huge ending gift for which I am most grateful, but anyhow it worked and because of it, I thank you!"

"That's OK Sebastian, you are a good guy, I'll do what I can about these issues! – Are you doing OK yourself now?"

"Yes I'm fine now thanks, Michael, a month or so convalescence did me fine!"

"Your step-whatever in Nigeria is doing fine too, yes the French came back on this Boko Haram project, think it's great, persuaded the Nigerians and your step-what…"..

"Brother"

"Yes Step-Brother has liaised in setting up the camp!"

Stephen White later commented to Michael Morgan which soon became public knowledge, around the Cabinet Table, "What a strange person he is. One moment dealing with literally world affairs, ticking off Heads of State and the next sorting out prisons and oh yes immigration, he doesn't seem to mind the change in status at all, does he?"

"No not at all!"

"The Prison reform seems to be going OK, we will know better in a few months! We still need him for the derogation thing for the EU, he's still widely respected there and could carry the day! I suppose he could go after that!"

Chapter FIFTY-SIX – Prison reform, continued

Sebastian reported back to the group. The rest of the team saw the gradual reductions which came through Sebastian's interventions, slower than expected but they dribbled through and with it a process that would speed up all future transfers too..

It acted as a huge spur to their work, something would happen, they knew it.

The Questionnaire to Governors. Emboldened the team circularised all Prison Governors and with an average of 3-5 for each of the 121 prisons, that was a lot of work, they asked the Governors what changes they would make to the paperwork, the manual and indeed operating procedures. They were flooded out, a couple of the Governors offered to rewrite the manual. Some suggested to wait and see the other changes, perhaps smaller units can be managed with fewer rules, giving more freedom for Governors to act with more latitude.

Review of the Forms used. One Governor suggested a composite Prison Entry Form consolidating 5 forms into one, background, offences, medical, education, training Of course it would take longer, but it saved much repeated items like, name address etc etc. It was also capable of being digitally read and could be placed directly on file and was instantly available for use by the experts.

Review of the Manual. Certain sections of the manual, for example on the 'number of sheets of music' a prisoner could keep in his cell, caused as much amusement to the team as it had when the press first picked up on it from the then Prime Minister's speech in 2016. After a guessing game around the table – it was conceded as 12 Sheets

Certain parts of the Manual that were Mandatory were in RED with a stripe in the corner, the Governor had no discretion, others that were Advisory, where the Governor had discretion were GREEN and those that were prohibited were MAUVE.

Governors pointed out, that if complaining, prisoners all knew the exact number of sheets of music in every cell on the floor, if it suited their case. Applying the rule book simply meant the Governor didn't have to adjudicate and get drawn into cell v cell arguments and could spend time more profitably doing other things. So the full manual was always to be kept as a back-up. But some Manual sets were removed. Smaller units would use a pared down version.

Reviewing Prisoner Complaints. The Prison Inspectors were asked to reveal the most frequent cause of complaints. These were generally, excess time lock up, no training, limited hobbies allowed, limited association time, wives waiting for visits, libraries often closed, lunch too early, tea the same, poor quality food, inadequate cleaning, queuing to phone home, laundry late so having to wear prison kit though having privileges not to, drugs availability and means of entry reviewed plus group penalties for failures of whole wings to stay 'clean' through random checks.

The Prison Inspectors promised to investigate the reasons for these checking back with the prisons and finding out if it was a process or equipment failure and what could be done to correct matters.

Prisoner Involvement, in the system. Another line of questioning was whether it was possible to upgrade the prisoners view of his own self-worth in prison, at present of course any prisoner has the right to complain to the Governor, but all Prison Inspection reports also asked for prisoners views on certain matters like, fear of being attacked in prison, but this it was agreed a very pale reflection of what genuine 'consumer involvement or feedback might be'. The idea was that before matters became 'complaints' they could be openly discussed, reported to the officers and corrected.. Sebastian suggested that It was just this lack of communication which might allow minor problems to escalated. Used in some countries appeared to have facilitated the running of prisons. Governors were generally defensive one said "we know what most of the problems are, the difficulty is in getting them sorted, the last this we need is for the wing manager to be faced with a gang leader who threatens to smash the place up if we don't do what he wants.. It was agreed that more modern and less overcrowded prisons might experimentally use that process.

Sebastian draws the line. At this point Sebastian drew the line, saying "If we wander off course any further that will hold back the main thrust of our report and will water down its impact, so we are not going to tread on any political toes here like allowing more prisons to be run by contracted services or by rebranding then as was done for schools, that's another argument for another day.

Remember we still have to cost all proposals and agree that they are practical and do-able, We have a rough budget, but that's also to cover new prisons. Deputy Chair we need soon building and capital costs and the bill for extra staffing and yes we will have to guess at reduced recidivism.

So I need another update in three months' time, remember you have to send it first to the management board here. Remember to push them on the 'principles letter'? Then I am due to see the PM after that, can we do it guys?

Draw in the heads of any experts you need, just tell me who they are and I'll get them for you!

I will tackle the points you raised upwards, the principles, and make sure they reply. they reply.

Angela seems to be doing a good job and I cannot praise you enough for what you are contributing, but I am here in support and I pledge I will do what I can, but we have to use our own self-filter, send me in please with good solid stuff that I can sell OK?"

Sebastian meets the PM again. In due course the meeting took place in the Downing Street. Sebastian had in his left hand a very modest 10 page document, on his right side a stack of ten files.

Stephen good humouredly listened to the shortened version.

"There seems to be quite a lot of things to do, Sebastian? Are you sure it can be implemented?"

"Yes, pretty certain, I have been part of the filter process you know and thanks to you we have had first call on experts from all other Ministries!"

Stephen frowned, Sebastian continued "Yes I heard on the grapevine you told them all, 'do what it takes!' isn't that right?"

"Yes because I didn't want people to think I had deliberately side lined you into these jobs that you are doing, everyone expected you would be back up dealing with NATO or the EU or the UN?"

"Nah!" said Sebastian, "this'll do me fine!"

"So how do you know it's going to be a success, Sebastian?"

"Look, Stephen, I have a folder on my desk in the office, 100 news clippings, every goddamn politician coming near the prison services has had his penny-worth, me included, 'You should do this or that, or run it this way, or change the name, or alter the number of sheets of music a prisoner can have, or what he should wear. But nobody asked the bloody governors!. We have 121 prisons that's over 360 Prison Governors, all managers with 20 plus years of dedicated service, that's over 7200 years of experience. Did anyone ever ask them?

"But we would go outside to seek advice at the drop of a hat? Just look at this review 'Unlocking Potential – a review of education in prison by Dame Sally

Coates'. Lovely little paper, full of good stuff, but totally and hopelessly impossible to implement, there's no delineation between slow learners and the rest, no idea even how to distinguish the two, no ideas about facilities needed apart from 'distance learning', no idea of how this sits alongside a core of often violent, aggressive, serial offenders, and of course another bloody form, another assessment, another plan for the prisoner and the warders to complete, and of course more retraining so that staff know what learning really is. Oh Yes? But in reality Governors are told absolutely clearly that their Number one Duty is Security so Prisoners don't escape, Number two Duty is Security to make sure Staff are safe, Number Three Duty is to make sure Prisoners don't attack each other. Number four duty is Security to make sure Prisoners don't kill themselves. Next is to make sure they are fed and clothed.

So where is all that in the Dames report? It's another bloody chatterbox just like the other 100 newspaper clippings! Until there is a reduction of over-crowding none of these well-intentioned schemes will be possible. NONE!

I mean Coates makes it seem as if she is trying to arrange a cake making party at a kindergarten school! It's all marvellous stuff I can assure you, but as it stands you couldn't do anything with it and I guess those Governors could have done twice as good in half the time!"

"Well those are brave words in support of your team, Sebastian, can you do it?"

"Stephen, I know you better than that, you will already have taken soundings!"

"Yes well er, actually yes, it seems to be going OK!"

"Right I'll take that as a Yes, give me half a day in three months' time, come and meet the team, ask them anything you like, I am happy to share any success with you. Call it the White/Edwards report, because I know you have helped in the background, one thing only I beg of you, there's a large number of proposals, whatever you do, please just don't ditch the lot? Don't destroy the real energy for change they are trying to create. Don't let them down?"

"Ok I promise!" Stephen seemed serious.

It was of course a considerable success by March 2020, it was accepted, as the saying goes 'done and dusted'.

It was based on units for purpose, so that drug and alcohol abuse were treated in new, separate smaller semi-prisons designed first to register and record an individual then deliver a plan with a period of 'cold turkey', followed by outside probation with call ins and tests. If these tests proved contaminated then there would be a period inside with more 'cold turkey' and the sequence would be repeated several times thereafter the stays got progressively longer. Separating the drug addicts, who were generally the suppliers also within prisons, reduced the volume of drugs in the remaining prisons and made them much less volatile.

These were locally based units, directly attached to the new regional probation offices.

Younger 'theft' re-offenders were treated in much the same way, using newer aversion therapy ideas, which at the very least had a similar disruptive element enough to change the subtle equation for the reward for the theft.

All prisoners were to be assessed for mental health before being removed from the court system, a special test was devised so that the most obvious cases were abstracted immediately, as nearly 47% were suggested as partly coming within this category, this still left a huge number for proper assessment. This would have to take place later on. Several hundred additional places in existing mental health hospitals would be needed in the regions and a special regime established for their care and rehabilitation.

All of those with Learning Disabilities, unable to read or write were assessed before going near prison using a specially adapted, numerical and picture test, these were sent to another 'local unit' and set up much on the basis of a small boarding school, with lessons and sports and training in 'useful' jobs according to ability, these prisoners were told that it was necessary to pass reading and writing tests and do well in some employable job training if they wanted to gain early release.

The ex-military prisoners were assessed; a. good army men, fallen off the rails, the Army were prepared to open a small prison, on the basis that after serving their sentences they might re-join the Military. b. those with a poor record in the army, who were then returned to prison, c. those who might have had battle fatigue, and with lower levels of criminality and who, although not injured were to be handed over to small semi-open units for treatment by specialists, these amounted to no more than a dozen.

All those destined for despatch were sent to a holding prisons near extradition points. These units had limited exercise areas, fewer visitors and a simpler management arrangement.

Jihadi jails were again separated units, their purpose was to pre-select there, those that were deemed likely to try to contaminate the first offender Muslim, these jails were regarded as more dangerous than the average and more likely to be subject to mass escapes, the prisons were therefore more heavily fortified. Substantial grants and early release were offered to those who publicly renounced the jihad and were prepared to relocate to other prisons to spread that news to other prisons where there were many Muslins.

Transgender units were to be set up in each Region attached to existing low violence prison units. It is recognised that fear generated in being in a male prison might directly lead to higher prisoner suicide rates.

This now left the over 1 year, mostly 1-4 year offenders and the target was that each person would be expected to learn a trade suitable to be able to find a well-paid job reasonably quickly, all the prisons were assessed for suitability in terms of facilities, the major dividing was between building Trades and Vehicular trades. To the surprise and no little amusement of the average prisoner, who had all along complained of there being no training in prison, the system seemed to have been turned on its head. Any prisoner wanting early release had to prove he had learned a trade which would support him outside!

Other Degree type courses were available and these were concentrated on several smaller prisons. All these opportunities were offered and had to be 'bid' for in the sense that the prisoner had to 'opt in' and say why he wanted to take the course. Career specialists and placement advisers were to be used to ensure their marketability. Early release was entirely dependent on achieving their planned learning targets.

Those who rejected the training, were next designated for work gangs, the government had brokered a deal with gangmasters for open field work and a small 'barracks' type unit was set up in Lincolnshire, a proportion of the prisoners' earnings could be saved for use on release.

Those that remained were largely the more violent, serial offenders who would substantially remain within the existing prison structure unaltered. But even here although teaching a trade to a lifer meant very little, the opportunity was taken to develop a wider range of hobbies and create smaller scale craft units for prisoner sale.

Key to many of the proposals for change was that several categories of prisoner had to be assessed before entering the prison system and a new joint review system was proposed, chaired by the local probation service but which could have access to the courts to reconfigure the sentences passed given the new information from these assessments. In effect this would vary the terms depending on the new suggested treatment and institution to be used, although with equal weighting to the sentence proposed.

Of course it didn't hit the headlines because it was to be implemented over 3 years and the press, wary of past eye-catching revolutionary 'STARTS' to prison reform promised by successive previous governments, were, of course, waiting for the equally reliable 'STOPS' or 'ON HOLD' which they thought would surely follow soon after.

By June 2020 Sebastian had given up the Minister of Justice role, eventually taken over by Bill Bennett, his faithful ally and friend.

Chapter FIFTY-SEVEN - At the Home Office – Immigration Review

Sebastian was now updated with all the woes of the immigration control systems.

Although the UK Government had attempted to put in place an immigration control mechanism based on a 'points system', this failed as some, including the former Home Secretary, had predicted it would. It failed because it let in a number of well qualified people for whom there were no jobs, and conversely employers like those farmers in Lincolnshire were unable to hire sufficient temporary workers to help cut and pack their produce as the vetting procedure took so long.

The Government's support plan of using a 'needs based system', that's to match job vacancies to be filled with people available and then source the shortages needed from outside immigration also failed. This was mainly because many jobs were not notified in time and it took weeks to advertise all the jobs in the UK and find out if there were suitable UK applicants and, if there were not, to then proceed to fairly assess all external candidates.

When he arrived it was thought that the Home Office may have to revert to a visa system but it is recognised that it's very difficult to control immigrants who may simply pass themselves off as UK subjects and, if they lose their own passports or visas, then we are back in the same mess as before and it could take weeks to track down who they are and if they have a valid visa. It may need completely rethinking and integrating with the introduction of identity cards throughout the UK. Sebastian realised that was highly controversial not only in Parliament but for Liberal Democrats who see it as a measure of increased state control and at a huge cost.

The Liberal Democrats opposed the Identity Card Act 2006 saying that 'identity cards don't work' the move was subsequently withdrawn by the Conservative Lib Dem Coalition.

With the arrival of the Labour MP who was in fact an IT buff, Sebastian had another point of reference. His actual assigned manager from the Home Office was Roger Boot. A long server in the Ministry he had started some 20 years previously and only acquired his IT knowledge after joining, he had been on an IT appreciation course and realised he rather liked it, it was something in which he could bury himself. However he had become a bit obsessed by numbering systems and was always worried about systems linking in with one another. Given a list of products or services he would try to ensure that all the numbers meant something so that the first number meant 'product code' the next 'type' service or goods and so on. He was cautious because as Sebastian learned, people were always asking him to tweak systems which he was concerned would not later 'talk' with other programmes. His first instinct when faced with change was "why?" suggesting the information could be provided in other ways, or at least most of it! He was terrified of being blamed for a total seizure of the Passport immigration control systems and stubbornly refused to change them at all. However he knew exactly what information his systems contained and how they were arranged and was always helpful in producing data, seemingly in a trice.

Sebastian arranged for a small team of Senior Home Office staff to be found from the Managers, these were to simulate 'users' and they were asked to summarise, what they thought they needed in control systems and what the shortfalls were.

He interrogated them for hours and tried to simulate in his mind at the same time, how he could prepare for another 'derogation' round battle with the EU in barely 15 months' time.

After a short time Sebastian realised the measure of the problem, they could not define what they wanted because they didn't know what the end objective was. Sebastian knew he had to pull together a rough plan and 'sell it' to the PM then drive it through.

Sebastian realised that he had to state clearly what he was looking for, before any further work could be done. In other words he had to assume that political decisions would be required first and the changed systems would hold that in place. He now used his influence to bring in David Roberts the UK's top IT civil servant. He argued that there were likely to be at least six separate databases each with their own interfaces and choke points with other existing IT Systems, such as police.

He sat thinking about the problems during one weekend at home and returned the following week to test out his plan with his existing team and the head of immigration.

He told them all "In fact I have a three level task.

The first is to actually find out more about the mysteries of immigration, if we can see more clearly what is happening then we shall be more able to face the changes we need to make. I have made representations to 'Homes and Communities Ministry' to carry out in depth research for us on the actual impact of immigration and make recommendations as to how we might improve any damaging effect of their arrival here. This will bore down in 20 areas thought to have been most affected. We need to know the real effect on Education, Health, and Housing provision, in those areas. Next we need to know the real impact on wages and on the local jobs market, the real impact on House prices and on Crime and on disruption generally caused by large numbers of immigrants. If such numbers are likely to continue we need to know how best to accommodate change and work with it rather than allowing unsubstantiated rumours to affect the process. Such half-truths may simply create exaggerated comment which under certain circumstances could shut off all immigration politically despite an element of immigration being needed because as a large country trying to bring in and develop top class companies we can never exactly match the people we need from the stock of people we train. So that project is ongoing and as need not concern ourselves with it further at this stage.

The second is to make recommendations for changes in the immigration rules themselves, in effect looking at the reasons for and need for immigration and in that light perhaps making changes to our existing practices. I have engaged one well respected professors to carry out a brief background report and I will be testing out my ideas on him initially using our existing statistics. I will be ready to pull something together even next week!

Finally the task is to look at the existing systems in place and make recommendations for changes. This is where we will spend most of the time, because the systems are both the monitoring and control systems but also provide the data by which immigration itself is to be judged."

Sebastian then had a number of private meetings with Vivien Thompstone, a person of considerable experience of serving on several tribunals including those on family unity appeals but also dealing with 'outraged' leaders of industry consistently rubbishing the immigration rules. They met up at Vivien's house, a modern architectural glass and cement with a lot of little quirks inside, it had been designed by her husband. Vivien herself, a slight figure, grey haired, at first seemed rather withdrawn and timid until drawn into the topics Sebastian put to her, when her interest and concern became immediately apparent. Outside there was a small patch of grass with a couple of trestle tables and it was here that the next fundamentals of the immigration system were to be laid out.

Sebastian began, "As far as I can see we have at the moment in the UK five effectively competing systems.

First there is still operating the almost pre-EU, Tier system, this does not apply to EU immigrants, unless subject to any derogations which we have obtained from the EU

Tier 1 is for entrepreneurs, those investing here and those with exceptional talent capped at a few thousand

Tier 2 is for those skilled with a job offer, usually these are compatible with the governments skill shortage list, capped at 20,700 unless earning more than £150,000.

Tier 4 is for all types of students

Tier 5 is for temporary and youth mobility

These are operated by points systems.

Second, there is the EU system itself with its avowed freedom of movement of people. Most of the current immigration waves have come under this rule.

Third, there is the family unity concept which allows, foreigners, non-EU, to come here to look after relatives, this clause is often invoked to allow British subjects to bring brides into the UK. There are fees payable and other criteria such as a minimum income threshold for a Partner applying under this Appendix FM from 9 July 2012

Fourth, there is the 'hidden' system used by the EC, in theory there is freedom to move between jobs in the EU, but this is in effect highly restrained by several factors. Certain jobs are specifically stated as being transferrable and there is a list of them, however many are, in effect, closed for all practicable purposes, this is because there may be a language attachment, eg, 'German necessary', or the job may be closely defined with a particular grade of training at a particular level or with a particular module at a college, or even that it is linked in with a particular apprenticeship to which a foreigner may simply not have access.

Fifth, there is a Universities scheme, the UK is proud of its educational heritage and is consistently willing to take in large numbers of foreign students to add to the melange of multicultural learning here, provided that is they go home eventually.

So with all that, it seems sensible to ask what it is that we here in the UK are trying to do?

The idea that around 20,000 are actually bought here, sponsored, invited in under Tiers 1 and 2, and not from the EU, suggests that we do have what seems like a persistent shortage in critical areas of professionally trained specialist staff, without which, if the Inst of Directors would have it, the UK would fall apart.

Witness here the huge argument between Mrs May over 800 Filipino nurses, not skilled for the short list, but not through the EU system either.

But at the other end, there is a huge increase of EU workers coming here, usually under a gangmaster sponsor system, agricultural pickers and packers as well as factory untrained staff.

Nobody appears to believe that we can do without work immigrants. The UK seems like a giant ship constantly having to be fed with people supplies of all kinds both to keep ahead of technology and provide world class companies with world class people but also even to keep the food systems working properly.

We know we have a massive shortage of engineers, and yet we have significant unemployment amongst graduates.

For example in some areas in the north general unemployment is still a considerable concern.

There even successive generations have been unemployed, leading to a view from up there that immigrants do take 'their jobs'. We also know we have a critical shortage of construction workers which appears as soon as there is a housing start boom, then collapses but during that time it's a severe constraint on building work which merely seems to result in exaggerated pay.

To me this smells of a massive jumble and that here in the UK we don't even have rudimentary manpower planning. We leave most of it to 'Market forces' and the extent of that, failure comes through in the high level of immigrants called here to enable the 'UK Machine' to work. In a sense immigration is the 'safety valve'.

So at the same time as trying to drag technical people here, we try to prevent the motley coming if we can.

Let's just imagine if we could what would happen if a) we invested a huge amount in training, filling all the gaps, in technical and trades and using apprenticeships then surely b) we would have nothing to fear from immigration?

If we were to do that we would have to massive improve our forecasting techniques and, attune training at colleges and Universities to that, but we would also 'sell' that to the younger people, to make them understand that it's better to do something of practical use which they might be persuaded to do, rather than the more glamourous more impracticable dreams which are less rewarding?

On the other hand there is a view that people planning of any kind is not required because the UK is an absurdly complex beast and that it's the creative, inspirational, random occurrences which in fact create the major leaps forward, like ICT here in the UK, which cannot be predicted. 'So fluidity with technically trained people as a skill, not planning is the real aim.'

They debated the issues for hours, one major problem was the use of English. As the number 2 European language, most people were prepared to say they could speak English, even if it was only bits and pieces of films and the facility of the language, no male female endings etc was such that it was remarkably tolerant of abuse, a robust language. German however was different, it had to be declined etc etc, such that a written professional report was expected to be of a high standard, an average foreigner particularly from the UK would almost certainly be excluded from higher level technical jobs. In that sense the German jobs were protected.

They decided that the EU had sort of 'fallen' into the free labour market, but it was far from complete, this was blindingly apparent in the Services sector which was of closely linked to the people freedom because much of it was contractual-people driven. Wherever there were different standards, national security, nuclear, electrical supply, railways, foreigners were, by and large excluded. That area was the inner sanctum of each country. Whereas in the UK key industries had been sold off or merged and we had no inner sanctum left, like getting the French to build our nuclear power station or operate our railways, the French and Germans were still incapable of opening up their inner sanctum. This meant that there was no level 'playing field' although the UK was, in fact, well placed to gain work there.

They then discussed at length the family united agreements. Sebastian had two major points, firstly that still a large number of these immigrants were in effect child brides, mostly of Pakistani origin, but that seems to have been an overhang from years past, there was no cultural or religious reason why the spouses should not in future be found here in Manchester or Birmingham. The second is that these particular immigrants are bringing in here just the sort of culture that we do not want. We try to give Muslim boys and girls the same opportunities but every time someone comes in from 'old Pakistan' that holds the modernisation back and the next generation also has to fight for their girls to be educated and get a job. We don't need that, this has to be phased out, maybe by increasing the incoming tariffs set?

Sebastian prepared a short paper and went to see the PM.

He gave Stephen White the key elements, 'All Sponsoring', 'more training in skills linked to schools', 'Shortage list really represents a failure to train our own', 'masses more apprenticeships', 'capitation', 'more free degrees for skills we need', 'target too our advantages for IT skills development', 'move onto attack re EU services not delivered'.

"Phew!" Stephen sat back, "I thought you were mostly just going to change some forms and categories and such? I hadn't imagined that you would somehow turn it on its head. Are you sure, Sebastian? Do we really need to do all this?"

"Well Stephen, it's like this, you can piss about, tinkering, it will not impress the EU, you will always be on the wrong side dithering, they will pick you off realising that the proposal is a complete mess, they won't simply agree to an extension because we have done absolutely nothing at all in the meantime to even show we are trying. If I have shown you anything about the EU, Stephen, it's that you have to have a pretty good case and then ram it home unmercifully, preferably by getting some champion to stand up for you and help drive it through. I know you have kept me on because of my useful contacts, but I am afraid there really is a job to be done and this is it! Why not let me make a presentation to the whole of the Cabinet, it'll take about 4 hours to go through it all?"

Stephen looked again at the A4 sheet which Sebastian had given him and tried to track back the jumble of phrases he saw into the coherent and lucid plan Sebastian had just given him. "Hmmh!" he coughed, "Are you sure Sebastian? This is the right way to go?"

"Yes absolutely, it will kill the problem for good, its surely a radical approach and it's that which will give you the moral and technical advantage, at the same time it will knock the others to the ground. Did you manage to get the 'enhanced co-operation' by the way?"

"Yes we did!" Stephen admitted.

"And do you now feel more confident of your position in the EU?" Sebastian asked,

"Yes! I am sure so!"

"Then you'll see, this will be a game changer that will set in place and kick start the next phase of the EU development, with this you will be set fare for the next 5 years!"

"OK Sebastian you were right three times, so this is on your reputation! OK I'll back you, I must say I don't understand the half of it. How much will this cost?

"Oh! £ Billions I should think" Sebastian replied blithely "I'll grab some figures for the meeting."

"But all the training and databases, Sebastian will it all work?"

"Frankly, probably not maybe just 66% but that'll be worth it that's the bit we need, you'll see!"

"But why?" Stephen was getting concerned at what me might have let himself in for!

"Well two main reasons, first UK PLC is a massively complex structure, you know I used to work in Russia, planning was simple you took 50,000 by weight out of the ground using a certain bucket whose running costs were so and such. Bob's you uncle you have a budget. But the USSR couldn't even plan or monitor on that. it becomes so complex that then the smallest adjustment has large ramifications. So we know that the detailed labour planning is next to impossible. But the second reason is that we here in the UK don't like planning, indeed we tend to hate it! Everyone gets the impression we are trying to malevolently prevent a businessman for doing something or that by agreeing to help draft a manpower plan, they are actually part of a constraint. The last Plan attempted was by George Brown and it was hated by most and was out of date in 18 months. You will find, Stephen, that individuals will take a delight in screwing it up!

But in our case we are just looking at manpower, even if we just use the 'junior bit rather than senior executives' to work out approximately how many engineers or radiotherapists, it will have done us good!

The high cost is because we desperately need more apprentices, engineers, tradesmen, we ought to have been training them for years but we have not, we are way behind, the catch up will cost us."

"And the illegal immigrants?" asked Stephen " why do we have to go for that?"

"Because it is expected, people don't know the difference between legal and illegal immigrants, We have not the slightest idea how many there are, even official estimates vary some say 750,000 in practice it could be less than half that! But we need to kill the problem, I suspect France will pick up a number of these proposals and borrow them because their own info is so poor and they seem to know even less than we do. It will probably spark off a complete 'count' across the EU and enable us to draw a line, make real decisions on migrants in Syria and finally tackle Turkey!"

"Oh!" said Stephen, It's your call I suppose! Let's do it!"

They assembled the following week for a full discussion, many openly expressed the view that it couldn't last long, this was after all Sebastian's' swansong! He surely couldn't, wouldn't, land them with another huge change for his final months?

Sebastian started off by identifying what it was that 'immigration control' was trying to do? Are we trying to get useful people to come in? or are we trying to keep various people out?

Our previous Tiered policy was aimed at allowing in those from a 'shortage list'

Tier 2 Shortage Occupation List – Government approved version – valid from 6th April 2014. This list identifies the shortages, they are mostly managerial/technical, but also cover a wide range of engineers in various industries, aerospace, railways, oil and gas, aerospace, nuclear, and carry appropriate salary rate. Another block is in computer animation and films, medicine, radiographer, haematology, paediatrics. Teachers, social workers. Orchestral musicians, dancers, classical ballet dancers. Chefs with 5 years' experience. In effect a UK sponsor proposes hiring someone on this list and within the assumed earnings described.

However if we now look at another paper, 'Skills shortages in skilled construction and metal trade occupations'. At first sight this little paper seems misplaced, but it indicates how difficult it is to get the data and interpret it. Vacancies come from Jobcentre Plus, which is limited in that it covers less than half employers with more than 5 employees; but also from ESS, Employer Skills Survey, but it is not a standard yearly study although it covers wider ground. This paper was partly directed at the construction industry, but it's clear within that 'shortage' there are problems in understanding the particular business cycle, which means that demand ebbs and flows within a range, but also that there may well be structural problems underlying the statistics. A finding was, that although it had been thought that the higher grade job professional grades were where the shortages were, in fact the skilled trades occupations 'stand out as having the highest share of all recruitment problems'.

So whilst the 'shortages list' was an assumption of what shortages were, they did not apparently gauge the real difficulty which was in the provision of skilled trades.

However, to Sebastian, the problem when applied to the real world is twofold.

1. How is it that we are failing to train such a huge range and number of professionals as they appear on this shortage list, are they really needed? In which case does the lack of these people affect our lives here or are radiographers simply retrained from other similar work where there is an over-supply perhaps? Why do we apparently give priority to these people?

2. Does it reflect immediate needs? As shown in the paper above the real difficulty was in hiring skilled trades. An interesting example was where the NHS wanted to hire 800 Pilipino nurses for which there was a stated urgency but this was rejected by immigration because they were not the higher category of staff shown on the 'shortage list', they were mere nurses.

Thus the practicalities of defining whether we actually need more specific jobs is extremely difficult.

The only 'real' facts are whether a job has been offered to someone abroad who has accepted it. But do we permit that? Is it right that we spend megabucks training staff only for one of our number simply buying abroad? Do we owe ourselves any responsibility for living in the same country?

The case of the 800 nurses is more complex than it appears. Trained Pilipino nurses can be hired at about 66% of the cost of training new staff here in the UK. So what we were going is buying in cheaply, but why didn't we train our own?

In a sense that throws into question why, if we are able to 'plunder' other countries' skilled or professional staff, we need to train anyone in anything?

We will return to this theme later.

A major concern is less that of people coming to work here for specific jobs, for what there appears to be a proven need but of those who roll about 'job searching', there is little doubt that these people do depress hourly wages, create problems in neighbourhoods as without work they have nowhere to reside, they do use facilities which do compete with locals needs. I am still awaiting a definite report from the regions minister to actually nail the impact of immigration accurately, partly of course to put in place a funding proposal should it re-occur.

For the moment I need to prove to the EU that we can, in effect, allow full EU access to the UK jobs market but avoid those coming to the UK to look for work.

I hope that this will still count as 'free movement of people' job hunting.

We will be offering on-line access from the person's home EU state, using PCs based in British Embassies, I will show that it is not discriminatory and offers exactly the same opportunity as if the job seeker were in the UK applying from a local job centre.

Applying from the original state means that language skills can be tested and police checks carried out before they come to the UK, if some do still arrive with records they can be turned around and sent home. So the UK can claim to be 'in control' of its borders.

Direct access to those coming to the UK means also more knowledge of where they are going through a knowledge of where the job is located and which gangmaster they might use. This means the those local authorities with the largest immigrants incoming can be identified and supported. It also gives the UK border controls a massive database for later feedback from these individuals, for example that they too are paid the minimum wage, that's import to prove they are not undercutting our people.

However if the system is to be based on 'vacancies' then this has to be a genuine real time database of jobs. For this reason I have to shake up the 'vacancies', every business over 5 employers has to identify new vacancies and employment agencies must also extent the range of managerial jobs. So that the list is much more than just fieldwork and packing through the gangmasters which was the staple of the migrant trade from for example Poland. But the Tier 2 is capped at 20,700. I want to eliminate that!

But here in the UK it's not merely a matter of jobs, it's a matter of accommodation, we neither have surplus housing nor do we have space to put the houses we need. Letting in large numbers of immigrants simply exacerbates an already very difficult housing problem.

Accordingly there must be a cap on work migration perhaps a net figure of 150,000 based on the lack of housing and other facilities due to the UK's reducing available land area for building. It may well be the sort of 'churn' which we can accept. We know roughly the numbers of seasonal workers and we have worked on the 20,000 higher grades which have been nearly taken up. But we cannot get much nearer than that, so cannot base a cap on knowing how many workers we will need to run the country smoothly without causing some employment gaps that cause problems, and we don't know either the benefit of the extra few we do or do not let in, it's probable that they could rearrange shifts or buy new equipment.

What we are clear about is that we cannot absorb large numbers without it impacting on housing and causing other disruptions to local areas.

This is radical step to take as we know other countries are not troubled by space limitations. And neither care now worry about our housing obsession. But we do have limitations we cannot accommodate everyone who wants to come here, we have to make that point clearly and head on, no prevaricating!

However to bring the vacancies real time on-line within the EC will necessitate many changes internally within the UK if we are not to be disadvantaged in our own land.

Right from school leaving age they will have to be assessed for work, initial benefits may be withheld until the individual is taken on to a registered scheme of training or apprenticeship.

All degree courses that appear on the shortages list are to be free for all tutorial fees. We must begin to target and prioritise those skills and expertise we need rather than those which the individual prefers.

A huge apprenticeship will be required perhaps 50% funded by the government for all employers with more than 40 employees, in order to provide consistent continuity of supply of staff needed into the future just to stay standing. These will tend to be local recruits.

A massive training programme is put into place for all those on the hospitals skills shortage list, all training is to be on a bursary basis, since charging of fees appears to have restructured the market even further.

In order to ensure absolute equality, I intend to introduce a 'sponsorship' of £100 for all incomers whoever they are, this makes it more difficult for 'casuals' to get into the UK. It is paid back on leaving but any infringement like car parking, other penalties come off the amount. Universities are to be charged the same for incoming students and they are responsible for making sure they get back as well, fines are to be based on the numbers and length of time on 'the run'.

As mentioned earlier if, as I propose, all immigration controls for work is removed, except in total where we would take seasonality into account by a pre-booking arrangement, then it would be quite possible for an unscruplerious UK business man just to hire from abroad at a cheaper rate than could be done by training in the UK.

In order to act as a counterweight, I am introducing the concept of 'a capitation'. This 'capitation' turns on its head the convention that the UK can hire whoever and whenever trained staff as if plucked from a tree. All engineers or radiographers are trained somewhere, it does the giving country no good for it to be plundered of all its skilled staff which it needs to grow its own GDP. There are estimates that Romania has lost 5% of it GDP just for that reason. Capitation payments are to be calculated by the ppn from end of training to the expected useful job-life. It is to be paid to the original state where the training took place, it is designed to enable that country to train a replacement. The application form will declare the trained status of the person, this will be assessed and charged to the sponsor.

It thus obliges the sponsor to bring this into the equation when calculating if it is better to buy abroad or train in the UKWe would expect the principle of 'capitation' to be made an EU wide concept and also involve the Commonwealth which has been a regular taker of highly qualified Health Service staff for decades and paid nothing back!

Of course you all relate to the net immigration data that you read about. Unfortunately bits of it are just estimates, and not even random tests either just samples, and it would be a tragedy if we found that later we had been using spurious figures to come to a define conclusion which proved incorrect?

Accordingly the emigration documentation will change to give more clarity to the data which is not reliable. This uses the copy of the outward boarding card which I have yet to negotiate with 400 carriers.

We are looking at reducing all unnecessary imigration, one of those is the well-known   NHS medical 'runs'. Accordingly the NHS must establish the country of origin of every patient and that heavy penalties will be enforced for attempted medical tourism.

Part of the problem with the 2016 derogation was that we had to admit that some of the problems related to our poor handling , monitoring and control of gangmasters, where abuse was found to be very high. So the gangmasters and employment agencies' rules will be tightened, enforcing closure for any major infringement and immediate transfer of those on the books to a government agency.

Adding to the general immigration are the arrivals joining family units, i.e. foreign spouses. I believe this is an unnecessary a hangover of another era, there are plenty of good stock of people to choose from in the major cities in the UK. A problem too is that each spouse brings with them the older version of culture where women are second best, which is a part of their culture which we have been trying to change for 20 years. Furthermore it's just another 20,000 to the problem. At the very least I expect that to be phased out over 3 years.

However although that concludes the immigration matters, that freedom of movement of people is indirectly linked to the fourth freedom, Services. We must now press ahead and demand that these be bought into line and opened up to outside competition. It is well known that the Germans hide behind its language barrier. Accordingly we now have to insist that all contracts be in the main language plus English as the most used second language. All other covert protection measures have to be declared. There is an estimated 50% more work to be carried out in services, this needs exposing and ensuring there is direct access for us to maximise our EU membership.

I now want to take the final plunge, to finally 'cleanse the pot'.

I have already persuaded the PM to introduce through an emergency 'strangers' Bill in the House of Commons, a rule that on a specific date there will be a counting of all illegal immigrants. A moratorium is declared and for a period of one week, no new visas of any kind may be used at incoming arrivals, any attempt to evade the new rules will be met with immediate return to country of origin. Within the UK itself an amnesty is declared. All those presenting themselves to selected meeting points will be assessed and provided they have not breached certain conditions, like living on illegal earnings or being repeat offenders returning, they will be allowed to remain and after a period become British Citizens. Employers of illegal immigrants may suffer penalties if they have been deliberately withholding information concerning their staff, they are obliged to notify all staff of this amnesty, if they do not then they face a jail sentence. Registered immigrants within the system will also be assessed to remain, those that pretend not to have documentation or know of their country of origin will not be granted any amnesty and will be sent to holding pens.

All work is expected to be carried out during one week-end, police leave cancelled and military back up units will be located at meeting points to hold those coming forward until relieved.

The Cabinet meeting took all day and was hotly debated.

"Do you think that the Germans will go for this 'English as the other format?' One asked

"Sure!" said Sebastian. "The Germans are anxious to prove they are not the Hegemon, it has language and cultural overtones, by accepting the use of English, which they use already by the way extensively throughout their exports industry, they are proving they are not the Hegemon."

"But can we obtain the right information for the real-time online vacancies you suggest?"

"Well we can expand the Jobcentre work by sending out surveys to a wider number of different companies, but we would also need to obtain the backing either better by persuasion or worse by legislation instructing all vacancies to be made available. If it simply serves to give the agency more customers it is difficult to see why they would not comply!"

"Will industry leaders support this? Sebastian" another asked.

"Frankly probably not! They regard any government interference as an unneeded intrusion and don't want to make comments of commitment they might later regret. Basically take retailers for example, they believe they live in an unrestrained world buying and selling, free to do their business as they wish, no constraint is welcomed, manpower planning is notoriously difficult to do for complex companies and they make their way largely by fluidly finding a way around problems. Many of the FTSE100 are no longer UK based, they are heavily into Mining operations worldwide, they can pluck mining Engineers from where they please. They see us thinking of planning, they immediately imagine large levies imposed on them as another tax they don't want!"

"Is it worth doing at all then?" Asked another gloomily.

"Of course, at the top we have to put the case properly, many specialist technically driven companies will support this, most of the next group down will also be keen to help, also we need here to interject our own business sector strategy, we know we are ahead in all ICT and apps and games development so we concentrate on those to help us develop a plan for that area which can run right back to assess the future need in terms of degree and non-degree courses and the number of students we need to stay ahead. You all know it's difficult even to define what exact training is needed, the enthusiastic person with aptitude can quickly outclass the best first class degree man, so it's a question of providing the environment that allow skills to be taught and provide a reservoir of digitally trained people to be called on for this sector. There are other sectors like construction, housebuilders and infrastructure and that includes brickworks, concrete, plumbing supplies, joinery and plasterboard, I used to work in that area you know, you should be able to pull these together but it will be hard work, you'll have to bully them or they will just ignore you! We haven't even started the Health Service sector yet? And so on you get the picture now?" Sebastian paused.

"So what happens below that?"

"Well having some idea of needs, you then have to set up the supply side, you need to link into an extensive network of apprentice providers, maybe here you could use a privatised version, so apprentices are spread over several small employers, although the earlier ICT trainers proved to be complete rubbish, charging and not training. And then linking up with colleges, Universities, you really need a monthly update and quarterly full round table formal review. This has then to be fed back to schools with career advisers touring and persuading well before "A" level or whatever taken, we need flexible work placements also we may need a stick, benefits dependent on taking up opportunities available. It's null point = hairdressing I am afraid, that's a hobby isn't it?" he ended jocularly hoping for some sort of response.

"If we don't do it?"

"According to one report if we do nothing there will be a serious gap by 2022, 9.2 million people chasing 3.7 million low skilled jobs; 12.6 million people with intermediate skills chasing 10.2 million jobs; 14.8 million high skilled jobs with only 11.9 million skilled workers.

It says this could restrict economic growth if employers cannot recruit the skills and capabilities needed.

So there appears to be a huge mismatch already. I have no idea of the accuracy it seems pessimistic!

But it seems if you do nothing, then the frontiers will simply implode as UK business demand to get supplied from abroad those talents we don't have here as we haven't trained enough.

Your internal systems will collapse as they no longer get the signals to coordinate their training.

Opening up immigration fully to Europe anyhow, probably to the world, means that unless you do try to put in place this work, there will be an increasing mismatch between skills learned and skills needed, that will attract even more immigrants.

It will add to chaos, but you cannot in my opinion avoid doing something.

Look over the last 40 years several huge industries have been wiped out, textiles, textile machinery, coal mining, steel working, shipbuilding, we, you have put nothing in place of remotely sufficient size, nor have you bothered properly to retrained those flung out of work. unless you do there will be trouble ahead! Big trouble, Regional assemblies are…"

Stephen White interjected "Sebastian!" he clearly didn't want this to drift into party political matters.

"OK! PM, I won't get into that, but it is a hope for the future, to move away from the London Centric model of the past?

But you all understand whatever we do here we will not outstrip the Germans, we may occasionally have flashes of creative inspiration driving new business sectors like ICT and of course in Financial Services Deregulation although also with some dire consequences, but that doesn't match for a moment the remorselessly efficient German industrial machine. There you see give a man £500 K and he tries to invest in and build a business, here we just buy a bigger house with the £ 500 K.

We are simply wrongly configured to compete with them! But then, you all know that?"

There was a pause, then a rather timid Pamela Tressider put the final cap on it, "yes I am afraid I agree with almost all of it, we have to do it, I was always hoping for an opportunity to get some reforms going and as you see it has needed an all-around approach, I thought perhaps…." Her voice tailed off.

Stephen White looked around the table, calling out ministerial titles as if on a school register. "Any comments?... No? So we go ahead, and thanks Sebastian. You'll give us a plan soon I suppose?"

"Yes, couple of weeks I hope if you let me keep the ICT chap he has a lot to do! I think John Wires should be able to do a good job here, it tied in directly with the work he was doing in the 2010/15 coalition on business sectors, just up his street! Oh! And would you like me to sound out the Unions, you know we have had a Labour Shadow in here, he's very positive about it, I'd like to use him to put in to them PM?"

Stephen White seemed really passed caring and waved his hand in assent. Sebastian and half the Cabinet left immediately, Stephen was still at his seat.

"Bastard-fuckinggenius-shitbag-fuck-bastardgenius-shite-balls-arseholes-fuck-FUCK!" he exploded pounding the table furiously.

Bill Bennet who was due to take over the Ministry on Sebastian's departure was still sitting there, collecting his papers in a pile.

"Sorry Bill it's not meant personally, I didn't see you there, but I do find him difficult to read, he is annoyingly successful in his political judgement of what can be done! I find it exasperating somehow? I thought we were playing around with categories and things, but now suddenly it's a massive rescue operation, needing a huge investment! He's right of course; but no-one else seemed to have noticed!"

"Yes, Stephen, it's frustrating, isn't it, to try to follow how he's thinking? He calls himself a Radical, you know? He seems to enjoy turning things on their heads, it makes things a bit unsettling perhaps?"

"You can say that again!"

Of course, that's exactly what Bill did when he reported back to Sebastian later.

Chapter FIFTY-EIGHT – Run up to the December 2022 General Election

Sylvia now took control of Sebastian's three days Friday to Sunday, they followed a set pattern, on Fridays they entertained at home usually Lib Dem supporters, financial funders and councillors and invited business or religious leaders, sometimes they would visit nearby constituencies. On Saturday mornings they started off at the new Car Park in Middleton, a local Lib Dem member was assigned as assistant in case public interest became a problem, they walked to the Lib Dem offices shopped and then returned home. Sebastian exchanged a friendly wave with those who recognised him and stopped to sign autographs. In the afternoon or evening they went to a film, exhibition or a play. On Sundays they took a walk usually to Wollaton or nearby stately home like Chatsworth.

Sylvia told Sebastian that she relished these long week-ends, she knew she could relax him and prevent a recurrence of his nervous periods, under this care Sebastian was soon restored to working fitness and be became more confident.

Sebastian eschewed other Lib Dem appointments, rarely went to conferences and if he did only spoke at fringe meetings, he always gave Dan Stirling, the Party Leader his full support, he refused to get involved in any political infighting, he was constantly on hand to help Sarah Driscoll with problems arising with the Regional Assemblies and was a reference point even for Civil Servants seeking interpretation of certain clauses.

Sebastian's work on Prison Reform was completed by March 2022 and he relinquished the Ministry of Justice Role. The Immigration work wound down by September 2022. In a Cabinet Reshuffle he stood down from the Home Office and took over again Minister without Portfolio, largely he suggested a 'sinecure' but both Tories and Lib Dem were anxious that he was still associated in the Cabinet. It seemed to offer the continuity the government wished to portray to the EC.

Bill and Madge were married during that first Summer, it was well attended. At the posh country Hotel where they all stayed over-night, Sebastian and Sylvia went to bed early. Sebastian turned over in bed with a serious frown.

"Sylvia I have something to confess, I have been meaning to come clean.."

She put her finger to his lips. "You mean about Madge?"

"Yes so you know then already?"

"Yes Seb on the way down to London, took me hours, remember before the family re-union? but I eventually got it out of her, you knew I always had my suspicions about her?!"

"She just said, you were both so exhilarated on virtually 'owning' Chevening, that you both went a bit potty, had a couple of drinks and fell into bed fully clothed, she said you passed out before you could do anything! It made her determined to get a younger model!"

"That's what she said, was it?" he asked.

"Yes, she promised, you know, cross my heart thing!"

"But did that satisfy you?"

"Oh No! I checked it through with Bill, later, he had it out with her too, it was that which prompted him to promise to marry her after his divorce went through."

The Elgin marbles were duly restored to Greece amidst much pageantry. Sebastian received a formal invitation as the principal guest but declined.

So Sebastian didn't take a leading part in the Lib Dem campaign leading up to the December '22 General Election.

He had been required to back up the general Lib Dem TV advert covering his period as PM where his successes had, he felt, been elaborated a bit.

He had a lot to do locally however, he led off four, local public engagements, in Derby, Nottingham, Leicester and Lincoln. At these he had been the main speaker and surprisingly, Sebastian noted, they had all been complete sell outs!

Madge commented to Sylvia that she thought Sebastian's hearing was going as he miss heard several questions from the audiences, but he refused to wear hearing aids, at home he just turned up the TV.

He did some token and very public canvassing, he was recognised everywhere and was surprised by the public's general level of awareness. There was, Sebastian thought, anxiety over the shape of the unitary councils; ' Who would run Planning Applications?' was a frequently asked question; or "How would home care run by the Unitary Councils merge with NHS Services?' was another.

It was Tim Holland who did, as Sebastian conceded, the lion's share of the work, and he proved to be diligent and resourceful; always making sure that he informed Sebastian before any Focus were sent out or PR releases issued. After his 'confession' to Sebastian about being gay, Sebastian imagined that Tim intended to deal with that problem in his own way.

The suggested voting preferences were made clear in all their literature.

TIM HOLLAND   1

SEBASTIAN EDWARDS   2

So if the Lib Dem voters followed that advice Tim should win.

Sebastian used his influence to try to get Madge O'Connor moved up to first preference position in her home town of Lincoln, so that he felt she now had a good chance of winning there.

Soon the Election Day arrived, as soon as the polls closed all politicians eased up, if just for an hour or so.

Sebastian relaxed in his old chair; the old slatted swivel chair that had arrived with other bits and pieces of his father's belongings, some African war clubs and his Colonial Office uniform.

He eased himself back and put his feet on a stool.

He contemplated the world around him.

He could see some of his step-nieces playing on the patch of grass outside his window.

One of the few remaining houses on the cul de sac where they lived had come up for sale. Sebastian had acquired it and given it to Ahmed's widow, Sylvia's sister and her children.

The last house was bought by Sylvia's charity just weeks before, both for use where the charity's limited administration work could be done, and as extra beds if there was a need caused by an overspill from the main charity 'Safe House'.

Sebastian contemplated the last few hectic, adrenalin fuelled years, the power he had found both exhilarating and exhausting.

He ran over their successes, Devolution getting the people more involved in big local decisions, NATO reform and moving UK further away from a global perspective, EU reform and UK taking a leading role there at last, Prison reform and Immigration reform, affordable housing numbers growing.

Of course just putting up proposals didn't mean that the work would be carried through.

As a consequence, it seemed, of Sebastian's high poll ratings and perhaps the energy generally of Lib Dem ministers, particularly Sarah Driscoll who was seen as an upcoming star; the pollsters had recorded Lib Dems as variously 20 or 30% of the vote or nearly double the 2017 result. However the managers at Lib Dem HQ thought the party would be subject to a squeeze and pessimistically suggested 17%, having failed for two General Elections in a row to getting anywhere near their predictions.

Sebastian mulled over the possible outcomes.

He had never made any secret of his objective of wanting to create a meritocracy and, good governance without the violent political shifts which Sebastian had always felt meant too much hot air and not enough creative and imaginative thought being applied to the urgent need constantly to improving government.

He told his followers, soon after he entered politics that what he wanted was a strong, creative, radical centre party. They must capture the centre ground. If that could be achieved then Lib Dems would likely be at the centre of power for decades. Of course therein lay a paradox, to be radical meant that the party had to be open to new ideas, perhaps ideas that competed with those already as party policy, that mean internal conflict and divisions, but he was well aware that centre parties tended to split because they held to no outside ruling ideologies, on the basis of personalities which could easily degenerate into personal wars. Independent minded MPs were, he knew, very difficult to control, often holding their own views above those of the Party. But if they didn't re-invent and stay ahead in the ideas 'game', they would become static, stand for a weaker left or right and easily be overwhelmed by larger parties, whose 'ticket' was much easier to sell and logically whose broader membership gave it a 'hinterland' into which they could retreat, recharge batteries, drop poor policies and return refreshed. Lib Dem's hinterland, Sebastian knew was in contrast but 5 to 7% . Sebastian knew they had to keep constantly on the boil, if they stopped they would shrink and sink, Sebastian wanted to make the Lib Dems a 'factory of ideas' constantly challenging the existing way of doing things, constantly looking for better, cheaper more efficient ways of working in government, he wanted innovation, innovation, innovation.

Tony Blair had tried hard to plunder the middle ground but had failed to take his party with him. John Major and even David Cameron had tried with phrases like the 'Big Society' but the public quickly twigged that it was an empty phrase.

Sebastian reflected that he had not been an ideal Lib Dem. He had often come to his own conclusions over the EU over NATO and then driven them home, he hadn't really been a team player, he had survived and climbed using his whits.

He had been lucky, very lucky.

The Russian Mineral business had made him enough money to invest in a little research group, the local MP changing to UKIP and causing a by-election, gave him his opportunity to get elected, being in Lib Dem HQ when the Prime Minister asked for a price for a coalition and Sebastian in the background had insisted on a Constitutional Royal Commission, his helping Robin Turnbull and pushing into the Chamber 'for his own Bill' had earned him some favours, his rise in the Coalition was, in part, due to that. He, and the then current Prime Minister, were opposites in character but worked well together. He couldn't be sure but thought maybe that Robin Turnbull disliked Sebastian's pillorying was also luck, so on the spur of the moment had made him Deputy PM. Admittedly Sebastian already had begun to raise the UK's profile and there seemed nobody else likely to do it.

Sebastian's dedication to continuing Robin Turnbull's main projects had earned him considerable Tory respect, when his time came to go, the Tories had treated him with equal respect, also allowing Sebastian his legacy projects. Perhaps Sebastian mused 'This was how coalitions should work picking out the best of both parties projects, rather than fighting to hold back or deny the other's party's worst projects?'

Finally of course the Tory Party leadership election had given him the chance to get stuck in. Projects bounced around in his head, he had just done it and his earlier successes had meant that there were few Lib Dems who challenged what he did. In fact, he thought on taking High Office, his directness of approach would rub too many of his allies up the wrong way and that, in the end they, would pull him down. It had been his biggest fear, but that had not happened

So yes, he had been lucky.

But the puzzling thing about politics was that the public seemed to like, not middle parties, maybe they were too dull and boring, but those to the right or left of centre. Maybe those were the parties whose message was easier to sell and which often showed a dynamic thrust? With Labour it had been easy for them to evoke the betterment of the working man, us working for and with you With Tories advancement of capital (though actually not business) and how you could hold onto it, that was a war cry in itself

In comparison, Sebastian gloomily noted. 'Let's face it- 'selling the middle is a muddle.'

France seemed to go like that and the German Liberal Free Democrats had ultimately been squeezed out by a mind boggling left/right coalition. The Americans seem positively to rejoice in their bipolar politics.

But anyhow the electorate were changing, getting more impatient of poor decisions, increasingly unwilling to allow big party blocks to foist change on them for party political reasons, the electorate wanted more say and they would switch parties more readily, government had to justify itself and had to sell what it was doing.

Would the electorate deliver Lib Dems a massive wedge of MPs to Westminster that perhaps would at last permanently 'Break the mould of British Politics once, for all'?

Or would Lib Dems be punished for obliging everyone to accept and vote in the new Regional Assemblies, whose polls were on the same day?

Would they go with a radical centre party?

So he sat and waited for the results on TV.

Sylvia had long since gone to bed, bored by the whole process.

He touched the signet ring on his finger, but he was no longer worried. In or out of parliament, he had done his bit!

In any case had he not been recently lobbied over his possible selection for posts, admittedly minor, in the EU, NATO, the Commonwealth and even the UN?

Of course under the all-seeing scrutiny of his wife he had turned them all down, or at least fobbed them off, at least initially, but....

Just before the results streamed in he received a call from Lord Israel Jacob, Sebastian had no idea how he had managed to get his private land-line yet again " Hello Sebe'son, good just caught you! Sending you another large cheque, I hope these people are worth it! Anyhow the campaign went well, though tailed off over the past year. Can't do it again! any more of this success will bankrupt me, you realise I make 5% gross margin less on all your kit? Anyhow happy new Year. Oh yes and 'mazal tov', good luck!"

As usual Sebastian couldn't get a word in edgeways.

He remembered to call his step-brother Massa Gombe thanking him for the work setting up the Chad Lake Camp. "Well Sebastian, you have done it! Your dad would have been so proud!" They promised to meet early in the new year.

Finally a call from his son Rupert Edwards "Hi Dad, just called to say Good Luck and...." He paused " I just want to say sorry about not trying to find you years earlier, I should have tried harder to find you, we could have done so much..." Sebastian cut him short "Yes, I made the same mistake and bitterly regretted it. So we have both suffered. But the past is gone Rupert! We have wasted nearly twenty years, we can still catch up! Let's work on the future. Can you come up and see us over Christmas?"

They were discussing dates when the TV jingle came on announcing the start of the counts.

"Sorry Rupert got to go, call me tomorrow eh?"

He quickly called Madge, he thanked her and Bill for all their work "I could not have done it without you and Bill, you were my rock, thank you so much!"

He turned his attention back to the TV. At least they would get a bit of news tonight, the turnout and the exit poll that's all. As both Regional and General Elections were being fought under proportional Representation, the full General Election results would not be available till tomorrow noon, and the Assembly election results not till 8.00 or 9.00 pm.

'Blast' mumbled Sebastian to himself 'I'd forgotten – must make a note to introduce voting machines – it would save time and money – we should try that 'spinning down' to see what the research groups think!' He sat back in his chair and waited.

A couple of hours later Sylvia was awoken by the hissing from the TV for which she knew Sebastian had set the volume up high.

She saw him sitting in the chair, she nudged him thinking he had fallen asleep, but his head rolled to one side, his eyes were open, she realised something was wrong, she tried for a pulse, nothing, she grabbed a mirror to see if there was a mist that would show he was breathing, felt again for a pulse on the neck, but he was cold, quite cold, she pulled him to the floor and tried resuscitation, nothing, she, of course, called the ambulance.

She remained at his side and gently raised his head and cradled him in her lap. "Oh my dear, my darling Sebby, the suitcase PM, the Comet, my hero, my protector, my soul-mate." Her tears cascaded onto his face, "Good bye my love, and thank you for a full life of love!"

NOTES to the previous Books in the series

Book One describes Sebastian Edwards' progress from his adult years on. The first exposure is where Sebastian moves with his first wife to Belfast. There he has an idea to set up a Guest House which he describes as a 'Safe House' which he hopes will appeal to visitors from both sides of the political/religious/nationalistic divide. Whilst this is apparently successful the IRA are intending to hunt down British security staff who are believed by then to use the place. An IRA attack results which is beaten off but the building is destroyed and Sebastian realises that his wife, prompted by her father, no longer supports the project. In any case in order to make the place really profitable Sebastian would have to build on more rooms, which his father-in-law, a wealthy retired businessman, is unwilling to fund.

Sebastian takes another job in Scotland but his outspokenness sets him against the other directors and when a fraud is discovered to have taken place, initiated by his subordinate, Sebastian realises that the other directors may have been plotting against him and no longer support him. He resigns in high dudgeon whilst the Court case is ongoing. He finds his applications for new positions are rebuffed. He eventually takes on a position below his capabilities but is sacked from that company when the directors learn of his involvement in a company where the fraud case is not yet resolved.

He can no longer afford the expensive boarding school fees for his two children. Sebastian is unemployed for many months and he begins to deteriorate mentally. This culminates when he has several drinks whilst taking medication for depression. This leads to him being completely drunk and, arriving home he accidentally hurts his son Rupert. Sebastian's father-in-law, accuses Sebastian of causing harm to his grandson and being incapable of providing for this daughter, Sebastian's wife. He now tells Sebastian that he will prefer legal charges against him on behalf of his grandson unless Sebastian hands over his two children and promises never to speak to them again. If he does that, he tells Sebastian, he will take over their education.

Sebastian agrees and, although his wife attempts a reconciliation, the family splits and this has a dreadful effect on Sebastian. He continues to deteriorate.

Eventually his GP asks him to carry out some 'pro bono' work for two charities. This proves to be the turning point. Eventually he gets a hum drum job way below his capabilities, as an Internal Auditor. He spends years carrying out that work which he finds extremely limiting.

He begins a political career with the Liberal Democrats being elected District Councillor at a by-election and this work increases.

One year he takes a holiday on the Trans-Siberian Railway but his journey is mysteriously cut short when he inadvertently steps off the train and falls dazed into a snowdrift. He comes to a rail crossing and sees that a car lying crushed at the side of the road was possibly the cause of the train halting. He follows tracks in the freezing snow and finds an injured policeman lying in the road. They spot a ruined wooden church and hole up there for the night during which Sebastian beats off a pack of hungry wild dogs. Sebastian mentally goes through the message from his HQ, he believes that he is being set up by several senior directors to take on a role in a small Russian company to protect the interests of the Company Directors and some of their friends who invested unwisely. He is tipped off by Sylvia, his faithful Secretary, who later becomes his second wife. He turns the table on the directors and instead takes on the role of effectively running that operation, Siberian Minerals, which ultimately yields him significant financial rewards.

Sebastian 'inherited' in the deal an English executive, Geoffrey Pardoe, who was previously employed by Siberian Minerals to vet any new acquisitions in Russia. In May 2015 he goes missing and Sebastian resolves to find him and bring him home. He finds him near the site of a recent acquisition in Rostov. He is injured and in getting him out it becomes clear to Sebastian that this role of sourcing new acquisitions has merely been a cover for his real work as a spy for British Intelligence Services who are determined to evaluate Russia's intentions in the Ukraine.

Sebastian is thanked by the British Ambassador who explains when Geoffrey arrives in Kiev that Geoffrey Pardoe is not his real name and that the mission and the current discussion he is having with Sebastian never took place. It is for rescuing Geoffrey Pardoe that Sebastian is later awarded an OBE. He is told that he can never explain to anyone the reason for this award.

It is during the long walk from Russia into Ukraine that Sebastian dwells on the reason for the collapse in the Lib Dem vote of May 2015 where he too is unsuccessful as a candidate. Spurred on by his party's, and his own, humiliation, he formulates a plan for his party's resurrection.

He decides to launch a local paper giving local information which he knows to be hidden, or at least obscured, such as the low level of provision of affordable housing, this is pushing many new families into short term rental accommodation. Due to the increase in house prices new families are unable to buy houses as the cost/earnings multiple has grown out of their ability to pay.

He believes that the reason for part of his Party's collapse is failure to bring such failures to public view.

Sebastian is lucky, the sitting Conservative MP for Middleton decides to join UKIP and is hounded by the press to resign and fight a by election. This he does and Sebastian comes out the winner but with a delicate majority in June 2016.

He joins the few Lib Dem MPs at Westminster. The Tory Prime Minister sees his majority ebbing away, the stock exchange collapses. The Conservatives offer Lib Dems a coalition for survival. Sebastian is instrumental in demanding, as a price, the setting up of the Constitutional Commission to recommend a change to the voting and representation systems. The condition is that all parties will agree to accept the findings and put these in place; this they do.

The EC referendum goes ahead since it is now too late to stop a public consultation on the matter which had been long promised. It results in a very narrow defeat by the Government. The Prime Minister refuses to accept that such a narrow majority can cause so massive a change in direction and instead uses the defeat as a weapon to oblige the EC to give ground on Immigration, being granted a derogation, and granting the City of London important future consultation rights however the EC should develop.

A second referendum takes place and at the same time some of the other constitutional proposals recommended by the Commission are put up for approval in the same referendum. Chief of these are, the abolition of the House of Lords and the establishment of Regional Assemblies throughout England which, in effect, mirror that in Wales. One key item that is included within the assembly's remit is the governance of the NHS in each region.

It appears to be 'ownership of their NHS' which results both in the acceptance of the second EC referendum and the acceptance of Regional Assemblies.

The Prime Minister consulting all political parties agrees to break the 5 year parliament and he resigns, being unwilling to stand in the way of change, and the country moves to a General Election.

Sebastian is made Lib Dem Party Whip

Book Two took the story from the start of the new mix in the House of Commons thrown up by the change in voting. No party has an overall majority and inevitably Lib Dems are drawn into Coalition discussions.

A new Coalition is established in December 2017 when Sebastian is made Deputy Government Chief Whip. In this role, for which he is not ideally suited because of his difficulty in restraining himself within the rigid rules that the job demanded, he accidentally helps Robin Turnbull, a senior Tory Minister, from making a fool of himself. This is, later on, to play a key part in Sebastian's rapid rise when Robin Turnbull became Prime Minister.

In the Spring of 2018, the House of Commons comes under the attack of terrorists and Sebastian plays a minor role in pulling a couple of wounded people to safety.

Sebastian is then moved to Minister without Portfolio and he is put in charge of the remaining Constitutional changes that had been agreed in the Constitutional Referendum. This involves replacing the House of Lords, setting up regionally elected English Assemblies and reforming local government by introducing Unitary Councils throughout the country, this leads him into various unexpected peripheral problems.

Sebastian sees that the existing, much vaunted, unwritten constitution has become warped and is no longer fit for purpose. Incidentally this author realised that, in simply shadowing the constitutional changes that would be needed to carry out this work, they would absorb a huge amount of Parliamentary time; one reason, this author suggests, is why no root and branch like this was ever seriously attempted before, especially since all Prime Ministers can abuse the system to ensure they have a near majority in the House of Lords.

Never-the-less this seems to have been successful and, after a year in this role, Sebastian is moved to the Department for International Development principally because the Conservatives had been concerned that the agreed budgeted spend of 0.7 of GDP was being wasted and was not bringing expected rewards, either for the recipient countries or for the public perception that the money was well spent. Sebastian reviews many projects taking Nigeria as a sample (in the book these were actual real live DfID cases). He manages to redirect policy to target reasons for systems blockages in recipient countries, which have prevented their normal economic development. In the case of Nigeria it is in rooting out corruption that was endemic throughout the ruling class in that Country. Eventually he becomes Foreign Secretary and begins an immediate programme to reawaken the UK's skills in diplomacy, raising the UK's profile worldwide significantly.

Sebastian's excellent and close working relationship with the Prime Minister grows.

Sebastian suffers a major political jolt as, out of the blue, he comes under vicious attack from figures in his past and current life.

He is helped out of his 'bumpy ride', not by his Lib Dem Cabinet colleagues who have resented his rapid promotion, but by a junior Lib Dem MP who started with him on the same day as MP but whose political career has not taken off. This MP, Bill Bennett, his flat-mate, stiffens Sebastian's resolve to continue. Sebastian is eventually exonerated of all accusations. Realising that Sebastian has talents which go beyond his role the Prime Minister appoints him Deputy Prime Minister.

Soon after this Robin Turnbull, the Prime Minister, tactically put himself in a political 'hostage to fortune' position refusing to release a report on an obstruction in the Thames which could impact the new airport project and, when an explosion occurs and lives are lost, he is obliged to resign immediately.

He advises the Queen to appoint Sebastian as his successor perhaps partly because Sebastian has promised to continue with a project with which Robin had been closely associated, development of Heathrow Airport into a significant Green Garden suburb and relocation of that Airport to the Thames Estuary site.

Alongside all this, this Sebastian's Asian wife's brother in law, Ahmed took advantage of the laxness in control of her charity, of which Ahmed was director, to steal clients' money, Sebastian has agreed to provide what funds are necessary to resolve the situation.

Or better still why not buy the original books yourself

NOTES to this Book

Chapter ONE - The call to the Palace –

Excerpts concerning the succession of Prime Minister are indeed taken from 'The Cabinet Manual' dated October 2011 – a guide to laws, conventions and rules on the operation of go prepared by the Cabinet Secretary Sir Gus O'Donnell sections 2.9, 2.10, and 2.11 refer.

Chapter FOUR – Sebastian's own situation

Control of the Diary

Helen Jones in her book 'How to be a Government Whip' Page 109 states 'The Civil Service operates by keeping ministers busy so that they have little time to think. It mistakes activity for achievement and only very confident ministers are able to buck the system. In fact the first rule for any minister should be to get control of their diary, but I have known only a few who manage to do this. One insisted that nothing was put in without his approval, others that they would eat in the members' dining room on a certain night each week, or that papers be brought to them for a decision during the day instead of being placed in their boxes for them to work on late at night. All of these victories were gained after long battles, and so many ministers don't even try.'

Chapter SEVEN – with the Cabinet Secretary

Information on the 'Trio' is taken from Notes issued by the EU 'Presidency of the Council of the EU'.

Details of the Presidency is taken from EU – ABC, the UK were originally earmarked for President July to December 2017. The draft table of forward Presidents gives Portugal (January to June 2017) and Slovenia (July to December 2017). I have assumed that the Presidency for the UK would be reintroduced following this novel's assertion that a second referendum did take place which endorsed the UK remaining in the EC. The formal removal of the UK from the list was taken by the Council decision EU 2016/1316 of 26th July 2016 although that decision made clear that it was 'without prejudice to the right and obligations of that member state'.

Chapter NINE - Xmas Day – Visit to Prison

The information and background is based on several sources.

This is a fictionalised account, it does not attempt to explain the workings of a jail nor to assess the efficiencies of the system or the people who work it.

This Author can certainly give testament to the extraordinarily detailed and carefully prepared reports of the Prison Inspectorate on which this fictionalised account is based. The main items are drawn from the Inspection Report on HMP Nottingham by HM Chief Inspector of Prisons 1-5 February 2016.

This author has no doubt about the sincerity and dedication of the vast majority of staff whose job is made the more difficult due to prisons crammed full of potentially aggressive people, substantial overcrowding, a regime which locks prisoners away for large periods of time and which fails to give them even the vocational training in simple jobs available in the outside world.

The description of the external aspect of the Prison was taken from a photo of Nottingham Prison.

Nottingham Prison is run by HMPS (the Prison Service) and is not subcontracted as are some prisons.

The grades of staff and what they do and distinguishing epaulettes was taken from the website 'doing time.. prison-officers' and 'how prisons work' the same website deals with governors "within any prison there may be as many as 10+ governors of various grades and specialities … they will report to a top governor usually described as 'the No. 1 Governor'.

The process of admitting visitors is from 'doing time.. hmp-nottingham' this indicates the searches undertaken, including rub down, metal detector 'much the same as done at every airport' and information required for identification. (HMP Oakwood managed by G4S has a much more comprehensive list). These rules for visitors appear to be rigorously enforced. Nottingham is a 'local prison' but other prisons may have an intake up to 100 miles away, so forgetting the right pieces of paper to establish identity e.g. concerning an accompanying child, could result in a costly and time wasting trip (in some cases costs are refunded see PSO 4405). Visitors have to obtain a 'Visiting Order' which designates the date of the visit.

The origins and history of HMP Nottingham comes from 'doing time', the new prison which was completely rebuilt has been in operation since 2010, the 'accommodation' given in the text comes from 'doing time'.

The different cell bed types/configurations are taken from 'doing time… first weeks' – 'if you are lucky you will get a single cell' and 'who your cellmate will be is a matter of luck' and 'both cell inmates have to compromise and adapt and this is difficult over the first weeks of your sentence'.

Overcrowding of nearly 50% comes from 'Annual NOMS digest 2015/16 – July 2016' 'Male Local' prisons are by far the most overcrowded in the system. Overcrowding is strictly defined as "where the number of occupants exceeds the uncrowded capacity – this basically appears to mean the number of prisoners held more than one to a cell. In the case of HMP Nottingham it has a 'certified normal accommodation' of 718 and an 'operational capacity' of 1060 as stated in the text (so an in principle overcrowding of 342 times 2 = both people in a two man cell are overcrowded), nearby Lowdham Grange, subcontracted to Serco, a Male Category 'B' prison but a 'training prison' appears to have an overcrowding of just 32, 'certified normal accommodation' is 900 and the 'number held' is 920.

HMP Inspection reports that this author has seen (Nottingham and Lowdham) do not appear to place any importance on the overcrowding factor. This author suggests that for some reason this "Elephant in the room" is never mentioned in the reports! Presumably this is because the Governor cannot use overcrowding as an excuse for any deficiencies provided it comes within the set limits. The HMP Nottingham Inspector's report of February 2016 states in the Summary section S 1 'Despite a more strategic approach to addressing violence, levels remain far too high and many incidents were serious' this is amplified in S 3 concerning a prisoner survey: '61% said they felt unsafe at some time in Nottingham which was one of the highest figures we have seen' (in Lowdham Grange the comparable figure was 48%) and in S 8: '56% of prisoners believed it was easy to get drugs in the prison which was a very high proportion' (this compares with 33% at Lowdham Grange). And exceptionally S 18 stated 'Many cells were cramped with inadequate toilet screens' that was just about the only acknowledgement that the basic cell configuration itself might be an issue. It's difficult to extract from this how prisoners react to the cell conditions compared with the regime suffered by them that is the number of hours a day when they are trapped in the cell. Frances Cook, Director of the Howard League suggests 'The lack of staff means that prisons have become much more violent places. If you lock up young men for days on end, as one prison officer said to me, 'they come out fighting', 'they go stir crazy.' According to the HMP Nottingham visit report Item 1.13 'strategies to deal with the perpetrators of violent and anti-social behaviour are mostly punitive'. Under 'Discipline' item 1.44 'The number of formal adjudications averaged about 380 a month, which was high' and under 1.48 'There was a high level use of force with 346 cases in the previous 6 months'.

This author wrote to the HM Prisons Inspectorate questioning why overcrowding was scarcely mentioned and not addressed directly. I received a very helpful response from the Chief Inspector on September 26th 2016 to the effect that a) overcrowding was a complex issue, b) my comments were relayed to the inspection team and c) they are completing a thematic report on overcrowding in prisons which will be available for public view.

To this author the problem that the Inspectorate faces is that the reason for overcrowding is almost wholly political and comes directly from the importance that the public places on this service compared with other competing services – too many criminals incarcerated – too few prison cells – restricted capital spend, restricted operational budgets – too much pressure on officers – too few officers – too much banged up time – too many stir crazy prisoners – too much violence - too little useful practical training in prison.

The daily timetable was taken from 'doing time' and is that for a typical Cat B Prison, individual prisons can vary.

Number of Prison officers comes from the Howard League of 31st August 2016 'Prison numbers fall again...' Nottingham shows Prison Officers; 230 for 2013 to March end; 160 for 2014; 200 for 2015; and 166 for 2016. Since this appears to be well after the date the prison was rebuilt, it's not obvious why there is such volatility in numbers, staff veering by 20% must be very difficult to cope with, but there again it's possible it was due to a reclassification somehow.

The two types of vocational training actually mentioned are; firstly, the HMP website boasts '100% of students who entered BICS qualification passed .. for those seeking work in the industrial cleaning sector' this is from 'doingtime/hmp-nottingham' but which also states 'spoof data for test purposes' which is disconcerting, so one cannot be quite sure; secondly from the HMP Nottingham Inspector's report item 3.14 'Staff provided good quality training in industrial cleaning and bicycle maintenance'. The report states item 3.10 'Prisoner feedback regularly included requests for training in trades such as painting and decorating, bricklaying and plastering, but these requests had not been met'. It's not clear to this author why training is so limited, there does not appear to be an overwhelming shortage of bicycle maintenance jobs whereas the building trades offer a huge potential and, in times of shortage, of such skills, earning can be very good, probably more than could be earned through nicking things!

From the visit report 'There had been 5 Governors in the Space of 4 years' (introduction) from which this author took the nervousness of the fictional Governor insecure in dealing with the 'Wing' prison officer whose attitude in the novel is supported 'However too many wing-based staff remained distant and somewhat dismissive of the men in their care' (introduction)

Time in or out of cell came from this report (purposeful activity) item 3.2. 'The Library was only open on weekdays during the day, which limited access for prisoners engaged in full time activities' (S37).

The report item 2.94 'Meals were served too early, lunch sometimes as early as 11.00 am and dinner between 4 and 5 pm, and 2.95 'Breakfast packs were issued in the evening on the day before they were eaten', it's not clear to this author who they are issued to and therefore it might mean that the pack was stored somewhere, or if the inmates had the ability to eat it the night before (which they might well do if dinner was served at say 4.00 pm). The recommendation was that lunch should not be served before noon and dinner not before 5 pm.

From 'The Sunday People' 13th December 2014 'Statistics show that prisoners' re-offending rates are 39% lower if family ties are kept up'

At Christmas, Barlinnie jail takes part in a "Santa Run" raising funds which sends children in hospices to Lapland 'It also runs quizzes for the inmates, allows more time for association and runs pool competitions' Independent 24th December 2014.

The description of the layout of a cell was deduced from a photo of a cell in Barlinnie jail in Scotland.

The characters of David and Tom were taken from an article in Independent "Christmas time in prison" of 24th December 2014.

'Jayne said 'So we spend Christmas Day waiting for him to phone'" 'Her daughter said she and her younger brother get just a couple of minutes each to speak to their dad during the short phone call he is allowed on Christmas Day' Daily Mirror 13th December 2014.

The meeting with John Wallace is an entirely fictional account but based on an incident related to this author by a psychologist who was visiting a prison some years ago as part of his normal job. He was told to use a room for a prisoner meeting. The guard left and almost immediately the client/prisoner began to behave strangely and the psychologist became worried. He pressed the alarm, nothing happened, so he did it frantically, still nothing happened. He said he became extremely anxious. Eventually the prison guard arrived some 10 minutes later. This author asked the psychologist if he thought that it was a deliberate ploy by the guards. He said he didn't know and went through the rationalisation process mentioned in the text and decided to do nothing about the incident.

There is a significance of the bolt being 'shot' since it defines whether the visitor is in a protected area or not. This extract below is taken from the Prison Inspectorate's own rules for the safety of their own staff:-

'**3.26** Always make sure that the bolt is 'shot' on a cell door before going into a cell to ensure you cannot get locked in. If you do not know how to do this or do not have a cell key ask a

member of staff to do it for you or invite the detainee to talk to you in a different location'.

In this novel the prison guard seems to have breached the rules and the Governor would know this.

There is also particular significance in the seating arrangement within a room and again this extract is from Inspectorates rules:

'**3.27** If you are speaking to a detainee in a separate room or office make sure you are aware of the location of the alarm. Always seat yourself rather than the detainee closest to the door.'

Mis-categorisation of prisoners does occur, item S 60 in the Inspectors report on HMP Nottingham 'We found a case in our sample where the risk of harm level had been wrongly assessed as medium when it should have been high. In S 57 'Some of these men had a combination of mental illness and very challenging behaviour'.

It's significant in the story that the last prisoner, John, was wearing prison uniform. Although the rules governing the wearing of prison gear does not appear to be completely standard throughout the service (at some prisons, sometimes apparently the laundry service cannot cope with demand, so prisoners' own clothes might be delayed in the wash, obliging them to resort to prison garb) it is most likely to be worn either by new arrivals or by those who are 'on basic in the IEP' status. IEP is the Incentives and Earned Privileges scheme which provides some perks to prisoners who behave well. Other privileges like automatic access to daytime TV and gym equipment can also be withdrawn (The Guardian 1ˢᵗ November 2013).

John would probably be a seasoned offender and be obliged to wear prison clothes at all times. (Sebastian would not have known this).

Barnardo's have estimated that there are 'more than 200,000 youngsters with a parent in jail this Christmas' Daily Mirror 13ᵗʰ December 2014. 'One nine-year-old girl starting stealing was asked why 'If I'm really naughty and get caught I can go to prison and spend Christmas with Dad'. 65% of boys with a jailed dad go on to offend.'

Violence in UK prisons appears to be endemic, but it's not just a word. The Times reported 22ⁿᵈ Sept 2016. 'Official figures show there were six apparent homicides in jails in 2015/16 the largest number … since current records started in 2000.' The prisons' Ombudsman was quoted as saying 'The cases we studied had little in common beyond their tragic outcome. Never-the-less what is clear is that the increased number of homicides is emblematic of the wholly unacceptable level of violence in our prisons'.

This author suggests that ending capital punishment perhaps salved the consciences of the ruling classes but successive governments are clearly complicit in these prison deaths for which they ought to have a duty of care. The question is are they doing enough? The Prison Ombudsman clearly does not believe overcrowding is the issue.

A newer category of prisoner (Islamic extremists) is likely to be created and inmates will be housed in 'prisons within prisons' to prevent them radicalising other prisoners, particularly vulnerable young men who have previously been open to radicalisation once in prison. There are currently around 130 convicted Islamist terrorists. In future specialist units will be based in eight high security prisons in the UK.

The text in the book was sent to HM Prisons in case it breached any rules. A standard reply was received in October 2016 to the effect that *"You may re-use this information free of charge in any format or medium, under the terms of the Open Government Licence".* That Licence insists that the items are identified to the reader which we have now done.

Chapter TEN – Boxing Day - A family problem

The procedures by the various bodies when dealing with fraud or complex cases such as this was related to this author by a very recently retired police officer,

Giles Orton. This author is very grateful for his response to what must have seemed a silly question, that of the problem of a character in a mere novel, but it was important to the story. Thank you!.

Chapter SEVEN - Ministerial Cars

The responsibility for Ministerial Cars was passed in 2012 from the Cabinet Office to the Department of Transport. The Prime Ministers cars and those for certain departments appear to be treated differently from the GCS (Government Car Service).

The Prime Minsters' cars are believed to be 'Armoured Jaguar XJ Sentinel' supercharged 5.0 litre V8 models. The cars are used by specially trained close protection drivers and are escorted by unmarked Range Rovers. They are believed to cost £300,000 each, they have a range of protective devises, kevlar lined cabins and armoured windows etc. They are believed to be stored and maintained at Downing Street.

Certain Departments have their own pool cars, these are DfID, FCO, Min Def and Scotland Office

There are 85 pool cars. Since 2012 cars are contracted to the department that the minister works for rather than the minister themselves. This reduced the cars from 136 to 85, but top up cars are also used. The annual cost of the other ministries is detailed by department and this is the league table published in the press. It comes to around £2 M per annum (taken from 'GOV.UK Charges for GCS supplied ministerial cars between 2012 and 2015).

The PM, Home, Foreign, Defence and Northern Ireland Secretaries of State use Metropolitan Police drivers, the Chancellor uses a pool driver.

The wife of Cabinet Minister Michael Gove wrote 'The red box arrives unannounced at all hours in a chauffeur-driven car, the engine purring deferentially as her handler walks her to the front door, she deposits herself on the sofa to await her master' (from the Daily Telegraph mps expenses/ministersred boxes)

Chapters – EIGHT and TWENTY-TWO - Chilcot Report review and Cabinet meetings

The basic material is taken from the Chilcot Report itself which can be downloaded – most comes from the questioning of the Cabinet Secretary on 13th

January 2010, who was then Lord Turnbull, by the Chairman and the committee.

His view of his role is from page 2.
He was questioned if the Cabinet should have had more ownership on page 15.
He agrees that it was not set up as a Cabinet Office Committee; page 26.
He agrees they were rather familiar with 'that style of working'; page 32.
He agrees that once ministers had coalesced... page 33.
He describes the Ad Hoc groups; page 34.
He discusses the time spent on Iraq on page 42.
He describes the osmosis in the Cabinet office; page 46.
He rephrases a question 'you think I should have been more challenging? page 46.
He attempts to suggest it wasn't just updates but 24 key moments of endorsement; page 48.
He indicates that sharing information would not have made much difference; page 84.
He says 'the only way it would have happened, somewhere close.. you need to think about'; page 84.

Robert Peston 6th July 2016 itemises some of the main 18 points of the Chilcot findings, most go into the factual mistakes but some were relating to procedural matters.

Point 6, there was a grotesque and systematic absence of proper cabinet oversight of almost all important Iraq decisions.
Point 10 Cabinet did not discuss the military options or their implications.
Point 13 Blair did not establish clear ministerial oversight of UK planning preparation.
Point 14 the British governments preparations failed to take account of the magnitude of the task....
Point 15 Whitehall departments failed to put collective weight behind the task (post conflict).
Point 17 UK Defence resources were chronically overstretched by deployment in both Iraq & Afghan.

Sebastian believes that, in part it, was the failure of the Cabinet system which was the direct responsibility of the Cabinet Secretary.

Since Chilcot:

Apparently the Secret Intelligence Services (the SIS formerly MI6) have since re-instated internal checks on the the quality of intelligence that had been removed in 1990s

The Coalition government published its position on the legality of military action in Syria providing some of the legal reasoning (missing over Iraq).

It has been agreed that since then Cabinet Committees would be used, (but nothing about allocation of a Permanent Secretary or other Civil Service oversight structure), (or Ministerial oversight) which the Chapters in this book discuss, nor about the quality of Cabinet reviews!

According to Ken Clarke's latest memoirs 'she (Margaret Thatcher) ran a collective government. Although Margaret would speak for at least half of any Cabinet meeting and was a poor chairman on that account, she did let other ministers express their views and could be prevailed upon to change her mind or even, occasionally, be overruled.'

But Ken (or Kenneth to Margaret) has a lot to say about David Cameron's style of government. Initially it appeared that he wanted to revive 'collective policy making in Cabinet' but never delivered it, instead adopting Tony Blair's style of personal decision making by the Prime Minister. He suggests that the 90 minute Cabinet meetings were an 'almost comically inadequate time within which to discuss any important subject', he used to raise topics which he felt junior ministers 'would otherwise have been debarred from debating'. The agenda items gradually shifted to being updates which David Cameron justified to Ken Clarke as being due to the coalition 'frank and open discussion was more difficult…and increasingly all the big decisions were finalised by the… Quad'.

He suggests that the Presidential style of government with 'short and cursory collective meetings' had been in place since 1997 and that 'far too many senior civil servants also believed that this was the normal process'.

(excerpts of excerpts of Ken Clarke's memoirs – this from Times 2 of October 3rd 2016.)

On interventions generally.

It's not unusual to want to create attention by bringing on ideas. Sebastian's idea of course is to have a continuous flow of discussions and ideas, the basis of a radical approach, so that it is seem as a party of, or factory of, ideas. In 'Call me Dave' Ashcroft & Oakshot recall page 385 'In the early years of Cameron's leadership, Hilton had been the energy and originality in the top team, injecting a constant flow of fresh, zany ideas designed to wow voters.'

Chapter TWELVE – European Discussions ONE

The events in this novel leading up to the First Euro Referendum, its result and then the Second Euro Referendum and that result are fully developed in the first book SEBASTIAN, basically the result was very tight and the Prime Minister used it as a negotiating ploy to drag more concessions from the EC.

How this novel shows that it might have been done follows the line of argument used in the book 'The Future of Europe – towards a Two-Speed EU' by Jean-Claude Piris who served as the Legal Counsel of the Council of the EU and Director General of its Legal Service from 1988 to 2010. This was taken from page 84 and 85 and is a general discussion on partial opt outs rather than specific to this case mentioned. This author is not a lawyer steeped in Euro rules and law and frankly has no idea if an opt out for such relief from what is seen as one of the fundamental principles would be acceptable, but it would seem to be very likely that the British Government might have used such an escape clause.

The case here would be a temporary 'derogation' and it might therefore be subject to the Qualified Majority Voting system. Since 2014 this means that, if the proposal comes from the Commission itself, it would require the assent of 16 of the 28 Member States and Member States with 65% of the population. It could be blocked by 4 Member States with 35% of the population. Although it is possible for a country to appeal directly to the Council but the bar is increased to 72% of the population of Member States.

The point is that it would not then itself have to be subjected to parliaments or referenda in Member States. This change proposed, if made permanent, might then be presented alongside future constitutional changes.

An important element is that the UK, if challenged by a Member State to the effect that it is discriminatory, would have to justify its 'derogation' before a Court of Justice, rather than in political terms.

The Sunday Times of 25th September 2016 explains what actually happened to David Cameron's negotiations with the EU. In order to control immigration the PM had two options a) a temporary cap or b) an attack on migrants benefits. Despite Angela Merkel's opposition to a cap the PM was prepared to pursue it knowing that it was a high risk policy. According to the article Theresa May and Philip Hammond were invited to a meeting by the PM and spoke against it.

The PM apparently said 'I cannot do it without their support. We'll just have to go with the benefits plan. If it wasn't for my lily-livered colleagues...'

It was to prove a fatal mistake. He was never likely to convince voters with his rather weak attack on migrants' benefits, and he didn't.

In my case the Prime Minister in this novel now turns the tables on the EC, 'Unless you agree we will have no option but to leave!' and so obliges the EC to evaluate a temporary cap or the withdrawal of the UK. Individual member states who objected to the restriction placed on their people coming to the UK could therefore evaluate between a cap or possibly none coming at all, this will have diffused the arguments of those that stood simply on the issue of the fundamental principle. Others not so concerned about that right could evaluate the potential loss of a stable trading partner.

The 'Derogation Case' depends on a number of points and issues which this author justifies by the following information

Housing Shortage and Green Belt

There is estimated to be a shortage of 250,000 houses in England.

There are 14 Green Belts in England covering 13% of the total land which is supposed to be protected from development. But this is now being built on. In 2009/10 some 2,258 houses were built on Green Belt land, but in 2014/15 this has increased to 11,977 houses. (source BBC.

Comparative Growth Rate

GDP Growth rate since 2004 to 2015 UK 1.4% average Eurozone 0.8%

EU House Prices compared

Price of houses in London is 4.999 per sq. m and Paris 4.911

But Brussels is 2.094 and Berlin 2.082

(source thisismoney.co.uk of 11 June 2016) Infuriatingly this author cannot see from the extract whether the currencies are in Euro or £. They can only be indicative unless you define exactly what 'London' is, it covers an area 15 times that of Paris and the differences of house prices are massive, take one definition of London and it could be wrong according to another. However it seems probable that this 'average' used is probably rather low!

Information on the Social impact of Population change, Boston (links) used as an example.

It is remarkably difficult to pick up material on the impact of such changes generally. People intensely dislike being categorised as racist which has prevented sensible discussion on the problems arising from immigration. This Author attended a seminar hosted by East Midlands Councils on 17th June 2014 'The impact of Migration in the East Midlands – Understanding Social Impact of Population change'.

The senior executive of the Boston Council, responsible for housing, exclaimed 'The system is broken and I cannot fix it'! He was clearly at his whit's end and was facing the nitty gritty problems of the situation there. He said that there was no national leadership of the problem, this meant the District Council on its own coping with a surge in Eastern European arrivals, 25% of whom could not speak English well, they included unaccompanied minors (technically up to 25 years old). Many people turned out to have alcohol problems which in turn drove increased violence or at lease public incidents resulting in a high level of Anti-Social Behaviour Orders (Asbos). Up to 20% didn't have passports, most were seeking 12 months residence and not migrant workers. Many had to be repatriated to their countries of origin. There was little assimilation. This surge completely altered the local demographics. It was even unclear how many of this group there were in the vicinity.

On the other hand the Council had to cope with rogue private landlords who took advantage of the surge and shortage of housing. Many of the newcomers appeared to be well able to access local services and to be aware of their rights. The general behaviour of immigrants appeared to lead to a massive increase in support for UKIP. Drinking bans were proposed.

It's clear that the speed of change had caught Boston Council by surprise and they were finding it very difficult to cope.

This problem was raised at the highest level through the MP to the Prime Minister. A Task and Finish group was created by Boston Borough Council and the very detailed and well prepared report was adopted on 19th November 2012.

It stated firstly that the population had increased from 55,750 in 2001 and to 64,600 using the 2011 census. Many thought this was an underestimate as migrants were deterred from completing forms by their landlords.

Contrary to models which suggested that the able bodied males come first in any immigrant wave, this report asserted that 'birth rates have increased locally and school admission numbers have gone up significantly'. Community tensions have increased. There is a strain on local services. Many residents believe that there should be a cap or limitation on free movement of labour, many believe 'that most of our social challenges are a direct result of EU migration in our town and rural parishes.'

There is clearly a problem with urination in public places. The police had a problem with vehicles as foreign cars can be brought into the UK for six months without showing a disk but there are no records available to show police when the vehicle arrived making it difficult to track persistent offenders. Boston claim to have repatriated the second highest number out of 6 pilot organisation schemes. Information disclosed that in Boston there were 57 licenced gangmasters and their representative suggested that they were able to control the amount of rent the worker pays if the gangmaster were also their landlord. The MP suggested that the UK's failure to use powers to delay the free movement of the new EC countries had 'effectively funnelled migrant workers into this country'. Inadequate funding for GPs and the hospital. Members of the public identified 'grot spots'. One resident reported that she had been sexually attacked 'by a group of EU men.' 'Time the government woke up to the fact that we are full to breaking point.' 'Multi-culturism is not a great success.' 'Difficulty in identifying illegal immigrants and in enforcing deportation.', 'some revoking of trading licences, one caused by counterfeit or non-duty paid goods'. 'Applications from EU citizens for affordable homes increased from 5% in 2008 to 13% in 2012', 'Littering 70 fixed penalty notices issued'. 'removal of benches in town' this it is understood to prevent the area being used as a drinking focal point, 'Foreign owned shops unaware of UK food regulations'.

But they also concluded that there were very few economic migrants claiming JSA and the local Job Centre suggested that there was no evidence that 'migrant workers take away local jobs'. A local farmer suggested that the work ethic of indigenous people 'is very poor' as evidenced by 'lack of work ethic, lack of enthusiasm and lack of engagement'. The lack of non-English speaking children has not had an adverse effect on attainment in schools even where 62% of the children were from migrant households. Primary and Secondary Schools and the College are all proactive in promoting integration. Schools receive substantial funds to support migrant children. Lincolnshire County Council is to spend £4.8 million on new school places in Boston. Boston's Pilgrim Hospital the maternity unit, would not be viable without migrant births (nearly 40%). 'Police state that there's no evidence that a disproportionate number of crimes are committed by foreign nationals.'

According to the MP 'Young men asked me, when I would be putting a stop on immigration and I replied when you are prepared to work in the packhouses and fields.'

Professor Craig, Professor of Social Justice at Hull.. ... 'the impact on Boston must have been considerable. Why did this happen? Who was responsible or to blame? What can we do? This happened because of a lack of planning by the Government, especially the Labour Government up to 2004 when 50-70,000 migrants were expected, it was actually a million over the period, since then though some have gone back, but we don't know how many because migrants only register when they enter but not if they go back! For many of them their dream has turned into a nightmare, for some its modern slavery. Most gangmasters are legal and operate properly. The rate for the job is better than in Eastern Europe but in many cases it's below the minimum wage and conditions are poor. The work is Difficult Dirty and Dangerous, so local people don't want to do it!'

He continued....

Some say they are taking our jobs – that's not true

Some say that migration leads to unemployment – there's no evidence for this either

People say they are taking our houses – that's not true though there might be some local effects – amongst the migrant worker population half a dozen people might share a house; 4 share a room by hot-bedding.' An MP published an article in the DT about the appalling conditions in which the migrant workers lived

This author's note. This Task and Finish report is one of the very few attempts to rationally identify the effects of immigration on a particular area. But the conclusions one could draw are in some ways baffling.

Whilst the Police assert that the crime rate has not increased, the Job Centre asserts that jobs were not lost, the Schools assert that there was no effect on standards, the Hospital asserts that without immigrants the maternity unit would close.

Yet the townspeople seem to suggest that their town is being taken over, there is clearly loutish behaviour, with a bench removed to prevent immigrants congregating and a large number of Asbos which suggests recurrent misbehaviour and sending some immigrants back for unstated transgressions, areas of the place now classed as 'Grot Spots', there's disquiet about gangmasters and if they are abusing their role as landlords and suggestions of overcrowding of the immigrants, a large number of 'foreign shops' have opened catering exclusively to migrants because of the language, the migrants on the lists for affordable homes have increased so locals do have to compete with them for cheaper housing, the officer in charge of housing says his system is broken.

There is a lot we don't know, for example, in the areas affected, have house prices collapsed? If they have then locals could see the nest egg of increased house prices built up into a profit over years, available elsewhere might have collapsed. If immigrants buy food in their own shops and in effect replace local traders in parts of the town then local shopkeepers are going to be affected. The town deteriorates locals can see that!

It's a picture of a Town under stress but not necessarily damaged, changed but not for the better according to the traditional townsfolk – a result of rapid increase in migrants (the council didn't know how many immigrants there were!) it's not a picture of joyful integration! The citizens turned against the EU in this author's view because the EU don't appear to care about the impact of their rules and because no one in the UK is bothered to help them. The District Council was unable to cope.

The referendum in Boston was lost 75/25, one of the highest Brexit votes in the Country on a 77% turnout.

The Economist of 16th July 2016 in an article 'Straws in the Wind' was concerned by the paradox as to why areas with few foreigners should be so keen to curb immigration and vote leave. They carried out an analysis and found that 'Where foreign born populations increased by more than 200% between 2001 and 2014, a leave vote would follow in 94% of cases'. The town of Boston showed as the highest such population gain and highest vote leave.

<u>Do immigrants bring economic or fiscal gain to the UK</u>?

It's a complex picture. 'Migration Watch paper 386, item 16 'recent migrants arrived since 2001 from the old member states of the EU 14 made a net fiscal contribution estimated to be £1.4 billion in 2011/12 and in 2014/15 it was £2.8 billion'.

The same paper, item 17, 'Recent migrants from the new East European States of the EU 8 and EU 2 have however a net fiscal cost estimated by MW as £1.5 billion in 2014/15.'

MW quote item 19 from the House of Lords Select Committee on Economic Affairs who stated 'We have found no evidence for the argument, made by the Government, business and many others that net immigration, immigration minus emigration, generates significant economic benefits for the existing UK population'.

The surge in EU immigration

The period from 1945 through to 1995 saw very little net migration in the UK mostly much less than 50,000 per annum, whereas the period from 2001 to 2010 it was over 200,000. (shown in their chart 5)

Immigration from the EU in 2014 represented between 40 and 46% of all immigration to the UK. (item 2.4 table 1)

Net migration of EU nationals rose from 65,000 in the year ending September 2012 to 184,000 in the years ending March 2015 and 2016 (item 2.4 and chart 7)

The United Kingdom is among the EU countries with the largest inflows of foreign nationals but it is not unique. In 2014 the EU countries with the largest inflows of foreign nationals were Germany (790,000), then UK (551,000), Spain (264,000) and Italy (248,000) (chart 11)

The reasons given for coming to the UK, apart from visitors and short term visas, were; study, work, family and dependant joining. (chart 9)

The work visas granted were: tier 2 sponsored skilled workers with a job offer 92,000; Tier 5 temporary workers 45,000; Tier 1 high skilled and high value people 5,400 (chart 10)

(source House of Commons Library – briefing paper Migration Statistics)

Integration Problems

(Source - UNRISD briefing paper No 1, World Summit for Social Development, March 1994, page 12)

'In major receiving Countries, international migration creates enormous problems of social integration and cultural adaptation which are currently at the centre of the policy debate. The juxtaposition of people who often share neither a common language nor a common religion and who have very different customs, makes unusual demands on human tolerance and understanding. The arrival of large numbers of foreigners also creates unusual strains on existing social services and local economies.

Merkel says German multi-cultural society has failed

This is dealt with in more detail under 'TURKEY' below. There is sadly little evidence that there has been meaningful integration of Turks in Germany or indeed of the Muslims in France. Sebastian, and indeed this author, is aware that certain groups can be highly resistant to integration. The Catholic/Nationalist population of Northern Ireland successfully resisted absorption into 'British' culture for 70 years, they felt different and were determined not to be integrated.

Multi-Cultural London

In absolute terms London is by far the most cosmopolitan European city. More than a third of its inhabitants, almost three million people, were born in a country other than the UK (source voxruop/4958456–map–cities–most–number-inhab)

Comparative GDPs – causing the migration moves

The GDP EU average in 2012, before the accession of several 'new EU members' was about $30,000, Bulgaria and Romania had GBP of less than 50% of that, other potential entrants like Albania and Bosnia have GDPs of less than 33% of that average.

By contrast in 2004 the older EU members had GDP of roughly 10 to 20% of each other (with the exception of Luxembourg) so there was little financial gain in moving between countries.

(Source Roger Bootle – The Trouble with Europe Pages 39 and 40 using World Bank and IMF sources)

Population density

Migration watch (Migration watch UK/MW356: Population Density Brief) looked at the density in larger EU Countries in 2012. Netherlands head the list with 497 persons per square kilometre with England second on 410. (Incidentally as of 2013 Wales has 149, Northern Ireland 135 and Scotland 68)

However some countries have a considerably faster population growth than others and on current projections; in 2050 England will become the most densely populated in the EC with over 500 persons just ahead of Belgium, with the Netherlands falling back. France, Germany and Italy will all have a density less than half that of England. On the Eurostat projections the the size of the UK population will overtake that of France by 2030 and Germany in 2050.

Number of illegal immigrants in the UK

The Daily Express (using fullfacts an information gatherer) of 2nd June 2014 suggested 800,000, in the UK.

A Home office Study based on the 2001 census suggested 310,000 to 570,000

A later update of the Home Office figures by the LSE suggested 417,000 to 863,000

Migration Watch later estimated the number as 1,100,000

UKIP's estimate as disclosed in the Daily Express of 28th August 2015 was 1,000,000.

Some suggest that, although Migration Watch itself says that it is strictly neutral, others say it is a right wing pressure group. It's unclear, if that were the case, if that bias would contaminate its statistics and net costs of immigration which appear to be very detailed, or only its rhetoric.

It's impossible to say with certainty how many illegals there are, it's unlikely to be lower than the lowest LSE figure and, due to the ongoing migrant rush to the UK, it could be substantially higher than LSE's highest.

This author goes for a figure between 600,000 and 1,000,000, maybe 750,000, but it is a significant number. (In a TV hustings meeting in 2010 Nick Clegg suggested 1,000,000). By definition these people do not pay taxes since to do so would likely mean exposure and return. A tax benefit of £1bn might accrue if they were to be legalised, on the other hand they don't use public services either and it is probable that these might cost much more, say £3bn, in terms of medical, pensions and social benefits. But it's unclear if the UK might not have to pay those costs anyway. Right now many immigrants are young and fit but as they get older they will need some services, it seems unlikely that we in the UK can or will refuse them? Will we be willing to see illegal immigrants aged 65 and sick with no money, homeless just starve? I think not! So we may have to pay those extra costs anyhow.

The Economist of 13th August 2016 gave details on the negative impact of migrants leaving their home countries, including the fall of 4% in GDP.

Romania's population they suggest declined from 22 million in 2000 to below 20 million today. Most emigrating Romanians went to Italy and Spain.

The Times 'Foreign students are welcome, say overwhelming majority of voters', this revealed that a YouGov poll of 1658 adults indicated that 51% saw foreign students as having a positive impact with only 9% seeing a negative impact. The article also took issue with the government for it failing to release data which showed that only 1% of foreign students here break the terms of their visas by failing to return home after 4 months. Less than expected.

A Mr Kidd of London W4, writing to the Sunday Times 2nd October 2016 did not agree with the proposal the author uses here; saying that 'securing an emergency brake on immigration ….. would have been totally inadequate. Any such break would have been under the control of Brussels'. Calling it a 'pathetic supplication (which) as an act of political courage tells us all we need to know about the weakness of his EU negotiating stance…..'

He's partly right, Sebastian has to make up much lost ground!

Others have questioned why, if the EU refused to negotiate with the UK September 2016 before Article 50, the negotiations in this book could have been possible.

The difference is that in this book the UK was negotiating to stay in, not to get out!

Corrective referenda are not at all unusual, several times countries have used a negative referendum result to go back and renegotiate the terms of an opt out, they hold the referendum again and pass it at the second go; Denmark in 1992 on Maastricht; Ireland in 2001 and 2002 on the Nice Treaty, Ireland in 2008 and 2009 the Treaty of Lisbon. Greek Bailout Referendum but this was overturned by the Greek Parliament. So there is a clear precedent for such bargaining with the EC. Recently Holland at the second go passed bringing associates status to the Ukraine.

Chapter THIRTEEN – European discussions TWO -   TURKEY

The bulk of the information comes direct from the 2004, Commission of the European Communities, 'Issues arising from Turkey's membership perspective' COM(2004) 656 Final.

This makes clear that, if the then current assessment were accepted, then negotiations with Turkey would proceed. It is thus the pivotal document.

Certain information on Turkey's completion of 'acquis' Chapters is taken from a summary of Wikipedia.

Information on Turks in Germany is taken from several sources.

Germany's Turkish-Muslim Integration Problem by Soeren Kern June 24 2016 'gatestoneinstitute.org/8321/germany-turks-integration is based on a statistical survey of Germany Datenreport 2016: Social Report for the Federal Republic of Germany… 'Turkish migrants are poorly integrated' and several similar pages.

Survey shows an alarming lack of integration in Germany, several authors, SPIEGELONLINE 26th Jan 2009.. A Study prepared by the Berlin Institute for Population and development. 'But immigrants from Turkey… are very poorly integrated' … 'they formed ghettos' etc. etc.

Young Turks Increasingly Favour Integration and Religion. SPIELGELONLINE 17th August 2012. (based on interviews with 1011 people). Although this is a more hopeful piece as it suggests that 75% say they want to belong to German society; but it also indicates a trend to radicalisation 'those who identify themselves as strictly religious rising from 33% to 35%' and 'the number who say they eventually plan to return to Turkey has risen from 42% to 45%.

Merkel says German multi-cultural society has failed   17 October 2010, Berlin (AFP) Germany's attempt to create a multi-cultural society has failed, Chancellor Angela Merkel said at the weekend calling on the country's immigrants to learn German and adopt Christian values (the latter seems to this author, a particularly potty idea or at the very least a potty way of trying to explain something)… Merkel spoke after talks with the Turkish Prime Minister in which they pledged to do more to improve the often poor integration of Germany's 2.5 million-strong Turkish community.

Slovakia received in 2015 £485 per head from the EU (House of Commons briefing paper September 22 2016) if applied on admission to 70m Turks in Turkey the cost for the EU would be very substantial.

The Economist of 6th August 2016 'Old Faultlines' suggested 'of the roughly 570,000 German Turks who voted in 2015, 60% chose Mr Erdogan giving him a higher share in Germany than at home, … Relations between the two countries have been deteriorating for months. Since the German Parliament voted in June to call the Turkish massacre of Armenians a century ago as a 'genocide'. Many German politicians now doubt the loyalty of their country's largest minority.'

This author assumes the Germans feel they can do nothing, turning Turkey down would upset the large minority and destabilise the immigrant deal.

Chapter FOURTEEN – European discussions - THREE MILITARY

Excerpts were taken from the following:-

UK Strategic Defence Review of 2015.
Common Security and Defence policy from 'Wikipedia'.
Military of the European union from 'Wikipedia'.
Berlin Plus agreement also from 'Wikipedia'.
UK Defence Spending from the Mirror 3 September 2014.
'These NATO Countries are not spending their fair share on defense' 8 July 2016 – money.cnn.
EPP group position paper of 2016.
Sunday Telegraph 28 August 2016 'RAF takes on bandits over the Baltics'.
Daily Telegraph 15 September 2016 'EU Army Plan sets alarm bells ringing on NATO's front line.'
The Times 'EU Parks its tanks on NATOs lawn…' prior to Bratislava meeting 2016.
The Financial Times 10 July 2016 'Russia attacks NATO's decision to strengthen defences in Poland'.
Euobserver, April 2015 A Rettman 'US says no to Poland for new NATO bases for presence, presence.'
sputniknews 8 October 2015 'US signs Heavy Military Equipment base deal with Poland'.
The Economist of 13th August 2016 ' Go Home Yankee' quotes the number of USA soldiers in Germany and their cost over and above costs as if in the USA.

Chapter SIXTEEN – Euro Discussion FOUR What's wrong with the EC and also Chapter TWENTYONE Euro Discussion SIX Possible Solutions EC.

The main books referred to were;

Roger Bootle 'The trouble with Europe' 2014. Good up to a point and lists reforms needed then just gives up when he realises they are unobtainable. A frequent and probably natural writer for the Daily Telegraph.

Simon Hix 'What's wrong with the European Union & How to fix it'. 2008. Some sensible points but it's not obvious that his solutions would work.

Jean-Claude Piris, Director General of the EU Legal Service 1988-2010 'The future of Europe – towards a Two-Speed EU?' 2012. Sebastian eventually bases his proposal on this, though the book is rather written from the point of view of the Euro Group.

Thomas Piketty 'Chronicles – on our troubled times' 2016

Thomas Piketty 'Capital in the twenty first century' Belknap Press of Harvard University – 2014. The immediate post war growth and forecast from 2012 is to be found on pages 95 to 102.

Vince Cable 'After the Storm' Chapter 4 - The Eurozone 2015

Martin Sandbu 'Europe's Orphan – the future of the Euro and the politics of debt'. It's interesting in that he suggests that the form and structure were not to blame for the disastrous performance of the Euro (unlike Piketty Currency with no State = Disaster) but the problem was the people who drove it.

David Marsh 'The EURO – the battle for the new global currency' He wades through acres of disagreements before the Euro is launched, he sees it 2012 beset in an area from which it simply cannot now escape. Reading this it was impossible to misunderstand the clear fissure between the German and French positions, which German dominance made even more obvious, the tensions between growth rates put huge pressure which would have been possible only by internal currency revaluations, for which there was no mechanism. Though part of Sebastian's 'solution' is based on a throw-away line in the final chapter, splitting the Eurogroup into North (based surely on the old D-Mark) and South.

The main reports used were;

Review of the Balance of Competencies between the UK and EC – Single Market. HMG July 2013. 'It is led by HM Treasury. It is a reflection and analysis of the evidence submitted by the experts, NGOs business people and other interested parties,…, as well as a literature review. Where appropriate, the report sets out the position agreed within the Coalition Government…'

Review of the Balance of Competencies between the UK and EC – Economic & Monetary Policy. HMG December 2014. 'It is a reflection and analysis of the evidence submitted by the experts, NGOs business people MPs and other interested parties,…, as well as a literature review. Where appropriate, the report sets out the position agreed within the Coalition Government…'

Review of the Balances in competencies etc the Single Market, Free movement of Services, same series as the above two.

These three reports were initially to be part of a series prepared by the Government presumably to help provide ideas for David Cameron on his 'EU renegotiation'. This author was unable to find any others so presumes they were later cancelled. They would not have given him much help although undoubtedly accurate and well researched. They did not, as it were, pick up nice juicy points as to how the UK was disadvantaged in the EU, so there is nothing much in these papers which David Cameron could pull out to 'Reform' the EU which appeared to have been his earlier intention.

Lisbon Strategy report of the High Level Group from EC 2004 Under Wm Kok, the former PM of the Netherlands. 'The Group was composed of a limited number of highly qualified individuals able to reflect the views of all stakeholders.

The Lisbon Treaty, 10 easy-to-read factsheet. Foundation Robert Schuman, December 2009.

Discussion on the EURO and trade, Information and excerpts from:

Prof Jeffrey Frankel, Harvard University, 'NBER conference on Europe and the Euro' 17th October 2008.

Mark Havel, Senior Sphister, Trinity College Dublin 'The Euro at 10: its effect on the Eurozone trade'.

Telegraph, Allister Heath 27th August 2014 'The Euro has failed to boost trade between the countries that adopted it.'

Elena Pantelidou EC326 2nd April 2014 'Economics of the EU'.

Francesco Mongelli, 1st May 2010 'Some benefits and costs from participating in a monetary union'.

European Commission 'Why the Euro'.

Juliana and Moise Cindea, Procedia, 8th International Strategic Management Conference. 'The Euro effect on international trade'.

Gianluca Cafiso, European Central Bank working paper no 941 September 2008 'The Euro's influence upon trade – Rose Effect vs Border Effect' Unfortunately Rose's hugely optimistic assessment, had a catastrophic effect, it gave credence to what seemed like a sure fire success, quite why he was not drummed out of his post, is a mystery to this author.

EC File: Intra and Extra EU 28 trade 2015 (imports plus exports)

Economics – Help – Benefits of the Euro.

Tal Sadeh, senior lecturer at Tel Aviv University, blogsies, 'Despite the crisis the euro has more than doubled trade among Eurozone members 2014.

'Europe at a Crossroads? How to achieve efficient economic governance in the Euro area?' March 22nd 2016 Governor of the Bank of France.(suggests an inner core of Eurozone countries cutting out non Eurozone members)

EuroCom, Eurobar 386, A review by the EC 'Europeans and their languages'. Published June 2012, indicated that in 19 of 25 EU states, English was the most wide spoken other language, 67% of Europeans consider English as one of the two most useful languages compared with 17% German and 16% French. English dominates as the foreign language at 38% (three times higher than the next language at 12% French.

BRIC GDP values were taken from Los Angeles Research Group web site which suggested the source as the IMF.

As far as Solutions proposed were;

IIEA The Euro Crisis Ins and Outs – Multispeed Europe Working Paper 3 Dr Paul Gillespie – partly from Irish perspective. (IIEA is based in Dublin)

IIEA European Banking Union, positions as of 2012.

IIEA Legalities of Eurozone Exit giving the view that the only way out of the Euro Group is to exit the EC using Article 50.

IIEA The Euro Crisis The Fiscal Treaty Working Paper 5 Peader o Broin

'Enhanced Cooperation', Wikipedia gives details of several-inter governmental agreements. The device was introduced by the Treaty of Amsterdam as amended by the Treaty of Nice and the Treaty of Lisbon. It was designed to allow those wanting faster travel to do so, these are often later incorporated into Treaty changes. It requires a minimum of 9 member states, it cannot extend the powers beyond the Treaties of the EU. It may not discriminate against member states. It has to be filed with the Commission who have to approve it and it then must pass the QMV. Any one member state may not veto the establishment of such an agreement. Matters previously covered; Divorce Law, Unitary Patent, Property regimes of International couples, Financial transactions tax. There are other arrangements between EU Members. This author found it to be extremely complex to work out which country is within which agreement and why others are not.

An example of the Assembly of the European Regions works to (item 1) 'share experiences and continuously innovate in the public sector'. Reinventing Democracy of 22 June 2016.

Chapter NINETEEN A quick trip to France.

The largest amount of information on Boko Haram, a Sunni, Salafist-jihadi militant Islamist guerrilla Group, comes from views expressed at a Conference, published in April 2014 by the Canadian Security Intelligence Services in Combination with the UK Cabinet Office called 'Political Stability and Security in West and North Africa', it deals with a country by country analysis and particularly with Boko Haram and the various attempts by Nigeria to co-ordinate activities around Lake Chad and ECOWAS. The report also indicates the nature of the heavy handed and arbitrary nature of Nigerian soldiers' control of the local population.

Wikipedia 'Boko Haram', suggests that it is responsible for 20,000 deaths and displacing 2.3 Million of which 250,000 have left Nigeria,

The notion that famine was imminent in the area because of terrorist attacks and lack of NGOs operating there, was taken from The Economist of September 3rd 2016.

The Economist of 20th August 2016 in an article 'The March of Democracy slows' assessing the states where the people live under various bands of 'freedom', categorises Nigeria and Niger as 'partly free' and Chad and Cameroon' as 'Not free'.

The Times of October 14th 2016 reports the exchange, negotiated through the International Red Cross, of 21 of the 219 girls kidnapped by Boko Haram for four Boko Haram commanders. The swap took place near the Cameroon border.

The idea that the UK is intending to establish a base there with the French is unfortunately pure fiction even if it is plain common-sense.

The Times of 6th January 2016 revealed that 'Hollande ordered deaths of 40 jihadists' in Middle East and Africa, using the DGSE. The President and Military want to show that France retaliates against all attacks against its interests and tracks down tirelessly the commanders in order to eliminate them.

Between 2008 and 2013 they captured or killed nearly 100 jihadists in Mauritania, Mali and Niger outside any legal military operation. 'We have neutralised 7 out of 8' leaders of an attack on an oil refinery in Southern Algeria in 2013.

The UN forces in African made up of African Countries' soldiery had a pretty terrible reputation, so for example in 2007 there were hundreds of cases of sexual exploitation and abuse by UN troops while on duty in the areas they were sent to protect. Happily the system and training was steadily improved up to 2014 where the cases were in the dozens.

The UK Government would be aware that the French Government is usually much further advanced in assisting the development of the Francophone Group, for example with commercial contracts than is the UK of its Anglophone former colonies. For example the French Government is presenting a case to COPP 22 the Climate Change Group, on behalf of the African Renewable Energy Initiative covering 17 African countries.

The 'Joint Deal on Drone' was agreed between David Cameron and Francis Hollande, it was for a £1.5 Bn joint investment 'to build a prototype of the next generation of unmanned aircraft' so it seems that the drones are actually larger than one would imagine them to be, so it's a pilotless aircraft with full capabilities. The agreement actually also covered potentially fitting a Brimstone 2 guided missile to its attack helicopter and potentially fitting Aster Block 1 missiles to the UK Type 45 destroyers.

The UN Reform proposal for which Sebastian requests French support comes from a report by Ramesh Thakur, previously a director of the UN Secretariat reported in 'The Japan Times'. The dissatisfaction with the UN structure comes from 'The Hindu' of 28 July 2016. Both Japan and India have been faithful UN members but have been denied positions as Permanent Members, their elevations are opposed respectively by Korea and Pakistan.

A reform of the Security Council was proposed by Kofi Annan in 2005, but all changes have been regularly blocked, the main problem being that the Veto can be arbitrarily used by any one of the big Five (USA, China, France, UK and Russia) which can and does end many initiatives prematurely.

The idea that Hinkley Point will fail is this author's own view, despite it having been initially negotiated by a Lib Dem in the 2010/5 Coalition! In 2016 several power stations using that technology were revealed as being already years behind schedule. The worst case for UK is that not only does it not deliver on time but, when it eventually does, the subsidy will be astronomic. The price will be £92.50 a unit for 35 years (plus inflation) well over the current £35 cost. The estimated capital cost was £18Bn in 2016, any alteration to that contract will immediately result in an international 'incident' as it is being built by France with Chinese money so it will be very difficult to extract the UK from it, even should it be hopelessly out of date and behind hand. The only way out is if France agrees that its design is impossible to deliver – it's never likely to do that. Meanwhile if it is seriously delayed we will run out of electricity. Of course the price of oil and therefore energy has dropped 50% since the contract was first considered.

This author believes the likelihood of UK receiving Electricity on time and at cost is extremely remote. Compare instead what the UK might have done in getting a wave machine into operation. Let's put it this way, can you seriously believe that if we were prepared to push £18 Bn of research into its development we couldn't invent a world design beater? (before the Chinese do). Has the Pelamis, the Scottish Wave Power prototype lingering through lack of funds, been copied by the Chinese? (Times 11th October 2016)

Chapter TWENTY – How the German motor industry coped with change

The chunk of this chapter is based on a paper prepared in Spring 2014 for Maison des Sciences de L'Homme – Paris/Nord by Martin Krzywdzinski (Revue de la Reculation).

Supporting information on the current 2015 German Auto Industry, numbers of units etc, comes from. 'Industry Overview' The Automotive Industry in Germany, by 'Germany Trade & Invest' a foreign trade and inward investment agency of the Federal Republic of Germany, supported by The Federal Ministry of Economic Affairs.

Dates of EC enlargements from Wikipedia,

JLR's determination to proceed with an electric car was announced by The Times of Saturday November 26th 'Jaguar plans 10,000 jobs in electric car revolution'. They also indicate that that the R & D capability is based in the UK.

Chapter TWENTY-ONE – EC Solutions.

This Chapter was originally part of the main Book but was taken out as it severely distracted from the narrative of the story. What it does is to respond to the queries and proposals made in the 'What's wrong' section and the reader can see here exactly how these points are treated.

So let's pick out what we have discussed?

First as we saw Turkey is a problem, logically it should be excluded from the enlargement process because it's so large and different, but no-one dares to do that because of the possible downside, specifically to Germany.

Next we saw that there seems to be an increasing desire within the EU for a common Defence Policy, the UK has done its best to block this to the frustration of its friends, allies and foes in the EU. In my opinion its unsustainable and it's an area where the UK could gain considerable kudos by encouraging it to happen but in doing so making sure the the USA in adequately involved in the overall structure.

For most of the rest, we have to work out a) what we can actually change, b) which are a high priority for the UK and c) what other changes within the EU we would encourage.

Let's first consider the comments of the three experts;

Roger Bootle appears to be in favour of reform when he lists the 'requirements for fundamental reform which he says is partly based on David Cameron's speech at Blomberg on 23 January 2013, these are:

Competitiveness At heart must be the single market including services, energy and digital coming under a Single Market Council (both agree)

Trade deals to be completed with US, Japan and India (agreed)

Smallest companies in the EC should eventually be exempt from further directives from the EC because the cost stifles young innovative and creative start-ups. (we need some exemption somehow?)

The Commission's budget should be reduced (yes but what logic do we use, shouldn't we challenge them more on their poor performance?)

Flexibility The EC should encompass countries with different levels of Integration, which appears to mean a multispeed EC (agreed – this is the basis of Sebastian's arguement)

Transfer Powers back to member states recognising that not everything needs to be harmonised (yes we have to test some items and fight for change)

National Leaders should remain accountant able to their national parliaments which should have a bigger role. (yes we need a list of what the EC will not do?)

Any new (structural?) arrangements should should work fairly from those members states whether they are in the Eurozone or not. (agreed otherwise multi stage will not work)

There is no reason why the single market and single currency should comprise the same countries. (agreed)

There are suggestions of the 'Fresh Start' British MPs as;

An emergency brake regarding future EU legislation affecting Financial Services (not clear why? Iut needs opening up further!)

A repatriation of EC competencies in the area of social and employment law back to member states (but not at the expense of downgrading personal benefits and rights, this is probably designed to reduce things like paternity leave?)

An opt-out from EC Policing and Criminal Justice not already covered in existing opt-outs (not clear why?)

Safeguard for single market, so there's no discrimination of non-Eurozone members (agreed)

Abolition of Strasbourg as an alternate seat and end to Economic and Social Committee and Committee of the Regions. (OK but it's just a thorn without this what would the UK press do? Have to go into real EU detail mi oh my!, not a real problem)

Bootle toys with the idea of having a core and outsiders or an outer ring of non-Eurozone states (agreed).

Ultimately he suggests that these reforms are unachievable basically because such a development 'would effectively tear up the legal basis of the EC and require a new set of treaties, which would be a nightmare if not downright impossible to renegotiate' (we hope not)

Simon Hix's solution is completely different, he sees the fundamental problem as a lack of democratic politics in the EU. So he wants a fight out between, Socialists, Conservatives and Liberals. (its not clear what the result would be? As there is no such platform – let's say Socialists won and tried to drive for an even more worker friendly set of rules and lets say this was contrary to the UK government's view – that would simply add further muddle and contempt. It would appear that could only arrive AFTER a federal structure were in place and there was some real political concensus)

President of EP elected for 5 years (doubling the term) (possibly – not clear what that would do? Schmultz did not improve matters and doesn't seem to understand the problems at all!)

Changing the method of allocating committee chairs to give more chairs to stronger parties (seems odd as the MEPs don't have a common average voter per MEP, this might make it even more cockeyed)

Make all the Council's documentation public and open deliberation to public (why not? It seems probable that this would have more fully disclosed the French/German battles before the Euro and explained why the structure was so weak that it collapsed at the first rough patch. Sebastian uses this lack of openness and clarity to throw back 'secrecy' at the leaders)

Restrict the right to propose amendments to the Council to a minimum number (not clear of benefit)

Put all legislative decisions to a in the Council to a public vote (which public? how? Might cause even worse chaos if national votes gave different results?)

Allow rival candidates for commission president to be proposed by groups BEFORE EP elections (it's not at all clear, that this would help, it might create another battleground)

Make these candidates set out their 5 year programme 'manifesto' (OK but it's the President who runs things?)

Hold live debates between rival candidates (yes good idea, but for what exactly? If they don't then form a 'government')

Allow manifesto commitments of the winner to guide Commission portfolios (maybe)

Jean-Claude Piris is yet again completely different he concludes the major problems are;

The depth of the EU's current crisis and the difficulty in solving it is due to the EU being confronted with 3 fundamental issues;

the crisis due to the euro areas imbalances;
the political gap between the EU and public opinion and;
the dysfunctionality of the decision-making.

He concludes that the Lisbon Treaty Reforms did not go far enough

(well it sounds interesting?)

He offers in effect four solutions

Substantial revision of the existing treaties (but that needs referenda majorities which no one can be certain of?)

Continue on the current path, which already provides differentiation, opt outs, co-operation, strengthening efforts to solve the euro crisis and using the treaties provisions on enhanced co-operation more frequently (yes we agree)

Move to a 2 speed EU in two formats, softer, or bolder (yes we agree)

In addition we should perhaps consider a Paper prepared by eminent EU thinkers under the chairmanship of Guthram Wolff a Director of the Bruegel Group in the Summer of 2016. It was written in the expectation of the UK Brexit but the suggestions are still important. The main themes were;

The proposed a new form of collaboration called a 'continental partnership'

The UK would have some control over labour mobility without the EU's supranational decision-making (yes why not?)

There would continue to be a market in goods, services, capital mobility and temporary labour mobility (yes agreed)

There would be a new system of intergovernmental decision-making and enforcement of common rules to protect the homogeneity of the deeply integrated market (yes agreed)

The UK would have some say but ultimate formal authority would rest with the EU ('suppose so?)

This would result in an inner circle the EU with deep and political integration (yes)

An outer circle with less integration which could develop into a method for handling Turkey, Ukraine and other Countries. (yes)

Solution to the single Market slow down.

There is a solution. Britain has been the biggest champion of driving the single market deeper and wider. There is an opportunity here for the UK to drive this forwards and turn the EC's eyes away from catchy changes which often do more damage when getting headlines than the rather more boring and tedious work of nailing down common qualifications for architects at the same time we can ensure that our own Financial Services are properly identified and registered to prevent longer term copying of skills by those with no qualifications. The English language gives us considerable advantage – it's the most popular language used in the EU after the mother tongue. The imminent report, Sebastian, on the City might help to establish new standards. So there is still a lot move efficiency to squeeze out of the EU, much of potential gain for the UK into the future. But as the Economist says 16th July 2016 'momentum has stalled'. (OK)

Solution – Country Interest Differentials

There is a solution; to 'mutualise the debt' create Eurobonds, move away from country specific bonds with variable interest rates, however unless there is control of the issue of such bonds, Germans might fear that other countries will just continue spending as before, so that will compel a Federal Authority to take control, in effect creating a Federal Finance Ministry which in turn will lead directly to further integration and political union. (Hmmh under German Rules?)

Problem Germany's Trade Surplus - Solution.

There is here a solution too, Germany (for Germany read any other surplus Euro country) must, in effect, be persuaded to buy Greek (for Greek read any other EU deficit country) factories, Greek plant, Greek equipment, have longer Greek holidays, station troops there buying Greek goods and services or open a naval base or as possibly for Germany to finance development banks there. They will also have to increase wages in Germany and spend, spend, spend.
Unfortunately this hits at the bedrock of the German psyche drummed into every German in the wake of the second world war, spend prudently, save, produce efficiently, balance their books and try to oblige the Greeks to do the same.   There is evidence that wages in Greece are declining whilst those in Germany are increasing. This in effect mirrors the effect of a Greek devaluation but it has been a painful process.   (yes but how to persuade the Germans?)

On Sebastian's interventions generally.

It's not unusual to want to create attention by bringing on ideas. Sebastian's idea of course is to have a continuous flow of discussions and ideas, the basis of a radical approach, so that it is seem as a party of, or factory of, ideas. In 'Call me Dave' Ashcroft & Oakshot recall page 385 'In the early years of Cameron's leadership, Hilton had been the energy and originality in the top team, injecting a constant flow of fresh, zany ideas designed to wow voters.'

Chapter TWENTY-THREE – The Train Trip

This is where this author has to be much more careful, criticism of a party or nation or a department of government, like the prison service is fair game but dealing with a 'live' powerful company with 'live contracts' and a reputation to protect, is potentially much more hazardous from a legal point of view. Whilst it's possible to fictionalise members of the public, how they might react to situations of overcrowding and even put in replacement politicians, it's legally dangerous to simulate conversations with real directors of a real company, even with made up directors of a 'new co' if it's intended to be simply a cover. This is what this author was intending to do. That is to fictionalise a discussion with a director of Go-Ahead which is the real owner of 65% of 'Southern'. The main problem is that the author cannot access the actual franchise documents – the web-site just goes blank and says 'cannot download as parts missing' which, as will be seen, is crucial to the discussion. So it's difficult to get inside the problem, which is to judge to what extent did the new franchisee acknowledge the existing overcapacity and what future growth did it use to estimate new carriages needed and new timetable to accommodate it? An option might have been for this author to fictionalise a Rail Operator but that would be to deny that there is a real problem and would also mean not being able to use the data or the press cuttings available. As a lesser option this author felt obliged to use the data and use the hapless Transport Minister as the punch bag, thus ensuring that all discussions are at one remove from reality. Problems from 2016 are therefore here simulated forward into 2020 as if no changes are made by Govia; given that the Thameslink 2000, north-south cross London project, was 18 years late that does not sound too pessimistic.

The selection by this author of that trip and that time was partly due to a 'Seat on the train' feature in 'Times2' which highlighted the interplay between house prices and journey times into London. House prices fall from £741,919 in Central London to £294,903 an hour outside the capital. (An annual rail season ticket would in comparison cost around £6,000). The article (Sunday Times of 2nd October 2016) quotes the 7.00 am (actually it's appears to be the 6.57 train) Govia Thameslink service from Brighton to Bedford as the most overcrowded service last year, with 513 'excess passengers a day'. It appears to this author as a rather odd service, but it's the Brighton to London bit that's over capacity. So this assumes that the whole train empties itself in London, and proceeds north to Bedford. At that time it would, one assumes, be nearly empty anyhow.

An article in the Daily Telegraph of 28th July 2016 states that the train 'is designed to carry 420 passengers but regularly crammed 960 on board during a 'typical weekday.' It gives a photo of an overcrowded compartment which the author used for the description in the text. That article goes on to state 'It comes after MPs expressed fury with Govia Thameslink Railway'.. and 'suggested it was not 'fit' to operate Southern rail'. Passengers suffered months of delays, cancellations and station overcrowding. The real Lib Dem spokesperson said 'We would not treat animals like this, so how can we treat commuters like this? The Government needs to put passengers at the heart of their franchise'.

The Department of Transport, Railways have a frequent 'Statistical Release' the one used for data below is dated 28th July 2016, and it is actually very detailed and well presented. This reveals a 'PiXC' factor which it defines as passengers in excess of capacity = the proportion of standard class passengers that are above the capacity on their service at its busiest point. The numbers on each service are added together and shown as a % of standard class passengers on all peak services. The capacity includes all standard class seats and also included a standing allowance if passengers are standing for 20 minutes or less. This implies that overcapacity is the number over and above that normal standing allowance (which is not quantified).

The statistics suggest a 5% increase in passenger journeys over the last year into London. London and the South East accounted for a massive 70% of all train journeys. Govia carried 327 million people. 'In 2015 London saw just over 1 million passengers (581,400 in the 3 hour peak) arriving into the City Centre on a typical day'. Ten times the arrivals at next nearest large City, Birmingham. In numbers, 155,000 passengers had to stand on trains arriving in London during that peak. The report says dryly 'the worsening crowding levels show that capacity provision is not coping with rising levels of passenger demand'. London Bridge had the largest number of passengers arriving in the morning peak accounting for 24% of all London stations. London Blackfriars had the largest % of crowding of all major London Stations with 14.7% PiXC

The PiXC for London and the South East operations is 5.9%. This author's note – though the actual effect on some journeys may be a lot worse than this; because the 'peak' covers a period of 3 hours from 7.00 am to 9.59 am but within that the 8.00 am to 8.59 am overcrowding is very much worse, there is capacity in the 9.00 am to 9.59 am which is, in effect, netted off against the earlier hours PiXC.(Times are arrival times into London – NOT the setting off times from the country stations).

'The travellers on Southern Rail face 14 days of strikes' (Times 23rd September 2016) the walk-outs are in protest at the move towards driver only operated trains on Govia network.

'Southern promises rail revolution (in 2018) (Times 20th September 2016). Thousands more seats on busy services at peak times are being promised' 'We are proposing a complete redesign of the timetable'. Govia has experienced months of delays and cancellations caused by strikes over changes to the role of conductors and high levels of staff sickness.

'A third of rail passengers are dodging their fares. (Times 24th September 2016) costing the rail industry as much as £200 M a year.

'Southern Rail owners reveal profits of £100 M after months of cancellations. (Times 3rd September 2016) .. posting a 27% profit increase and raising its dividend by 6.5%. The Go-Ahead group owns 65% of Govia the franchisee. Tim Faron, the Lib Dem Leader, branded the results a 'national scandal – it's the ugly face of capitalism getting government cash one day then creaming in massive profits the next.' The company has cancelled hundreds of trains a day to cope with staff shortages and increased sickness.

'Folding seats offer solution to railway overcrowding (Times 21st September 2016) – could be incorporated into existing commuter trains within a year. The flip up seat results in an increase in capacity of 15 to 20%. There's also a super-skinny seat which allows for 30% more rows of seats. Design costs of this was £900,000. This article also quotes the spokesman of 'railfuture' as saying 'the bottom line is that most people want a comfortable seat', presumably that's a joke? – any seat would do? – any comfortable standing space would do? Go Ahead just wants a good bottom line! Ha! (that's this author's joke!)

An even more brilliant idea thought up by this author; why not have poles, hanging straps and bum pads as suggested, then forget seats! Stick a weight load limit indicator monitor by the door so there's a carriage limit, introduce air-con and ticker tape style news screens, plenty of radio points for ear plug ins and you are nearly there. At least if you are obliged to stand why not make it bearable? After all just gutting an existing carriage and gutting it can't be that difficult? Maybe launching a standing only ticket price on specific trains would be possible and at least reduce the pain in the pocket?

'Investors pour £12 bn into roads and railways' (Sunday Times 18th September 2016) an example was quoted 'Sources inside L & G said it had £7 Bn to spend in the next two years which comes from an existing £15 Bn infrastructure fund'.

The Department for Transport has a 'Single departmental plan 2015 – 2020' published on 19th February 2016. The 'Vision … to make journeys better, simpler, faster, more reliable.' Objective 3 is to 'Improve journeys'. Whilst HS2 is mentioned at least a dozen times, there is nothing about the dreadful overcrowding. Most of the 'opportunity' stuff relates to building the 'Northern Powerhouse' and it suggests that 'Economic growth has been too dependent on London'. But they claim 'We are improving the travel experience.'

This author adds, it smugly claims that '83% of passengers (are) satisfied with their journey in autumn 2015' – see they too can write novels! Presumably they avoided the service Sebastian tested! However the basic problem with the plan is the failure to understand that in the Midlands and North the dominant transport system is the Car and Motorway, whilst in the South East it's the Railway network, they are indeed independent pools. In the South several millions of people are dependent on one poorly performing operator – railways are much less flexible than roads – in the South, the tension in the system is thus borne by the poor long suffering passengers. Some of these passengers give up jobs or withdraw from urgent medical care because the railway service is unreliable. Yet nothing is done!

There isn't an integrated Transport Plan for the South East, (the Regions were disbanded as one of their first acts of the Coalition in 2010/11). There are bits and pieces covering various towns and LEDs and for different types of transport, so it's impossible to see if there are any alternatives Brighton to London eg buses and what the estimated capacities are that were used for infrastructure planning. It's difficult to describe it in any other way but a terrible shambles.

The Economist of 3rd September 2016 mentions 'overcrowded trains travelling into London' and the severe effect of the reduction of public-sector net investment. From 'Right kind of budget' and 'The government calculated that the cost-benefit ratio for expanding rail capacity on existing lines was almost 50% higher than for building HS2' From 'Infrastructure – Ropey roads, rail and runways'.

His later visit to see his son and discussions with mathematical and behavioural experts suggests that he has however come to the wrong solution and doubling trains would be better – keep the guards double the trains.

Notes on purpose of these interventions generally.

These are Sebastian's attempts to draw the press away from his weakness in stand-up debates in the House of Commons where he's concerned he will be exposed by Conservative backbenchers he cannot control, so instead he exploits his position drawing attention to other issues.

It's not unusual in political terms to want to create attention by bringing on ideas. Sebastian's idea of course is to have a continuous flow of discussions and ideas, the basis of a radical approach, so that it is seem as a party of, or factory of, ideas.

He then uses these items to run up through the Lib Dems topical debates to broaden the intellectual capacity away from the mind-numbing 'filling the pot-holes, emptying the   bin' content of Focus, the all pervading Lib Dem doorstep newsletters.

In 'Call me Dave' Ashcroft & Oakshot recall page 385 'In the early years of Cameron's leadership, Hilton had been the energy and originality in the top team, injecting a constant flow of fresh, zany ideas designed to wow voters.'

Chapter – TWENTY-FOUR – Interventions – ONE – Selection of Archbishop of Canterbury and Christian belief in the UK

There is a Privy Counsellors' Oath which Sebastian by now would have had to have assented to, see below. Apparently its existence and wording was only revealed in 1964, so it's quite possible that all PMs might have an additional special oath which has not been made public.

'You do swear by Almighty God to be a true and faithful Servant unto the Queen's Majesty, as one of Her Majesty's Privy Council. You will not know or understand of any manner of thing to be attempted, done, or spoken against Her Majesty's Person, Honour, Crown, or Dignity Royal, but you will lett and withstand the same to the uttermost of your Power, and either cause it to be revealed to Her Majesty Herself, or to such of Her Privy Council as shall advertise Her Majesty of the same. You will, in all things to be moved, treated, and debated in Council, faithfully and truly declare your Mind and Opinion, according to your Heart and Conscience; and will keep secret all Matters committed and revealed unto you, or that shall be treated of secretly in Council. And if any of the said Treaties or Counsels shall touch any of the Counsellors, you will not reveal it unto him, but will keep the same until such time as, by the

Consent of Her Majesty, or of the Council, Publication shall be made thereof. You will to your uttermost bear Faith and Allegiance unto the Queen's Majesty; and will assist and defend all Jurisdictions, Pre-eminences, and Authorities, granted to Her Majesty, and annexed to the Crown by Acts of Parliament, or otherwise, against all Foreign Princes, Persons, Prelates, States, or Potentates. And generally in all things you will do as a faithful and true Servant ought to do to Her Majesty. So help you God.'

This is largely about secrecy rather than duties to be performed and in what spirit.

Several Republicans notably, recently John McDonnell, the Shadow Chancellor have subordinated themselves to this Oath. As the Tories joked at his expense 'another sort of little red book!' Referring obliquely to his attachment to Mao's Little Red Book.

The parts concerning Ministerial Code of Conduct come from 'The Cabinet Manual' 1st edition 2011, prepared by Sir Gus O'Donnell, Cabinet Secretary, item 3.46

On a new set of 10 commandments:- There are several people who have attempted to devise codes for life guidance. One of these is 'The Universal Moral Code', by Kent Keith.

Information on Church attendances come from the C of E's own statistics – 'religious trends'

Procedures for the appointment of an Archbishop also comes from the Church of England web site

The C of E has a '£72 M programme for renewal and reform' per The Guardian Feb 17th 2016

The Economist of August 13th 2016 gives examples of churches closing etc. in their article 'Britain is unusually irreligious, and becoming more so. That calls for a national debate.'

The Times December 23rd 2016 'Belief in God slumps after turbulent year' Suggests that those who don't believe there is a God increased to 38% (up from 33%) with only 28% believing there is a God (down from 32%) from a YouGov poll of 1,595 adults.

The note about Gordon Brown's suggested reforms of 2007 came from Wikipedia 'appointment of Church of England Bishops'.

David Cameron appeared to be a rather more traditional Christian, 'I am a typical Church of Englander and I believe that there is a power greater than us and the life and work of Jesus Christ is an important guide to morality and action, but went on to describe himself as a 'racked-with-doubt-and-scepticism believer'. To many observers, his faith is primarily cultural. One theologian argues that Cameron has 'lectured' the Archbishop of Canterbury to be liberal on homosexuality and told the Pope to alter Roman Catholic moral teaching to permit contraception and abortion. Cameron actively supported Gay Marriage much to the surprise and annoyance of many Tory Constituency Chairmen. From 'Call me Dave'. The unauthorised biography of David Cameron. Bb 2016..

Chapter TWENTY-FIVE – visit to community and ethnic schools and a Muslim suburb.

The Junior school was based on Greenfields Community School based in the Meadows Nottingham and the information was taken from its Web Site, as it says not only was it rated 'outstanding' by Ofsted but 'Best school in Nottingham' by the Nottingham Post.

The Senior school is based on Tauheedul Islam Girls High School based in Blackburn. It has girls from 11 to 16 it says 'mainly from Indian but also Pakistani heritage' so it seems illogical to have 'Islam' in the title – that's baffling, but the comments are from the Ofsted report.

The poorly rated school is based on Jamia Al-Hudaa Residential College, which seems to have two units, in Sheffield probably Secondary and, the Primary School in Nottingham. The school appears to have been downgraded by Ofsted as 'Inadequate', some pupils calling it 'utterly cruel' this excerpt from the National Secular Society 8th Sept 2015

The bulk of Sebastian's questions are from a reading of the 'Casey Review - A review into opportunity and integration' dated December 2016. In this author's opinion it is a brilliant paper, perhaps pulling its punches in places. It was immediately derided as being anti-Asian or anti–Pakistani. It's simply the result of lots of data, quite brilliant. Go read it yourself!

Sebastian's experiences in Northern Ireland, and the cultural divide there, are dealt with in the first Sebastian book. His other comments on Muslims are from Sebastian, the first book.

A main concern of all UK politicians in granting licences to 'faith schools' was the problem disclosed in the Birmingham 'Trojan Horse' where several 'plotters' were said to have imposed an 'intolerant and aggressive Islamic ethos' in 6 non-faith schools which had allegedly been taken over by governors wanting to oust the heads and impose a hard-line Muslim agenda. These were then placed in special measures, as of writing hearings are proceeding that might mean the 5 plotters may be unable to teach, at least one of these seems totally unrepentant seeking to reduce the syllabus in line with 'conservative Islamic teaching. Sunday Times 1st January 2017 happily amplified by that on 6th January, revealing that anonymity previously given to witnesses may now be broken as names and evidence is revealed of the whistleblowers, some of whom had been subjected to intimidation, death threats or even lost their jobs.

Chapter TWENTY-SIX – Interventions TWO - the Elgin Marbles.

The Description of the Elgin marbles and Caryatid were taken from 'Treasures of the British Museum, edited by Sir Frank Francis KCB, a former Director and Principal Librarian of the British Museum.

The Bill referred to is 'Parthenon Sculptures (Return to Greece) Bill – a private member's Bill.

The dates of the Bill are as shown in the lists of Bills 2016-17 published by Parliament.

The % shown was an Ipsos-Mori Poll for the Times reported by the Independent July 2016.

Of course this author does not know if this was successful in 2017 but Private Members' Bills rarely are, since if the Government of the day had wished it to succeed they would probably have taken it over which is what in effect Sebastian is doing.

Chapter TWENTY-SEVEN – Interventions THREE -Whose right to die?

'Debating the right to die and assisted suicide: key issues for the 2015 Parliament' from the parliament UK website. Lord Falconer's Private Members' Bill 'Assisted Dying Bill' – it did not progress beyond committee stage in the Lords.

Assisted Death in Europe and America; Four Regimes and Their Lessons by Guenter Lewy, This is the main source..

Philip Nietsche 'How the face of voluntary euthanasia campaign became its outcast' experience of Northern Territory in Australia.

Belgian Act on Euthanasia of May 28th 2002.

The guardian 'What if Parliament were to follow the advice of right-to-die campaigners and legalise assisted dying?' July 2016

'Assisted Dying' The Humanist Association website extract.

'Dignity in Dying Poll' 11-19th March 2015 by 'Populus' 10 pages

The Economist August 6th 2016 'the right to die 'What is unbearable?'' survey of 180 patients at a Philadelphia Hospital.

Chapter TWENTY-EIGHT – Interventions FOUR – CEO pay and Performance.

The main supporting evidence comes from 'No Routine Riches – reforms to Performance Related pay' it's a damning report, published by the 'High Pay Centre' dated May 2015. It calls itself an independent non-party think tank. Like most who get into the detail they find that the correlation between pay and performance is incredibly weak, however they are not really able to say STOP it! as it would end their ability to later review anything, so in this paper they rather despairingly propose some changes that might improve the connection. Some of those items are taken up to show that not only might there be a conflict between the targets on which the CEO is paid and the desired results, but also between that and what the Government wants.

This author believes that there is a clear disconnect Industry/Government. Take the most basic, most famous Guru, Porter and his 5 forces. It's about getting into a position where the company concerned dominates a niche and controls buyers, suppliers and where the number of players in that niche are limited, all designed to reduce competition and to use that to improve profits and prevent others getting into that niche using patents and any other devices. The British Government wants industry to invest heavily in new equipment and products, create improved productivity, enabling it to compete in foreign markets, train staff to get world class managers in technologically advanced world sized companies, innovate products, expand the markets rather than consolidate, increase healthy competition, use and bring on other UK suppliers, export.

This author has picked up most of the criticisms in the 'high pay centre' paper and presented it in a confrontational way to make the narrative better and bring in the element of conflict.

'Executive Pay – the problem with Agency Theory' by Alexander Pepper. 7th July 2014.

UK Corporate Governance Code April 2016 Financial Reporting Council. This lays down the rules of, for example, the remuneration committee and does suggest that performance related pay should 'promote long term success of the company' but it says nothing about whether Performance Related pay is desirable or effective..

'Pay Ratios just do it' By Paul Marsland High Pay Centre CEP ration as Multiple of Average Employee earnings come from page 48

'Directors' Remuneration' Cranfield School of Management 2004 Dr Ruth Bender to whom I am also indebted for introduction to all the above articles and papers in this Chapter.

Also Guardian article April 18th 2016 'Sir Marin Sorrell defends £63 M pay package ahead of AGM.'

'CEO and their Salaries' article in daily telegraph by Alistair Osborne Jan 1012

Chapter TWENTY-NINE – Interventions FIVE 'A UK version of Posada or Parador Group'.

Sunday Telegraph 30th October 2016 'Last Chance to save Wentworth'

Posadas de Portugal – Wikipedia

Parador - Wikipedia

Chapter THIRTY – Interventions SIX 'Productivity is Everything.'

The main data and statistics are taken from a House of Commons, Library, Briefing Paper Number 06492 of 9th September 2016 'Productivity in the UK.'

A couple of items on the list of possible reasons were also taken from Vince Cable's 'After the Storm' pages 198 to 200, there it is termed the 'productivity puzzle'.

The Sunday Telegraph of 30th October 2016 suggested 'Finding ways to boost productivity is seen as the holy grail for boosting living standards and growth.'

Chapter THIRTY-TWO - The Royal Commission on Banking and Financial Services

Of course there was no real Royal Commission on Banking and Financial Services so this Chapter is fictional. It's something that aggressive Lib Dem

MPs might well have pushed for. It's likely it would have faced the same sort of 'brush off' as I indicate here although the Royal Commission would not have been so blunt, nor would the banks have been outright obstructionist as they are shown to be here, for dramatic effect. Very occasionally the Financial Press themselves wonder how the banks escaped being pilloried and they sometimes do a 'where are they now?', following the careers of the several directors of the large Bank Corporations which crashed. Most lefter-winged parties wanted them exposed. It must be said that it's probably quite difficult to go back more than a decade, responsibilities would have changed, staff would have switched between banks, the organisational structures would have changed, ring-fencing has altered responsibility reporting, moreover it would have almost certainly gobbled up huge amounts of Bankers, Lawyers and Police time.

Some of the comments in this chapter are based on comments from Vince Cables book 'After the Storm' particularly chapter 10 British Banking after the Banking crash.

One of the 'massive frustrations' was, he says, the failure of the system...... to lay a finger on the most egregarious villains of the banking crisis' (page 253) He elaborates this 'It is striking that,…,virtually no banker has gone to jail and few have been financially penalized.' (page 265) and 'There has been a lot of sound and fury, but so far little pain to those who directly caused the disaster' (page 266). 'Mr Carney's launch of the Fair and Effective Markets Review was intended to establish senior executives personal responsibility for their banks but it will rely on voluntary, not legal, enforcement.'

He says 'With hindsight, however, it was a mistake not to have had a full judicial inquiry which could have produced a definitive set of conclusions.'

He quotes the UK Financial Services sector at 8% GDP in 2000 but that grew to 12% in the following decade, out of proportion of that in most other countries.

He mentions the 'disconnect between the financial sector and the domestic economy, (created) a dual economy enclave'.

He bemoans that the cross party agreement for senior bank executives to be made responsible – but the proposal is 'now to be weakened' 'Other rules like extending the application of the Bribery Act to the sector, have been shelved'.

'Greater stability through raising capital, has been bought at the expense of lending to smaller companies…' resulting in more lending to operations with underlying assets like bricks and mortar.'

He mentions 'living wills' to convert debt into equity to better absorb losses in crisis conditions, as being required but not yet done. This author did not pursue this particular avenue.

He lists the various problems PPI, swaps etc. suggesting these are 'inherent in the business model used by the leading banks.'

He mentions the EU interventions on bonuses as 'counterproductive'.

In concluding the chapter 'There are tentative signs of a change in banking culture towards more socially responsible behaviour but there is a vast legacy problem of miss-selling and abuse… and the Conservative government has drawn a line under attempts to impose bank 'culture'. (page 273).

The names given to 'toxic assets' sold as a bundle, came from an article in The Economist of January 25th 2013, having seemingly named that particular batch as 'Shitbag' it was then renamed and sold to a Chinese Bank, it seems they thought they all knew it was rubbish but decided to carry on till they were stopped, like stupid schoolkids, which of course is what they were!

The Code of Professional Conduct is that of the Institute of Chartered Bankers issued dated January 2016. It doesn't strike this author as being very testing but the terms are defined elsewhere.

Sebastian deals with the development of more local investment banking for smaller businesses such as the Handelsbanken and British Business Banks and Catapults in the final stages of the Consolidated Constitutional and Regional Devolution bill.

On 15th September 2016 the Times reported that an 'Ex-Barclays currency trade sues the bank for unfair dismissal' he was fired but never charged. It seems very likely that individuals would have reacted strongly if they were to have been named in the fictional Royal Commission report.

The Times of September 14th 2016 tracked the careers of those involved in the Lloyds Bank/HBOS take over, these included Eric Daniels, Sir Victor Blank, Jan du Plessis, Helen Weir, Archie Kane, Tim Tookey, Martin Scicluna, Lord Leitch, Dame Carolyn McCall. They all deserve to be remembered and as Patrick Hosking wrote 'What rankles is that for the most part, none of them has ever publicly acknowledged it was a mistake.'

In an article 'Insolvency experts to be quizzed over fees fraud' former employees of P & A partnership were to be interviewed by HMRC following whistleblowers reports of falsifying billable hours and of 'time-dumping' falsely claiming work done on insolvency cases.

In an article 'What's wrong with Bankers? Money.' Julian Birkinshaw ridiculed Barclays for hiring a top lawyer to review the banks corporate culture. 'The problem here is not Barclays, it's the entire investment banking industry. The underlying problem, of course, is money. If you pay big individual bonuses, you get results. You also get a toxic corporate culture'.

There are so many examples of banker self-enrichment that they appear in the Press almost every week. The Times of November 12th 2016, revealed 'that three City workers were said yesterday to have been arrested as part of an investigation into alleged insider trading' this seems to have resulted from the leaked 'Panama Papers', this would be the second operation since the conclusion of the £13 M insider-dealing ring which lead to the convictions of several senior City bankers.

The Sunday Times of November 13th ran an articles 'Huge scale of insider Bank fraud revealed' they suggested that about 50 instances of fraud are reported to the police every year, with a loss of £27 M but but also that banks are hiding the full impact of the number of people they employ who are helping to fuel Britain's fraud epidemic.

This author is surprised that The Sunday Times is surprised. First you hire bosses on bonuses which everyone regards as not justified (except of course to the Boards and to the shareholders who are anything but disinterested or an objective assessment body); you see Directors walking away with careers intact having been directly involved in ridiculous take overs; hardly anyone is brought to book who individually or as a group nearly bankrupted the country, who allow dozens of rotten practices mostly at the expense of their own clients with no comebacks, probably keeping their rotten ill-gotten bonuses, allowing massive managers' bonuses which banks are not willing to own up to or justify in terms of profits earned. And what? Complain about junior staff who earn say £500 by handing a few confidential details each to crooked outsiders? Nobody suggests the bankers earn the huge wages they are paid, it's just that one other equally rubbish bank is prepared to pay more for that manager's employment!

The problem mostly comes from the usual business assumption that banking is not a zero sum game, if you make cars or industrial products for example, you can always improve or develop the products and sell a better or differentiated one, but with money, the pound is a commodity just as gas or electricity. In most cases then, dressing a financial deal in package is a zero sum game, if there is some little additional item, like guaranteed lower interest or deferred covenant then it can only be obtained by reducing the benefit to the other party, to squeeze something additional comes at the expense of somebody else, that and the issue of asymmetric power, where banks sell products to uninformed customers, makes the banking industry abnormally open to abusing its power in any transaction for the benefit of the bank and, if they are on a bonus, for themselves as individuals.

The Economist does not agree with this author, in an article of May 1st 2015 'What's wrong with finance'. They suggested that 'the best hope for progress (in the balance between economics or financial theory) is the school of behavioural economics, which understands that individuals cannot be the rational actors who fit neatly into academic models. More economists are accepting that finance is not a 'zero sum gain', not indeed a mere utility, but an important driver of economic cycles. Indeed, finance has become too dominant a driver.'

The information on Banks bonuses paid comes from an article in the Guardian (date unknown).

Further information on earnings was published by the group 'CITYA.M' This revealed in an article dated 13th May 2016 that the highest earning specialists in Banking were M & A Bankers who earned Salary of £178 K and bonus of £148 K = £326 K, whereas a 'Trader' would earn Salary of £161 K and bonus of £120 K = £281 K. In further revelation dated 20th May 2016 it showed that Associates – presumably below Director level, earned from £100 K, to £110 K, whilst MDs earned from about £400 K to £900 K.

Accounting Web of 4th August 2014 disclosed that a survey of the top firms of Solicitors and Accountants; Of the 4,500 equity partners (2,726 accountants and 1,774 lawyers) analysed, average pay in 2013 was £700 K for accountants and £1,100 K for lawyers.

CITYA.M revealed that Fund Managers earnings were; Associates £75 K, VP's £100 K, Directors £180 K, MD £240 K, with Hedge Fund Managers earning 10 to 15% more.

Information on the number of UK bankers earning over Euro 1 M comes from EBA as related by Business Insider (date unknown).

The Times of September 1, 2016 'Can another Bank Scandal be prevented?' highlights the money laundering problem ' The National Crime Agency estimates that hundreds of billions of pounds of ill-gotten gains are washed through the UK Financial system every year, with only a tiny proportion facing scrutiny.' It also reported comments from bankers who were caught out and imprisoned. 'Tom Hayes the first trader convicted over his role in the Libor Scandal echoes Leeson's complaint that traders do only what they see others doing. 'The issues with all of this is that I didn't know that I was doing was wrong because actually it was market practice.''

Chapter THIRTY-THREE - The Visit to Poland

The earlier trip to Poland when junior health Minister and his proposal for a Locum Agreement were covered in 'Sebastian' the first book, Chapter 21.

The continuing relevance of this NHS part of the trip was shown by an article in the Times 6th January 2017 Chris Smyth. 'Locum Doctors are still earning £300,000 as NHS curbs fail'. NHS tried to cap stand in staff to no more than 55% of normal rates. The proposal in the novel was to set up a 'virtual' training ward in Poland, linked directly to a database, providing locums on a capitation paid system.

The next trip to Poland is related in 'Sebastian – Sea-Bass' the second book Chapter 45 when he deals with a problem in Belarus.

Payunk Wask is somewhat modelled on Donald Tusk a Pole and former Prime Minister of Poland who became one (they have 5) of the Presidents of the EU. Judging by his comments released to the Press recently. Donald Tusk might not in fact be the Anglophile this author took him for, although he might just be following orders.

'Golonka' and 'Flechki' are two local country dishes served in Poland on special occasions. For centuries Pole were the subjects of variously Germans, Austro-Hungarians and Russians who presumably took the most tasty cuts of meat so the country folk made the best of what was left, a tradition similar to black puddings, jellied eels and indeed tripe, in the north country here in the UK. Even long after the command economy disappeared this author can confirm that despite the millions of cows in Poland it was almost impossible in country districts to buy a steak.

Poles make what they believe is the finest vodka in the world, a colleague of mine on a trip there asked a President of the Polish company he was visiting, whether on his next trip the Prezes would like him to bring in something like Vodka perhaps? First there was a frown on his face then an enormous grin "Yes" he said "Like you bringing in local Whisky from India!" There probably is somewhere a teetotal Pole but on all my 40 trips there I never met one. The meetings with Polish boards of companies which this author attended ended up rather similar to the President's dinner with the UK group!

The Times revealed on September 3, 2016 'Army falls to lowest level for two centuries' 'The army has fallen below the symbolic threshold of 80,000 full time soldiers. A Colonel Richard Kemp suggested ' We depend on the US for significant security cover but there has been a sign for some years of their exasperation with European Countries for not doing enough to help themselves. If this continues it could lead to a reduction in US Defence support to us'.

The UK Strategy Defence Review has no doubt about its direction of travel, Chapter One item 1.1 'Our Vision' says;

'Our vision is for a secure and prosperous UK with global reach and influence'. No hesitancy or doubt about it, generations of the military have been fed on such snuff!

There has been a Common Security and Defence Policy for the EU for many years. The Berlin Plus agreement was established to cover concerns that European Policies might detract from NATO. EU forces are described as 'separable but not separate'. Successive EU Treaties like the Lisbon Treaty have tried to address the problem of whether to have a co-ordinated defence and how it should integrate with NATO. Basically the UK has consistently stymied any attempt to create a European Army. Sebastian aims to break that habit and force the UK into a leading role.

Article 42 of the EU treaty does provide for a 'permanent structured cooperation between the armed forces of a subset of member states'. So what Sebastian is suggesting is within the rules of the EU.

Wikipedia 'Military of the European Union' gives details of most EU countries military strength. Poland has 48, F-16 but still 31 older Mig-29, whilst the UK has 160 Typhoons and 87 Tornado, the latter also used by the Italian and German Air forces. Britain and France have much larger navies than any other EU states. The UK has in comparison a very small force of main battle tanks at 253, Challenger 2 the UK's main battle tank has a rifled bore and Cobham armour thought to be the best in the world, its life has been progressively extended, but a replacement will be due in 2030. compared with France 484 (Leclercs) and Poland 984 many of the latter are older ex Russian T Tanks some of the more modern are Leopard tanks of German design.

The Times of 4th January 2017 revealed that the UK had been offered and rejected some 100 to 400 second hand Leopard 2 German tanks on a special deal. A source said 'We invented the tank, we have to have a British Tank.' Unfortunateatly the unrifled German tank hits further, travels faster. In 2016 the UK were considering buying the German designed armoured 'Boxer' vehicles. 800 of these might cost £3 bn made by a consortium led by Rheinmetall. (The Times October 15th 2016)

In November 2015 the UK government announced the withdrawal of the final British Army units in Germany. This author has assumed that the decision to transfer to the UK the 20 Armoured Infantry Brigade may well have been deferred and it is this force that Sebastian suggests should be relocated. (from Army Technology market & Customer insight)

Chapter THIRTY-FIVE and THIRTY-SIX – NATO REFORMS

The information on the new US Embassy in London is from the London Evening Standard 20th September 2012.

Details of the places in which the President of France and the German Chancellor work come from Wikipedia.

The details of the various armies in Europe comes from 'The Military of the EU' from Wikipedia. The numbers of population within Army Group, North and South were also derived from that.

The mixed NATO Naval unit under British Command was from the Times of November 26th 'Navy takes Gulf command from US.'

Chapter THIRTY-SEVEN - Final Passage of the Constitutional Bill.

Vince Cable in his Book 'After the Storm' repeatedly comments favourably on the Handelsbanken; p27, 'seems autonomous', 'community based', p75, 'ethical banking' ,p263, 'excellent model', p265, 'out-lawed sales-based bonus, steady growth' p270 'expanding rapidly p272, 'devolved decision making'. But the model appears difficult, if not impossible, for others to replicate – see below. It seems likely that it's a unique cultural/financial model which cannot be used except by the Handelsbanken itself.

Handelsbanken was founded in Stockholm in 1871. It began to expand abroad when currency restrictions were lifted in 1989

Handelsbanken is indeed in the UK Market, opening operations in London in the 1980's, by 1990 it was in Manchester, then later in Birmingham. In 2002 the UK was designated it's third 'Home Market' in terms of its being a regional Bank. It is also in the Netherlands; and Norway, Finland and Denmark which gained the status of separate regional banks in 1998. By 2009 it served 60 communities across England and Wales. In 2010 it opened in Scotland. The Bank's 100th and 200th branches were announced in 2011 and 2015. In 2013 it acquired a UK Wealth and investment management co.

A study by a Danish banking group 'Can the business model of Handelsbanken be an archetype for small and medium sized banks?' A comparative case study. (with Danish banks) is only partly revealing – Journal of Applied Business Research May/June 2014 volume 30, number 3. However the study suggested that the model could not be copied at least to medium sized Danish Banks, quoting higher costs of 'default risk' and also its operating procedures based on culture, including no budgets and some difference in Banking customers. The continued increase in branches and similarity of Euro Financial Banking controls, suggests that maybe the report writers were simply unable to understand how it could operate, with higher returns, devolved decision making, with lower costs and happier clients. It appears to be entirely cultural, everything appears to depend on the Manager on the Branch involved

Information on Regional Venture Funds particularly the Regional Venture Capital Funds is from an article in The Economist Aug 3rd 2013 'Misadventure capital'.

Some information on Corporate Venture Capital came from BVCA (British Venture Capital Association) Guides. It seemed to have been written in 2012, sadly it's pretty poor quality stuff although it gives a broad spectrum of some major Corporate Investors.

In a Government note describing the HMRC 'Capital Venturing Scheme – introduction to National Statistics' is revealed that the tax scheme lasted between 1st April 2000 till 31st March 2010 and was not renewed.

The more detailed Archived HMRC related document suggests that tax reliefs were available by the Investing Corporate Venturer of 20% of the amount which it subscribed for the invested company's shares. There were a number of conditions; for example that the invested subject had to carry on a trade, can have assets no greater than £16 M and that 20% of the invested co.'s shares have to be held by individuals other than directors or employees. It's unknown if these restraints made it difficult to use this system.

The UK has never been able satisfactorily to handle parts of the Country on an arm's length basis. This was certainly true of Ireland. It took decades for an Irish Home Rule Bill to pass, delayed by personal problems with Leaders, switching Political sympathies, and the Great War. This Author is one of many who believed that the vicious and violent Irish insurrection and civil war was totally unnecessary. There were around 80 MP's from Southern Ireland at Westminster, given the British Politics of the 20th Century many believe that all they had to do was to await their opportunity as they would sooner or later have been the balancing power and able to directly influence events.

Chapter FORTY-TWO – Sebastian's speech to the EU – The HEGEMON

It's not just this author that gets obsessed with Luxembourg which has a GDP several times that of its neighbours. Thomas Piketty does as well an eminent French Economist recounts in 'Chronicles' he reports that Junker explains to a 'dumbstruck Europe in the wake of the LuxLeaks revelations that as Luxembourg's prime minister he had no choice but to siphon off his neighbours' tax bases; the manufacturing industry was declining, you see so a new development strategy had to be found for my country; what could I do but become one of the worst tax havens on the planet?'

Sebastian if he engineered the break-in in Luxembourg might have needed a list of such legal tax haven agreements sending profits through Luxembourg at reduced rates, if his own position was attacked.

The key points Sebastian intends to make

1) Dedication to the European Ideal
2) His temporary nature
3) His part mostly free from major EU decisions
4) His objectiveness and personal integrity
5) His disappointment at the current position, secrecy bad democracy
6) The Euro both badly constructed designed to fail?
7) Teutonic Star Chamber
8) People and countries humiliated
9) German Swabian contract re Deutsch Mark not co-operation
10) One size fits all = loss of 7% GDP
11) Hegemon Established, supported by helot states
12) The Price the Hegemon now has to pay for leadership, or leave
13) Contrast the Marshall plan
14) The EC return to follow the Economic goals
15) Its failure to open the free market in Services
16) WE and THEY – the fatal flaw – The Swabian Promise
17) UK has to protect its position in the nastier vindictive Europe
18) We are all Europe, nobody owns Europe
19) Setting up the 9 member enhanced group for those traveling multispeed
20) Never will be in Euro, we will never submit to the Teutonic star chamber

21) Furthermore on a wider front, the UK says No to turkey, Belarus and Ukraine, not tomorrow, not next year, never, ever, instead set up meaningful associated status
22) No to sloppy budgets and paying poor quality euro servants like the king of the corporate tax thieves, we will pay by tariff on increased Euro trade at 1%

Sebastian is to use hand signals to his staff to prevent shut off of his speech, he has posted key staff to prevent this. He issues instructions as exactly when to issue parts of his speech labelled 1,2, 3 and 4 to waiting press, each of these contains notes eg Failure to stress test Euromodel, Hegemon, helot what are they? Marshall plan details. Why Turkey is different?

Euro managers are not noted for openness. One interested Euro-observer saw the swarms of MEPs crowding into the chamber to register last minute for attendance, instead of addressing the problem, ie did 5 minutes justify a full days allowance, the Euro Managers simply refused to allow any press to photo the scramble – the gravy train!

In an interview 'Guardian 6th January 2017' the outgoing MEP President accuses 'National leaders have failed to sell EU vision' This author comments; Like perhaps transferring powers under the Euro and finding the one size fits all reduced GDP by 7%? Does he mean that pushing the whole area into recession? Or does he mean the invention of the Teutonic Star Chamber? He says 'people talk as if Europe is attacking their countries' Well who would believe such a thing? He says Brussels is treading water. Martin Schultz thinks he is the solution, in reality he is part of the problem!

As part of a larger article 'Guardian 6th January 2017' on Europe 'there is no idea what to do about the single currency. No major initiatives are in the pipeline to resolve the incompatibility at the heart of the project. Governments are terrified of scaring financial markets- and voters. Finance ministers' meetings are an unedifying succession of stalemates. Southern powers want more pooled sovereignty to insulate their vulnerable economies. Northerners demur, until their balance sheet risk is reduced.

On the Turkish deal for immigrants 'it has created a deep unease in European Institutions. It may have served to stop the migrant influx, but at a heavy cost, taking a toll on the cardinal EU value of openness. To avoid taking in populations fleeing war zones, the EU preferred to give billions in Euro to a government that is violating the principle of freedom of expression. Held to ransom by populist governments of Eastern Europe that are implacably opposed to taking their share of refugees, the EU opted for realpolitik. Jennifer Rankin in Brussels. This author – or maybe it should be fudge?

Chapter FORTY-THREE - Repercussions of Sebastian's European Speech

The Trading with the Enemy Act 1939 makes it a criminal offence to conduct trade with the enemy in wartime, with a penalty of up to seven years' imprisonment. The bill passed rapidly through Parliament in just two days, from 3 to 5 September 1939, at the beginning of the Second World War. It is still in force today.

Under a Sequestration Act; Land, firms, shops, investments, ships, goods, shares, bank accounts, patents and trademarks, and personal belongings owned by citizens of enemy nationality were sequestered and then sold by state custodians to citizens of their own countries. These actions, which started at the very beginning of the conflict, were eventually legitimised by the peace treaties.

Chapter FORTY-SEVEN - The Chancellors Spring Statements.

The key comments on the UK housing Market are mostly abstracted from Chapter 9 'The British Housing Obsession' from the Book 'After the Storm' by Vince Cable.

The information on Engineering degrees was from a report and summary of 'Engineering UK' prepared in 2016, this contains the need for doubling the number of engineering graduates to 2020 and the benefits of doing so, increasing manufacturing, improving exports. Improving productivity and creating other jobs from that increase of engineering graduates..

Details of a new university seemingly to be called 'New Model in Technology and Engineering' wants to set up in Hereford, based on project groups of 30 students, divided over 13, 3 week blocs with less lectures more practical. The idea to bridge the gap between the normal output from academia and what employers really want, solution of practical workplace problems. 6th December 2016..

Chapters FIFTY-THREE and FIFTY-FIVE - Home Office Prison Reform.

Relevant documents researched included.

Labour Party on Prisons, 'Labour to put work at the heart of prisons.' 26th March 2014

Prison Reform Trust 'Crispin Blunt MP speech to all party Penal Affairs group' 6th July 2010

Prison Reform Trust 'Simon Hughes MP outlines Lib Dem plans for Prison Reform 19th November 2014. This brief article has provided the bulk of the ideas that Sebastian deploys to reduce the prison population, looking separately at those with mental health issues, focus on education and skills needed, doubling youth prison education, identifying those with special education needs, though Simon Hughes deals with drug addiction by not imprisoning them in the first place. Sebastian decides he will tackle first those matters than he can change, he knows that to alter sentencing is something that he cannot justify, there is for example no proof that non-custodial sentences actually reduce the prison population.

Prison Reform Trust 'The most overcrowded prisons twice as likely to be failing' November 2016

The Guardian 'Michael Gove announces plans for 'reform prisons'' 16th March 2016

Gov UK 'Prison Reform: Prime Minister's speech' 8th February 2016

House of Commons Library 'Briefing paper Prison Population Statistics' 4th July 2016

Howard League papers, .

What if police bail was abolished?

What if imprisonment were abolished for property offences? . This is a rather odd paper so it suggests that there should be no imprisonment for theft instead using fines and community sentences. It points out that 80% of youths re-offend anyway, but it doesn't say that the replacements they suggest work either, since most simple theft is carried out to get cash, it doesn't explain who is going to pay the fines, this leaves just community service.(for this see other note below) The basic problem of recidivism for youth, it that no-one has provided yet a realistic solution, all tagging does is work out where the individual is, it cannot prevent him doing anything.

Rethinking the Gateway: Using evidence to reform the criminal justice system for victims and people who offend

Prison Watch UK 'Why do so many ex-servicemen end up in prison?' April 12, 2016, by Jordan Elizabeth Milne.

The information on the 'Forlorn Hope' comes from the book, "Rifles – Six years with Wellington's legendary sharpshooters" by Mark Urban. Pages 166 and 167,

Unlocking Potential – A review of Education in Prison, Dame Sally Coates May 2016 from the Ministry of Justice. This author pans the thin work she carried out.

Prime Minister's Speech on Prison reform 8th Feb 2016 which contains the notes on prison reform intended, academies model, 49% of prisoners have mental health problems, 47% no qualifications , mentions Dr Alm and HOPE, tagging using GPS, 40,000 pages of rules and the one about the number of sheets of music a prisoner can keep in his cell.

Prime Minister 18th May 2016, speaks of £1.3 billion spending on new Prisons up to 2020, replacing old. It's this budget which Sebastian hopes to use. Mentions 9 new build prisons and 8 police forces using upgraded GPS tagging.

Phil Wheatly, (undated and un attributed – must find!) former director general of prison service says reform plan won't work without reducing the prison population, saying the idea of giving governors greater powers could simply prove a distraction to the real business of running effective gaols. This seems to this author exactly right, so the proposal here is to get out of main prisons those who shouldn't be there, then treat the reduced numbers to training.

Liz Truss new justice secretary, 7th September puts the whole Cameron/Gove plan on hold

European Observatory, December 2013 contains discussions on the use of Prison Councils noting at Albany when used it had led to a 37% reduction in complaints. It gives details of the Scottish Video visits, it's not clear if this is a 'virtual' connection or one like Skype, it is said to be an internet service, unclear exactly.

European Prison Observatory 2015 'Reducing the prison population in Europe, Do Community based sentences work? 'Unfortunateatly the results of our observatory did not produce evidence on a connection between the development of community sanctions and the decrease in prison population rates'.

Hawaii's Opportunity Probation with enforcement, HOPE set up by Judge Steven Alm, seems mostly related to drug crimes. Wikipedia

'Unlocked' Guardian 21st December 2016, scheme to hire 2,500 extra prison staff seemingly under a two year graduate scheme, rather muddled article.

Proven Reoffending Statistics, Quarterly Bulletin Jan to Dec 2014. Ministry of Justice. And Annex A.

From the Crime Prevention Website

Methods of Property Marking and Tagging

Bicycle Security.

From the Sunday Times 1st January 2017, a more humorous note but one which shows clearly that installing protection apps in the sale of phones and PCs could massively reduce theft. A 23 year old aspiring Dutch Filmmaker Anthony van de Meer, had one 'I pad' stolen, intent partly on revenge, he placed an App 'Cerberus' in an identical one, which he then deliberately managed to get stolen. The App allowed him to secretly film and record the thief, this, he made into a film.

House of Commons Library, briefing paper, 4th July 2016. Prison Population statistics.

'Caged fervour' Jihadism in French Prisons The Economist September 17th 2016, in a long and rather rambling article, Muslims are estimated to be 8-10% of the French Prison population, expresses concern is partly a 'failure to make isolation watertight', deradicalisation programmes are still experimental, prison watchdog not in favour of segregated units looking at exchanges of those who have renounced jihad.

Chapter – FIFTY-SIX – Immigration Review

Sources used

Election briefing 2015 removals and voluntary departures migrationobservatory 2015

The UK, EU citizenship and free movement of people, migrationobservatory 2014

Migration to the UK Asylum migrationobservatory July 2016

Would leaving the EU reduce immigration into the UK – answer maybe but probably not enable the net migration to fall below 196,000.

Realising Talent, employment and skills for the future, a report for the Local Government Association July 2014. Main summary is that if we do nothing there will be a serious gap, 9.2 million people chasing 3.7 million low skilled jobs; 12.6 million people with intermediate skills chasing 10.2 million jobs; 14.8 million high skilled jobs with only 11.9 million skilled workers. This could restrict economic growth if employers cannot recruit the skills and capabilities needed-

Written Commons Question 30373 Nurses training, 'how many nurses commenced training in each of the last 5 years. 2010; 20,092; 2011 17,741; 2012 17,219; 2013 17,568; 2014 19,147; 2015 20,333. The implication here is that there were not enough training places made available, NHS then found itself short and attempted to recruit the 800 Pilipino nurses which May turned down. It's impossible for this author to come to definitive conclusions but it's an example of how immigration fills the #UK shortfall, is it just bad planning? Or the effects of a cut back? Maybe in hospital beds?

Guardian august 2016, Australian points based system.

BBC June 2016 Immigration points based systems compared.

Mirror 2016 'where do foreign migrants choose to live in the UK?'

Australian visabureau, skilled points test.

Migration watch – Vanishing students from outside the EU? MW 387

Daily Mail 11th February 2015. Britain hit by worst skills shortage in 30 years, construction industry turning down work, 44690 entrants needed to maintain industry but has only 7,280, need 75,000 engineers, only 22,000, construction industry 7% of GDP hard hit, lack of tradespeople in London. Hiring foreign brickies at £1000 per week.

UKCES Employer Skills Survey 2015, 'skills in the labour market' but here also questions the use we are making of existing workforce eg failing to train existing managers for wider briefs.

Economist 20th August 2016 ' keep off truckin' lobby groups suggest a shortage of 45,000 drivers, only 17,000 new truck-drivers licences are issued each year, but oddly this shortage has no lead to an increase in pay since the margins are too thin, competition particularly intense for retail delivery, only 3.3% miles run by foreign vehicles so far, fleets are getting older but UK hauliers are now employing Polish drivers. But it costs £3000 to train and pass exams so that unemployed cannot get a job that way, but its classed as a low-level skill so unemployed cannot get 'advanced learner loans', there may be an apprenticeship scheme available perhaps.

Economist July 30th 2016 OECD report suggests that the UK has been a 'stingy spender' on 'active' labour market policies, ie. Those that seek to improve the skills of the unemployed, not just let them languish. One paper estimated that British spending on active policies adjusted for GDP was about one-fifth that of Germany. Only about 15% of those on unemployment benefits receive any sort of training. Those displaced by free trade thus get little help towards becoming the model employees of tomorrow.

Immigration by Category; workers ; Students ; Family Members ; Asylum Applicants. By migrationobservatory 17th Feb 2016.

Non-European Migration to the UK' Family Unification and Dependents by migrationobservatory 21st March 2016.

National Statistics feature   March 2004 'Skills shortages in skilled construction and metal trade occupations'. At first sight this little paper seems misplaced, but it indicates how difficult it is to get the data and interpret it. Vacancies come from Jobcentre Plus, which is limited in that it covers less than half employers with more than 5 employees; but also from ESS, Employer Skills Survey, but it is not a standard yearly study although it covers wider ground. This paper was partly directed at the construction industry, but it's clear within that 'shortage' there are problems in understanding the particular business cycle, which means that demand ebbs and flows within a range, but also that there may well be structural problems underlying the statistics. A finding was that although it had been thought that the higher grade job professional grades were where the shortages were, in fact the skilled trades occupations 'stand out as having the highest share of all recruitment problems'.

Tier 2 Shortage Occupation List – Government approved version – valid from 6th April 2014. This list identifies the shortages, they are mostly managerial/technical, but also cover a wide range of engineers in various industries, aerospace, railways, oil and gas, aerospace, nuclear, and carry appropriate salary rate. Another block is in computer animation and films, medicine, radiographer, haematology, paediatrics. Teachers, social workers. Orchestral musicians, dancers, classical ballet dancers. Chefs with 5 years' experience. In effect a UK sponsor proposes hiring someone on this list and within the assumed earnings described.

However, to this author, the problem when applied to the real world is twofold. 1 How is it that we are failing to train such a huge number of professionals, are they really needed in which case does the lack of these people affect our lives here or are radiographers simply retrained from other similar work where there is an over-supply perhaps? 2 Does it reflect immediate needs? As shown in the paper above the real difficulty was in hiring skilled trades. An interesting example was where the NHS wanted to hire 800 Pilipino nurses but this was rejected by immigration.

Any proposal needs to prove to the EU that the UK can allow full EU access to the UK jobs market but avoid those coming to the UK just to look for work, it's this bit which is unplannable, unpredictable and appears to show that local authorities are unable to cope with the influx.

The proposal for offering on-line access from the person's home EU state, using PCs based in British Embassies, aims to show that it is not discriminatory and offers exactly the same opportunity as if the job seeker were in the UK.

Applying from the original state means that language skills can be tested as well as police checks before they come to the UK, it maybe that identical questions have to be asked of UK applicants to avoid discrimination. Should those with records arrive they can be interviewed here turned around and sent home immediately. So the UK can claim to be 'in control' of its borders.

Direct access to those coming to the UK means also more knowledge of where they are going to and which gangmaster they might use. It also gives the UK border controls a massive database for later feedback from these individuals, particularly to ensure that minimum wage rules are not broken, which is rightly a major concern, this is needed to prove that immigrants are not undercutting the locals rates.

For this to work it is necessary to shake up the 'vacancies', every business over 5 employers will have to identify new vacancies and employment agencies must also extent the range of managerial jobs. So that the list is much more than just fieldwork and packing through the gangmasters which was the staple of the migrant trade from for example Poland.

But the Tier 2 is capped at 20,700, can the proposal also cap the EU and total immigration?

A proposal is made of 150,000 based on the lack of housing and other facilities due to the UK's reducing available land area for building. There is simply no calculation that can be brought to bear on immigration limits to state that either the UK needs xxxx thousand to function fully or that yyyy thousand coming here will or will not damage the country culturally, except using past data where immigration was controlled to within 100,000 for many many years, this is a 'comfort zone' 'in the tens of thousands', David Cameron kept repeating.

A great many suggest that a complete 'open door' for immigrant workers simply reflects very sloppy, childlike UK management mentality, instead of rethinking the job and managing efficiently or investing in faster machines, we just open the door and shout 'more please'! Completely careless of any other infrastructure costs.

The Times 4th January 2017 the Inst of Directors claim the 20,700 limit is not being broken 'because the restrictions are so high that employers are prevented from applying, showing that UK immigration policies are not fit for purpose.' This is because the Tier 2 uses also uses a points system based on current earnings, here they say it's too high.

January 1st 2017, Sunday Times, 'Starmer tightens rules on immigration' he said there should be a fundamental rethink on immigration rules from start to finish, there's a consensus that when we leave the EU the immigration regime will have to change. Corbyn appeared to disagree.

There is a paper prepared by Migrant Watch for the referendum debate. It indicates the 'Top 10 problems in evidence based immigration' it suggests that there is no available regular emigration controls or information, that's partly because most in the UK can exercise their right to leave and return anyhow, at any time, without restraint. But without any actual system in place to capture the info, it's only possible to guess at one side of the equation, the headline screaming figures are based on the net migration. As this 'top 10' list points out the only source for the emigration are some rather limited interviews of samples of passengers leaving, which cannot be described even as a proper random sample. The paper suggests 'data on emigration is particularly scarce' which makes the whole thing not only 'fluffy' but unhelpful too, places like Boston had no idea how many of their immigrants left or stayed, so they found additional numbers impossible to plan for at all.

Other key items in the 'Top 10 Problems in the Evidence Base for Public Debate and Policy Making on Immigration in the UK' Items, 5, 7 and 8 relates to the need for info on the impact of immigration on public services, housing and for local areas with larger immigrant communities. This is also in the proposal for some detailed research to be carried out, to be able to either counter rumour with fact or put in place more rigorous coping policies.

But to change the documentation, anything put in place has to be non-discriminatory vis a vis the EU so it has to apply to everyone going everywhere, breach of this would jeopardise the derogation already granted.

The EU derogation earned in this novel was a time based one which gives about a year or else face the issue once again being seen as a weathervane within the UK as to whether or not the UK was, or was not, in control of its borders.

It's not too difficult even to devise an exit document of some kind for emigration monitoring. Probably a docket prepared by the carrier at the same time as a 'boarding pass' which is now standard for all carriers, air, ports and rail, at all ports of exit. So his proposal is that everyone will complete this and hand to the carrier before boarding. This would need to be negotiated with the possible 400 carriers to agree to print and supervise collection. It's probable HMG would have to pay maybe 10p per completed form would do, a huge cost but it would give a resulting real figure.

This author doodled a layout for the new ticket; he drew 5 lines across a thin bit of paper about half the size of an original punched card. Each of the 5 he labelled at the left hand side, in turn 'UK Citizen', 'EU Citizen', 'USA Citizen', 'Rest of World', 'FCO Designated'. Now along each row there would be a small box and alongside each; 'holiday', 'work', 'visitor visa', 'long stay abroad', 'long term live abroad'.

This author suggests that it would be quite possible to make such small changes quickly at a top ministerial meeting, and someone with extended powers, able to cross ministerial boundaries as in his remit, could make changes which might otherwise take years.

A main change is 'Sponsorship for all incoming people' everyone must be sponsored by somebody already in the UK and guaranteed to the effect of £100. This means everyone, the vast majority would be holiday returnees, and their sponsor would be the carrier, to do this some sort of credit system might be required. So let's say an outgoing holidayer from the UK goes to Mallorca, pays the deposit at the time and on the return to UK is repaid £100. Then any people who have been long term living in the South of France would have to find someone in the UK to sponsor them and pay the £100. EC workers hired through agencies would presumably act as sponsors and pay the £100.

In fact all Tier2 immigrants have to be sponsored anyhow right now, so this merely extends the principle.

Under this proposal Casual visitors and temporary workers would still require a sponsor and £100 without which they would not be admitted.

This proposal might appear to single out any visitors here who are just casually seeking work, whilst those coming for a specific job would presumably be sponsored by those through whom the job has been obtained. These would be employment agencies and often gangmasters. They would be monitored to ensure that they pre-register, there have been several cases of them abusing the EC workers, saying one thing in an ad, then the job being different, giving the rate of pay in the ad but finding huge deductions for very simple crude and dirty lodgings and no food, or crammed into the gangmasters own premises, illegal retention of passports, not even attempting to pay the minimum wage. The list of failures is extraordinary, really poor, a lot of abuse.

In order to get a gangmasters license there are 8 basic requirements, these need to be on the real time on line application so that immigrants can see the standard intended and can make complaints direct themselves this, regularly monitored, will provide feedback. The derogation based used our own poor supervision of this area, that is saying the EC workers were open to abuse, the same argument cannot be used again!

The same sponsor system will work for each University, they will be responsible for monitoring the return of the students in accordance with the agreement, or if they fail then the deposit will be lost and they in turn might lose their own sponsorship status, or have to pay double for the next cohort of incoming students.

This next element was originally in the text but was taken out because of the detail which threatened to swamp it. But it's necessary to the understanding of the existing rules, so apologies readers here.

Underneath the EU immigration there is our own UK based points/categories which still continue;

There are several completely different but interlinking groups of people to monitor and control, some of these will clearly have to link in with other databases, others less so!

The main Categories are.

a) <u>Students</u>. There's no intention of shutting them out, or reducing their number, all that the proposal does is to make sure that, soon after their course finishes, they return home, they are pretty good at doing so anyhow.

b) <u>Family re-union</u>. There are several smaller sub-categories, but many relate to mainly Asian families here returning to find brides or grooms from family groupings in India and Pakistan, this group has been reducing but it could be further curtailed by increasing the tariff they have to pay, so the proposal is looking not only at, a control mechanism but also perhaps, to change the ability of foreign individuals to come here at all, so to tighten the rules perhaps

c) <u>Specialist Foreign experts</u>. We here have always considered that we should be able to attract the 'best in the world' if we are to keep in the top flight in all branches of what we do here, so there must always be an ability to hold the door open for such people, medical experts, research boffins, creative artists writers, but also specialists that are needed when any FDI factory starts up here which needs initially dedicated staff from the home base to get the equipment installed and running. Since these are by definition one-offs, all that's required here is some analysis to make sure the system is not being abused and it's not letting in thousands who should be covered by other rules. Tier2 Up to about 20,000 are let in using the Special lists and points within that. Some rationing system would be required to keep sufficient places for EU.

d) <u>EU Citizens seeking work.</u> This is the most controversial, in this novel the UK already has a derogation so a renewed derogation we will have to prove that any system we use is non-discriminatory and also in its widest sense it offers opportunities for EU citizens to work and live here once residence is permitted here. There may be constraints that we wish to propose but we may also have to provide evidence of what jobs are available so as to allow applications for jobs from those within the EU, but this also gives us another problem, it's not just restricting those coming here but ensuring that employers here have access to foreign workers to encourage them to come here to ensure that the UK employers can produce, if the locals cannot or will not provide the necessary people to do the work.

e) <u>The General Mass off visitors</u> have to be validated in and out otherwise large numbers might try to evade all immigration controls and just land here and never go back home, some of these might be NHS Tourists like the well-known Nigeria Maternity London run. So some interconnecting might be needed. There are a huge number of tourists arriving every year. It would be vitally important to ensure that the ins and outs, were tracked monitored and followed up for any immigration policy to succeed.

f) <u>British Citizens leaving and returning</u>. As mentioned this is the least monitored and understood. Basically those leaving, leave and those returning, return. We know almost nothing more about them than that. They could be gone for days, weeks, years or even decades and similarly when they return we don't know where they have been or how long they have been away. This is addressed in the proposal.

Many of these require links into Police and Security modules, to be able to track potential terrorists and maybe to link in with other EC security systems. So it's actually a very complex and complicated series of databases which has to be available in real time but with sufficient control points to ensure that only certain parties have access to each section.

Would the proposals made actually be acceptable? This is a novel surfing on the fringes of reality but to my surprise it seems likely that they might.

A letter in 9th January 2017 of The Guardian suggests that there are already clauses within the original treaty of Rome which have been overlooked, it's worth quoting in detail;

'The answer to the question on how to combine a border regime that is fluid enough to preserve economic dynamism and rigorous enough to inspire public confidence lies in articles 48 and 49 of the original treaty of Rome.

Article 48 states that 'freedom of movement for workers shall entail the right a, to accept offers of employment actually made; b, to move freely within the territory of the member state for this purpose'. Article 49 calls for the 'achievement of a balance between supply and demand in the employment market in such a way as to avoid serious threats to the standard of living and level of employment in the various regions and industries'. In other words is not a neo-liberal free for all. Freedom of movement is specifically tied to agreed, contracted employment and recognises the need to balance labour supply and demand. Here is the basis for a serious negotiation between the UK and the rest of the EU. These articles offer the framework for Andrea Leadsom to argue for seasonal agricultural labour and for hospitals and care homes to be able to recruit staff as required. Returning to the original principles of the Treaty of Rome would be in the interests of all parties. It would permit a migration policy managed according to the needs of the economy. Are the British and European politicians up to the task? – Jon Bloomfield – Birmingham...

Another letter same paper & day suggests that EU citizens may circulate for only 3 months freely before declaring intent, something the UK government has never enforced – Pat Witacker – London. Says this is another May failure. This author agrees.

Chapter – FIFTY-EIGHT – The run up to the Election

Sebastian here is drawing a parallel between Schumpeter's 'creative destruction' usually applied within economic circles to its use here in changing how government departments are run. In its simplistic version it's that innovation which is a continuum, think IT, usually brings with it change in business, creative destruction occurs often when an industry collapses and from within that other units crowd in maybe using using new technology to resurrect something else in its place, for a time the rivalry to occupy the market can be intense. He says the same should apply within government units as they are, in effect, subject to much the same innovative pressures, but the problem is how to control it?

For example one prison reform system might be based on using one set of behavioural experts who define their view of how prisoners might be rehabilitated, it might be completely different from another reform, based on say the prisoner self-realisation, where the prisoner might set his own rehabilitation plan. Competing but possible answers?

Sebastian wants to see this as a regular pattern, he sees Lib Dems as a 'factory of new ideas', constantly producing new innovative models which take over from old ones, Sebastian's idea is that it should result in better government and it would also create a uniquely radical asset for Lib Dems.

The problem is that nothing is ever settled for long, nothing is sacrosanct and everything is in flux so it is a concept which is highly destructive of existing processes and is unsettling.

Over the past two centuries, the Western nations that embraced capitalism have achieved tremendous economic progress as new industries supplanted old ones. Even with the higher living standards, however, the constant flux of free enterprise is not always welcome. The disruption of lost jobs and shuttered businesses is immediate, while the payoff from creative destruction comes mainly in the long term. As a result, societies will always be tempted to block the process of creative destruction, implementing policies to resist economic change.

The ironic point of Schumpeter's iconic phrase is this: societies that try to reap the gain of creative destruction without the pain find themselves enduring the pain but not the gain.

Notes and changes after writing Books, I, II & III., views from this author.

These books are written some years before the dates to which the actions relate and this might lead the reader into some black holes.

Constitutional Changes – an event in the first book, recopied here because of its importance to SEBASTIAN THREE –

This was the summarised report as shown in the first book 'Sebastian', a novel. It is the result of the Royal Commission on the Constitution agreed by a referendum in November 2017.

Regional Assemblies will be accepted in all areas of the England subject to a simple majority in the referendum. These will have powers similar to Wales, covering health, transport, education, fire, police and culture. Income will be allowed from Road Fund Tax, a proportion of the tax on motor petrol and diesel, all business rates, all registration fees. Regional Assembly members will be elected on STV with agreed ratio of Councillors per 1000 of the population

Unitary Councils below that will be based on County Councils with the abolition of District Councils and enhanced powers for Parish Councils still with unpaid Parish Councillors. They will cover all physical maintenance in their areas.

Scotland will receive additional income from North Sea oil tax on a basis to be agreed but the Bennett formula will be adjusted to reflect their new financial income.

There will be an English Parliament run under the existing Cabinet system.

There will be a UK Parliament made up of the representatives of MPs from England and proportionately of Wales, Scotland and Northern Ireland. Its decision making powers to be determined by legal experts.

The House of Lords, will number not more than 200 and will be largely elected. It will be agreed by the first UK Parliament as representing the widest cross section of the population as possible with sufficient experience. Peers will be limited to two terms.

In this book in the Chapter 'The Final Passage of the constitutional Bill' Sebastian reminds himself that he has failed to address the problem of English/UK parliament, now more urgent when devolved units in Northern Ireland and almost Scotland are not represented in the UK Government. He

realises that he has no ready way of getting around the 'Cabinet collective responsibility'. It's not possible to be a Cabinet Minister but assume a political position to oppose Cabinet decisions, as for example, SNP would have done on Austerity if it had been invited to join the Cabinet. All Sebastian can do is to invite leaders of the devolved nations to attend some cabinet meetings, indeed to give then a right to do so. But he realises this still falls far short of representing the genuine views of those areas and he sees that this lack of linkage between rulers and ruled, will inevitably lead to break up of the UK.

Commonwealth Meeting was set up and held in SEBASTIAN TWO

The Commonwealth CHOGM is scheduled to be held in Malaysia in 2020, Baroness Scotland is the current Secretary General and the Agenda items are likely to be as indicated.

However since writing the bit about CHOGM in Sebastian TWO, two things have happened which might have caused a blot on proceedings 1) An enormous black hole was found in the Malaysian Sovereign fund, someone has apparently had their finger in the pie and a very large finger too, it's not clear whose, but it dents the idea of Malaysia being a beacon of virtuous political behaviour. 2) Also the Baroness has had acres of headlines devoted to her supposedly doing up the Commonwealth office at huge expense. It was later reported that the normal buying procedures were not followed in granting this work, staff left and the police were informed.

So maybe the venue and characters would have been changed but no reason to think the Agenda would!

DONALD TRUMP wining the USA Presidency was not foreseen in SEBASTIAN ONE but it appears that this NATO proposal from Sebastian would have been much more likely to succeed under Trump than Clinton, if the former's published views are anything to go by.

THE LEADER OF THE LABOUR PARTY as Sebastian correctly analysed in SEBASTIAN ONE remained. When put to the test conviction politicians are hard to get rid of, they appeal ever more strongly to extreme supporters. One should not blame the Labour Party. Tony Blair's idea of moving to the centre to win power worked, unfortunately he forgot to leave any real legacy for Labour members, whose representatives eventually became indistinguishable from Leftish Tories. The glue of the Unions had been destroyed. This author remembers canvassing in a coal Mining large village. All miners were directed to the Social Club before the vote to remind them what to do and why. Union reps would stand within 20 feet of the entrance to the polling station, they knew each miner by name. They counted them in. They didn't black ball the odd Lib Dem or Tory but the expectations were clear. The same was true on the red Clyde. Tony Blair did not seem to notice that it was all swept away, he did nothing to replace it or to tell those people that they still counted as they had done before.

UNITED NATIONS. Development of the United Nations – the suggestion of a new UN unit put forward by Sebastian in SEBASTIAN TWO comes from 'Divided Nations' by Professor Ian Goldin, page 61 on migrants. Unfortunately, time and space did not allow this author to develop the idea of a half-way house between intervention militarily in a war situation and doing nothing except picking up the pieces. In effect Sebastian's proposals would allow the UN to seal off part of that state (at war or in turmoil), creating camps and if necessary towns there protecting civilians in their own country, building infrastructure and providing the people with a means to earn a living. Eventually the UN would negotiate with the rulers when the war had ended. and charge them with costs! This, if it worked, would prevent the need for hundreds of thousands of migrants desperately seeking refuge swarming across frontiers. A 'Safe House' in their own land. If necessary the UN might have temporarily to take over such failed states. The UN has consistently fought shy of unilateral intervention in states in that way, but places like Syria and Rwanda illustrate the terrible costs of doing nothing but dealing with the outcomes. The UN is like a huge liner, requiring the application of a huge force to change direction.

Wikipedia - COPYRIGHT NOTE

People in this Story	Relationship to Story
Douglas Finlay	Close childhood school friend & confidant lives in Northumberland, Sebastian visits every Easter, suffered a stroke recovering. Sebastian is attacked visiting this house.
Alexander Edwards	Sebastian's elder son – a banker – had no contact for over 20 years
Rupert Edwards	Sebastian's younger son – kept apart from Sebastian for decades by a deal enforced by his father in law, reunited, later SPAD to Sebastian in 2018, Lecturer in Local Government at Unity College, Camford, sees Sebastian frequently.
Sylvia Edwards	Sebastian's second wife, Muslim parents, Set up in 2016 charity and 'safe house' for Asian women fearing forced marriage or 'honour' killing
Tim Beaumond	MP leader of the LD not in 2010/15 coalition but in 2017 became Foreign Sec, Helped advance Sebastian's career, died January 2019
Tim Holland	LD County Councillor – Middleton – once time rival, Sebastian later supports him as No 1 preference for LD for the STV 5 member seat.
Madge O'Connor	LD District Councillor PA to Sebastian in 2017, now SPAD to Sebastian as Prime Minister 2020. Becomes personal secretary, married Bill Bennet who is the PPC.
Mohammed Rahmam	LD District Councillor, Chair of Middleton Parish Council, early supporter of Sebastian funding his earliest campaigns
Norman Dodgson	LD Local Treasurer
Sally Jones	LD Middleton Activist – Focus Routes
Rod James	LD Middleton Activist – Posters and signs

Bill Bennett MP	LD MP Sebastian's friend, flat mate, elected at same time, Manchester – later Whip, later Sebastian's Private Secretary when PM. Totally loyal to Sebastian
John Denny	Police Inspector in Middleton, promoted to Superintendent and part of the local Ministerial Protection Squad (MPS)
Dan Stirling MP	LD MP Min in LD 2010/15 Coal, defeated, re-elected. Chf Sec Treasury, elected Leader of the LIB Dems after the death of Tim Beaumond
Dave Billingham MP	LD MP Min in LD 2010/15 Coal, defeated, re-elected, Sec Int Devel, then Foreign Secretary, 'released' by the PM
John Wires MP	LD MP Min in LD 2010/15 Coal, defeated, re-elected, Min Climate, promoted to Minister Without Portfolio by Sebastian, is used to beef up the UK manpower planning part of immigration.
Saxon Bull MP	LD MP Min in LD 2010/15 & Coal 2017 undefeated, Sec Housing and the Regions, promoted to Foreign Secretary by Sebastian.
Jim Spiggot MP	LD MP Junior Min in 2017 Coal, undefeated, later Deputy Whip
John Key MP	LD MP Junior Min in 2017 Coal, undefeated. Min Educ
John Forbes MP	LD MP Junior Min in 2017 Coal declined new posts
Sarah Driscoll MP	New LD MP from South West. Min for Housing, considered a rising star, oversees building surge promoted to Secretary of State for Communities and Regions responsible for the new regional assemblies. A coming star in Lib Dems carries the day in the complex 'devolution Bills'
Rashid Ahmed MP	New LD MP from Yorkshire, Min Cabinet Office, promoted to Minister for Housing

John Andrews MP	New LD MP from London with 'refer back' to constituency
John Smithson MP	New LD MP from Scotland Minister without portfolio, then Scotland
Baroness Sal Thrumpton	LD Leader in the House of Lords, ex Junior Minister 2017, Depty Lords, in 2020 member of Sebastian's inner core.
John Corn	LD Former Chief of Staff to LD Leader and reinstated in 2017 in 2020 member of Sebastian's inner core
Jo Dyson	LD Former Deputy Chief of Staff to LD Leader, in 2020 member of Sebastian's inner core
Liz Dunnet	LD Former SPAD to LD Leader of House of Lords – rehired SPAD 2018
Anne Dewsbury	LD Former SPAD to Deputy PM on constitutional matters also 2018
Veena Peech	LD Press Secretary, in 2020 member of Sebastian's inner core
John Thorne	LD Chair of Executive Committee
Anne Dewsbury	LD SPAD ex Constitutional Adviser 2012-15 and also from 2018
Jeremy Chambers	LD SPAD to Saxon Bull Sec of State Housing Communities & Regions
John Blaney	LD helped set up Daedalus, info paper on Local stats, NHS Adviser
Pamela Tressider MP	Cons MP, Sec of State Home, Interim Prime Minister from Dec 2017, the Home Secretary again, until Deputy PM in December 2020, defeated by Stephen White in Tory leadership election March 2021
Michael Morgan MP	Cons MP ex Secretary of State for Defence (Welsh Seat), confirm as such in Coalition, Eventually agrees with Sebastian about NATO. In effect he realises the

	'Strategic Defence Review' does nothing and that global reach is impossible with reduced manning. and it is his support which proves crucial in persuading the other NATO members
Stephen White MP	Cons MP ex Chancellor of Exchequer, confirmed as Chancellor, wins Tory leader ship election in March 2021 becomes PM
Robin Turnbull MP	Cons MP generally 'leaver' Leadership Election then PM, resigned December 2020 after explosion of Ammunition ship in the Thames.
James Robertson	Cons Former Chief of staff to Conservative Leader
Sir John Hopkins MP	Cons Former Chief Government Whip - then Chief Whip, Sebastian served under him but not easily, still in position in 2020, sends Sebastian 'Ides of March' letter March 2021
Simon Gibson MP	Cons also a Whip tries to help Sebastian, tries to defect.
John Dabbs MP	Labour Leader of the Party
Pamela Brown MP	Lab Leader of Labour Party in Scotland
Sir James Knotwood	Cabinet Secretary and Head of Civil Service, still in position in 2020, clashes with Sebastian over Chilcott changes.
Patrick O'Brian	Second Permanent Secretary Head of UK Governance Group, still in position 2020
Annabel Smythe	Director Constitution Group, still in position 2020
Stuart Jones	Deputy Director UK Governance and Devolution, still in position 2020
James Smith	Landlord of Middleton Constituency Office, now a member of Sebastian's Executive Committee in Middleton
Lord Bridgeford	Conservative Peer – lodged complaints about Sebastian, later resigned as Conservative Leader of the

	House of Lords
Andrew Laws	Ex Conservative Middleton MP – changed to UKIP – lost by-election, still friendly with Sebastian, supported him in his 'bumpy ride'
Nichole Harris	One of the Country Managers at DfID, went with him to Nigeria, subsequently promoted to Head of Africa post in DfID
Leonard G. Edwards	Sebastian's father who died tragically in Nigeria, after an affair with the daughter of a highly respected local chief.
Massa Edwards Gombe	Sebastian's half-brother, the result of his father's affair now director of a development fund in Kaduna, Nigeria. They meet in London.
Dr Singh	Sebastian's GP introduced him to his charity became LD donor. Also a Trustee in Sebastian's wife's charity. Tries to help a reluctant Sebastian with medical advice. Insists he works only 4 days a week and gives up High Office later.
Dr Cottee	Sebastian's consultant for stomach ailments treated him in 2016 and in 2019 for Tropical Sprue
Walter Jefferies	CEO of the NHS from 2016 with whom Sebastian tussles on Regional Assembly and competition rules. Still in position in 2020, goes with Sebastian to Poland.
John Stewart	Permanent Undersecretary at the Ministry of Health 2016 onward still in position in 2020
Keith Williams	Permanent Undersecretary at the Foreign & Commonwealth Office, had ambivalent working relationship with Sebastian when he was Foreign Secretary, goes with him to Poland, supports him when asked by Payunk Wask
John Voss	Sebastian's minder in the West Bank. Helps with the Hegemon speech arrangements.

Tadeusz Polakov	Polish Prime Minister, Sebastian met him during Belarus 'feint', by Russia. And again on the later trip to Poland.
Sergey Kramrenko	Special Russian envoy dealing with Ukraine, previously in London, met earlier over attempts dealing with Ukraine, met again over Belarus and further at the secret meeting in Sweden, a confidant of Medvedev and is eventual promoted Deputy Foreign Minister
Jeffrey Pardoe also Major then later Colonel Collingham	Sebastian's former Assistant at Siberian Minerals, worked for MI5, a.k.a Major Collingham, he had contact with Sebastian in Belarus as UK military attaché at Polish Embassy, now attached to NATO, helps Sebastian on second trip to Poland and when ill on way back from Germany. Helps with Hegemon speech arrangements.
Jacques Dupuis	French MP, Contact in the French Government initially over Sebastian's comparative analysis on NHS and later on Nuclear Military co-operation. Meets Sebastian again on the latter's trip to France.
Rob Murphy	Features Editor of a high circulation broadsheet Sunday Paper. Analysed Sebastian's bumpy ride after his impeachment, gave him support. Helps launch 'Lines in the sand'.
Ahmed	Sebastian's wife's brother in law, who has stolen cash from girls in the Charity's 'safe' house. Tries to kill Sebastian in Northumberland and is himself shot dead.
Ranjit Singh	Partner in a major London firm of solicitors who successfully defended Sebastian in his impeachment and assists now over the family problem with Ahmed.
Roger Collingham-Smith	Sebastian's SPAD on EC matters a former Lib Dem MEP on sabbatical from a London University where he is Senior Lecturer on EC affairs. He is Sebastian's mentor trying to work a way for the UK through the EU maize.

Payunk Wask	Former Polish Prime Minister, then President of the European Council from which he retired in 2019. Agreed to help Sebastian in his mission for a two speed Europe. Sebastian's success is largely due to his constant promotion flitting between states.
Lord Israel Jacobs of Golders Green	CEO of the largest clothing retailers in the UK, S & G, who does a deal with Sebastian, launching for Charity a new clothing brand which carries Sebastian on 1500 bill boards across the country. This raises millions for the 'Looked after Children's charity.
General Sir Charles Winterbotham	Senior MOD General visits Poland with Sebastian
Cedric Elsworthy	USA Secretary of State, discusses NATO with Sebastian
Col Jacques Moulin	Sebastian's chosen (French) commander for base in Northern Nigeria for BOKO HARAM operations, previously led similar in Mali
Angela Stone	Sebastian's designated assistant in the Justice Department, former prison governor, proves to be a huge help to Sebastian
Roger Boot	Sebastian's designated assistant in the Home Office – immigration. A careful, cautious, infuriating but ultimately resourceful help.
David Roberts	The UK's top IT Civil servant, responsible to the Cabinet Office.
Professor Vivien Thompstone	Expert on immigration, served on several tribunals adjudicating different family related cases, advising on Tier 2 interpretations.

'It's all far too accurate to be real' this author!

End piece, Dear reader,

When I killed off Sebastian, I wept, I fiddled with the wording, tried to read it aloud and was unable to complete it before bursting into tears again.

My brother, one of the few who seems to have read the first book, doesn't think Sebastian a particularly nice character anyhow, he is probably right. Sebastian rather lets down his first boss getting easily diverted to his hobby, when it fails and he subsequently hits real trouble, and here in the 'terrible times' there are parts which are autobiographical, he too easily sacrifices his blameless children. Soon after becoming a local councillor he disdains Edna Leggs who has tried to help him and he pays the price for that. Tim Beaumond, the Lib Dem leader goes out of his way to help and support Sebastian, but is not well repaid, Sebastian doesn't do too good a job as Deputy Whip and creates unnecessary tensions within the small Lib Dem group of MPs much to Tim's frustration, even though the latter is under stress. Sebastian undermines the next Lib Dem leader Dan Stirling, in effect pushing him away. Sebastian appears to have only one leading Lib Dem ally and that is Sarah Driscoll. Although Bill and Madge are his closest political friends, Madge seems not to notice Sebastian's 'bumpy ride' only Bill does anything to really support him. So Sebastian does not either create loyalty or support. He doesn't really help his wife's charity as much as he might have. Apart from Sarah he doesn't bring on people, indeed his chosen replacement at DfID splits on him. So why weep for such an unsympathetic, though perhaps brilliant, character?

Two years ago I was diagnosed again with a returning cancer, NHL a cancer of the lymph glands. I started to write Sebastian, angry at the unwarranted pounding handed out to Lib Dems in May 2015 and I started on this incredible adventure. Then another treatment for cancer, but soon it had returned. There was one very dark day when the gloom oppressed me, I called it 'melt down day', I suppose every cancer patient has it? In my case it came out 'Well, no need to buy another shirt then!' But in a couple of days, there was Sebastian again, waiting. When my leg became so swollen that I could scarcely put it in the car, Sebastian and I could fly into the Russian President's private dacha or walk along a dusty lane out of Russia into Ukraine. When hospitals insisted I wait for hours to have tests carried out, within minutes Sebastian and I were walking up the Grand Staircase of the Foreign Office. When a biopsy became infected, Sebastian and I were finding out what really went wrong with the EU or working out who the hell thought up PFI? When a partial blockage developed in my bowel, Sebastian and I were rebuilding NATO, or on an overcrowded train from Brighton to London, or visiting a Muslim neighbourhood. When ill, lying prone in Hospital infusing Rituximab,

Sebastian and I were reforming prisons or the immigration system or rewriting the Hegemon speech for the 10th time. While waiting medical reports, we were creating names and building characters, or inventing new bits of plots.

Sebastian has been my companion, for between 3 and 5 hours a day, often very much more, for two years, forced me into endless research, and reading books I would never have dreamt of even looking at. It's been wonderful, every minute of every day, a journey of a lifetime. So good-bye, my faithful friend, and thank you for a magnificent time. I would not have missed it, or you, for the world.

So there I go again, dribbling away, reaching for the hankies.

www.ingramcontent.com/pod-product-compliance
Lightning Source LLC
Chambersburg PA
CBHW062148270326
41930CB00009B/1477